Dreamweaver® MX 2004 For Dummies®

Cheat Sheet

Properties Inspector

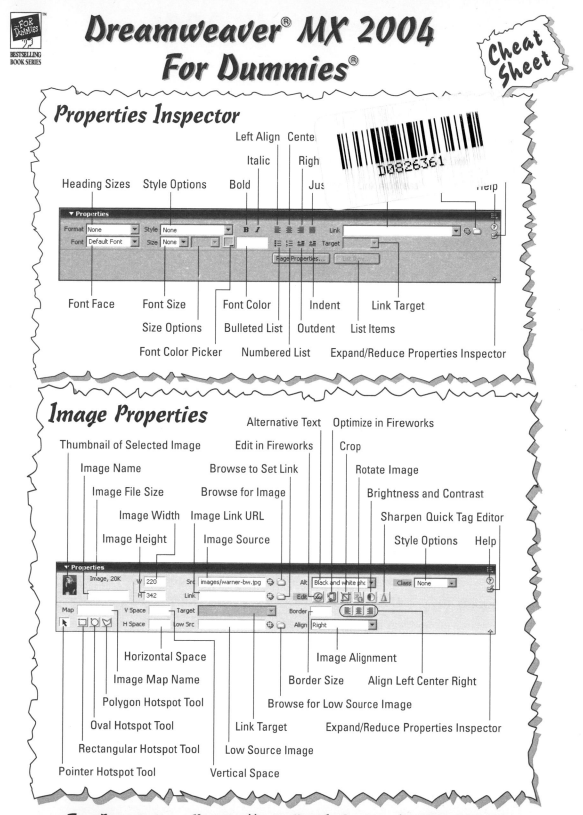

Heading Sizes · Style Options · Bold · Italic · Left Align · Center · Right · Justify · Help

Font Face · Font Size · Size Options · Font Color Picker · Font Color · Bulleted List · Numbered List · Indent · Outdent · List Items · Link Target · Expand/Reduce Properties Inspector

Image Properties

Thumbnail of Selected Image · Image Name · Image File Size · Image Width · Image Height · Image Link URL · Image Source · Browse to Set Link · Browse for Image · Edit in Fireworks · Alternative Text · Optimize in Fireworks · Crop · Rotate Image · Brightness and Contrast · Sharpen Quick Tag Editor · Style Options · Help

Pointer Hotspot Tool · Rectangular Hotspot Tool · Oval Hotspot Tool · Polygon Hotspot Tool · Image Map Name · Horizontal Space · Vertical Space · Low Source Image · Link Target · Browse for Low Source Image · Border Size · Image Alignment · Align Left Center Right · Expand/Reduce Properties Inspector

Dreamweaver® MX 2004 For Dummies®

Cheat Sheet

Table Properties

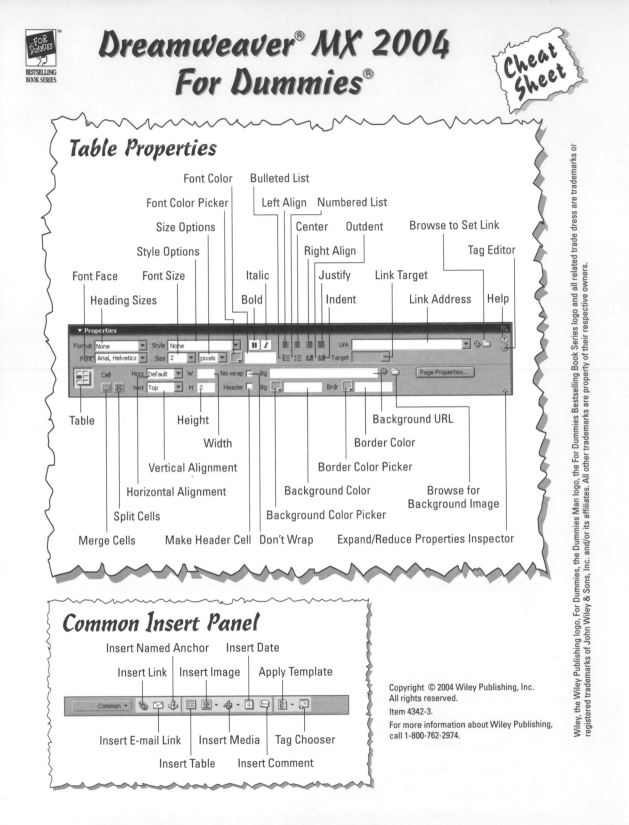

Font Color
Bulleted List
Font Color Picker
Left Align
Numbered List
Size Options
Center
Outdent
Style Options
Right Align
Browse to Set Link
Tag Editor
Font Face
Italic
Justify
Link Target
Font Size
Heading Sizes
Bold
Indent
Link Address
Help

Table
Height
Width
Vertical Alignment
Horizontal Alignment
Split Cells
Merge Cells
Make Header Cell
Don't Wrap
Background URL
Border Color
Border Color Picker
Background Color
Background Color Picker
Browse for
Background Image
Expand/Reduce Properties Inspector

Common Insert Panel

Insert Named Anchor
Insert Date
Insert Link
Insert Image
Apply Template

Insert E-mail Link
Insert Media
Tag Chooser
Insert Table
Insert Comment

For Dummies: Bestselling Book Series for Beginners

Dreamweaver® MX 2004 FOR DUMMIES®

by Janine Warner
and
Susannah Gardner

WILEY

Wiley Publishing, Inc.

Dreamweaver® MX 2004 For Dummies®

Published by
Wiley Publishing, Inc.
111 River Street
Hoboken, NJ 07030-5774

www.wiley.com

Copyright © 2004 by Wiley Publishing, Inc., Indianapolis, Indiana

Published by Wiley Publishing, Inc., Indianapolis, Indiana

Published simultaneously in Canada

For general information on our other products and services or to obtain technical support, please contact our Customer Care Department within the U.S. at 800-762-2974, outside the U.S. at 317-572-3993, or fax 317-572-4002.

Wiley also publishes its books in a variety of electronic formats. Some content that appears in print may not be available in electronic books.

Library of Congress Control Number: 2003113082

ISBN: 0-7645-4342-3

Manufactured in the United States of America

10 9 8 7 6 5

1O/ST/RQ/QT/IN

 is a trademark of Wiley Publishing, Inc.

About the Authors

Janine Warner is a best-selling author, professional speaker, syndicated columnist, and strategic Internet consultant. She is the author or coauthor of several books about the Internet, including *Managing Web Projects For Dummies, Dreamweaver For Dummies, 50 Fast Dreamweaver Techniques,* and *Macromedia Contribute For Dummies*.

Janine has been featured on technology news specials on NBC and TECHTV and has been interviewed on numerous radio programs in the United States and abroad. Her syndicated newspaper column, "Beyond the Net," appears in print and online, including in *The Miami Herald*.

As a consultant, Janine serves a broad range of clients from Internet companies to bricks-and-mortar businesses in the United States and abroad. Her expertise in multimedia, technology, and education has taken her on consulting assignments from Miami to Mexico and speaking engagements from New York to New Delhi.

Janine has been a part-time lecturer at the University of Southern California Annenberg School for Communication and at the University of Miami. She currently serves as Multimedia Program Manager for The Western Knight Center and The University of Southern California Online Program.

From 1998 to 2000, Janine worked for *The Miami Herald*, first as their Online Managing Editor and later as Director of New Media, managing a team of designers, programmers, journalists, and marketing staff for *The Miami Herald, El Nuevo Herald,* and Miami.com. She also served as Director of Latin American Operations for CNET Networks, an international technology media company.

From 1994 to 1998, Janine ran Visiontec Communications, a Web design business in Northern California, where she worked on such diverse projects as the corporate intranet for Levi Strauss & Co., an extranet sales site for AirTouch International, and e-commerce solutions for many small and medium-size businesses.

An award-winning former reporter, she earned degrees in Journalism and Spanish from the University of Massachusetts, Amherst, and worked for several years in Northern California as a reporter and editor. She speaks fluent Spanish.

To learn more, visit www.JCWarner.com.

Susannah Gardner is the founder and creative director for Hop Studios Internet Consultants (www.hopstudios.com), a Web design company specializing in custom Web solutions.

Susannah is also a freelance writer and a part-time faculty member at the University of Southern California School for Communication.

Prior to running Hop Studios, Susannah worked in the Online Program at the University of Southern California, writing curriculum, teaching, and conducting research in the intersection of technology and journalism.

Susannah also spent four years working for *The Los Angeles Times*, where she was one of the first designers to work on the newspaper's Web site, before being promoted to multimedia director.

Susannah earned bachelor's degrees in Print Journalism and American Literature at USC. Today she is pursuing a master's degree in Public Art Studies. Susannah loves cats, food, books, and travel, but not all at once.

Frank Vera is a Web development consultant who specializes in programming solutions for dynamic Web sites.

With more than seven years of programming experience on the Web, Frank specializes in high-end Web site development using HTML, XML, Vignette StoryServer and Syndication Server, PHP, Tcl, C++, Visual Basic, Java, Perl, ASP, Oracle, and MySQL. He also has extensive experience with Web design programs, including Macromedia Dreamweaver and Microsoft FrontPage.

From 2000 to 2002, Frank worked for ZDNet Latin America, first as Publishing Operations Manager, and later as Director of Technology, where he managed technical operations, wrote documentation on proprietary systems, and conducted training programs for staff in the U.S. and Latin America. Prior to that, he served as System Administrator for PP Corp. in Miami, Florida.

Frank studied Computer Animation at the Art Institute of Fort Lauderdale and is a Microsoft Certified Systems Engineer.

Dedication

To all the dreamers who work on the Web. May Dreamweaver provide you with all the tools you need to publish your ideas, and may this book make it easier to use this powerful program so that you may focus your time on your words and your dreams.

Authors' Acknowledgments

Janine: I always thank many people in my books — former teachers, mentors, friends — but I have been graced by so many wonderful people now that no publisher will give me enough pages to thank them all. So I focus here on the people who made *this* book possible.

Above all others, I have to thank my wonderful coauthor Susannah Gardner for helping to maintain a high standard of quality in this book, even on a tight deadline, and for gracing these pages with examples of her own beautiful design work (see it on the Web at www.hopstudios.com).

Thanks also to Frank Vera, who is a great programmer with real communication skills who deserves credit for revising the three most complex chapters in this book: Chapters 13, 14, and 15, on dynamic database features in Dreamweaver. I have no doubt they could both write their own books and any publisher would be lucky to have them. Thanks also to Paul Vachier for taking a little time out from his own books to lend a hand to this one.

Thanks to Becky Huehls, our ever-understanding editor, for keeping us on track and helping with all the details that make these books make more sense. Thanks to Bob Woerner for shepherding this book through the development and publishing process. Thanks to Margot Maley, my wonderful agent, for helping me get this book deal in the first place.

I've written acknowledgements for so many books now I think my parents have lost count, but I always send them copies and I always thank them. I love you all — Malinda, Janice, Helen, and Robin. Thank you for your love, support, and understanding.

And finally, let me thank the beautiful stars that this book is finally done. Complete. Finished. This is it. (And don't even tell me those aren't complete sentences.)

Susannah: My thanks go first to Janine Warner, friend and colleague, who gave me the opportunity to work on this book with her. She has shared her expertise and advice at all hours of the day and night. I daydreamed for years about writing a tech book, but without Janine it would have been several more years before it ever happened. Thanks, Janine, for the kick in the you-know-what!

Some day I hope to write a book where my amazing husband, Travis Smith, can get a dedication page all his own, because he deserves it. Travis may have been more excited about this project than I was (I wonder if that had anything to do with not having to write the book himself) and kept me motivated and working hard to meet deadlines. He knows the way to my heart is late-night sushi dinners.

I also want to say thanks to the many clients and friends who allowed me to use their photos and Web sites in this book and who have let me come back to do work for them once, twice, sometimes even three times! My thanks go to Deborah Nathanson, Tracy Dominick, Suzanne Berg, Ted Gest, Kathryn Lord, Patti Rayne, and Jay Willis.

It is, of course, thanks to my wonderful parents that I have the brain to use for writing at all. I also have them to thank for my love of books and reading. So, kudos to Jan and Phil Gardner, and also to my siblings, Matt and Debbie Gardner, whose brilliant minds and stunning good looks cannot be denied.

Life would be undeniably poorer without my two cats, Aimee and Lukaska. Our frequent arguments about whether they belong on my desk or not made me stop and take breaks while writing this book. Aimee has been especially dedicated to keeping me company while I write by sleeping on top of the monitor.

I have some friends to thank for assistance with technology and simple common sense: Lance Watanabe, Jae Sung, Karin Sung, Elaine Zinngrabe, Jim Sabo, and Zipporah Lax.

And finally, thank you to all the fine people at Wiley whose attention to detail has kept things spelled right, labeled right, and best of all, right on the bookshelf.

Frank: These thanks are amazingly similar to thanks I've given before. However, what am I to do? I remain ever so grateful to all of the people in my past and present that helped me get to where I am today.

I am thankful to Janine for asking me to help her with this book. In the years that we've known each other, you have been a welcome addition to my life. Your encouraging words and optimism have, at times, pushed me along when nothing else would (even though you didn't know it at the time). Janine, thank you for being my friend and for being the only person you know how to be: you.

My family has always been an incredible source of support and drive in my life. My parents, Elsa and Francisco Vera: Thank you for bringing me into this world. Without your love and example, I never could have accomplished anything in my life. My little sister, Dr. Dinorah Vera, MD: Dee, you are without question the best example of how to reach for the stars and actually get there. Your persistence, and maybe downright stubbornness, has always impressed me. I measure my success, or sometimes my lack thereof, by comparing myself to you. Thanks, Dee. To my older sisters and their husbands, Susy and Sergio Morales, and Magda and Peter Portilla: Thank you for listening to my mindless ramblings and guiding me when I needed it. To my nephews and their wives, Danny Portilla, Gabriel Alvarez, and Sandy and Fabian Portilla: Thanks for putting up with my oh-so-exciting discussions about computers; but especially to my nephews' wives: Thanks for letting me take so much of your husbands' time with silly things. I love you, Melissa Romanowicz, for putting up with my silly notion that I have to work all the time; you are so kind to me and it never goes unnoticed.

Finally, I want to thank friends and people who have influenced me along the way: Ivonne Berkowitz (I borrowed this idea from her again!), Generosa Gonzales (Tia), Norys Hernandez, Thomas Santanta, Adriana Peña, William James King II, Drew Gilliland (look the spelling's right this time!), Farrell and Jan Ackerman, Francisco Rivera, Warren Van Der Woude, Tatiana and Bernardo DeAraujo, Manuel Alonso (Senior and Junior), Peter Schmidhoffer, Justo Sardiñas, Dave Marcotte, Robinson Mejia, Rene Ruiz, and countless others. Thank you for being a part of my life and helping to make me who I am.

Publisher's Acknowledgments

We're proud of this book; please send us your comments through our online registration form located at www.dummies.com/register/.

Some of the people who helped bring this book to market include the following:

Acquisitions, Editorial, and Media Development

Project Editor: Rebecca Huehls

 (Previous Edition: Andrea Boucher)

Acquisitions Editor: Bob Woerner

Copy Editors: Rebecca Senninger,
 Rebecca Whitney

Technical Editor: Danilo Celic

Editorial Manager: Leah Cameron

Senior Permissions Editor: Carmen Krikorian

Media Development Specialist: Kit Malone

Media Development Manager:
 Laura VanWinkle

Media Development Supervisor:
 Richard Graves

Editorial Assistant: Amanda Foxworth

Cartoons: Rich Tennant
 (www.the5thwave.com)

Production

Project Coordinator: Maridee Ennis

Layout and Graphics: Seth Conley,
 Kelly Emkow, Heather Ryan, Janet Seib,
 Mary Gillot Virgin, Shae Lynn Wilson

Proofreaders: Andy Hollandbeck,
 Carl William Pierce, Dwight Ramsey
 TECHBOOKS Production Services

Indexer: TECHBOOKS Production Services

Publishing and Editorial for Technology Dummies

 Richard Swadley, Vice President and Executive Group Publisher

 Andy Cummings, Vice President and Publisher

 Mary C. Corder, Editorial Director

Publishing for Consumer Dummies

 Diane Graves Steele, Vice President and Publisher

 Joyce Pepple, Acquisitions Director

Composition Services

 Gerry Fahey, Vice President of Production Services

 Debbie Stailey, Director of Composition Services

Contents at a Glance

Table of Contents

Introduction

*I*f you're like most of the Web designers I know, you don't have time to wade through a thick book before you start working on your Web site. That's why I wrote *Dreamweaver MX 2004 For Dummies* in a way for you to find the answers you need quickly. You don't have to read this book cover to cover. If you're in a hurry, just go right to the information you need most and get back to work. If you're new to Web design, or you want to really get to know the intricacies of Dreamweaver, skim through the chapters to get an overview and then go back and read what's most relevant to your project in greater detail. Whether you are building a simple site for the first time or working to redesign a complex site for the umpteenth time, you find everything you need in these pages.

Why Choose Dreamweaver?

With each new version of Dreamweaver, this award-winning program becomes more efficient and powerful. Yet somehow, Macromedia continues to make Dreamweaver intuitive and easy to use, even as its programmers work long hours to keep up with the latest innovations in Web design and release a new version of this program nearly every year since its creation.

The high-end features and ease of use of Dreamweaver make it an ideal choice for professional Web designers, as well as for those new to working on the Internet. And the new features in version 2004 make Dreamweaver better than ever!

I've been reviewing Web design programs since the first ones hit the market in 1994, and I can assure you that Dreamweaver is the best one I've ever worked with. But don't take my word for it — Dreamweaver has already won a slew of awards over the years, including Best of Show at Internet World, the prestigious five-mouse rating from *Macworld*, and Best Web Authoring Tool in the Readers Choice Awards by *PC Magazine*.

Among all the Dreamweaver features, these are some of the best:

✔ Dreamweaver has clean HTML code and sophisticated support for the latest HTML options (such as Dynamic HTML and Cascading Style Sheets — improved in the 2004 version).

✔ Dreamweaver MX 2004 even makes adding high-end features for creating database-driven Web sites easier. These features used to be sold separately in Dreamweaver UltraDev, but since Dreamweaver MX 2004, they're integrated into this one powerful program.

✔ As in previous versions, you find a state-of-the-art integrated text editor that makes switching back and forth between Dreamweaver and a text editor easier (if you prefer to look at the code, behind your pages you find some great enhancements to the text editor in this version).

If you've never written HTML before, don't be intimidated by these fancy features. The Dreamweaver graphical design environment uses sophisticated palettes and windows to enable beginners to create high-end Web sites that include such features as animations, interactive forms, and e-commerce systems, even if you don't know HTML.

Foolish Assumptions

Although Macromedia assumes that you're a *professional* developer, I don't. In keeping with the philosophy behind the *For Dummies* series, this book is an easy-to-use guide designed for readers with a wide range of experience. Being interested in Web design and wanting to create a Web site is helpful, but that desire is all that I expect from you.

If you're an experienced Web designer, *Dreamweaver MX 2004 For Dummies* is an ideal reference for you because it gets you working quickly with this program, from basic Web page development to the more advanced features. If you're new to Web design, this book can get you started and walk you through all you need to create a Web site.

About This Book

I designed *Dreamweaver MX 2004 For Dummies* to make your life easier as you work with this Web program. You don't have to read this book cover to cover and memorize it. Instead, each section of the book stands alone, giving you easy answers to particular questions and step-by-step instructions for specific tasks.

Want to find out how to change the background color on a page, create a nested table, build HTML frames, or get into the really cool stuff, such as style sheets and layers? Then jump right in and go directly to the section that most interests you. Oh, and don't worry about keeping all those new HTML tags in your head. You don't have to memorize anything. The next time you need to do one of these tasks, just go back and review that section. Feel free to dog-ear the pages, too — I promise they won't complain!

Conventions Used in This Book

Keeping things consistent makes them easier to understand. In this book, those consistent elements are *conventions*. Notice how the word *conventions* is in italics? That's a convention I use frequently. I put new terms in italics and then define them so that you know what they mean.

When I type URLs (Web addresses) or e-mail addresses within regular paragraph text, they look like this: `www.janinewarner.com`. Sometimes, however, I set URLs off on their own lines, like this:

```
www.janinewarner.com
```

That's so you can easily spot them on a page if you want to type them into your browser to visit a site. I also assume that your Web browser doesn't require the introductory `http://` for Web addresses. If you use an older browser, remember to type this before the address.

Even though Dreamweaver makes knowing HTML code virtually unnecessary, you may have to occasionally wade into HTML waters. I set off HTML code in the same monospaced type as URLs:

```
<A HREF="http://www.janinewarner.com">Janine's Web Site</A>
```

(That's the HTML code that makes a URL a link on a Web page.)

When I introduce you to a set of features, such as options in a dialog box, I set these items apart with bullets so that you can see that they're all related. When I want you to follow instructions, I use numbered steps to walk you through the process.

How This Book Is Organized

To ease you through the learning curve associated with any new program, I organized *Dreamweaver MX 2004 For Dummies* to be a complete reference. The following sections provide a breakdown of the parts of the book and what you can find in each one. Each chapter walks you through the features of Dreamweaver step by step, providing tips and helping you understand the vocabulary of Web design.

Part 1: Fulfilling Your Dreams

This part introduces you to Dreamweaver and covers getting started with the basics. In Chapter 1, I give you a handy reference to toolbars and menu options, and I also describe the new features in version 2004. And then in Chapter 2, I start you on the road to creating your first Web site, including setting up your site, importing an existing site, creating new Web pages, applying basic formatting to text, and even placing images and setting links on your pages.

Part II: Looking Like a Million (Even on a Budget)

Planning the design of your Web site is perhaps the most important part of Web site development — you'll save plenty of reorganizing time later. In Chapter 3, I start you out on the right foot with tips on Web site management, the principles of good design, and strategies that can save you countless hours. I also introduce you to the Dreamweaver site-management features. If you work with a team of designers, you'll be especially interested in the Dreamweaver check-in and check out features for version control and integrated e-mail for communicating with other team members. In Chapter 4, I introduce you to some of my favorite Dreamweaver features, including sophisticated template capabilities, Library items, Tracing images, the Quick Tag Editor, Design Notes, and the History palette.

Chapter 5 introduces you to Web graphics and shows you how to integrate graphic elements to your pages. You can find tools and strategies for creating the best Web graphics and tips on finding free images or buying graphics already optimized for the Web.

Part III: Advancing Your Site

In Part III, I show you how to use Dreamweaver with some of the more advanced HTML features. In Chapter 6, you discover how to use HTML tables to create complex page layouts that work in the most common Web browsers. A highlight of this chapter is the Table Layout mode, which makes creating complex Web designs easier than ever. In Chapter 7, you find all you need to know about designing a site with HTML frames. (This chapter helps you decide when you should and shouldn't use frames and gives you plenty of step-by-step instructions for creating HTML frames in Dreamweaver.)

Chapter 8 provides an overview of how Cascading Style Sheets work and how they can save you time. You find descriptions of all the style definition options available in Dreamweaver and instructions for creating and applying styles.

Part IV: Making It Cool

Now for the really fun stuff. In this part, you go for a walk on the wild side of HTML. In Chapter 9, I take you further into the Dynamic HTML features, such as layers and behaviors, which allow precise design control and new levels of interactivity. Chapter 10 introduces you to Fireworks, the Macromedia image program for the Web, and you can find out how to take advantage of the Dreamweaver integration with Fireworks to create complex images.

In Chapter 11, I help you use Dreamweaver to add multimedia to your Web pages and show you how to link a variety of file types — from Flash to Java to RealAudio — to your Web pages. Then in Chapter 12, I address HTML forms and how you can use Dreamweaver to add interactive elements, such as search engines, online discussion areas, and e-commerce systems, to your pages.

Part V: Working with Dynamic Content

Part V features three chapters that cover the most advanced features in Dreamweaver MX 2004. Chapter 13 is designed to help you understand how database-driven Web sites work and why they have become so important on the Web. Then in Chapter 14, you discover how to add dynamic content to your pages, define data sources, and display record sets. In Chapter 15, you pull it all together — find out how to build master pages, create pages to search databases, and test your work with a live connection.

Part VI: The Part of Tens

In The Part of Tens, you discover ten great Web sites created with Dreamweaver, ten great Web design ideas, and ten tips to save you substantial time and make your sites work better when you're using Dreamweaver MX 2004.

And finally, the About the CD appendix. In this appendix, you find a guide to the CD-ROM and all the great software that accompanies this book. On the CD-ROM you can also find a glossary of all the terms that you need to know when you work with Dreamweaver — and then some! And you get a bonus HTML chapter that introduces you to the HyperText Markup Language and helps you appreciate what's happening behind the scenes in Dreamweaver.

Icons Used in This Book

 This icon points you toward valuable resources on the World Wide Web.

 When I want to point you toward something on the CD that accompanies this book, I use this icon.

 This icon reminds you of an important concept or procedure that you'll want to store away in your memory banks for future use.

 This icon signals technical stuff that you may find informative and interesting but isn't essential for using Dreamweaver. Feel free to skip over this stuff.

 This icon indicates a tip or technique that can save you time and money — and a headache — later.

 This icon warns you of any potential pitfalls — and gives you the all-important information on how to avoid them.

Where to Go from Here

Turn to Chapter 1 to dive in and get started with Dreamweaver. You find a great overview of the program designed to get you up and running quickly, as well as a handy reference to all the new features in version MX 2004. If you're already familiar with Dreamweaver and want to find out about a specific trick or technique, jump right to the section you need; you won't miss a beat as you work to make those impossible Web design deadlines. And most of all have fun!

Part I
Fulfilling Your Dreams

The 5th Wave   By Rich Tennant

"What do you mean you're updating our Web page?"

In this part . . .

Stay awake for Part I, and I'll show you that you're not dreaming as I introduce you to the wonderful new advances in this powerful Web design program. The new features of Dreamweaver MX 2004 take care of many of the little complaints of designers and make Web design easier and more powerful than ever. And don't worry, if you're new to Dreamweaver or need a little refresher, this part offers a full introduction to the toolbars, menus, and panels that have made this an award-winning Web design program. Chapter 1 gives you the overview you need to appreciate all the features in this great tool, and in Chapter 2, you dive right into creating your first Web page.

Chapter 1

Introducing Your New Best Friend

*W*elcome to the wonderful world of Dreamweaver. If you're an experienced Web designer, you're going to love the power and sophistication of this HTML editor. If you're new to Web design, you'll appreciate its simplicity and intuitive interface. Either way, this chapter starts you on your way to making the most of Dreamweaver by introducing you to the menus and panels that make this program so useful.

Dreamweaver can help you with every aspect of Web development, from designing simple pages, to fixing links, to publishing your pages on the World Wide Web. Dreamweaver can handle the simplest HTML, as well as some of the most complex and advanced features possible on the Web, including Cascading Style Sheets and Dynamic HTML (see Chapters 8 and 9 for more information on these features). Dreamweaver also integrates a powerful HTML text editor into its easy-to-use graphical design environment.

If you already work in another Web design program, don't worry — you can use Dreamweaver to modify existing Web pages and continue to develop your Web site without losing all the time you already invested. All Web design programs create HTML pages, and those pages can open in any other Web design program. So, for example, if you've been working in a program such as Microsoft FrontPage or Adobe GoLive, you can still change to Dreamweaver to edit and develop your site further. At the end of this chapter, you find tips about some of the challenges in the section called "Working on Web Pages Created in Another Web Design Program."

In this chapter, you find an introduction to the new features in Dreamweaver MX 2004, get a tour of the desktop, and an overview of what makes Dreamweaver such a powerful Web design program. (If you don't understand a new vocabulary term as you read through this book, look it up in the comprehensive glossary included on the accompanying CD-ROM.)

So What's New in Dreamweaver MX 2004?

Now the good stuff. All those requests you make to Macromedia, all that wishful thinking . . . believe it or not, they heard you and many of the little — and not so little — things we all have been wanting in this program are finally here!

The following list provides you a quick overview of some of the new features you find in version MX 2004:

- ✔ The changes to the interface in this version aren't as dramatic as the changes to the Workspace made in the previous version, Dreamweaver MX, but you find some lovely enhancements. Beware that you no longer have the option of using the floating panels interface, the only option in the Dreamweaver versions prior to MX. You now have a choice between the Designer interface, which is graphical and features panels that lock into place, or the HomeSite/Coder-Style, which (as the name suggests) displays the HomeSite text editor. You have the option when you first turn on the program, and you can always make the changes in Preferences. If you choose the Designer interface, you can expand and collapse panels as needed and move them around to create a work environment that suits your preferences. Throughout this book, most of the screenshots and instructions reflect the Designer interface. If you're a code head (forgive me, someone who prefers working in the raw HTML), choose the HomeSite option, and you find many great features that make writing HTML code easy so you don't have to type all those tags in manually.

- ✔ The Designer interface is more streamlined and intuitive in its organization in this new version. You also find the interface easier to customize. For example, if you don't like the Properties inspector at the bottom of the screen, just drag it to the top and it locks into place.

  The Insert bar at the top of the screen is smaller in this version to take up less room in the work area. And, if you want to keep your favorite features handy, select Favorites from the pull-down list and right-click to easily customize the bar to hold your favorite features.

- ✔ Keeping up with the general trend in Web design, Macromedia greatly enhanced support for Cascading Style Sheets. You find many predefined style sheets to get you started and the Dreamweaver graphical interface renders those styles better so you don't always have to preview your work in a browser to see how it looks. The CSS panel and rules inspector are also improved to provide more options and make creating your entire design with CSS easier. You find more on these great features in Chapters 8 and 9.

✔ Dreamweaver is finally better suited to handling content from Microsoft Office documents. I have to say I think this one is long overdue, but now you can copy and paste content from Word and Excel and not lose the formatting. Dreamweaver even makes tables out of Excel spreadsheets.

✔ When you open Dreamweaver, you'll notice a new Start Screen. Anytime you don't have a file open, this screen reappears, providing quick access to a variety of page formats, premade templates and styles, and recently opened documents.

✔ Small, file-like tabs across the top of the work area make moving among open documents easy. In previous versions, the filename of open documents was at the bottom of the work area.

✔ No matter what language you speak, you can now work in Dreamweaver thanks to full Unicode support. Even languages that Dreamweaver is not localized for render properly in the work area.

✔ Dreamweaver is the best Web design tool for developing sites that work across multiple browsers, and Dreamweaver has great tools for checking your work to ensure that it displays well on the browsers you want to target. Now, those features work in real time thanks to Dynamic Cross Browser Validation. Specify the browsers you want to design for and Dreamweaver checks your work every time you save your pages.

✔ Want to crop, resize, or sharpen an image without launching an image editor? Now you can perform these common tasks right in Dreamweaver. You can also adjust brightness and contrast. Look for these new features in the Properties inspector and enjoy saving time on those quick image fixes and edits.

✔ You no longer have to use the Dreamweaver Site Setup before you can work on a Web site. If you prefer to just log in to a server and make quick changes or open files on your hard drive without setting up the main folder first, you can skip this previously required step.

However, if you want to use the Dreamweaver wonderful site management features, which allow you to easily move files and folders without breaking links and automatically fix links if they do get broken, you still want to use Site Setup. But don't worry, that's really an easy step, especially with the Dreamweaver Site Setup Wizard. You find detailed steps for setting up your site in Chapter 2.

✔ If you build your site with ASP, you will be pleased to find that ASP.NET server controls now include real objects and Properties inspectors. Look for the new ASP.NET tab on the Insert bar.

✔ A collection of new templates makes creating complex designs with a click of a button even easier. Templates are covered in detail in Chapter 4.

So, what's the big deal about Dreamweaver?

Dreamweaver has gotten great reviews and attracted considerable attention because it solves common problems found in other Web programs. Many Web designers complain that WYSIWYG design tools create sloppy HTML code, alter the code in existing pages, and make manually customizing pages difficult. Most of these problems stem from the fact that people who know how to write HTML code manually are used to having total control over their HTML pages. Unfortunately, many Web design programs force you to give up that control in order to have the convenience and ease of a graphical design tool.

Dreamweaver gives you both control and convenience by packaging an easy-to-use graphical design environment with a powerful HTML text editor, and in this latest version of Dreamweaver, the built-in text editor is even more powerful. Then Dreamweaver goes a step further with a feature Macromedia calls Roundtrip HTML. With Roundtrip HTML, you can create your HTML pages in any program, open them in Dreamweaver, and not have to worry about your original HTML code being altered.

Dreamweaver respects your HTML code. A big problem with many other Web design programs is that they can dramatically change HTML code if it doesn't conform to their rules. Unfortunately, the rules on the Web constantly change, so many designers like to break the rules or at least add their own variations to the theme. If you create a page with custom HTML code in a text editor and then open it in a program such as Microsoft FrontPage, you run the risk that FrontPage may change your design when it tries to make your code fit the rules of FrontPage.

Dreamweaver promises not to alter your code, which is one of the reasons it's become a best friend to so many professional designers. Still, Dreamweaver is not perfect, especially if you use the Clean Up HTML feature on custom code or special scripts. If you're a programmer creating advanced features, you may want to turn off some of the Dreamweaver automatic code rewriting features by choosing Edit⇨Preferences⇨Code Rewriting.

The challenge was in figuring out how to display HTML code created in any editor in the Dreamweaver graphical design environment without changing the code to match Dreamweaver's rules, even when you use some special code Macromedia has never seen before. The success that Macromedia has had in solving this problem is a big part of the reason why Dreamweaver has gotten so much attention, won so many awards, and attracted the loyalty of even the most die-hard HTML coders.

Introducing the Many Components of Dreamweaver

Dreamweaver can seem a bit overwhelming at first. It has so many features that all the panels, toolbars, and dialog boxes can be confusing when you start poking around. To help you get familiar with all the great options in this program, the next few sections introduce you to the interface and provide an overview of the basic functions of Dreamweaver. You also discover where to find most of the features and the functions of the buttons and menu options. All these features are covered in more detail in the rest of the book.

The Workspace

Creating a basic Web page in Dreamweaver is easier than ever, but it does take an extra step in this new version. When you launch Dreamweaver, the Start Screen appears in the main area of the program (and it reappears anytime you don't have a file open). From this Start Screen, you can choose to create a new page from one of the many Dreamweaver pre-made templates, or you can create a new blank page by selecting HTML from the Create New options in the middle column. When you select HTML, Dreamweaver creates a new blank HTML page in the main *Workspace,* as shown in Figure 1-1. You can type text directly into any page in the Workspace and apply basic formatting, such as bold and italics, simply by selecting Text➪Style➪Bold or Text➪Style➪Italics.

You build HTML pages, templates, style sheets, and so on in the Workspace, which consists of a main window that shows the page you're working on and a number of panels and windows that provide tools that you can use to design and develop your pages (shown in Figure 1-1). The Dreamweaver Workspace consists of the following basic components: the menu bar (at the very top), the Insert bar (just below it), the Document window (the main area of the screen, just below the Insert bar), the Properties inspector (at the bottom of the screen), and the Vertical Docking panels (to the right of the Document window) that expand and collapse as needed.

The Document window

The big, open area in the main area of the Workspace is the Document window, which is where you work on new and existing pages. If you use the Designer interface and are in Design View, you see your page as it would display in a Web browser, but if you look at the HTML code behind it (which you can do by clicking the Code buttons at the top of the work area), you see that it's a simple HTML file. If you choose the Split button, you can see the HTML code and the Design view simultaneously.

Pages viewed on the World Wide Web may not always look exactly the way they do in the Document window in Dreamweaver because not all browsers support the same HTML features or display them equally. For best results, always test your work in a variety of Web browsers and design your pages to work best in the browsers that your audience most likely uses. Fortunately, Dreamweaver includes features that help you target your page designs to specific browsers. (For more information on browser differences, check out Chapter 9.)

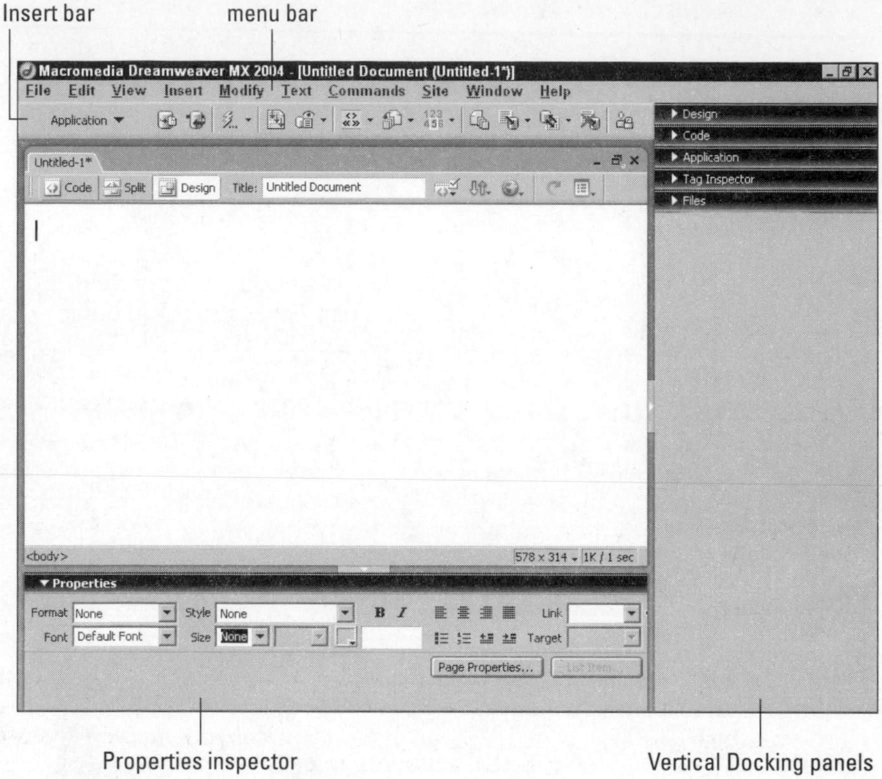

Insert bar   menu bar

Figure 1-1:
The
Workspace
includes a
Document
window,
menu bar,
Insert bar,
and the
Vertical
Docking
panels.

Properties inspector   Vertical Docking panels

Customizing the interface

The docking panels, palettes, and bars in Dreamweaver provide easy access
to many of the program's features. You can move these elements around the
screen by selecting them and dragging and dropping them. If you find that
having all these windows open distracts you from your ability to focus on
your design, you can close any or all of them by clicking the tiny icon in the
top right of all the main panels and selecting Close Panel from the pull-down
menu (it looks like three bullet points with lines next to them with a little
arrow underneath, and it's really, really small). You can close them all at
once by choosing Window➪Hide Panels, and you can access any or all the
panels through the various options on the Window menu. If you want to open
a panel — the CSS Styles panel, for example — choose Window➪CSS Styles
and it expands to become visible on your screen.

The Properties inspector, Insert bar, and panels are integral parts of this program, and you find a lot more information about them throughout the book.
Check out the Cheat Sheet at the front of this book for a handy reference to
the Properties inspector options. In Chapter 2, you discover some of the
most common features, such as inserting images (the icon for inserting an
image is in the Common Insert bar at the top of the page).

The Insert bar

The Common Insert bar at the top of the page contains buttons that provide quick access to many common features. For example, click the icon that looks like a piece of a chain and you insert an HTML link into your page. Click the little envelope icon and you insert an e-mail link.

The Insert bar has eight *subcategories* that offer separate sets of buttons for various functions: Common, Layout, Forms, Text, HTML, Application, Flash Elements, and Favorites. The Favorites Insert bar is blank by default, and you can customize it to hold your favorite options. Simply right-click in the bar and you can easily customize this bar. Throughout the book, I refer to these by their full names, such as the Forms Insert bar or the Layout Insert bar. You find more information on each of these in their relevant chapters. For example, the Forms Insert bar is covered in detail in Chapter 12, and Application is covered in Chapters 13, 14, and 15.

Use the small arrow to the right of the name to access the pull-down list and switch from displaying the buttons on one subcategory to showing the buttons for another. Figure 1-2 shows the pull-down list with the Common Insert bar selected. To change the icon display, choose Edit⇨Preferences, and select the Panels option.

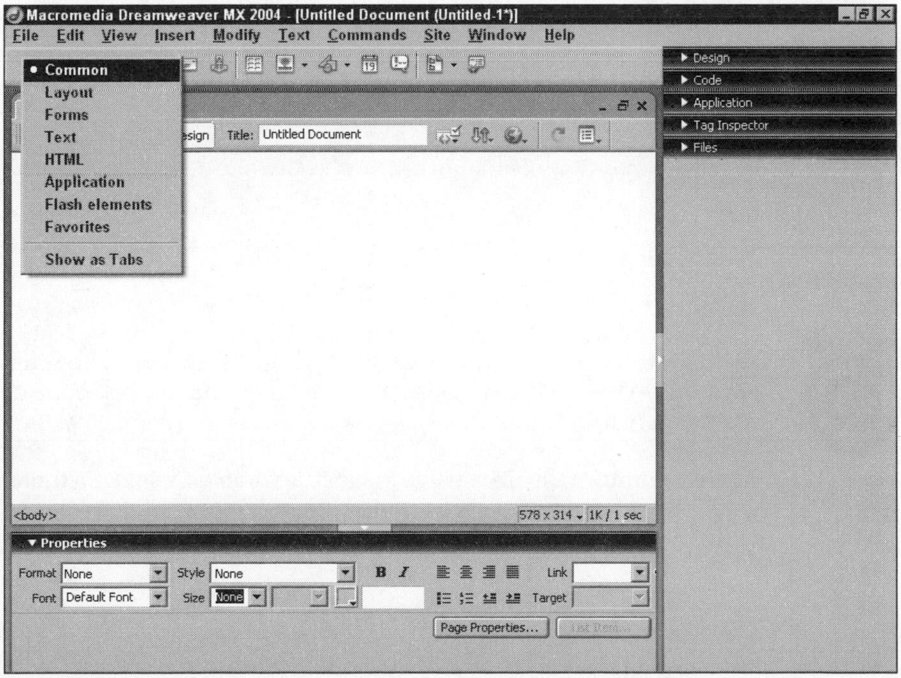

Figure 1-2:
The Insert bar provides quick access to options for forms, tables, images, and more.

The Properties inspector

The Properties inspector is docked at the bottom of the page in Dreamweaver. If you prefer it at the top of the screen, you can drag it up there, and it locks into place. The Properties inspector displays the properties of a selected element on the page. A *property* is a characteristic of HTML — such as the alignment of an image or the size of a cell in a table — that you can assign to an element on your Web page. If you know HTML, you recognize these as HTML *attributes*.

When you select any element on a page (such as an image), the inspector changes to display the properties, or attributes, for that element, such as the height and width of an image or table. You can alter those properties by changing the fields in the Properties inspector. You can also set links and create image maps using the Properties inspector.

Figure 1-3 shows the image options displayed in the Properties inspector, including height and width, alignment, and the *URL* (Uniform Resource Locator or, more simply, Web address) to which the image links.

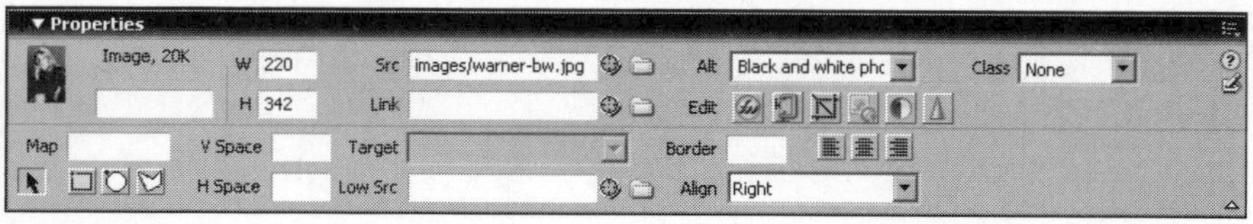

Figure 1-3:
The Properties inspector displays the attributes of a selected element, such as an image shown here.

▼ Properties							
Image, 20K	W 220	Src	images/warner-bw.jpg	Alt	Black and white phc	Class	None
	H 342	Link		Edit			
Map	V Space	Target		Border			
	H Space	Low Src		Align	Right		

At the bottom-right corner of the Properties inspector, you see a small arrow. Click this arrow to reveal additional attributes that let you control more advanced features.

Figure 1-4 shows the Properties inspector when you select a table. Notice that the fields in the inspector reflect the attributes of an HTML table, such as the number of columns and rows. (See Chapter 6 to find out more about HTML tables.)

The Vertical Docking panels

The Vertical Docking panels, shown in Figure 1-5, are located to the right of the work area (although you can easily move them to the left). The Vertical Docking panels display a variety of important features in Dreamweaver, including Files in a site, Assets, CSS *(Cascading Style Sheets)*, Behaviors, History, and the Application features (the Databases, Data Bindings, Server Behaviors, and Components). You can open and close panels by selecting the panel name from the Windows menu, and you can hide these panels by clicking the tab with the small arrow on the left of the panels.

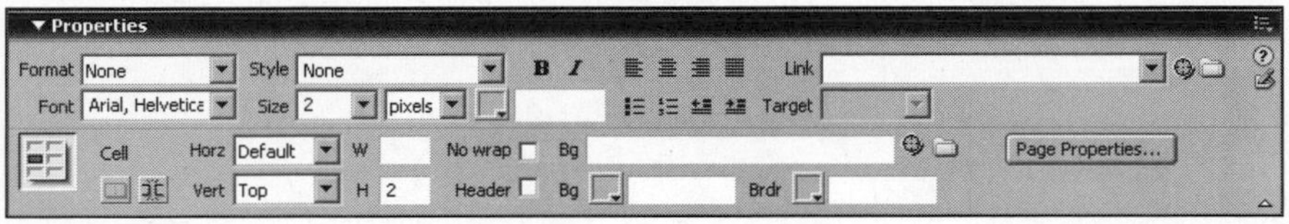

Figure 1-4:
The Properties inspector displays the attributes of a selected HTML table or cell when selected.

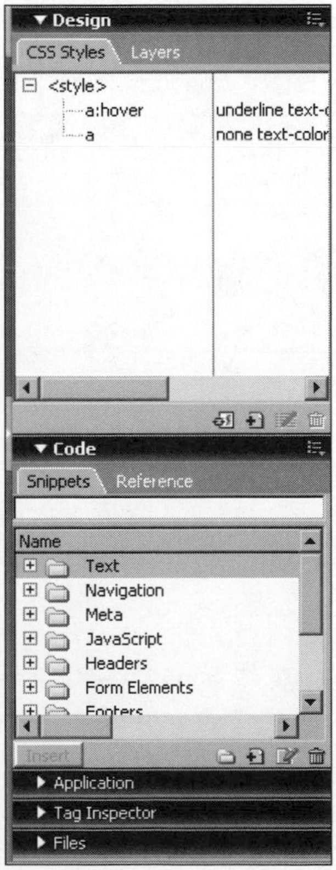

Figure 1-5:
The Vertical Docking panels provide easy access to various Dreamweaver features, including CSS, Behaviors, and Application features.

The following list offers a description of some of the elements that you access through the Vertical Docking panels (the others are described in greater detail in their respective sections of the book).

 ✔ **Files panel:** Shown in Figure 1-6, the Files tab in the Files panel lists all of the folders and files in a Web site and helps you manage the structure and organization of the site. The Files tab is also where you access FTP *(file transfer protocol)* capabilities. You can use the Connect button at the top of this dialog box to dial quickly into your server. The Get and Put buttons enable you to transfer your pages back and forth between your computer and the server. (See Chapter 2 to find out more about the Site panel.)

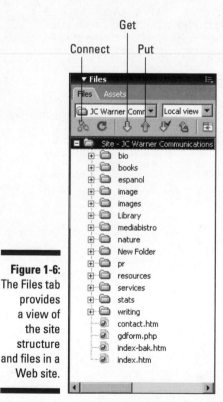

Connect Get Put

Figure 1-6:
The Files tab
provides
a view of
the site
structure
and files in a
Web site.

 ✔ **Assets panel:** The Assets panel provides easy access to the images, colors, external links, multimedia files, scripts, templates, and Library items in a Web site. The Library panel, shown in Figure 1-7, enables you to store items in a central place so that you can easily add them to multiple pages. After you store an element in the Library (you store an item simply by dragging the element onto the Library panel), you can then drag that element from the Library onto new pages. The Library is ideal for elements used throughout a Web site, as well as those that you must update frequently. The other parts of the Assets panel work in much the same way, providing easy access to related elements. You find more on the Library feature in Chapter 4.

These features work only if you define your site using the Site Definition dialog box, available by selecting Site⇨Manage Sites. If you find that the Library options aren't available to you, go to Chapter 2 and follow the steps for defining a site.

✔ **Design and Rule panels:** These two panels enable you to define styles by using Cascading Style Sheets (CSS). CSS styles are similar to style sheets used in word processing and desktop publishing programs, such as Microsoft Word and QuarkXPress. You define a style and name it, and the style is then included in the CSS Styles panel, which is accessible through the tab at the top of the panel (see Figure 1-8). The Design panel provides access to the CSS Styles panel, shown in Figure 1-8, where you can specify the type, size, and formatting of the style. After you define a style, you can apply it to text or other elements on a page. The Rules panel is a Tag inspector for CSS. Style sheets are a big time-saver because they let you set several attributes simultaneously by applying a defined style. (For more information about CSS, see Chapter 8.)

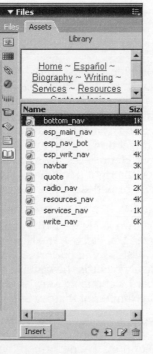

Figure 1-7: The Assets panel stores items in a central place, which makes placing the same element, such as a navigation row, on multiple pages easy.

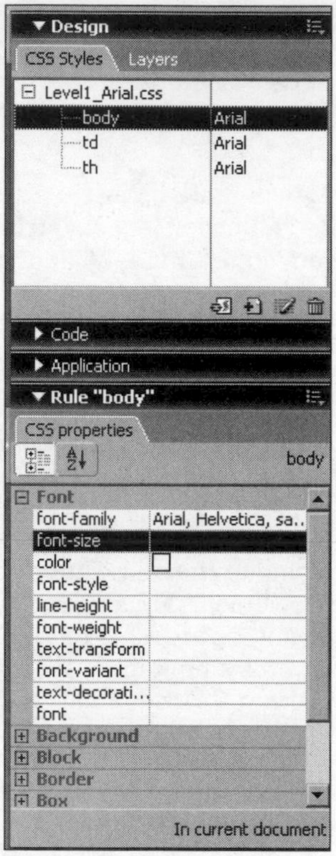

Figure 1-8:
The Style
Definition
panel
makes
creating
new combi-
nations of
formatting
features as
CSS easy.

- ✔ **Tag inspector:** The Tag inspector provides access to the Attributes, Behaviors, and Relevant CSS tabs. In Dreamweaver, *behaviors* are scripts (usually written in JavaScript) that you can apply to objects to add inter- activity to your Web page. Essentially, a behavior is made up of a speci- fied event that, when triggered, causes an action. For example, an event may be a visitor clicking an image or section of text, and the resulting action may be that a sound file plays. Figure 1-9 shows the Behaviors panel. The left pane displays events; the right pane displays the actions triggered by those events. (Chapter 9 provides more information on cre- ating and applying behaviors.)

- ✔ **History panel:** The History panel, shown in Figure 1-10, keeps track of every action you take in Dreamweaver. You can use the History panel to undo multiple steps at once, to replay steps you performed, and to auto- mate tasks. Dreamweaver automatically records the last 50 steps, but you can increase or decrease that number by choosing Edit➪Preferences➪ General, and changing the Maximum Number of History Steps.

- ✔ **Application Panel:** This is where you find Data Bindings, Server Behaviors, Components, and Databases options, but you use these only if you work with a database. These options are described in more detail in Chapter 14.

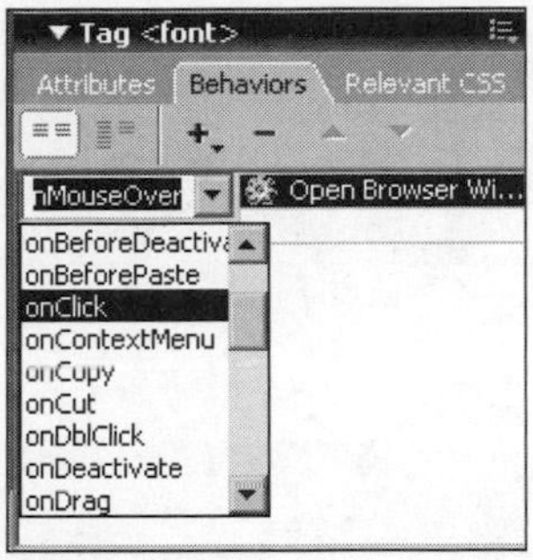

Figure 1-9:
Clicking
the + button
opens a
drop-down
list of
behaviors.

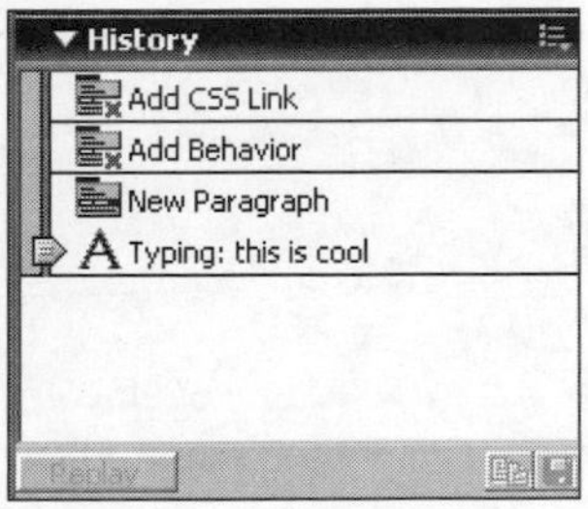

Figure 1-10:
The History
panel keeps
track of
all your
actions in
Dream-
weaver,
which
makes
undoing or
replaying
steps easy.

Code and Split views

The Code view in Dreamweaver reveals the best-integrated HTML text editor of any Web design program. In Figure 1-11, the Split View option is selected, which makes seeing the graphical design area and the HTML code at the same time possible. Notice that the highlighted text in the graphical area is also highlighted in the HTML Code view. Changes made in one immediately appear in the other. This integration makes moving back and forth between writing HTML code manually and creating it in the graphical editing environment nearly seamless.

The menu bar

At the top of the screen, the Dreamweaver menu bar provides easy access to all the features that you find in the Insert bar, Properties inspector, and panels, as well as a few others that are available only from the menu. The following sections provide a general description of each of the menu options.

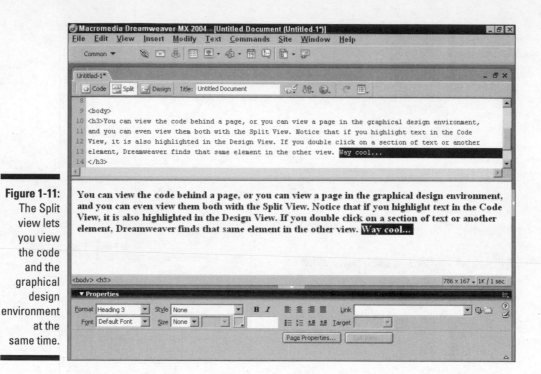

Figure 1-11:
The Split
view lets
you view
the code
and the
graphical
design
environment
at the
same time.

The File menu

You find many familiar options, such as New, Open, and Save, on the File
menu, shown in Figure 1-12. You also find a Revert option, which is similar to
the Revert feature in Adobe Photoshop. This sophisticated undo feature
enables you to return your page quickly to its last-saved version if you don't
like the changes you made. Dreamweaver automatically keeps track of up to
50 actions, but you can increase or decrease that number by choosing Edit⇨
Preferences⇨General and changing the maximum number of history steps.

The File menu also includes access to Design Notes, a unique feature that
associates private notes with HTML and other files. Take a look at Chapter 4
for more information about Design Notes and other Dreamweaver features
that make collaboration easier.

You can also find features useful for checking your work in Web browsers on
the File menu. Most Web design programs include some way of previewing
your work in a browser. Dreamweaver takes this feature two steps further by
enabling you to check your work in a number of browsers and even test the
compatibility of your pages in different versions of different browsers.

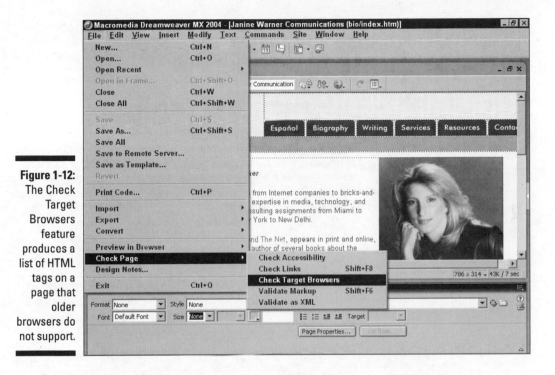

Figure 1-12:
The Check
Target
Browsers
feature
produces a
list of HTML
tags on a
page that
older
browsers do
not support.

Figure 1-12 shows the Check Page options, which includes Check Accessibility, Check Links, and Check Target Browsers — all great tools for testing your work. The Check Target Browsers option enables you to specify a browser and version, such as Netscape 3.0 (still a widely used browser on the Web) or Internet Explorer 3.0. When you do a browser check, Dreamweaver generates a report listing any HTML features you use that the chosen browser doesn't support.

The Check Links feature verifies all the links in a site and produces a report with all broken and unresolved links. The Check Accessibility feature checks to make sure the page displays properly in browsers for the blind and other systems for the disabled.

The Edit menu

The Edit menu contains many features that you may find familiar, such as Cut, Copy, and Paste. One feature that may be new to you is the Edit with External Editor option, which enables you to open an element in another program, such as an image editor, and make changes without ever leaving Dreamweaver.

You also find the Preferences settings on the Edit menu. Before you start working with a new program, going through all the Preferences options to ensure that the program is set up the best way for you is always a good idea.

The View menu

The View menu provides access to some helpful design features, such as grids and rulers. The Visual Aides option on the View menu gives you the option of turning on or off the borders of your HTML tables, frames, and layers, as well as controlling visibility of image maps and other invisible elements. This option is useful because you often want to set the border attribute of these HTML tags to zero so that they're not visible when the page displays in a browser. However, while you work on the design of your page in Dreamweaver, seeing where elements, such as tables and layers, start and stop is very useful. Checking the frame options in the View menu lets you see the borders in Dreamweaver even if you don't want them visible to your site's visitors.

The Insert menu

As shown in Figure 1-13, the Insert menu offers access to a number of features unique to Web design. From this menu, you can insert elements such as a horizontal rule, a Java applet, a form, or a plug-in file.

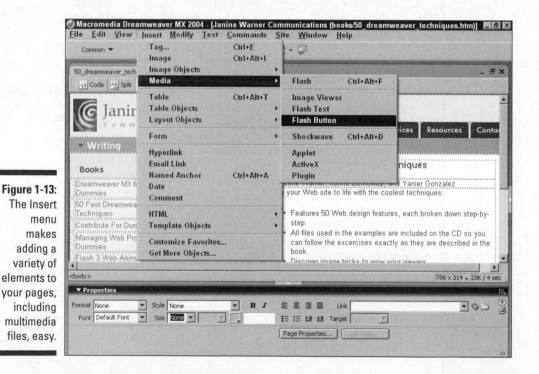

Figure 1-13: The Insert menu makes adding a variety of elements to your pages, including multimedia files, easy.

Dreamweaver offers extra support for inserting Flash and Shockwave Director files, both of which are products from Macromedia. (You can find out more about using multimedia files in Chapter 11.)

The Modify menu

The Modify menu is another place where you can view and change object properties, such as the table attributes shown in Figure 1-14. The properties (usually called *attributes* in HTML) let you define elements on a page by setting alignment, height, width, and other specifications.

Page Properties

You can also set individual attributes using the Properties inspector. To alter properties for an entire page, use the Page Properties dialog box, available from the Modify menu or by clicking the Page Properties button at the bottom of the Properties inspector. Changing page properties (see Figure 1-15) enables you to set link and text colors for the entire page and specify the background color or image.

Figure 1-14:
The Modify menu makes changing object properties, such as the table attributes shown here, easy.

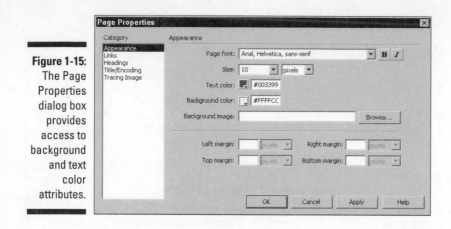

Figure 1-15:
The Page
Properties
dialog box
provides
access to
background
and text
color
attributes.

The Text menu

You can easily format text with the Text menu by using simple options, such as bold and italic, as well as more complex features, such as font styles and custom style sheets. Text formatting options have evolved dramatically on the Web. Just a few years ago, you didn't even have the option of specifying a particular font style or controlling leading and spacing. Today, although these options aren't yet universally supported, you have more control than ever over the look of your Web pages.

For example, if you choose a particular font for your text, that font must be available on the user's computer for the text to display properly. Because of this limitation, HTML enables you to specify several font possibilities to improve your odds that a font you want displays. The browser searches the user's computer for one of these fonts in the order in which you list them. Dreamweaver recognizes the importance of specifying more than one font and the safety of using the more popular fonts.

The Commands menu

The Commands menu, shown in Figure 1-16, provides access to a host of options in Dreamweaver. These options include the Start and Play Recording features, which let you quickly save a series of steps and then repeat them. To use this feature, choose Commands➪Start Recording, perform whatever actions you want to record — for example, copying and pasting some text — and then choose Stop Recording. Then to perform that action again, choose Commands➪Play Recorded Command. You can download an action by choosing Command➪Get More Commands, which automatically launches a browser and takes you to the Macromedia Web site. You can download new commands from the Web site that adds functionality to Dreamweaver.

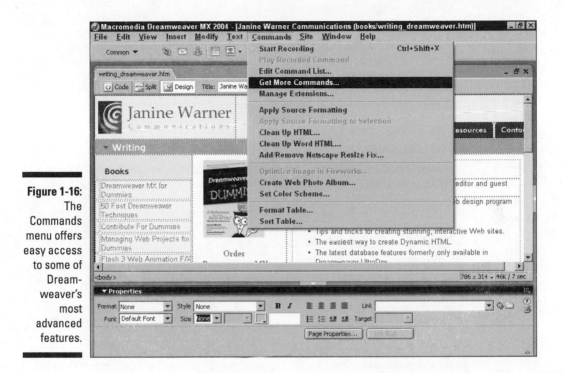

Figure 1-16:
The
Commands
menu offers
easy access
to some of
Dream-
weaver's
most
advanced
features.

The Clean Up HTML option on the Commands menu helps you correct bad HTML code, and the Clean Up Word HTML feature is designed especially to correct the common problems caused by the Save As HTML feature in Microsoft Word.

The Add/Remove Netscape Resize Fix option on this menu inserts or removes a JavaScript script designed to help correct a Netscape bugby automatically reloading the page when users resize their browser windows.

The Create Web Photo Album option launches Macromedia Fireworks and uses it to automate the creation of a photo album with a series of images. If you choose Optimize Image in Fireworks, a selected image automatically opens in the optimization area in Fireworks.

Another great feature on the Commands menu is the Set Color Scheme command. This option includes a list of background and text colors specially designed to work well together on the Web.

The Site menu

The Site menu provides access to the options you need to set up your site, a process required before many of the other Dreamweaver features work properly. (This process is covered in detail in Chapter 2.) The Site menu also gives you easy access to the Check In and Check Out features, which are options that can help you keep a team of designers from overwriting each other's work. (Chapter 4 also talks about this feature.)

The Window menu

The Window menu lets you control the display of panels and dialog boxes, such as Insert, Properties, and Behaviors. To turn on these features, select the panel name so that a check mark appears next to the feature you want to display; to turn the feature off, click again to remove the check mark. Other panels and dialog boxes, such as CSS Styles and HTML Code Inspector, are also listed on the Window menu for easy access.

The Help menu

The Help menu provides easy access to help options that can assist you in figuring out many features of Dreamweaver. You also find access to the Dreamweaver template and example files under Help.

Templates and examples provide visual samples of common HTML designs, such as tables and frames, and provide design ideas and great shortcuts for creating complex layouts.

The Status bar

The Status bar appears at the very bottom-left of the Dreamweaver screen. On the right end of the Status bar, you can see shortcuts to many other features. On the left end, you find HTML codes that indicate how elements on your page are formatted. If you run your mouse pointer over text that is centered, for example, the Status bar displays `<CENTER>`. This feature makes double-checking the kind of formatting applied to any element on your page easy.

You can also use the Status bar to identify a section on your page. For example, if you click the name of a tag in the Status bar, the section of your page where that tag is applied is highlighted. This makes selecting certain sections of a page easier, such as a table.

Working on Web Pages Created in Another Web Design Program

In theory, all Web design programs should be compatible because HTML files are, at their heart, just ASCII (or plain-text) files. You can open an HTML file in any text editor, including Macintosh SimpleText and Windows Notepad. However, HTML has evolved dramatically over the years and different Web programs follow different standards, which can cause serious conflicts when a page created in one program opens in another.

One of the reasons Dreamweaver is so popular is because it creates very clean code and is considered more accurate and more respectful of HTML standards than other programs. Dreamweaver is also better at creating pages that work in different browsers and on different platforms, but importing files created in another Web program can be challenging, even in Dreamweaver.

To help with the transition, Dreamweaver includes some special features, such as the Clean UP Word HTML option, designed to fix some of the common problems with Microsoft Word's HTML code.

Before you start working on a site that was developed in another program, you need to import the site into Dreamweaver. I recommend you make a backup of the site first so you have a copy of all the original pages. You find step-by-step instructions for importing an existing Web site in Chapter 2.

The following sections describe the most popular HTML editors and what you need to know if you're moving files from one of these programs to Dreamweaver.

Microsoft FrontPage

Microsoft FrontPage is one of the most popular HTML editors on the market, in large part because Microsoft Office is so popular. FrontPage also offers some powerful features as well as an attractive bundle of programs for Web developers, including Image Composer, a bundled graphics program designed for creating images for the Web. FrontPage also includes *Web components* that you can use to add interactive features, such as a simple search engine or a discussion area, to your Web site. Web components work only if their corresponding programs reside on the Web server that you use, but many commercial service providers now offer FrontPage Web components.

If you are migrating a site from FrontPage to Dreamweaver, first make note of any FrontPage Web components that you use, such as search engines or forms. Dreamweaver doesn't offer these same built-in features, and you won't be able to continue editing them in Dreamweaver the way you did in FrontPage. Though the components still work, thanks to the Dreamweaver Roundtrip HTML, which respects unique code, you sacrifice some of the convenience of the FrontPage built-in components for Dreamweaver's more standard approach to creating code. If you use a number of components, are used to the way they work in FrontPage, and feel that you can't live without them, you may be better off sticking with FrontPage for a while.

If you're ready to graduate to Dreamweaver (and I've spoken to many frustrated FrontPage users who are happy after they make the switch), you can re-create all the components you use in FrontPage by using CGI and other programming in conjunction with your pages in Dreamweaver. If you don't know how to do that yourself, consider hiring a programmer to help you make the transition and then maintaining the site yourself in Dreamweaver after those features are re-created.

If you use CSS or Layers in FrontPage, you need to pay special attention to those features as you convert your site to Dreamweaver. Microsoft FrontPage isn't as good as Dreamweaver at creating high-end features that work in both Netscape Navigator and Microsoft Internet Explorer, so you probably want to improve your code if you expect viewers to use any browser other than Internet Explorer. Because CSS and layers are more complex than HTML to code, you probably don't want to edit this code manually — converting from other editors to Dreamweaver can get pretty tricky. Tables can also get messy when you switch from one program to another. In some cases, you may find that the simplest solution is to delete the elements that you created in FrontPage and re-create them in Dreamweaver. (For more on CSS and layers, check out Chapters 8 and 9.)

Microsoft Word

Although Microsoft Word is a word processor and is not considered an HTML editor per se, it does have HTML output capabilities. As a result, you will likely encounter pages that have been output from Microsoft Word at some point. The problems you find in HTML code generated from Word are similar to the problems generated from FrontPage: They both tend to output verbose and redundant code that deviates from HTML standards. Because Word-generated HTML is so common, Dreamweaver includes a special Clean Up Word HTML command. To use this feature, choose Commands⇨Clean Up Word HTML and then specify the code you want altered in the Clean Up Word

HTML dialog box. When you use this feature, Dreamweaver removes excess code, which can help your pages load faster and work better in different browsers.

NetObjects Fusion

If you work in NetObjects Fusion, you face a more dramatic transition to Dreamweaver than you do coming from almost any other HTML editor discussed in this section. That's because Fusion took a unique approach to Web design and HTML code output. Although the program is not widely used anymore, many Web sites out there were created with it.

The biggest challenge with Fusion sites is that Fusion uses complex HTML tables and a transparent graphic to control spacing. The down-to-the-pixel design control enticed many graphic designers because they can create complex layouts with less effort, but those designs are not well supported by all browsers — meaning that the designs don't work well for broad audience sites.

The problem if you import a Web site created with Fusion is that it has very complex code that doesn't lend itself easily to further editing in any other program. Unfortunately, if you want the cleanest HTML code possible, which speeds up download time and makes editing pages easier in the future, your best bet is to re-create your designs from scratch. I'm sorry to break this to you, but if you import a site created in Fusion, you should probably start over with Dreamweaver; the transition process is just too daunting to be worth it. Move all your images into new image directories, set up a new site in Dreamweaver, and start over with your design work.

Adobe GoLive

Adobe GoLive offers some great features for easy page design and a lot of similarities with Dreamweaver, but it also brings some of the same problems as pages created in NetObjects Fusion (see the preceding section). GoLive makes using a grid to provide down-to-the-pixel layout control possible, in much the same way Fusion does. So, like Fusion, GoLive often outputs very complex code that is difficult to edit in other programs.

Because you can see the alignment grid in GoLive, you may be more aware of the complex table that GoLive creates in the background. The grid feature in GoLive is optional, and if the site you import was created without this feature, converting your pages to Dreamweaver is a much easier task. If the site was created using the grid, you may find that re-creating your pages from scratch in Dreamweaver is your best option. The code used to create the complex HTML tables that GoLive uses in its grids is extremely difficult to edit outside of GoLive. If you work with people who use GoLive, try to get them to avoid using the Layout Grid feature when designing their pages and you have an easier time working on the site with Dreamweaver.

If you add any JavaScript actions to your pages in GoLive, you can't edit them in Dreamweaver, either, but the actions still work. Likewise, CSS and other Dynamic HTML features created in GoLive do not work well in Dreamweaver unless you know how to edit the code manually. If your page contains any actions or DTHML features, you may find re-creating the page in Dreamweaver is easiest.

Other HTML editors

In the early days of the Web, lots of different visual HTML editors were being used. Today only a few major ones are left. The few that I discuss here seem to capture most of the market. Still, you may find yourself inheriting sites built in really old editors such as Adobe PageMill, Claris HomePage, or Symantec VisualPage, to name a few. Each of these programs present fewer problems than either Fusion or GoLive, because they aren't capable of creating the complex, high-end features that are hardest to migrate from one program to another.

No matter what program your site is originally created in, as you consider how best to convert your work into Dreamweaver, pay special attention to unusual code output, nonstandard rules about HTML tags and syntax, and sophisticated features such as CSS, Dynamic HTML, and sophisticated programming, such as ASP, Java, or CGI scripts. These Web page elements are most likely to cause problems when you import them into Dreamweaver.

For the most part, you can open any HTML page with Dreamweaver and continue developing it with little concern. If you run into problems, remember that you always have the option of re-creating the page from scratch in Dreamweaver — a sure way to get rid of any unwanted code. You may also want to use the Dreamweaver Clean Up HTML feature to identify potentially problematic code. To use this feature, choose Commands⇨Clean Up HTML and then select the elements you want to alter in the Clean Up HTML dialog box.

Also be careful if you use Adobe ImageReady to automatically output HTML with images, for example, if you use the slicing feature to break up a large image into smaller images arranged in an HTML table. ImageReady also relies heavily on the transparent image trick for alignment and makes heavy use of the Colspan attribute in tables. Both of these tricks are problematic if you change the table width values. If you have trouble getting your images to align the way you intend, you may again be better off deleting the original page and re-creating the table in Dreamweaver. The good news is after you migrate your site into Dreamweaver, your work goes much more smoothly and your sites works better for a broader audience in the future.

Chapter 2

Setting Up a Web Site with Dreamweaver

*I*f you're ready to dive in and start building your Web site, you've come to the right place. In this chapter, you find what you to need to start working on an existing Web site — or create an entirely new site. In the following pages, you find out some basics about planning your site and how to use the site setup features, which enable Dreamweaver to keep track of the images, links, and other elements in your site. In the second part of the chapter, you get into the fun stuff, creating your first page and adding images and text.

Before you start creating or editing individual pages, set up your site using the site-management features in Dreamweaver. Whether you're creating a new site or working on an existing site, follow the steps in the next section to get Dreamweaver ready to manage the site for you. The site management features enable Dreamweaver to keep track of the elements in your site, automatically create links, update your server, and even manage a team of developers. With the enhancements in this latest version, all these features are even more powerful and easy to use.

You can use Dreamweaver without doing the initial site set up explained in the following section, but many of the features — such as automated link checking and the ability to store commonly used elements in the Library — won't work without first doing site set up.

Visualizing Your Site

Before you get too far into building Web pages, take some time to plan your site and think about its structure and organization. Begin thinking about the following questions:

- ✓ What do you want to accomplish with your Web site? (What are your goals and objectives?)
- ✓ Who is your target audience?
- ✓ Who will be working on your site? How many developers do you have to manage?
- ✓ How will you create or collect the text and images you need for your site?
- ✓ How will you organize the files in your site?
- ✓ Will you include multimedia files, such as Flash or RealAudio?
- ✓ Will you want interactive features, such as a feedback form or chat room?
- ✓ What other software will you need for specialized features (for example, Macromedia Flash for animations)?
- ✓ What kind of navigation system will you have for your site (that is, how can you make navigating through your Web site easy for visitors)?
- ✓ How will you accommodate growth and further development of the site?

With at least a basic plan for your site, you're in a better position to take advantage of the site management features I discuss later in this chapter. In Chapter 3, you find more detailed tips and suggestions for planning and managing your site. Taking the time to get clear on your goals and objectives is time well spent and can save you lots of grief later. Set the tone for successful Web development from the beginning and make sure you spend your precious, time, money, and energy on the elements and features that best help you serve your audience and reach your goals.

Setting Up a New or Existing Site

The site setup process is important because when you finish building your site and upload it to your Web server, the individual pages, images, and other elements must remain in the same relative location to each other on the Web server as they are on your hard drive. The site-management features in Dreamweaver are designed to ensure that things work properly on the server by making certain that you set links and other features correctly when you create them. If you don't do site set up and use the site management features, you risk breaking links between pages. The site setup process also gets you ready to use the Dreamweaver FTP capabilities, which facilitate the transfer of your site from your local computer to your Web server and manage updates anytime you make changes to your site.

When you set up a new site, Dreamweaver automatically creates a new folder on your hard drive to ensure that you save all the pages and other elements of your site. If you prefer, you can change the location of that folder or create a new one yourself.

If you're working on an existing site, you follow the same steps, but instead of creating a new folder, you direct Dreamweaver to the folder that contains the existing site.

If you're an experienced Web designer and just want to make quick changes to a site or use the FTP features to access files on a server without doing the site setup steps, Dreamweaver now allows you to use these features without completing site set up. To access FTP features and set them up quickly, choose Site⇨Manage Sites and then choose New⇨FTP & RDS Server from the Manage Sites dialog box. This shortcut enables you to work directly on your server using FTP or RDS, but Dreamweaver does not manage links checking or any of the other site management features.

If you're a not so experienced Web designer or you are working on a site that you're building completely on your computer, take the extra three minutes and follow the steps to do site set up. The time you save in the long run is more than worth it.

Note: FTP *(File Transfer Protocol)* is used for copying files to and from computers connected across a network, such as the Internet. FTP is the protocol you use to send your Web pages to your Web server when you're ready to publish your site on the Web. (For a glossary of this and other terms, see the CD-ROM.)

Defining a site

The following steps walk you through the process of using the Site Definition dialog box to define your site. Whether you create a new site or work on an existing Web site, this first step is important to your Web design work because this is where you identify your site structure, which enables Dreamweaver to set links and effectively handle many of the site-management features explained in later chapters.

If you want to work on an existing site that is on a remote Web server, follow the steps in the section, "Downloading an existing Web site," later in this chapter.

To define a site using the Site Definition dialog box, follow these steps.

1. **Choose Site⇨Manage Sites.**

   The Manage Sites dialog box appears, as shown in Figure 2-1.

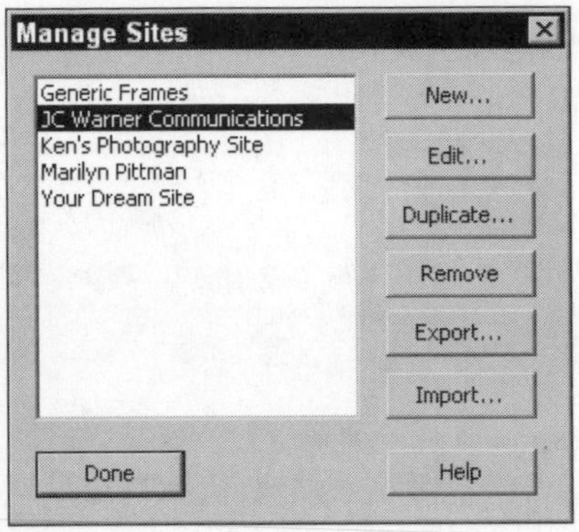

Figure 2-1:
The
Manage
Sites dialog
box keeps
a list of all
the sites
you set up
in Dream-
weaver and
provides
access to
editing
and setup
options.

Manage Sites

Generic Frames
JC Warner Communications
Ken's Photography Site
Marilyn Pittman
Your Dream Site

New...
Edit...
Duplicate...
Remove
Export...
Import...

Done   Help

2. **Click the New button, and then select Site.**

   The Site Definition dialog box appears, as shown in Figure 2-2.

3. **Click the Advanced tab.**

   The Advanced window appears. If you prefer, you can use the wizard that automatically appears, but I find you have much better control over the feature options by using the Advanced tab.

4. **Make sure that the Local Info category is selected in the Category box.**

5. **In the Site Name text box, type a name for your site.**

   You can call your site whatever you like; this name is only used for you to keep track of your sites. Many people work on more than one site in Dreamweaver so the program includes a way to name and keep track of them. After you name it here, the name appears as an option on the drop-down list in the Files panel. You use this list to select the site you want to work on when you open Dreamweaver.

6. **Click the Browse button (it resembles a file folder) next to the Local Root Folder text box to locate the folder on your hard drive that contains your Web site.**

   If you're working on a new site, create a new folder and designate that as the location of your site in Dreamweaver.

7. **If Refresh Local File List Automatically isn't already selected, click to place a check mark in the box next to this option if you want Dreamweaver to automatically update the list of all the new pages you add to your site.**

   This feature helps Dreamweaver work more efficiently by speeding the process of tracking and identifying files in your site.

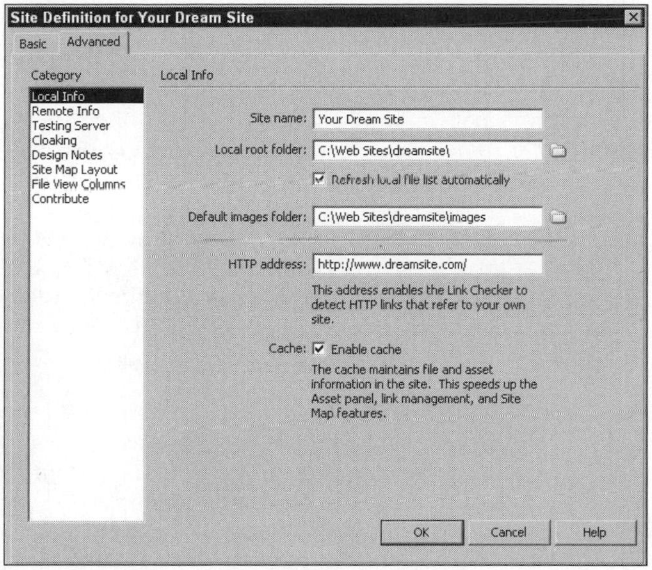

Figure 2-2:
The Site
Definition
dialog box
enables you
to set up
a new or
existing
Web site
in Dream-
weaver.

8. **Specify the Default Images folder by entering the location or using the browse button to locate it.**

   You do not have to identify an images folder. If you store images in more than one folder or if you have not yet created any images, you can leave this box blank. (You can find more information about images in Chapter 5.)

9. **Type the URL of your Web site in the HTTP Address text box.**

   The HTTP Address is the URL, or Web address, that your site will have when published on a Web server. If you do not yet know the Web address for your site or you do not plan to publish it on a Web server, you can leave this box blank.

10. **Check the Enable Cache option.**

    Dreamweaver creates a local cache of your site to quickly reference the location of files in your site. The local cache speeds up many of the site management features of the program and takes only a few seconds to create, unless you have a really content-heavy site or a very slow computer.

11. **Click OK to close the Site Definition dialog box.**

    If you haven't checked the Enable Cache option, a message box appears asking whether you want to create a cache for the site. Figure 2-2 shows what the Site Definition dialog box looks like when all the areas in the Local Info section are filled in.

Setting up Web server access

To make your life simpler, Dreamweaver incorporates FTP capability so that you can easily upload your pages to a Web server. Integrating this feature also enables Dreamweaver to help you keep track of changes you make to files on your hard drive and ensure that they match the files on your Web server.

You enter information about the Web server where your site will be published on the Remote Info page of the Site Definition dialog box. You access this page by selecting Remote Info in the Category box on the left side of the Site Definition dialog box. The Remote Info page opens on the right side of the box, as shown in Figure 2-3.

You'll find several options in the Remote Info section under the Access drop-down list. In the following section, you'll find instructions on how to set up FTP access, which is the second choice on the list. If you aren't going to publish your site on a server, choose None from the drop-down list. If you're going to send your site to a server on a network, choose Local/Network; then use the Browse button to specify that server's location on your network. The other options, RDS, Source Safe Database, and WebDAV, enable a version control system and help you keep track of changes when a team of developers is working on a site.

The most common way to publish a Web site after you develop it is to use FTP to send the site to a remote server, such as those offered by commercial Internet service providers. If that is how you're going to publish your site, the steps coming up help you through the process.

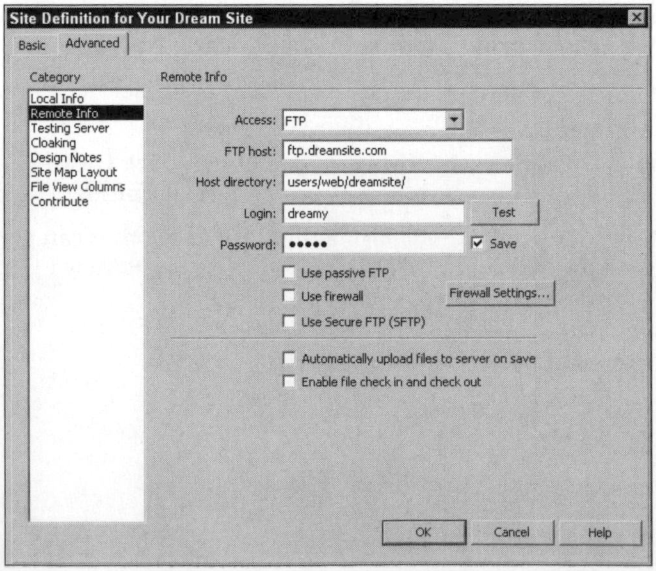

Figure 2-3:
The Site
Definition
dialog box
specifies
the access
information
for a remote
Web server.

If you're using a remote server, such as an Internet service provider, ask your provider for the following information:

- ✔ FTP host name
- ✔ Path for the host directory
- ✔ FTP login
- ✔ FTP password

Choose FTP from the Access drop-down list in the Remote Info page of the Site Definition dialog box, shown in Figure 2-3, and follow these steps:

1. **In the FTP Host text box, type the hostname of your Web server.**

   It should look something like `ftp.host.com` or `shell.host.com` or `www.host.com`, depending on your server.

2. **In the Host Directory text box, type the directory on the remote site in which documents visible to the public are stored (also known as the *site root*).**

   It should look something like `public/html/` or `www/public/docs/`. Again, this depends on your server.

3. **In the Login and Password text boxes, type the login name and password required to gain access to your Web server. If you check the Save box, Dreamweaver stores the information and automatically supplies it to the server when you connect to the remote site.**

   This is your unique login and password information that provides you access to your server.

4. **Put a check mark in the Use Passive FTP or Use Firewall options only if your service provider or site administrator instructs you to do so.**

   If you aren't on a network and use a commercial service provider, you don't need to check either option.

5. **If you don't want to check any other settings, click OK to save your Web Server Info settings and then close the Site Definition dialog box.**

   If you want to continue reviewing the settings in other categories, choose Testing Server, Design Notes, Site Map Layout, File View Columns, or Contribute from the Category box on the left side of the screen (I explain some of these settings in the following sections and others later in the book).

   If you're ready to dive in and start working on your first pages, you don't need to adjust any of these options. Just skip ahead to the section, "Creating New Pages," so that you can jump right into creating your Web site.

Using Check In/Out

The Check In/Out category is designed to keep people from overwriting each other's work when more than one person contributes to the same Web site (a valuable feature if you want to keep peace on your Web design team). When a person working on the Web site checks out a file, other developers working on the site are unable to make changes to that page. When you check out a file, you see a green check mark next to the filename. If someone else checked out a file, you see a red check mark.

To use the Check In/Out feature, check the Enable File Check In and Check Out option at the bottom of the Remote Info dialog box. The dialog box expands to expose other options. If you want files checked out whenever they are opened, check the Check Out Files When Opening option (see Figure 2-4).

Using this feature, you can track which files a particular person is working on. If you're the only person working on a Web site, you don't need this feature, but if you want to use this tracking mechanism, check the Check Out Files When Opening option and then fill in the name you want associated with the files (presumably your name or nickname if you prefer) in the Check Out Name field and then include your e-mail address in the Email Address field. (The Email Address field is needed for Dreamweaver's integration with e-mail, which facilitates communication among developers on a site. You find more information about integrated e-mail in Chapter 4.)

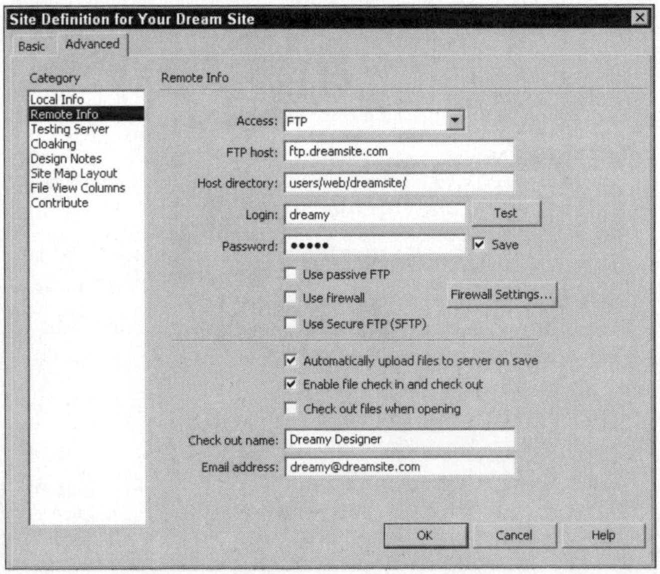

Figure 2-4: The Check In/Out feature helps you keep track of development when more than one person is working on the site.

Using the Testing Server

The Testing Server option enables you to specify a development server, a necessary step if you are creating a Web site using the Dreamweaver features with a database. You find more information about how to do this in Chapters 13, 14, and 15. If you are not creating a site linked to a database, you don't need to make any changes to this dialog box.

Using Design Notes

If you sometimes forget the details of your work or neglect to tell your colleagues important things about the Web site you're all working on, the Dreamweaver Design Notes feature may save you some grief.

Design Notes enable you to record information and associate it with a file or folder. They work like the HTML comment tag, which lets you add text to a page that doesn't display in a browser, so you can make notes in the code. But Design Notes takes this concept a step farther, enabling you to add comments to any element, including images, multimedia files, and even folders. And unlike the comment tag, which is embedded directly in the HTML code of a page, visitors can't see Design Notes when they view your Web site — even if they look at the HTML source code. You can choose to upload Design Notes so that they are available to others with access to your server, or you can prevent them from ever being loaded to your public site.

To access the Design Notes page, choose Design Notes in the Category box in the Site Definition dialog box (see Figure 2-5). The settings on this page let you control how Dreamweaver uses Design Notes:

- ✔ **Maintain Design Notes:** Select this option to ensure that the Design Note remains attached to the file when you upload, copy, or move it.

- ✔ **Upload Design Notes for Sharing:** Choose this option to include Design Notes when you send files to the server via FTP.

- ✔ **Clean Up:** This button enables you to delete Design Notes no longer associated with files or folders in your site.

When you create graphics in Macromedia Fireworks, you can save a Design Note for that file that is also available in Dreamweaver. To use this integrated feature, save the Fireworks image to your local Web site folder. When you open the file in Dreamweaver, the Design Note displays when you right-click the image (⌘-click on the Mac). This feature is a great way for graphic designers to communicate with other members of the Web development team.

Activating Site Map Layout

If you have trouble keeping track of all your files and how they link in your site, you're not alone. As Web sites get larger and larger, this task becomes increasingly daunting. Dreamweaver includes a Site Map Layout feature to help you keep track of your Web pages and the hierarchy of your site. This is not a Site Map like those you often see on Web sites that's visible to visitors of your site and provides links to all or many of the pages in the site. The Dreamweaver Site Map Layout is a site management feature in that you can visually manage the files and folders that make up your site.

To access the settings for the Site Map Layout feature, choose Site Map Layout from the Category box in the Site Definition dialog box. The Site Map Layout page opens on the right side of the box, as shown in Figure 2-6.

You can use the Site Map Layout feature to automatically create a site map of all the pages in your Web site. This is a useful management tool because you have a visual reference of the hierarchy of your Web site and all its links. You can use this map to make sure that your site is following the basic plan you created before you started creating pages. For more details on planning, see "Visualizing Your Site," earlier in this chapter, and see Chapter 3.

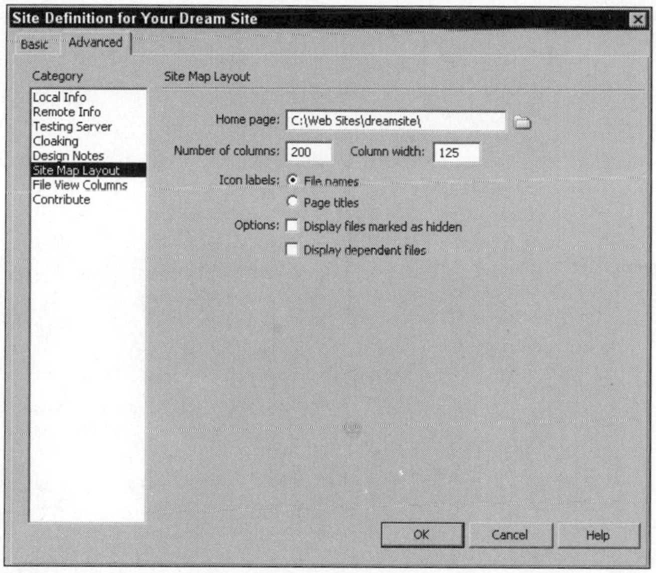

Figure 2-6:
The Site Map Layout page enables you to specify how the Site Map navigation window appears.

To create a site map from the Site Map Layout page of the Site Definition dialog box, follow these steps:

1. **In the Site Definition dialog box, choose Site Map Layout from the Category list.**

   If it's not already open, access the Site Definition dialog box by choosing Site⇨Manage Sites, and then double-clicking the name of the site you want to work on in the Manage Sites dialog box.

2. **In the Home Page text box, type the path to the main page of your site or click the Browse button (the icon that resembles a file folder) to locate it. If you already filled out the Local Info page, this field automatically is filled in.**

   This text box specifies the home page for the site map and provides Dreamweaver with a reference for where the Web site begins. If you don't specify a home page and Dreamweaver doesn't find a file called `index.html` or `index.htm` (the most common names for a home page), Dreamweaver prompts you to select a home page when you open the site map.

3. **Set the Number of Columns field to the number of pages you want displayed per row in the site map.**

   If you're not sure what you want for these settings, start with the default values. You can always come back and change these settings later if you don't like the spacing of the icons in your site map.

4. **In the Column Width text box, set the width of the site map's columns, in pixels.**

   Again, start with the default if you're not sure how wide you want this to display.

5. **In the Icon Labels section, click either the File Names option or the Page Titles option if you want the filename or page title of each page to display in the site map.**

   You can manually edit any filename or page title after you generate the site map.

6. **In the Options section, you can choose to hide certain files, meaning that they won't be visible in the Site Map window.**

   If you select the Display Files Marked as Hidden option, files you have marked as hidden display in italic in the site map.

   If you select the Display Dependent Files option, all dependent files in the site's hierarchy display. A *dependent file* is an image or other non-HTML content that the browser loads when loading the main page.

7. **Click OK.**

   A window appears asking if you want to create a cache file for the site. This helps Dreamweaver keep your links up to date and improves the performance of the site map.

8. **Click the Create button to generate a cache file and launch the site map process.**

   Dreamweaver scans all the files in your site and creates a cache, which helps make things work faster in the program.

9. **Click the Done button in the Manage Sites dialog box when you finish.**

10. **To view a site map, select the Expand/Collapse icon in the right-hand side of the Files panel. Then select the Site Map icon in the top left of the expanded display window and choose Map Only from the pull-down menu.**

    Alternatively, you can select Map and Files to display the site map on the left of the screen and the files list on the right, as shown in Figure 2-7.

Downloading an existing Web site

If you want to work on an existing Web site and you don't already have a copy of it on your local computer's hard drive, you can use Dreamweaver to download any or all of the files in the site so that you can edit the current pages, add new pages, or use any of Dreamweaver's other features to check links and manage the site's further development. The first step is to get a copy of the site onto your computer by downloading it from the server.

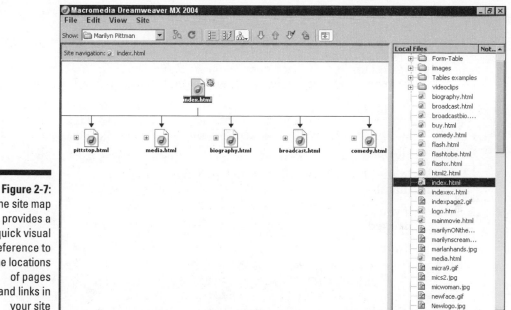

Figure 2-7:
The site map provides a quick visual reference to the locations of pages and links in your site structure.

To download an existing Web site, follow these steps.

1. **Create a new folder on your computer to store the existing site.**

2. **Specify this folder as the local root folder for the site with the Dreamweaver site setup features.**

   Check out the section "Defining a site," earlier in this chapter, if you're not sure how to do this.

3. **Set up the Remote Info dialog box.**

   I explain how to do this in the "Setting up Web server access" section, earlier in this chapter.

4. **Connect to the remote site by clicking the Connects to Remote Host button, which looks like the ends of two cables, in the Site window (located in the Files panel to the right of the Dreamweaver Workspace).**

5. **Click the Get Files button, which looks like a down arrow, to download the entire site to your local disk.**

   If you want to download only specific files or folders from the site, select those files or folders in the Remote pane of the Site window, and click the Get File(s) button. Dreamweaver automatically duplicates some or all of the remote site's structure, meaning the folders in the site but not all the files within them, to place the downloaded files in the correct part of the site hierarchy. Recreating the folder structure on your local computer is important because Dreamweaver needs to know the location of the files as they relate to other parts of the site in order to set links properly. The safest option is to download the entire site, but if you are working on a really large Web project, downloading a part and duplicating the structure enables you to work on a section of the site without downloading all of it.

If you are working on only one page or section of a site, you should generally choose to include dependent files, meaning any files linked to those pages, to ensure that links set properly when you make changes.

6. **After you download the site or specific files or folders, you can edit them as you do any other file in Dreamweaver.**

Creating New Pages

Every Web site begins with a single page. Visitors are first greeted by the front page — or *home page* — of your site and that's usually a good place to start building. Dreamweaver makes building a home page easy: When the program opens, you see a Start Screen with shortcuts to many handy features for creating new pages. If you just want to create a simple Web page, choose HTML from the Create New list in the middle row (see Figure 2-8). If you are creating a dynamic site, you may choose ColdFusion, PHP, or one of the ASP options. (If you don't even know what those options mean, you probably won't need to use them, but you can look them up in the glossary on the CD.)

To create a new page with a page already open, simply choose File➪New and then select Basic Page from the category list and HTML from the Basic page list. You find many other options in the Dreamweaver New Document dialog box, but for now, don't worry about all those. In this chapter, you start off by creating a simple HTML file. You find out about other options, such as predesigned templates covered in Chapter 4, later in the book.

Creating a new page to start a Web site may seem obvious, but consider this: You may want to create a bunch of new pages before you get too far in your development, and you may even want to start organizing the new pages in subdirectories before you have anything on them. Doing so enables you to organize the structure of your site before you start setting links. After all, you wouldn't want to link to a page that doesn't exist. If you plan to have five links on your front page to other pages in your site, go ahead and create those other pages, even if you don't put anything on them yet.

When I first start building a Web site, I often create a bunch of pages with nothing but a simple text headline across the top of each. I make a page like this for each area of my site and often place them in subdirectories. For example, if I create a site for my department at a big company, I have a page about my staff, another about what we do, and a third with information about the resources that we provide. At this initial stage, I create four pages — one for the front page of the site and three others for each of the subsections. With these initial pages in place, I benefit from having an early plan for organizing the site, and I can start setting links among the main pages right away. See Chapter 3 for more tips about Web site planning and organization. Chapter 4 guides you through the use of templates, a great way to develop multiple pages with similar designs.

Designing your first page

Before you get too far into design or organization, I want to give you a general idea about how to do basic tasks in Dreamweaver, such as formatting text and setting links.

If you're ready to plunge right in, click to insert your cursor at the top of a blank page in Dreamweaver and type some text. Type anything you like; you just need something that you can format. If you have text in a word processor or another program, you can copy and paste that text into your Dreamweaver page. After you enter the text on your page, dive into the following sections to find out how to play around with formatting your text.

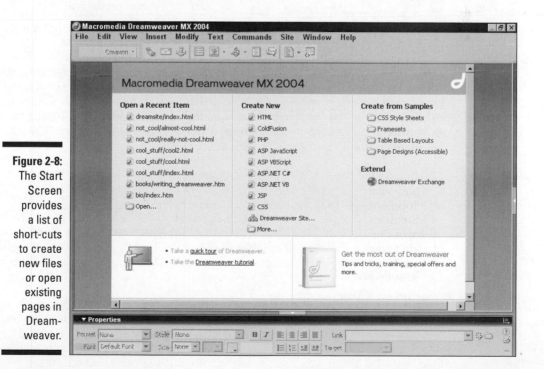

Figure 2-8:
The Start Screen provides a list of short-cuts to create new files or open existing pages in Dream-weaver.

You can collapse the panels on the right side of the work area by clicking the small tab on the side of the panel set. In the following figures, I collapsed the panels to create more room in the Workspace.

Creating a headline

Suppose that you want to center a headline and make it big and bold, such as the one shown in Figure 2-9. To create a new page with a page already open, simply choose File➪New and then select Blank page from the category list and HTML from the Basic page list. To create a headline, follow these steps:

1. **Highlight the text you want to format.**

2. **In the Properties inspector at the bottom of the page, select the B icon to make the selected text bold.**

   The heading becomes bold.

3. **In the Properties inspector at the bottom of the page, select the center icon.**

   The text automatically centers.

4. **In the Properties inspector, use the Size pull-down menu and select 36.**

   The text changes to font size 36 and you have a headline at the top of your page that looks something like the headline shown in Figure 2-9.

In general, I find the Properties inspector the easiest way to apply basic formatting, but some people prefer using the drop-down menus from the Text menu bar. Both achieve the same results with the exception that Dreamweaver now features font sizes in the Properties inspector that align more with what you see in a word processing program. Notice that in the Properties inspector, the font sizes are listed as sizes 9 through 36.

Indenting text

Type a little more text after your headline text. A single sentence is enough. To indent that text, follow these steps:

1. **Highlight the text you want to indent.**

2. **Choose Text➪Indent.**

   The text automatically indents. Alternatively, you can use the Text Indent and Text Outdent icons in the Properties inspector.

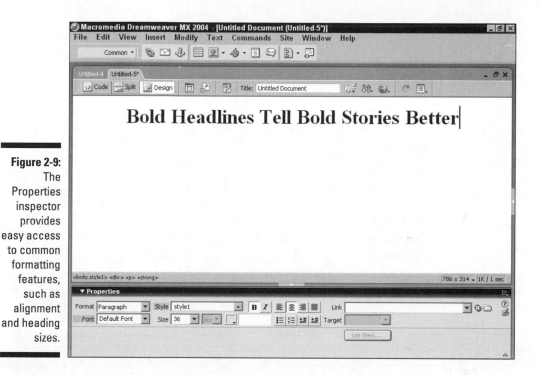

Figure 2-9:
The Properties inspector provides easy access to common formatting features, such as alignment and heading sizes.

If you want to continue adding text and you don't want to indent it, choose Text⇨Outdent to transition back to plain text mode without the indent. You can also use the small Indent and Outdent icons located at the bottom of the Properties inspector, just to the left of the Target field.

If you just want to indent a line or two, the Indent option in the Text menu is ideal. If, however, you want to create the effect of a narrower column of text on a page, you may find that putting your text in an HTML table is a better option because you can control the width of the column. You can find information about creating HTML tables in Chapter 6.

Adding images

Adding an image to your Web page is simple with Dreamweaver. The challenge is to create a good-looking image that loads quickly in your viewer's browser. You need another program, such as Photoshop or Fireworks, to create and edit images. Use Dreamweaver to place the images on your page. For more information on finding and creating images, as well as keeping file sizes small, see

Chapter 5. For now, I assume that you have a GIF or JPEG image file ready, and just walk you through the steps to link your image to your page. (The only image formats you can use on your Web page are GIF and JPEG, which is shortened to JPG.) If you don't have an image handy, you can find a few GIF and JPEG files on the CD-ROM included at the back of this book. You can use any image on your Web site, as long as it's in GIF or JPEG format.

PNG is also an accepted image format on the Web, but Web designers rarely use it because browsers have not supported PNG as well.

You need to do two important things before inserting an image on a Web page. First, save your HTML page in your Web site's folder on your hard drive. This step is important because Dreamweaver can't properly set the link to your image until it identifies the relative locations of the HTML page and the image. Until you save the page, Dreamweaver doesn't know what folder the page is in.

For this same reason, you need to make sure that the image file is where you want to store it on your Web site. Many designers create a folder called *images* so that they can keep all their image files in one place. If you are working on a very large site, you may want an images folder within each of the main folders of the site. An important thing to remember is that if you move the page or image to another folder after you place the image on your page, you risk breaking the link between the page and the image, and an ugly broken image icon appears when you view your page in a browser. If you move files or folders around in the Dreamweaver Files panel, it automatically fixes the links, but if you move them outside of Dreamweaver, the link breaks. If for some reason you do end up breaking an image link, simply click the broken image icon that appears in its place, and use the Browse icon to find the correct image to replace it.

Follow these steps to place an image to your Web page:

1. **Click the Image icon located in the Common tab of the Insert bar at the top of the work area. (*Hint:* It looks like a small tree.)**

   The Image dialog box opens.

2. **Click the Select button.**

   A dialog box opens, displaying files and folders on your hard drive.

3. **Navigate to the folder that has the image you want to insert.**

4. **Double-click to select the image you want.**

   The image automatically appears on your Web page.

If you haven't already saved your page, a warning box appears to tell you that Dreamweaver cannot properly set the link to the image until you save the page. You see this message because Dreamweaver needs to know the location of the HTML page relative to the image to create the link. If you see this box, cancel the step, save your page by choosing File⇨Save, and then repeat the preceding steps. Similarly, if the image is not located within your designated root folder, a dialog box opens asking if you want to copy the image to that folder. Click the Yes button if you want Dreamweaver to automatically copy the image to your root folder (this helps ensure the image transfers to your server correctly when you upload your site to your server).

5. **Click the image on your Web page to display the image options in the Properties inspector at the bottom of the page.**

   Use the Image Properties inspector to specify image attributes, such as alignment, horizontal and vertical spacing, and alternative text. (The image properties are visible in the Properties inspector in Figure 2-10.)

   The Image Properties inspector enables you to specify many attributes for images that you use in your Web site. Table 2-1 describes those attributes. If you don't see all the attributes listed in the table, click the triangle in the bottom-right corner of the Image Properties inspector to reveal all the image options.

Although you can resize an image in Dreamweaver by clicking and dragging on the edge of the image or by changing the Height and Width values in the Properties inspector, the options are not recommended because they don't actually change the size of the image, just the way it displays on the page. That's a problem because using this option to make an image bigger leads to distortion, and using this option to make an image smaller, requires your visitor to download a larger file than necessary.

You're almost always better off using an image editor to change the physical size of an image instead. Because this is such a common thing to do, the newest version of Dreamweaver includes a few shortcuts that incorporate Fireworks image-editing capabilities and enable you to actually edit the image without leaving Dreamweaver. You can find these options in the Properties inspector when an image is selected. See Chapter 5 for more on these new image-editing options.

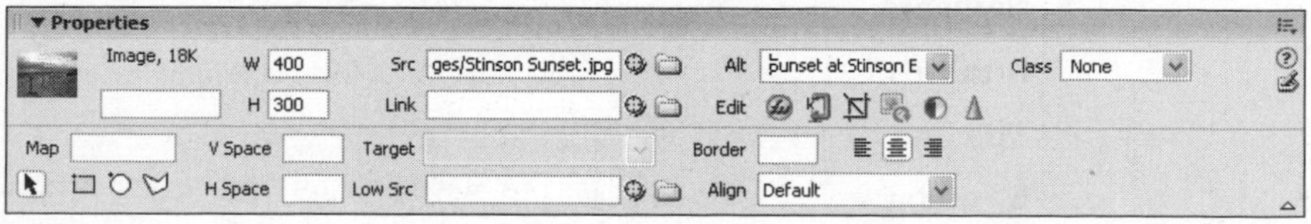

Figure 2-10:
The Image Properties inspector provides easy access to common image attributes, such as alignment and spacing.

Table 2-1	Image Attributes in the Properties Inspector	
Abbreviation	*Attribute*	*Function*
Image	N/A	Specifies the file size.
Image Name	Name	Identifies image in scripts.
Hotspot tools	Image map	Use the Rectangle, Oval, and coordinates Polygon icons to create image map hotspots on an image. (See Chapter 5 to find out how to create an image map.)
W	Width	Dreamweaver automatically specifies the width of the image based on the actual size of the image file.
H	Height	Dreamweaver automatically specifies the height of the image based on the actual size of the image file.
Src	Source	The *source* is the link or the filename and path to the image. Dreamweaver automatically sets this when you insert the image.
Link	Hyperlink	This field shows the address or path if the image links to another page. (For more about linking, see "Setting Links" later in the chapter.)
Alt	Alternate Text	The words you enter here display if the image doesn't appear on your viewer's screen because the viewer either has images turned off or can't view images. Special browsers for the blind also use this text and convert it to speech with special programs, such as screen readers.
Edit	N/A	Click the Edit button to launch an image editor, such as Fireworks, but you must first specify the editor you want to use in the Dreamweaver Preferences dialog box, available by selecting Edit⇨Preferences and then choosing the File Types/Editors Category. If you install Fireworks when you install Dreamweaver, then Fireworks is the default editor.
Reset Size	N/A	The Reset Size button enables you to automatically reset the actual image size. This is handy if you change the size of the image by clicking and dragging the edge of the image and then want to reset it.
Map	Map Name	Use the Map name text box to assign a name to an image map. All image maps require a name.
V Space	Vertical Space	Measured in pixels, this setting inserts blank space above and below the image.

Abbreviation	Attribute	Function
H Space	Horizontal Space	Measured in pixels, this setting inserts blank space to the left and right of the image.
Target	Link Target	Use this option when the image appears in a page where you want to control the target, such as when a page is part of an HTML frameset or when you want a link to open a new window. The Target specifies the frame into which the linked page opens. I cover creating frames and how to set links in frames in Chapter 7.
Low Src	Low Source	This option enables you to link two images to the same place on a page. The Low Source image loads first and is then replaced by the primary image. You may find this option especially useful when you have a large image size because you can set a smaller image (such as a black-and-white version) as the Low Source, which displays while the main image downloads. The combination of two images in this way creates the illusion of a simple animation.
Border	Image Border	Measured in pixels, this attribute enables you to put a border around an image. I nearly always set the image border to 0 (zero) and Dreamweaver makes that the default setting when linking an image because otherwise you will see a colored border around a linked image.
Align	Alignment	This option enables you to align the image. Text automatically wraps around images aligned to the right or left. The other options, including Baseline, Top, and Middle, control how text or other elements align next to the image.

Setting Links

Dreamweaver is truly a dream when setting links. The most important thing to keep in mind is that a link is essentially an address (URL) that tells a viewer's browser what page to go to when the viewer selects the text or image with the link.

If that page is within your Web site, you want to create a *relative link* that includes the path that describes how to get from the current page to the linked page. A relative link doesn't include the domain name of the server. Here's an example of what the code looks like when you create a relative link:

```
<A HREF="staff/boss.html">The boss</A>
```

If you link to a page on a different Web site, you want to create an *absolute link*. An absolute link does include the full Internet address of the other site. Here's an example of the code behind an absolute link:

```
<A HREF="http://www.janinewarner.com/books">Janine's
         Books</A>
```

If all that HREF code stuff looks like Greek to you, don't worry. The following section shows you how Dreamweaver makes it possible for you to set links without even knowing what the code means.

Linking pages within your Web site

Linking from one page to another page in your Web site — known as an *internal link* — is easy. The most important thing to remember is to save your pages in the folders that you want to keep them in before you start setting links and make sure that all your files are in the root folder, as described in the section "Defining a site," earlier in this chapter.

Here's how you create an internal link:

1. **In Dreamweaver, open the page on which you want to create a link.**

2. **Select the text or image that you want to serve as the link (meaning the text or image that will open the new page when a user clicks it).**

   Alternatively, you can double-click the image or text to select it.

3. **Click the folder icon to the right of the Link text box in the Properties inspector.**

   The Select File dialog box opens.

4. **Select the page that you want your image or text to link to, and then click the Select button.**

   The link is automatically set and the dialog box closes. If you haven't already saved your page, a message box opens, explaining that you can create a relative link only after you save the page. Always save the page you're working on before you set links.

If the page is part of a frameset, use the Target field in the Properties inspector to specify which frame the linked page opens into. (You find out more about setting links in frames in Chapter 7.)

Setting links to named anchors within a page

If you like to create really long pages, using anchor links to break up navigation within the page is a good idea. A *named anchor link,* often called a *jump link,* enables you to set a link to a specific part of a Web page. You can use a named anchor to link from an image or text string on one page to another place on the same page, or to link from one page to a specific part of another page. To create a named anchor link, you first insert a named anchor in the place that you want to link to, and then use that anchor to direct the browser to that specific part of the page when a viewer follows the link.

Suppose that you want to set a link from the word *Convertible* at the top of a page to a section lower on the page that starts with the headline *Convertible Sports Cars.* You first insert a named anchor at the *Convertible Sports Cars* headline. Then you link the word *Convertible* from the top of the page to that anchor.

To insert a named anchor and set a link to it, follow these steps:

1. **Open the page on which you want to insert the named anchor.**

2. **Place your cursor next to the word or image that you want to link to on the page.**

   You don't need to select the word or image; you just need a reference point that displays when the link is selected. For this example, I placed the cursor to the left of the headline *Convertible Sports Cars.*

3. **Choose Insert⇨Named Anchor.**

   The Insert Named Anchor dialog box appears.

4. **Enter a name for the anchor.**

   You can name anchors anything you want (as long as you don't use spaces or special characters). Just make sure that you use a different name for each anchor on the same page. Then be sure that you remember what you called the anchor, because you have to type the anchor name to set the link. (Unlike other Web design programs, Dreamweaver doesn't automatically enter the anchor name.) In this example, I chose *convertible* as the anchor name because it's easy for me to remember.

5. **Click OK.**

   The dialog box closes, and a small anchor icon appears on the page where you inserted the anchor name. You can move an anchor name by clicking the anchor icon and dragging it to another location on the page.

   If you're curious about what this named anchor looks like in HTML, here's the code that appears before the headline in my example:

```
<A NAME="convertible"></A>
```

6. **To set a link to the named anchor location, select the text or image that you want to link from.**

   You can link to a named anchor from anywhere else on the same page or from another page. In my example, I linked from the word *Convertible* that appears at the top of the page to the anchor I made next to the headline.

7. **In the Properties inspector, type the pound sign (#) followed by the anchor name.**

   You can also select the text and drag a line from the Point to File icon (next to the Link text box) to the anchor icon. The anchor name automatically appears in the Link box, saving you from typing the name again.

   In my example, I typed **#convertible** in the Link text box. The HTML code for this line looks like this:

```
<A HREF="#convertible">Convertible</A>
```

   If you wanted to link to an anchor named *convertible* on another page with the filename coolcars.html, you type **coolcars.html#convertible** in the Link text box.

Linking to pages outside your Web site

Linking to a page on another Web site — called an *external link* — is even easier than linking to an internal link. All you need is the URL of the page to which you want to link, and you're most of the way there.

To create an external link, follow these steps:

1. **In Dreamweaver, open the page from which you want to link.**

2. **Select the text or image that you want to act as a link.**

3. **In the Link text box in the Properties inspector, type the URL of the page you want your text or image to link to (see Figure 2-11).**

   The link is automatically set.

Although you don't have to type the http:// at the beginning of a Web site address to get to a site in most browsers, you need to use the full URL, including the http:// when you create an external link. Otherwise, the browser may think that the www.whatever.com is the name of a folder on your Web server instead of an external site address and results in a 404, Page Not Found Error. (See Figure 2-11 for an example of how you set a link to the Macromedia Web site, using its full URL.)

Figure 2-11:
To set a link
to another
Web site,
highlight
the text or
image you
want to link
and type the
URL in the
Link text
box in the
Properties
inspector.

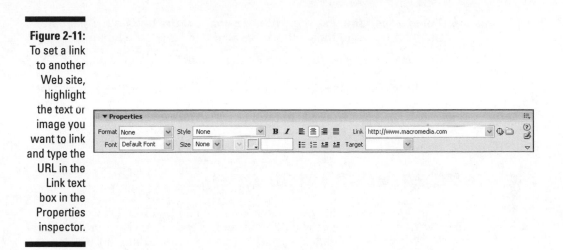

Setting a link to an e-mail address

Another common link option goes to an e-mail address. Visitors can send you messages easily with e-mail links. I always recommend that you invite visitors to contact you because they can point out mistakes in your site and give you valuable feedback about how you can further develop your site.

Setting a link to an e-mail address is almost as easy as setting a link to another Web page. Before you start, you need to know the e-mail address to which you want to link. The only other thing you need to know is that e-mail links must begin with the code mailto:. Here's an example of the full line of code behind an e-mail link:

```
<A HREF="mailto:editor@janinewarner.com">Send a message to
       Janine</A>
```

To create an e-mail link in Dreamweaver, follow these steps:

1. **In Dreamweaver, open the page on which you want to create an e-mail link and insert your cursor on the page where you want to create the link.**

2. **If you want to link an existing image or text block, select an image or highlight the text that you want to act as the link.**

3. **Click the Email Link icon in the Common Insert bar at the top of the screen. (It looks like a small envelope.)**

   The Email Link dialog box opens. If you selected text before choosing the Email Link icon, that text is automatically entered into the Text box in the Email Link dialog box.

4. **Enter or edit the text you want to represent the link on the page in the Text box, and then enter the e-mail address in the Email box.**

The text appears on the page with the e-mail link automatically set.

If you want to use the Properties inspector to create an e-mail link, highlight the text you want to link or select the image you want to link, and then type **mailto:** followed by the e-mail address into the link text area.

Previewing Your Page in a Browser

Although Dreamweaver displays Web pages much like a Web browser, Dreamweaver doesn't let you follow links, and the page you see in Dreamweaver doesn't always look exactly like every browser because different browsers display pages differently. That's why it's important to check your work in a Web browser regularly to see how it looks and to check links.

The simplest way to preview your work is to save the page you are working on, and then click on the Preview/Debug in Browser icon located at the top right of the Workspace (it looks like a small globe).

When you install Dreamweaver it automatically finds a browser on your computer and sets it up so that when you click this button, you launch the browser. If you want to be able to test your work in more than one browser, you can add more options to the list by choosing Edit⇔Preferences and then choosing Preview in Browser from the Category list. Use the plus button at the top of the screen to add more browsers to the Browser list.

Changing Page Properties

Dreamweaver provides access to many of the elements you can change across an entire page in the Page Properties dialog box. These include background colors, link and text colors, and the *page title*. (The page title is the text that appears at the very top of the browser, next to the browser name, and is also the text that is saved in a user's bookmarks list.) Notice in Figure 2-12 that the Page Properties dialog box also has a Categories list and that each of these sections reveals different page options. Some of these options are covered in other parts of the book, such as the Tracing Image feature, which is covered in Chapter 4, and the Background Image feature, covered in Chapter 5. For now, to keep things simple, this section focuses only on changing the background and text colors available from the Appearance category, shown selected in Figure 2-12.

To change the background and text colors on a page, follow these steps:

1. **Choose Modify⇨Page Properties.**

   The Page Properties dialog box appears, as shown in Figure 2-12.

2. **Click the Background Color swatch box to reveal the color palette. Choose any color you like. (Just make sure it will look good with the text color you select and that your text will still be readable.)**

   The color you selected fills the color swatch box. The color does not fill the background until you click the Apply or OK button.

3. **Click the Text Color swatch box to reveal the color palette. Choose any color you like. (But again, make sure it will be readable against your background color. In general, a light background color works best with a dark text color and vice versa.)**

4. **Click the Apply button to see how the colors look on your page. Click OK to finish.**

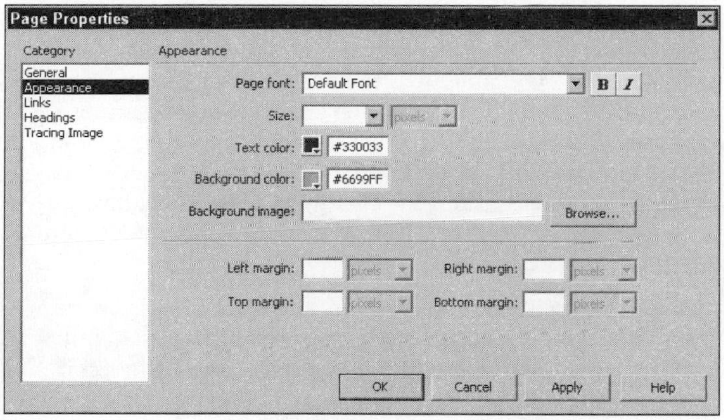

Figure 2-12:
The Page
Properties
dialog box
enables you
to change
text colors,
as well as
specify
a title for
the page.

Putting Your Web Site Online

In the section, "Setting Up a New or Existing Site," earlier in this chapter, I tell you how to set up a site and enter the address, login name, and password for your server. In this section, I show you how to put pages on your server and retrieve them by using the built-in FTP capabilities of Dreamweaver.

To transfer files between your hard drive and a remote server, follow these steps:

1. **Make sure you defined your site, as described in the "Setting Up a New or Existing Site" section in the beginning of this chapter, and make sure that that the site you set up is open. You can open an existing site by choosing Window⇨Files and then selecting the site from the Files submenu.**

If you do this properly, the files and folders of your site become visible in the Files tab of the Files panel on the right side of the work area. (See Figure 2-13.)

2. Click the Expand/Collapse button in the top right of the Files menu, just under the View pull-down.

The Files panel expands to fill the screen, making more options viewable. To collapse the panel, click the Expand/Collapse button again.

3. Click the Connect to Remote Host button.

If you're not already connected to the Internet, the Connect to Remote Host button starts your dial-up connection. If you have trouble connecting this way, try establishing your Internet connection as you usually do to check e-mail or surf the Web; then return to Dreamweaver and click the Connect to Remote Host button after your Internet connection is established. When your computer is online, Dreamweaver should have no trouble establishing an FTP connection with your host server.

If you still have trouble establishing a connection to your Web Server, refer to the section, "Setting up Web server access," earlier in this chapter and make sure that you specified the server information correctly. If you still have trouble, contact your service provider or site administrator to ensure you have all the correct information for connecting to your server. Getting all this information set up correctly the first time is tricky, and each service provider is different. The good news is that, when you get this right, Dreamweaver saves your settings so it connects automatically the next time.

After you establish the connection, the directories on your server appear in the Files panel. You can move between views in this panel by choosing from the pull-down menu at the top right, shown in Figure 2-13. The main options are Local view, which displays files on your local hard drive, and Remote view, which displays files on the server.

4. To *upload* a file (transfer a file from your hard drive to your Web server), select the file from the Local view panel (which shows the files on your hard drive) and click the Put Files icon (the up arrow) in the Files panel.

The files are automatically copied when you transfer them. You can select multiple files or folders to be transferred simultaneously and you can test your work by using a Web browser to view them on the server.

5. To *download* files or folders (transfer files or folders from your Web server to your hard drive), select the files or folders from the Remote view panel, (which shows the files on your server) and click the Get Files button (the down arrow) in the Files panel.

The files are automatically copied when you transfer them. When the transfer is complete, you can open the files on your hard drive.

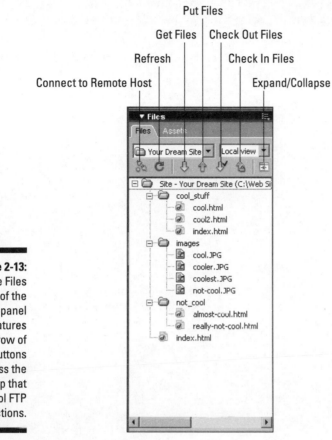

Put Files

Get Files | Check Out Files

Refresh | Check In Files

Connect to Remote Host | Expand/Collapse

Figure 2-13:
The Files
tab of the
Files panel
features
a row of
buttons
across the
top that
control FTP
functions.

The arrows with the check mark and the little lock are for the Check in/Check out feature, which enables you to keep track of who is working on a site and prevent more than one person making changes to the same page. You'll find this feature explained in Chapter 4.

If you're not happy with the FTP capabilities in Dreamweaver, you can use a dedicated FTP program, such as Fetch for the Macintosh or WS_FTP for Windows. You can download these shareware programs from shareware. cnet.com and download.com.

Part II
Looking Like a Million (Even on a Budget)

The 5th Wave   By Rich Tennant

"Games are an important part of my Web site. They cause eye strain."

In this part . . .

No matter how great the content on your Web site is, the first things viewers always notice are the design and the images. This part starts by explaining how to design a well-planned site. Then, you find out how to add graphics in ways that bring your pages to life. You also discover how to work with some of the most important, and timesaving, features in Dreamweaver, such as Templates and Library items.

Chapter 3

Designing a Well-Planned Site

. . . .

. . . .

*O*ne of the most common mistakes new Web designers make is plunging into developing a site without thinking through all their goals, priorities, budget, and design options. The instinct is to simply start creating pages, throw them all into one big directory, and then string stuff together with links. Then, when they finally test it out on their audience, they're often surprised when users say the site is hard to navigate and can't find the pages they want to use.

Do yourself a favor and save yourself some grief by planning ahead. By having a plan, you also stand a much better chance of creating an attractive Web site that's easy to maintain and update. In this chapter, you discover many of the common planning issues of Web design. You also find out how Dreamweaver makes managing a team of developers and getting the most out of the site-management features easy with features such as site synchronization and integrated e-mail. If you do find yourself in the unfortunate predicament of trying to fix broken links, you may appreciate how Dreamweaver makes that task easier, too.

Preparing for Development

One of the first things you should do is hold a brainstorming session with a few people who understand the goals you have for your Web site. The purpose of this session is to come up with possible features and elements for your Web site. A good brainstorming session is a nonjudgmental free-for-all — a chance for everyone involved to make all the suggestions that they can think of, whether realistic or not.

Not discrediting ideas at the brainstorming stage is important. Often an unrealistic idea leads to a great idea that no one may have thought of otherwise. And if you stifle one person's creative ideas too quickly, that person may feel less inclined to voice other ideas in the future.

After the brainstorming session, you have a long list of possible features to develop into your site. Your challenge is to edit that list down to the best and most realistic ideas and then plan your course of development to ensure that these ideas all work well together when you're done.

Developing a New Site

In a nutshell, building a Web site involves creating individual pages and linking them to other pages. You need to have a home page (often called the *front page*) that links to pages representing different sections of the site. Those pages, in turn, can link to subsections that can then lead to additional subsections. A big part of Web site planning is determining how to divide your site into sections and deciding how pages link to one another. Dreamweaver makes creating pages and setting links easy, but how you organize the pages is up to you.

If you're new to this, you may think you don't need to worry much about expandability in your Web site. Think again. All good Web sites grow, and the bigger they get, the harder they are to manage. Planning the path of growth for your Web site when you get started makes a tremendous difference later. Neglecting to think about growth is probably one of the most common mistakes among new designers. They jump right into the home page, add a few pages, and then add a few more, throwing them all into one directory. Before they know it, they're working in chaos. This becomes even more serious if the Web site expands so much that more people begin to work on it. Without a clearly established site organization and some common conventions for things like naming files, confusion reigns.

Managing your site's structure

Managing the structure of a Web site has two sides: the side that users see, which depends on how you set up links, and the behind-the-scenes side, which depends on how you organize files and folders.

What the user sees

The side that the user sees is all about navigation. When users arrive at your home page, where do you direct them from there? How do they move around your site? A good Web site is designed so that users navigate easily and intuitively through the site and make a beeline to the information most relevant to them. As you plan, make sure that users can

✔ Access key information easily from more than one place in the site.

✔ Move back and forth between pages and sections.

✔ Return to main pages and subsections in one step.

Setting links is easy in Dreamweaver; the challenge is to make sure that they're easy for visitors to follow.

What you see

The second side to managing your Web site structure happens behind the scenes (where your users can't see the information, but you want some kind of organizational system to remember what's what). Before you get too far into building your site with Dreamweaver, spend some time thinking about the management issues involved in keeping track of all the files you create for your site. *Files* are all the images, HTML pages, animations, sound files, and anything else you put in your Web site. As you create pages for your Web site, organizing them in separate folders or directories is best.

Many Web developers get 20 or 30 pages into a growing Web site and then realize that having all their files in one folder is a mistake. In fact, it's more than a mistake; it's a mess. And to make matters worse, if you start moving things into new folders after the site grows, you have to change all the links. Not realizing this, some people start moving files around and then find that they have broken links and don't remember where things go. Fortunately, Dreamweaver includes site-management tools that automatically fix links when you move pages around or create new folders, but starting out with a good plan is still better than having to clean up the structure later.

Before you build those first few pages, think about where you're likely to add content in the future (you always will!). After you put together a list of the key elements you want in your site, you're ready to create a storyboard or outline. Use the list and outline to create logical sections of a site that anticipates growth. For example, you may start with one page that lists all your staff; however, after they see how cool it is, staff members may want to develop their own pages. In that case, you may want a separate folder dedicated to staff pages. If you provide information for your sales team, you may find that you want a separate section for each product.

As you add new sections, such as the staff or product pages I mention here, create new subdirectories or subfolders to store their respective files. Creating subdirectories also makes managing a site that's built by multiple people easier. If each subsection has a separate folder, then each developer can better manage his or her own files.

Under construction? No hard hats here!

All good Web sites are under construction — always. It's the nature of the Web. But build your site in such a way that you can add pages when they're ready instead of putting up placeholders. Don't greet your viewers with a guy in a yellow hat who seems to say, "You clicked this link for no good reason. Come back another day, and maybe we'll have something for you to see." Instead of creating "Under Construction" placeholders, create directory structures that

make adding new pages later easy. You can let readers know that new things are coming by putting notices on pages that already have content — a message like "Come here next Thursday for a link to something even cooler" is a great idea. But never make users click a link and wait for a page to load, only to find that nothing but a guy with a hard hat is waiting for them.

Naming your site's files

An important element of planning your site is establishing file-naming conventions for all the files that will make up your site. By following the tips I mention in this section, you can save yourself time and frustration down the road.

First, make sure your files will work on your Web server. Dreamweaver lets you call your files any name that works on your operating system, even something like don't forget this is the photo the boss likes.htm, but your Web server may use a different operating system that's more restrictive. Many servers on the Web are run on UNIX machines that are case-sensitive and don't allow spaces or special characters, except for the underscore (_). If you use filenames that your Web server can't read, then your site won't work until you rename all those files.

Although coming up with names that work and that everyone else on your site development team will remember can be difficult, it's time well spent. In general, I suggest using names that are all lowercase and that use underscores or hyphens instead of spaces. For example, staff stuff.htm is not a good filename because it has a space in it, but staff-stuff.htm is fine, because the hyphen works on any server, and you still have a break between the words to make them easier to read.

A file-naming system can also help you keep track of the information on your site's pages if you develop a system that makes sense to everyone working on the project. For example, say your Web site is a newsletter that includes articles about the happenings in your town. Simple names like fire.html and truck.html may make sense to you this week because you're familiar with the top stories. But six months from now, if you look for that article on the big vehicle accident, you may not remember that you called it `truck.html`. Adding dates to the end of filenames can help you identify the files that you may need months — or even years — down the road. Remember that you can't use spaces, but you can use the underscore. A good filename may be `fire8_12_2002.html` or `truck8_19_2002.html`; using dates helps you remember that you added these articles in August of 2002.

Another option is to create a folder for each new update and name it with a date. For example, a folder named stories8_2002 can contain all the stories from the August 2002 issue. Then you can put `truck.html` and any other stories from that issue in the stories8_2002 folder, and you can find them by date as well as by filename.

As you develop a file-naming system, talk to other people who may work on the site and make sure you create a system that makes sense to everyone and is easy to explain if a new person joins the team. Whatever you do, don't name files randomly and throw them all in one directory. You should also consider documenting your naming system. Printing a list of all the filenames in your site can also provide a handy reference if you're looking for a particular file.

Organizing images

Many HTML teachers and consultants suggest that you place all your images in a single folder at the top level of the directory structure and call it Images or Graphics. You may also find that other HTML authoring tools require you to keep all your images in one folder. Dreamweaver doesn't require an images folder, but you can specify one when you set up your site (for more on that, see Chapter 2).

This approach has pros and cons. The advantage of keeping all your images in one folder is that the paths to all your images are the same, and you only have one place to look for them. However, using just one folder can also cause problems: If all your images are in one place, you'll likely end up with a long list of image files, and you can easily lose track of which image is which. When you want to change an image later, sorting through this list can be arduous work.

A good alternative is to store your images in multiple Images folders within the subfolders that hold the HTML files where those images appear. For example, keep all your staff photos for your staff pages in an Images folder within a Staff subfolder. If you have images that link throughout the site — a logo, for example — you may want to keep those images in an Images folder at the top level of your directory structure. This way, the images are easy to find from any folder in the site.

Dreamweaver makes no distinction between a folder called Images and a folder by any other name. You can call these folders whatever you like, even: Goofy_pictures.

Handling links

As you develop your site, the links only become more complicated, and of course, Dreamweaver includes tools that help you keep those links in good working order. Read on to find out how to put these tools to use.

Managing links

From the Files panel in Dreamweaver, you can move or rename local files, and Dreamweaver automatically adjusts all related links. This feature can save you tons of time, especially if you try to organize a large, haphazard site and decide to add new folders and move pages into them for better organization.

One thing to note, however, is that this feature works only on local files. In order to rearrange files and automatically correct corresponding links, you need to have your entire site, or a self-contained section of it, stored on your local hard drive. (You can use the FTP features in Dreamweaver to download a site before you work on it. See Chapter 2 for details.)

Before this feature can work, you have to turn on the link-management options in Dreamweaver:

1. **From the Dreamweaver menu bar, choose Edit⇨Preferences.**

   The Preferences dialog box opens.

2. **Select the General category from the left side of the Preferences dialog box.**

3. **Choose Always, Never, or Prompt from the Update Links When Moving Files pop-up menu. (It's the fourth option in the dialog box.)**

   Choose Always to automatically update all links to and from a selected document whenever you move or rename it. Choose Prompt if you first want to view a dialog box that lists all the files affected by the change. Choose Never if you don't want Dreamweaver to automatically update links.

   If you choose Prompt, you get the following two options whenever you move or rename a file: Update, to update the links in the file(s), or Don't Update, to leave the file(s) unchanged.

4. **Click OK to save your changes and exit the Preferences dialog box.**

If Check In/Out is enabled, Dreamweaver automatically attempts to check out the file before making any changes. (For more on the Check In/Out feature, see Chapters 2 and 4)

Changing and moving links

After you enable link-management options in the Preferences dialog box, you can use the Files panel to rename or rearrange files and folders with drag-and-drop ease.

To rename or rearrange files, follow these steps:

1. **Select the site name from the pull-down menu at the top of the Files panel and choose the site you want to work on from the list.**

   When you select a site, the folders and files of that site display in the Files panel on the right side of the Dreamweaver work area.

2. **Use the plus (+) and minus (–) signs to open and close folders in the Files panel.**

3. **In the Files panel, select the file or folder that you want to change (move and/or rename):**

   To move the selected file: Drag that file or folder anywhere in the panel. For example, you can move a file into a folder, and Dreamweaver automatically changes all the related links.

   This panel works just like the Explorer window on a PC or the Finder on a Mac, except Dreamweaver tracks and fixes links when you move files through the Files panel. If you move or rename files or folders in the Finder or Explorer, however, you risk breaking the links. In Dreamweaver, when you move a file into a new folder, the Update Files dialog box appears with a list of links that need to be updated, as in Figure 3-1. The Update Files dialog box appears when you choose Prompt in the Preferences dialog box.

   To rename the selected file: Click the selected file, and after the cursor appears at the end of the filename, type your new filename or edit the existing name. When you finish, press Enter.

Making global changes to links

If you want to globally change a link to point at a new URL or to some other page on your site, you can use the Change Link Sitewide option to enter the new URL and change every reference automatically. You can use this option to change any kind of link, including mailto, ftp, and script links. For example, if the e-mail address that you list at the bottom of every page on your site changes, you can use this feature to fix it automatically — a real timesaver. You can also use this feature when you want a string of text to link to a different file than it currently does. For example, you can change every instance of the words *Enter this month's contest* to link to `/contest/january.htm` instead of `/contest/december.htm` throughout your Web site.

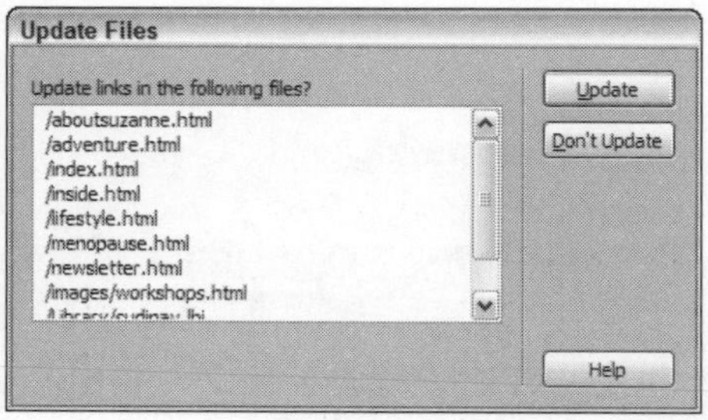

Figure 3-1:
The Update
Files dialog
box shows
you which
links change
when you
move or
rename a
file in the
Files panel.

Update Files
Update links in the following files?
/aboutsuzanne.html
/adventure.html
/index.html
/inside.html
/lifestyle.html
/menopause.html
/newsletter.html
/images/workshops.html
/library/sydney.lbi

Update
Don't Update
Help

To change all links from one page on your site to another using the Change Link Sitewide feature, follow these steps:

1. **Select the site name from the pull-down menu at the top of the Files panel and choose the site you want to work on from the list.**

   If you double-click a filename in the Files panel, the page opens in the Dreamweaver work area. But to make global changes, you don't have to select or open a page.

2. **Click the Expand/Collapse button on the right side of the Files panel.**

   The Site dialog box opens, showing both the remote and local views of the site.

3. **From the menu, choose Site⇨Change Link Sitewide.**

   The Change Link Sitewide dialog box appears.

4. **Click the Browse buttons to set the correct filenames in the Change All Links To and Into Links To text boxes. You can also type in a root-relative path.**

5. **Click OK.**

   Dreamweaver updates any documents that link to the selected file.

These changes occur only on the local site until you change them on the remote server. To automatically reconcile these changes, use the Dreamweaver Synchronize Files option I describe in the "Synchronizing Local and Remote Sites" section later in this chapter.

You can also use the Change Link Sitewide feature to change an e-mail link or a link to a remote URL, as shown in Figure 3-2.

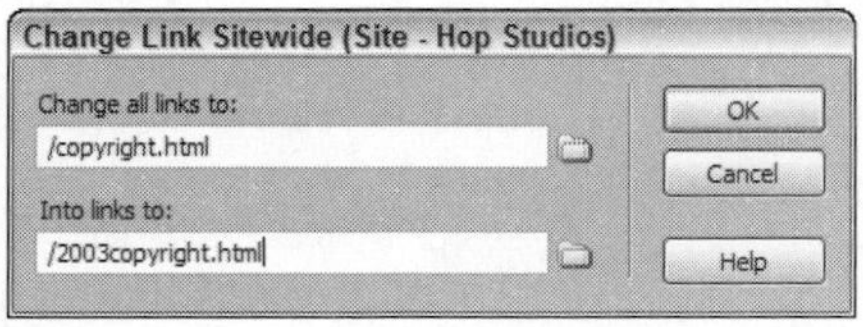

Figure 3-2:
You can
enter
any URL
or e-mail
address into
the Change
Link Site-
wide dialog
box to make
quick global
changes to
your site.

Change Link Sitewide (Site - Hop Studios)

Change all links to:

/copyright.html

Into links to:

/2003copyright.html

OK

Cancel

Help

Finding and Fixing Broken Links

If you're trying to rein in a chaotic Web site, or if you just want to check a site for broken links, you'll be pleased to discover the Check Links feature. You can use Check Links to verify the links in a single file or an entire Web site, and you can use it to automatically fix all the referring links at once.

Here's an example of what Check Links can do. Assume that someone on your team (because you would never do such a thing yourself) changed the name of a file from `new.htm` to `old.htm` without using the Dreamweaver automatic link update process to fix the corresponding links. Maybe this person changed the name using another program or simply changed the name in the Finder on the Mac or in the Explorer in Windows. Changing the filename was easy, but what this person may not have realized is that if he or she didn't change the links to the file when the file was renamed, the links are now broken.

If only one page links to the file that your clueless teammate changed, fixing the broken link isn't such a big deal. As long as you remember what file the page links from, you can simply open that page and use the Properties inspector to reset the link the same way you created the link in the first place. (You can find out all the basics of link creation in Chapter 2.)

But many times, a single page in a Web site is linked to many other pages. When that's the case, fixing all the link references can be time-consuming, and forgetting some of them is all too easy. That's why the Check Links feature is so helpful. First, it serves as a diagnostic tool that identifies broken links throughout the site (so you don't have to second-guess where someone may have changed a filename or moved a file). Then it serves as a global fix-it tool. You can use the Check Links dialog box to identify the page a broken link should go to, and then you can have Dreamweaver automatically fix all links referring to that page. The following section walks you through the process.

If you are working on a dynamic, database-driven site or if your site was altered with programming that was done outside of Dreamweaver, the Check Links feature may not report every bad link. Database-driven sites often use variables and other code instead of a straight link to a file. For example, a database-driven site may have a link to `response.write 'news_' + $stories + '.htm" where "fire0216"` instead of `news_fire0216.htm`, so a search for that filename won't be successful.

Checking for broken links

To check a site for broken links, follow these steps:

1. **Select the site name from the pull-down menu at the top of the Files panel and choose the site you want to work on from the list.**

   Link checking works only for sites listed in the Dreamweaver Site dialog box. For more information about the Site dialog box and how to set up a new site or import an existing one, see Chapter 2.

2. **From the menu, choose Site⇨Check Links Sitewide.**

   The Link Checker tab opens in the Results panel at the bottom of the page, just under the Properties inspector, as shown in Figure 3-3. The tab displays a list of filenames with broken links. The tab also lists any pages, images, or other items not linked to any other pages in the site, which is handy if you want to clean up old images or other elements you no longer use on the site.

Most service providers limit the amount of space on your server and charge extra if you exceed that limit. Deleting unused files helps you save valuable server space, especially if they are image or multimedia files. But remember, just because you delete them from your hard drive doesn't mean they are off the server. Dreamweaver removes them when you use the Synchronize option described later in this chapter, but double-checking is always good.

If you find broken links, the next section, "Fixing broken links," shows you how Dreamweaver automatically updates multiple link references to make fixing them fast and easy.

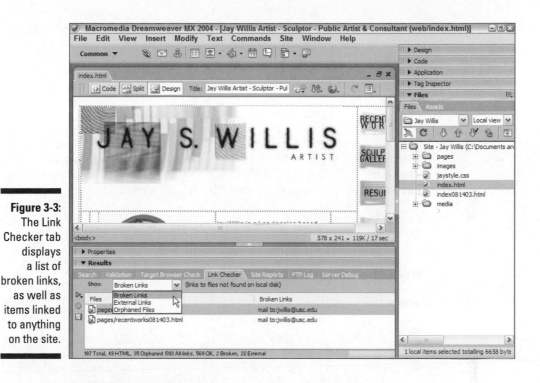

Figure 3-3:
The Link
Checker tab
displays
a list of
broken links,
as well as
items linked
to anything
on the site.

Fixing broken links

Broken links are one of the most embarrassing problems in Web design. After
you identify a broken link in your site, you need to fix it immediately. Nothing
turns off your users faster than clicking a link and getting a `File Not Found`
error page (also known as a *404 error* because that's usually the message
viewers see if they click a broken link). Fortunately, Dreamweaver makes fixing
broken links simple by providing quick access to files with broken links and
automating the process of fixing multiple links to the same file.

After using the Link Checker feature described in the preceding section to identify broken links, follow these steps to use the Results panel to fix them:

1. **With the Results panel open at the bottom of the page, double-click a
   filename that Dreamweaver identified as a broken link.**

   The page and its corresponding Properties inspector opens. The Results
   panel remains visible.

2. **Select the broken link or image on the open page.**

In Figure 3-4, a broken image was selected and is being fixed by using the Properties inspector to find the correct image name.

3. **In the Properties inspector, click the folder icon to the right of the Src text box to identify the correct image file.**

The Select Image Source dialog box appears. You can type the correct filename and path in the text box or browse to find the image.

You fix links to pages just like you fix links to images, except you type the name of the correct file into the Link text box or click the folder icon next to it to find the file in your site folder.

4. **Click the filename and the Select button; then click OK.**

The link automatically changes to reflect the new filename and location. If you replace an image, the image file reappears on the page.

If the link that you correct appears in multiple pages, Dreamweaver prompts you with a dialog box asking whether you want to fix the remaining broken link references to the file. Click the Yes button to automatically correct all other references. Click the No button to leave other files unchanged.

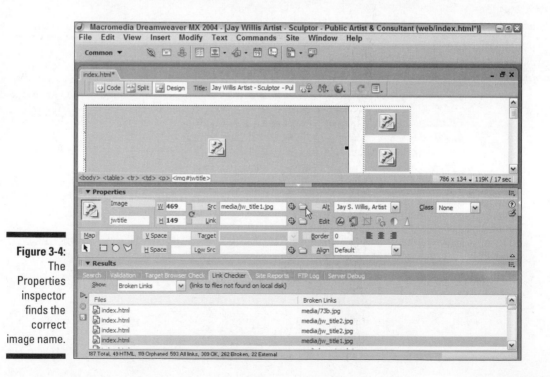

Figure 3-4:
The Properties inspector finds the correct image name.

Testing Your Work with the Site Reporting Feature

Before you put your site online for the world to see, checking your work using the Dreamweaver Site Reporting feature is a good idea. You can create a variety of reports, and even customize them, to identify problems with external links, redundant and empty tags, untitled documents, and missing Alt text. You can easily miss things — especially when you work on a tight deadline — and they can cause real problems for your viewers if you leave them unfixed.

Before Dreamweaver added this great new feature, finding these kinds of mistakes was a tedious and time-consuming task. Now you can run a report that identifies these errors for you and use Dreamweaver to fix mistakes across your entire site automatically.

Follow these steps to produce a Site Report of your entire Web site:

1. **Select the site name from the pull-down menu at the top of the Files panel and choose the site you want to work on from the list.**

   See Chapter 2 for step-by-step instructions for defining your site if you haven't done it already.

2. **From the Site menu, choose Site⇨Reports.**

   The Reports dialog box appears (see Figure 3-5).

3. **From the Report On pull-down menu, choose Entire Current Local Site.**

   You can also choose to check only a single page by opening the page in Dreamweaver and then choosing Current Document from the Report On pull-down menu. You can also run a report on Selected Files or on a particular Folder. If you choose Selected Files, you must have already selected the pages you want to check in the Files panel.

4. **Select the type of report you want by putting check marks next to the report names in the Select Reports section.**

   Table 3-1 describes the kind of report you get with each option. You can select as many reports as you want.

TIP

The Workflow options in the Select Reports section are available only if you already enabled Check In/Out in the Remote Info section of the Site Definition panel and selected Maintain Design Notes in the Design Notes section of the Site Definition panel's Advanced tab. You can read more about the Site Definition panel in Chapter 2 and more about Design Notes and the Check In/Check Out feature in Chapter 4.

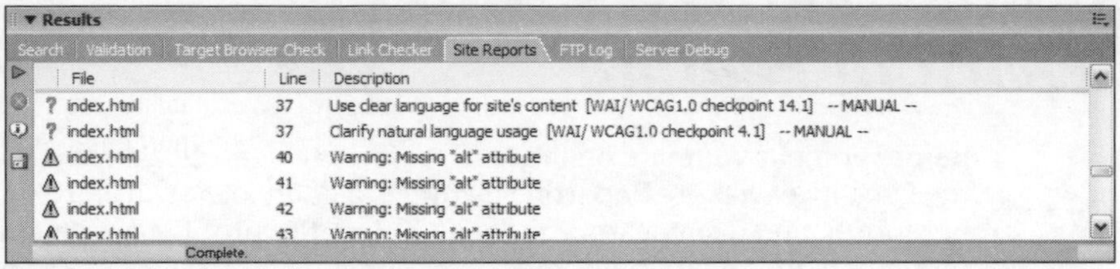

Figure 3-6:
The Results
panel
displays
a list of
problems
found on
your site.

File	Line	Description
? index.html	37	Use clear language for site's content [WAI/ WCAG1.0 checkpoint 14.1] -- MANUAL --
? index.html	37	Clarify natural language usage [WAI/ WCAG1.0 checkpoint 4.1] -- MANUAL --
⚠ index.html	40	Warning: Missing "alt" attribute
⚠ index.html	41	Warning: Missing "alt" attribute
⚠ index.html	42	Warning: Missing "alt" attribute
⚠ index.html	43	Warning: Missing "alt" attribute

▼ Results
Search | Validation | Target Browser Check | Link Checker | Site Reports | FTP Log | Server Debug
Complete.

5. Click the Run button to create the report(s).

If you haven't already done so, you may be prompted to save your file, define your site, or select a folder (see Chapter 2 for more information on defining a site in Dreamweaver).

The Results panel opens (see Figure 3-6 displaying a list of problems found on a site). You can sort the list by different categories (filename, line number, or description) by clicking the corresponding column headings. If you run several reports at the same time, you can keep all the results tabs open at the same time.

6. Double-click any item in the Results panel to open the corresponding file in the Document window.

7. Use the Properties inspector or other Dreamweaver feature to fix the identified problem and then save the file.

Your changes aren't applied to your live site until you update your server. Use the Synchronize feature, described in the next section of this chapter, to update all your changes at once.

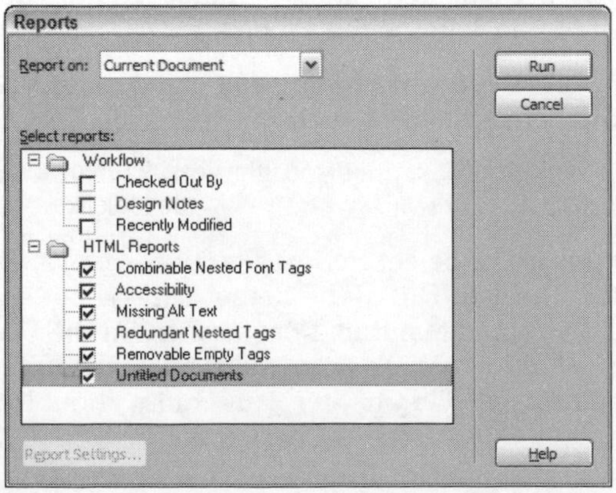

Figure 3-5:
You can
select any
or all of the
options in
the Reports
dialog box
to run simul-
taneously.

Reports

Report on: Current Document

Run
Cancel

Select reports:
- ☐ Workflow
  - ☐ Checked Out By
  - ☐ Design Notes
  - ☐ Recently Modified
- ☐ HTML Reports
  - ☑ Combinable Nested Font Tags
  - ☑ Accessibility
  - ☑ Missing Alt Text
  - ☑ Redundant Nested Tags
  - ☑ Removable Empty Tags
  - ☑ Untitled Documents

Report Settings...   Help

Table 3-1	Site Report Options
Report Name	*Results*
Accessibility	Produces a list of possible accessibility issues in a wide variety of categories. To set the report categories, click the Report Settings button.
Checked Out By	Produces a list of files checked out of the site and identifies the person who checked them out.
Design Notes	Produces a list of Design Notes (see Chapter 4 for more on how to use Design Notes).
Combinable Nested Font Tags	Produces a list of all instances where you can combine nested tags. For example, `<font color="#00000">` `<font size="2">Great Web Sites You Should Visit</font></font>` is listed because you can simplify the code by combining the two font tags into: `<font color="#00000" size="2">Great Web Sites You Should Visit</font>`.
Missing Alt Text	Produces a list of all the Image tags that do not include Alt text. *Alt text* adds alternative text to an image tag. If the image isn't displayed for some reason (many people choose to surf with images turned off), the Alt text appears in place of the image. Alt text is also important to the blind because special browsers that "read" pages to site visitors can't interpret text that is part of an image, but can "read" the Alt text included in the image tag.
Recently Modified	Produces a list of files recently updated or changed. You can set the time period for the report by clicking the Report Settings button.
Redundant NestedTags	Produces a list of all places where you have redundant nested tags. For example, `<center>Good headlines <center>are harder to write</center> than you might think</center>` is listed because you can simplify the code by removing the second center tag to make the code look like this: `<center>Good headlines are harder to write than you might think</center>`.
Removable EmptyTags	Produces a list of the empty tags on your site. Empty tags often occur if you delete an image or text section without deleting all the tags associated with it.

(continued)

Table 3-1 *(continued)*

Report Name	Results
Untitled Documents	Produces a list of filenames that don't have a title. The title tag is easy to forget because it does not display in the body of the page. The title tag contains the text that appears at the very top of the browser window and is also the text that appears in the Favorites list when someone saves your page in his or her browser. And if that's not enough, a good title tag is key to getting good placement in many search engines as well.

Synchronizing Local and Remote Sites

After you do all the cleanup and organization on the local copy of your Web site, you want to make sure that those changes reflect on the live site on your Web server. Fortunately, Dreamweaver makes that easy, too, by including a feature that automatically synchronizes the files in both places. Before you synchronize your sites, you can use the Site FTP dialog box to verify which files you want to put on or get from your remote server. Dreamweaver also confirms which files updated after you complete the synchronization.

Follow these steps to synchronize your Web site:

1. **Select the name of the site you want to work on in the Files panel pull-down menu.**

   See Chapter 2 for step-by-step instructions for defining your site if you haven't done it already.

2. **Click the Connects To Remote Host button to log on to your remote site.**

   Chapter 2 shows you how to set up this feature for your site.

3. **Click the Expand/Collapse button on the right side of the Files panel.**

   The Site dialog box opens, showing both the remote and local views of the site, as shown in Figure 3-7.

4. **From the menu bar, choose Site⇔Synchronize.**

   The Synchronize Files dialog box appears, as shown in Figure 3-8.

5. **Choose whether to synchronize the Entire Site or Selected Files Only from the Synchronize pull-down menu.**

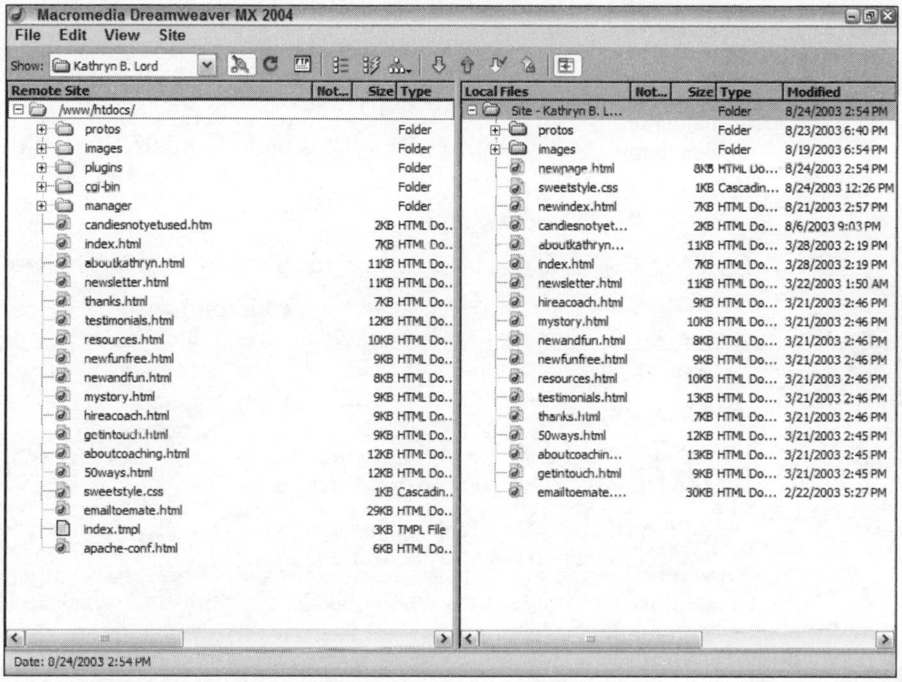

Figure 3-7:
The expanded Site dialog box lets you view both remote and local files at the same time.

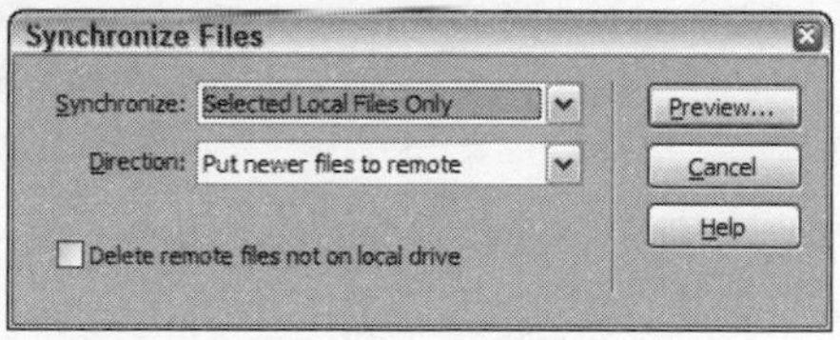

Figure 3-8:
The Synchronize Files dialog box ensures that your remote and local files are the same.

6. **From the Direction pull-down menu, choose which option you want to use to copy the files:**

   • **Put Newer Files to Remote:** This option copies the most recently modified files from your local site to the remote site. Click the Delete Remote Files Not On Local Drive box, if you want those files removed from your Web site.

- **Get Newer Files from Remote:** This option copies the most recently modified files from your remote site to the local site. Click the Delete Local Files Not On Remote Server box, if you want to remove those files from your local copy.

- **Get and Put Newer Files:** This option updates both the local and remote sites with the most recent versions of all the files.

7. **Click the Preview button.**

   The Site FTP dialog box displays the files about to be changed.

   Now you have the option to verify the files you want to delete, put, and get. If you don't want Dreamweaver to alter a file, deselect it now or forever live with the consequences.

8. **Click OK.**

   All approved changes are automatically made, and Dreamweaver updates the Site FTP dialog box with the status.

9. **When the synchronization finishes, you can choose to save the verification information to a local file.**

   Choose to save or not save the verification information. This information can be handy later if you want to review your changes.

Be very careful of the Dreamweaver Synchronize option if you have special administrative pages, such as stats files, which are often added to your server space by your service provider to track traffic on your site. *Remember:* Any files on your server not on your local computer may be deleted when you synchronize. The best way around this is to download those files before you synchronize so that Dreamweaver knows you want to keep them. Be careful, though! Sometimes those files are very large, particularly if they are usage stats. To be completely safe, consider using another method for sending your files to your server.

Cloaking Options

The new Dreamweaver Cloaking option enables you to exclude any specified folder or files from all site operations, meaning they can't be altered or uploaded to the live site. This feature is handy if you have sections of a site that you want to save but don't want visible to your viewers. For example, if you have a special Christmas section that you don't want visible during the rest of the year, you can use the Cloaking feature to save it, with the assurance that no one can alter, delete, or publish the files until you uncloak them.

Make sure you remove the files from your live server if you don't want them visible to your users.

You can also use cloaking to exclude certain file types from site operations. For example, you can cloak all your multimedia files so that they are not uploaded to your site every time you update your work to the server.

To use the Cloaking feature, follow these steps:

1. **In the Cloaking tab of the Site Definition dialog, select Enable Cloaking as shown in Figure 3-9.**

2. **If you want to cloak files of a certain type, select the Cloak Files Ending With box and enter the extension(s) in the text field.**

   For example, if you want to cloak all your JPEG and GIF files, you enter those extensions. Separate each file extension with a space. Do not use a comma or other delimiter.

3. **Click OK to close the Site Definition dialog box and then click the Done button in the Define Sites dialog box to close it.**

4. **In the Files tab of the Files panel, select the files or folders you want to cloak.**

5. **Right-click (Windows) or Ctrl+click (Mac) and select Cloaking⇨Cloak from the shortcut menu (see Figure 3-10).**

   To uncloak files or folders, repeat Steps 4 and 5 and select Uncloak from the shortcut menu. You can also use these steps to uncloak all the files in your current site, disable cloaking in the site, and change the cloaking settings.

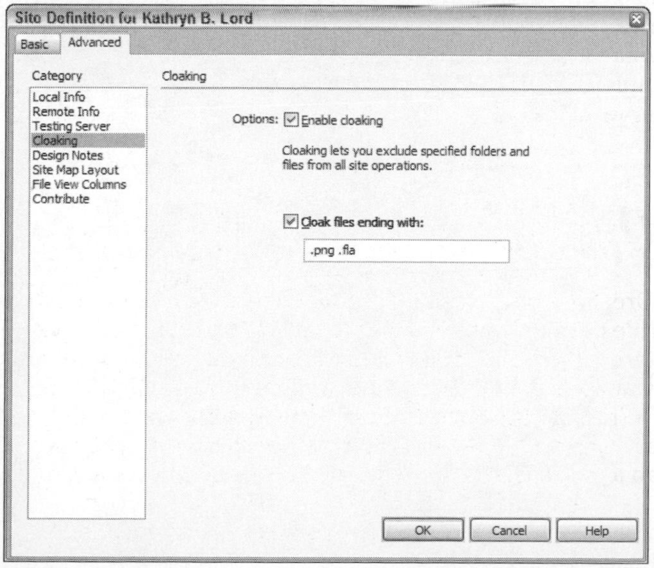

Figure 3-9:
The Cloaking feature enables you to specify files or folders that you don't want visible.

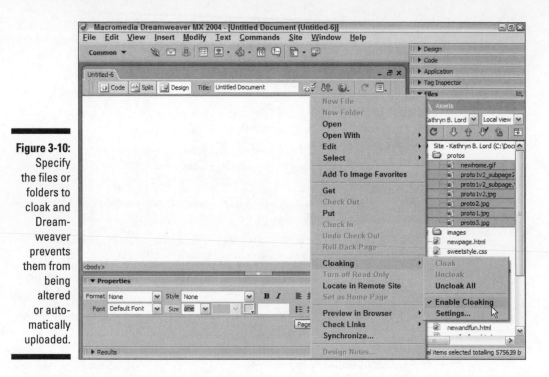

Figure 3-10:
Specify
the files or
folders to
cloak and
Dream-
weaver
prevents
them from
being
altered
or auto-
matically
uploaded.

Chapter 4

Coordinating Your Design Work

- -

In This Chapter

▶ Using advanced template features to speed development

▶ Saving elements in the Dreamweaver Library for easy access

▶ Designing a Web page with the Dreamweaver Tracing Image feature

▶ Introducing Design Notes

▶ Collaborating with integrated e-mail and version control systems

▶ Using the History panel and the Quick Tag Editor

- -

Strive for consistency in all your designs — except when you're trying to be unpredictable. A little surprise here and there can keep your Web site alive. But, generally, most Web sites work best, and are easiest to navigate, when they follow a consistent design theme. Case in point: Most readers take for granted that books don't change their design from page to page, and newspapers don't change headline fonts and logos every day. Books and newspapers want to make life easier for their readers, and consistency is one of the primary tools for doing this. Dreamweaver offers several features to help you develop and maintain a consistent look and feel across your site, whether you're working on a Web site by yourself or you're coordinating a team of developers.

In this chapter, you discover three of my favorite Dreamweaver features — templates, Library items, and the Tracing Image feature. Find out how they combine to make your work faster and easier to manage. This chapter also introduces you to Design Notes, the History panel, and the Quick Tag Editor — tools that you can use for adding notes to yourself or a team, retracing your steps in Dreamweaver, and tweaking HTML tags respectively.

Templating Your Type

Many Web design programs boast about their HTML templates. Often what they really mean is the program includes some ready-made page designs. Dreamweaver takes this concept a few leaps further by providing template design features that enable you to create the basic design of a page and then limit the sections that can and can't be altered. This is a valuable feature if you work with a team of people with varying skill levels, or if you have to create dozens of pages with the same basic layout. For example, if you're building a site for a real estate company and you want to let the employees update the sales listings without being able to mess up the page design, a template can be the perfect solution.

Templates are best used when you're creating a number of pages that share certain characteristics, such as background color or image placement. Later, edit the template and when you save, those edits are updated in any file made from the template. This can be a huge timesaver when you need to make changes to several pages at once. For example, templates are ideal when you need to change the logo for your company or add a new navigation element that you want to appear on every page in a section. Or, use a template when you have a section with all the bios of your staff, and only the image and text on each page is different.

A template has editable regions and locked (noneditable) regions. Use *editable regions* for content that changes, such as a product description or events in a calendar. Use locked regions for static, unchanging content, such as a logo or site navigation elements.

For example, if you're publishing an online magazine, the navigation options may not change from page to page, but the titles and stories do. To indicate the style and location of an article or headline, you can define *placeholder text* (an editable region, with all the size and font attributes already specified). When you're ready to add a new feature, you simply select the placeholder text and either paste in a story or type over the selected area. You do the same thing to create a placeholder for an image.

While you're editing the template itself, you can make changes to any part of the file, be it the editable or locked regions. While editing a document made *from* a template, however, you can make changes only to the editable regions of the document. If you go back and change a template after it is created, Dreamweaver gives you the option of having those changes updated in all the pages you created with that template.

You can create both *editable regions* and *editable attributes* in a Dreamweaver template. An editable region is one that is unlocked and can be changed in any way in files created from the template — you can add tables, images, text, and so on. An editable attribute is more limited. This tool lets you set editable attributes of specific page elements in a template. For example, you may lock down an image on the page, but allow the alignment attribute to be changed to left, right, or center in a file created from the template.

Dreamweaver MX 2004 includes a wealth of ready-to-use Web components that can be used as documents or templates. You find these in the New Document dialog box when you choose File⇨New. These components can help you get your site designed quickly, using sample page designs, style sheets, framesets, and table-based layouts.

Typing your template

Creating a template is as easy as creating any other file in Dreamweaver, as you see in the following steps. You can start with an existing HTML document and modify it to suit your needs, or you can create a completely new document. When you save a file as a template, the file is stored automatically in the Templates folder of the main folder for the Web site. Templates must be saved in this common folder for the automated features in Dreamweaver to work properly. If you don't already have a Templates folder in your Web site, Dreamweaver automatically creates one when you save your first template.

The template features work only if you define your Web site in Dreamweaver. If you aren't sure how to do this, refer to Chapter 2.

All elements in a template are locked by default, except the document head section, which is indicated by the <HEAD> </HEAD> tags. This allows you to change the title in a page created from a template, or to insert JavaScript if you use behaviors on the page. For the template to be of any use for building new pages, you must make other areas of the page editable as well. Remember that you can always return to the template and make more areas editable or remove the capability to edit certain areas.

Creating areas that can be edited

To create a template with editable regions, follow these steps:

1. **In the Files panel on the right, click the Assets tab and then click the Templates icon (see Figure 4-1).**

   The Templates panel opens.

2. **In the Templates panel, click the New Template button (a page with a plus sign on it) at the bottom of the panel.**

   A new, untitled template is added to the list of templates in the panel.

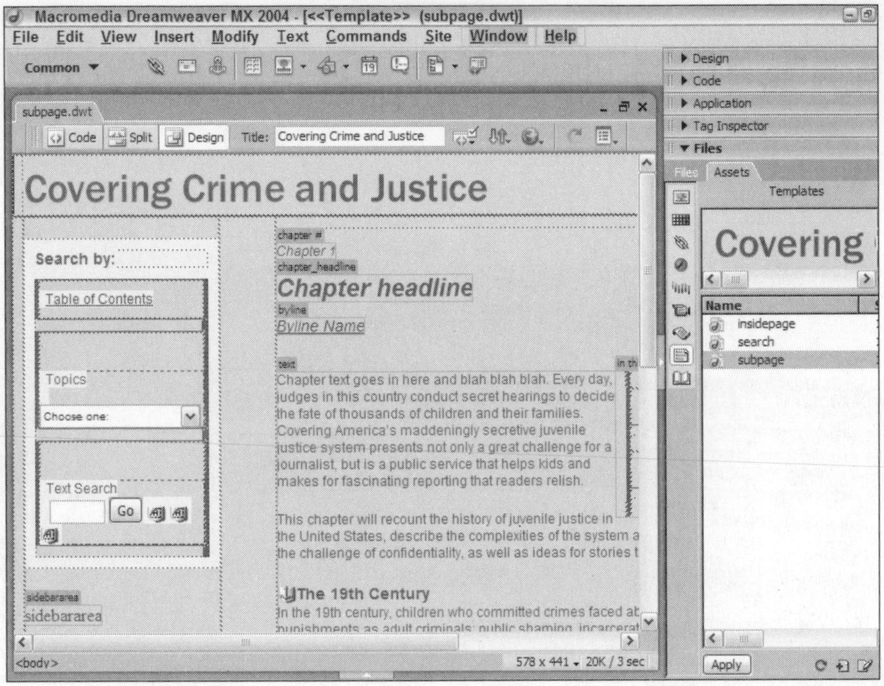

Macromedia Dreamweaver MX 2004 - [<<Template>> (subpage.dwt)]

File Edit View Insert Modify Text Commands Site Window Help

Common ▾

subpage.dwt

◇ Code □ Split □ Design Title: Covering Crime and Justice

Covering Crime and Justice

Search by:

Table of Contents

Topics

Choose one:

Text Search

Go

chapter #
Chapter 1
chapter_headline
Chapter headline
byline
Byline Name

text
Chapter text goes in here and blah blah blah. Every day,
judges in this country conduct secret hearings to decide
the fate of thousands of children and their families.
Covering America's maddeningly secretive juvenile
justice system presents not only a great challenge for a
journalist, but is a public service that helps kids and
makes for fascinating reporting that readers relish.

This chapter will recount the history of juvenile justice in
the United States, describe the complexities of the system a
the challenge of confidentiality, as well as ideas for stories t

The 19th Century
In the 19th century, children who committed crimes faced at
punishments as adult criminals: public shaming, incarcerat

sidebararea
sidebararea

<body>   578 x 441 · 20K / 3 sec

▶ Design
▶ Code
▶ Application
▶ Tag Inspector
▼ Files
   Files Assets
         Templates

Covering

Name
insidepage
search
subpage

Apply

Figure 4-1:
The
Templates
panel
shows you
a list of all
available
templates in
the selected
site.

3. **With the template still selected, type a name for the template just as you name any file in the Finder on a Mac or Explorer on a PC.**

   The new template is added to the Templates for Site list, as shown in Figure 4-2.

4. **Double-click the name to open it.**

   The template page opens in Dreamweaver as any other HTML page does, except that the filename ends with the extension .dwt.

   You can now edit this page as you edit any other HTML page, inserting images, text, tables, and so on.

5. **Choose Modify➪Page Properties to specify background, text, and link colors.**

   This works just like any other Dreamweaver document.

6. **To create an editable region, select the content you want to affect and choose Insert➪Template Objects➪Editable Region (as shown in Figure 4-3).**

   The New Editable Region dialog box opens. The region you define as editable becomes an area that can be changed in any page created with the template. You can have multiple editable regions in one template. Areas that you don't mark as editable become locked and can be changed only if you modify the template itself.

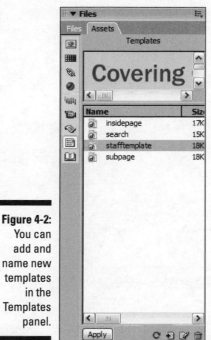

Figure 4-2:
You can
add and
name new
templates
in the
Templates
panel.

7. **Give the new region a name, usually something that identifies it by the kind of content it is, such as** *headline* **or** *navigation*.

8. **Click OK.**

The editable region is enclosed in a highlighted area with a tab at the top left, indicating the name of the region.

You can make an entire table or an individual table cell editable, and you can make entire rows editable. (For more about creating HTML tables, see Chapter 6.)

Setting attributes that can be edited

To create editable attributes in a template, follow these steps:

1. **In a Dreamweaver template, select an item you want to have an editable attribute.**

2. **Choose Modify⇨Templates⇨Make Attribute Editable.**

The Editable Tag Attributes dialog box appears.

3. **From the Attribute pull-down menu, choose the attribute you want to be editable.**

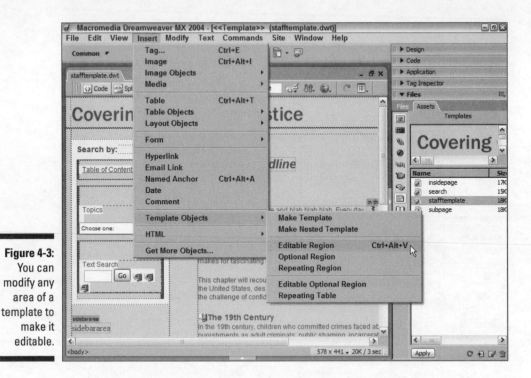

Figure 4-3:
You can
modify any
area of a
template to
make it
editable.

4. **Click the Make Attribute Editable box and fill in the Label, Type, and Default options.**

   The attribute options vary depending on whether you select an image, text, or other element on the page. With these options, you can control whether or not an image can be changed and what specific attributes of the image tag may be altered when the template is used.

5. **Click OK.**

Saving any page as a template

Sometimes you get partway through creating a page before you even consider the idea of making the page a template. Other times, you may have a page that someone else created, and you decide that you want to make it into a template. Either way, creating a template from an existing page is as easy as creating a new template from scratch.

To save a page as a template, follow these steps:

1. **Open the page that you want to turn into a template.**

   Choose File➪Open and browse to find your file. Or, open the site in the Files panel and double-click the file.

2. **Choose File⇨Save As Template.**

   The Save As Template dialog box appears.

3. **Select a site from the Site drop-down menu.**

   The menu lists all the sites that you defined in Dreamweaver. If you're working on a new site or haven't yet defined your site, Chapter 2 shows you how to define your site.

4. **In the Save As text box, type a name for the template.**

5. **Click the Save button.**

6. **Make any changes that you want and choose File⇨Save to save the page. Follow the steps in the earlier section, "Typing your template," to make editable regions or attributes.**

   Notice that the file now has the .dwt extension, indicating that it's a template. You can now make changes to this template the same way you edit any other template.

Using Templates

After you create all your great templates, you'll want to put them to use. You can use templates to create or modify all the pages in your Web site or just use them for specific areas or sections. Using a template to create a new page is similar to creating any other HTML page.

To use a template to create a page, follow these steps:

1. **Choose File⇨New.**

2. **Select the Templates tab.**

   The New from Template dialog box opens, as shown in Figure 4-4. You now have access to any template from any site you already defined.

3. **From the Templates For list on the left, choose the site that contains a template you want to use.**

4. **Select the template you want to use from the Site list in the middle of the dialog box.**

5. **Click the Create button.**

6. **Edit any of the regions of the page that are editable using regular editing features.**

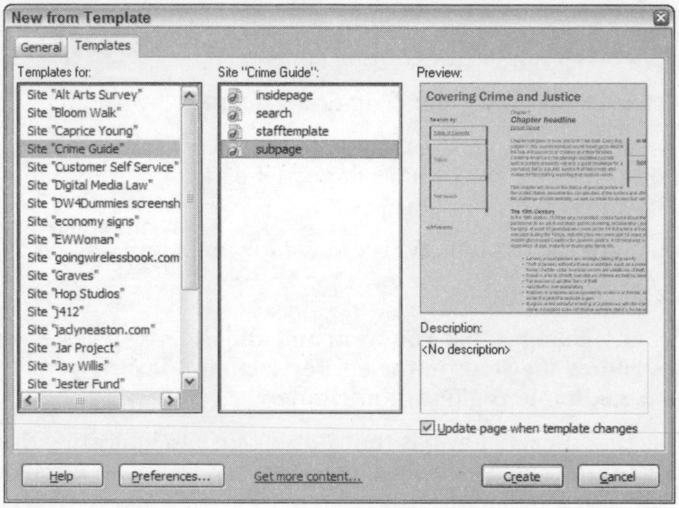

Figure 4-4:
The New
from
Template
dialog box
lets you
create a
new
document
from any
defined site.

New from Template

General | Templates

Templates for:

Site "Alt Arts Survey"
Site "Bloom Walk"
Site "Caprice Young"
Site "Crime Guide"
Site "Customer Self Service"
Site "Digital Media Law"
Site "DW4Dummies screensh
Site "economy signs"
Site "EWWoman"
Site "goingwirelessbook.com
Site "Graves"
Site "Hop Studios"
Site "j412"
Site "jaclyneaston.com"
Site "Jar Project"
Site "Jay Willis"
Site "Jester Fund"

Site "Crime Guide":

insidepage
search
stafftemplate
subpage

Preview:

Covering Crime and Justice

Description:
<No description>

☑ Update page when template changes

Help | Preferences... | Get more content... | Create | Cancel

You can only alter the editable regions of the template when you use a template to create a page. If you want to change a locked region of the page, you have to either remove the template association from the file or open the template and make that area of the file editable by revising the template itself.

You can remove the template association from a file by selecting Modify⇨Templates⇨Detach from Template. This action makes the file fully editable again, but changes you make to the template are not reflected on a detached page.

To edit the template of a document you are working on, choose Modify⇨Templates⇨Open Attached Template.

You can also apply a template to an existing page. When you apply a template to an existing document, the content in the template is added to the content already in the document. If a template is already applied to the page, Dreamweaver attempts to match editable areas that have the same name in both templates and to insert the contents from the editable regions of the page into the editable regions in the new template.

You can apply a template to an existing page by using any one of the following techniques:

✔ Choose Modify⇨Templates⇨Apply Template to Page and then double-click the name of a template to apply it to the page.

✔ Drag the template from the Template panel into the Document window.

✔ Select the template in the Template panel and click the Apply button at the bottom of the panel.

Making Global Changes with Templates

The greatest advantage of using templates is that you can apply changes to all the pages that use a template all at once. Suppose that you want to make a major change to the layout of your pages. If you built the site using a template, you can make the change and update the site page automatically — a real time saver. You can use the template update commands to update a single page or to update all the places that the template is used in the entire site.

To change a template and update the current page, follow these steps:

1. **Open a document that uses the template that you want to change.**

2. **Choose Modify⇨Templates⇨Open Attached Template.**

   The template opens.

3. **Modify the template.**

   For example, to modify the template's page properties, choose Modify⇨ Page Properties.

4. **When you finish making changes to the template, choose Modify⇨Templates⇨Update Current Page.**

   The page that you have open changes to reflect the changes you made to the template.

If you save a template after making changes, the Update Pages dialog box opens automatically, prompting you to choose the page or pages you want to update. Choose All to update all pages at once, or select one or more pages to update them individually. You can also choose Don't Update if you aren't ready to apply the changes.

To change a template and update all the files in your site that use that template at once, follow these steps:

1. **Open an existing template and make the changes that you want to apply.**

2. **Choose Modify⇨Templates⇨Update Pages.**

   The Update Pages dialog box appears.

3. **From the Look In drop-down list, choose one of the following options:**

   - **Entire Site:** Select the site name to update all pages in the selected site to all the corresponding templates.

   - **Files That Use:** Select the template name to update all pages in the current site that use that template.

Make sure that Templates is selected in the Update option.

4. Click the Start button to run the update process.

When the update process completes, the Updated Pages dialog box opens with a report on which pages were altered.

Reusing Elements with the Library Feature

The Library feature is not a common feature in other Web design programs, so the concept may be new to you even if you've been developing Web sites for a while. The more experience you have with this feature, however, the more likely you are to appreciate its value and the time you can save.

The Dreamweaver Library feature automates the process of inserting and changing elements that appear on multiple pages in a Web site. You can save any element as a Library item — for example, a logo or a navigation table of images and links. You can then insert that Library item on any page by simply dragging it from the Library to the new page. Create the element once and then use it all over the site — the Library is a great place to store navigation and other often-repeated content. Even better, if you ever need to change the Library item (by adding a link or image, for example), you can change the Library item and have Dreamweaver automatically update the change throughout the site. Libraries are not shared among sites, so each site you define must have its own Library.

A *Library item* is a snippet of code that can contain image references and links. Like templates, Library items are a great way to share the work of your best designers with less experienced ones. For example, one designer can create a logo and another the navigation elements, and then these can be placed in the Library and made available to the entire team. You have more flexibility with Library items than templates because they are elements you can place anywhere on any page, even multiple times.

Library items are any element from the body of a document, such as text, tables, forms, images, Java applets, and plug-in files. Library elements are efficient because Dreamweaver stores the snippet of code like a document in the Library folder and then updates the links to it from wherever you apply the Library element. Library items can also contain behaviors, but special requirements exist for editing the behaviors in Library items.

Library items cannot contain style sheets because the code for these elements is part of the Head area of an HTML file. (For more information on style sheets, see Chapter 8.)

Creating and using Library items

The following sections show you the steps for creating a Library item, adding one to a page, and editing a Library item when an element changes. For these steps to work appropriately, you must do them carefully, in sequential order. Before creating or using Library items, you must first define a site or open an existing site. If you're not sure how to do this, see Chapter 2.

Creating your Library item within an existing page is best because you can make sure that the item looks right before you add it to the Library. You can, of course, edit the item after it's in the Library, but the item may not look just like on the page. For example, a Library item does not have a `<BODY>` tag, so link and text colors in the Library item show as default blue and black. In the page, however, the `<BODY>` tag settings affect the link colors and text.

Creating a Library item

To create a Library item that you can use on multiple pages on your site, follow these steps:

1. **Open any existing file that has images, text, or other elements on the page.**

   A navigational row with images and links used throughout your Web site is ideal.

2. **From this page, select an element that you want to use as a Library item, such as your site navigation.**

3. **Choose Modify⇨Library⇨Add Object to Library.**

   The Assets tab of the Files panel opens and displays the Library. You new Library item displays as "Untitled."

4. **Name the element as you name any file in the Finder on a Mac or in Explorer on a PC.**

   When you name a Library item, you automatically save it to the Library. You can then easily apply the item to any new or existing page in your site. The Library section of the Assets panel lists all Library items, as shown in Figure 4-5.

Adding a Library item to a page

You can use elements from the Library as easily as you put them in. When you add a Library item to a page, the content (and a link to it) is inserted in the document.

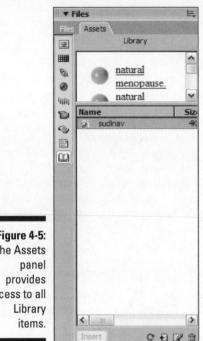

Figure 4-5:
The Assets
panel
provides
access to all
Library
items.

To add a Library item to a page, follow these steps:

1. **Create a new document in Dreamweaver or open any existing file.**

2. **From the Files panel, choose the Assets tab and then select the Library icon.**

   The Library panel opens in the Assets panel.

3. **Drag an item from the Library panel to the Document window.**

   Alternatively, you can select an item in the Library panel and click the Insert button.

   The item automatically appears on the page. After you insert a Library item on a page, you can use any of the formatting features to position it on the page.

Highlighting Library items

Library items are highlighted to distinguish them from other elements on a page. You can customize the highlight color for Library items and show or hide the highlight color in the Preferences dialog box.

To change or hide Library highlighting, follow these steps:

1. **Choose Edit⇨Preferences.**

   The Preferences dialog box appears.

2. **Select Highlighting from the Category section on the left.**

3. **Click the color box to select a color for Library items. Check the Show box to display the Library highlight color on your pages. Leave the box blank if you don't want to display the highlight color.**

4. **Click OK to close the Preferences dialog box.**

Changing a Library item

One of the biggest timesaving advantages of the Dreamweaver Library feature is that you can make changes to items and automatically apply those changes to multiple pages.

To edit a Library item and then update one or all of the pages on which you use that item, follow these steps:

1. **From the Files panel, choose the Assets tab and then select the Library icon.**

   The Library panel opens in the Assets panel.

2. **Double-click the item in the Library panel to open it.**

   Dreamweaver opens a new window for editing the Library item.

   Because the Library item is just a snippet of code, you don't find a <BODY> tag in which to specify background, link, or text colors. Don't worry over this — the Library item acquires the right settings from the tags on the page where it is inserted.

3. **Make any changes you want to the Library item.**

   For example, you can redirect the link of text items or images, edit the wording or font, or add images or text.

4. **Choose File⇨Save to save changes to the original item. Or, to create a new Library item, choose File⇨Save As and give the item a new name.**

   The Update Library Items dialog box opens, displaying a list of all pages where the Library item appears.

5. **Click the Update button to change the Library item on all the listed pages. To cancel without making changes, choose the Don't Update button.**

   The Update Pages dialog box appears and shows the progress of the updating. You can stop the update from this dialog box, if necessary.

Editing one instance of a Library item

As I say at the beginning of this chapter, you should strive for design consistency in almost all things. If you find that you want to alter a Library item in just one place, however, or make just a couple of exceptions, you can override the Library feature by breaking the link between the Library and the item in the document.

Remember: After you break that connection, you cannot update the Library item in the page automatically.

To make a Library item editable, follow these steps:

1. **Open any file that contains a Library item and select the Library item.**

   The Properties inspector displays the Library item options.

2. **Click the Detach from Original button.**

   A warning message appears, letting you know that if you proceed with detaching the Library item from the original, you can no longer update this occurrence of it when the original is edited.

3. **Click OK to detach the Library item.**

Using a Tracing Image to Guide Your Layout

The Macromedia Tracing Image feature is unique in the world of Web design tools, although the concept dates back to the earliest days of design. The Tracing Image feature enables you to use a graphic as a guide to your page design, much like an artist who creates a sketch and then paints the final picture over the sketch.

The Tracing Image feature is ideal for people who like to first create a design in a program such as Photoshop or Fireworks and then model their Web page after it. By using the Tracing Image feature, you can insert an image into the background of your page for the purpose of "tracing" over it. Then you can position layers or create table cells on top of the tracing image, which makes exactly re-creating your design in HTML easier. You can use JPG, GIF, or PNG images as tracing images, and you can create them in any graphics application that supports these formats.

Although the tracing image appears in the background of a page, it doesn't take the place of a background image and never displays in a browser.

To add a tracing image to your page, follow these steps:

1. **Create a new page or open any existing page in Dreamweaver.**

2. **Choose Modify➪Page Properties.**

   The Page Properties dialog box opens, shown in Figure 4-6.

3. **Select Tracing Image from the Category list on the left of the dialog box.**

   The Tracing Image options display on the right.

4. **Click the Browse button to locate the image you want to use as a Tracing Image.**

   The Select Image Source dialog box appears.

5. **Click the image you want to trace from.**

6. **Click OK.**

7. **Set the opacity for the tracing image with the Transparency slider.**

   Lowering the transparency level causes the tracing image to appear faded, which makes distinguishing between the tracing image and content on the page easy. You can set the transparency level to suit your preferences, but somewhere around 50 percent seems to work well with most images.

8. **Click OK.**

   A tracing image appears in the Document window, as shown in Figure 4-7.

A tracing image doesn't replace a background image. The tracing image itself is visible only when you edit the page in the Document window; it never appears when the page loads into a browser.

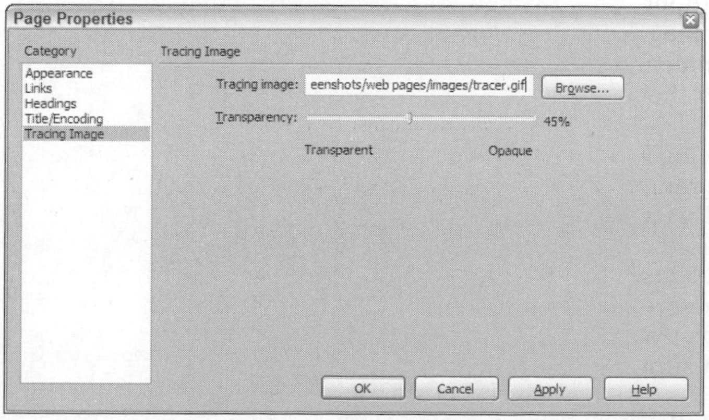

Figure 4-6:
The Page Properties dialog box lets you set a tracing image to use when laying out your HTML page.

Page Properties

Category	Tracing Image
Appearance	
Links	Tracing image: eenshots/web pages/images/tracer.gif Browse...
Headings	
Title/Encoding	Transparency: _____ 45%
Tracing Image	Transparent Opaque

OK   Cancel   Apply   Help

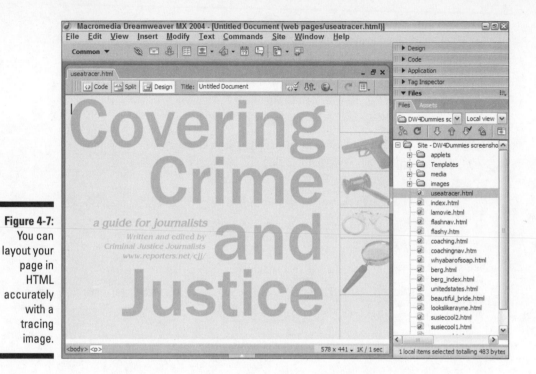

Figure 4-7:
You can layout your page in HTML accurately with a tracing image.

You have a few other options with the Tracing Image feature. Select View⇨ Tracing Image to reveal the following options:

✔ **Show:** Hides the tracing image if you want to check your work without it being visible but don't want to remove it.

✔ **Align with Selection:** Enables you to automatically line up the tracing image with a selected element on a page.

✔ **Adjust Position:** Enables you to use the arrow keys or enter X, Y coordinates to control the position of the tracing image behind the page.

✔ **Reset Position:** Resets the tracing image to 0, 0 on the X, Y coordinates.

Keeping in Touch with Design Notes

Design Notes are ideal for communicating with other developers who are working on your site, but aren't within shouting distance. This Dreamweaver feature works like the *comment tag* (HTML code that enables you to embed text in a page that won't display in a browser) but with a lot more privacy. Many developers use comment tags to share information with each other.

But anyone who views the source of your documents can see a comment tag, so it's not a very secure way to share information. When you use Design Notes, only those with password access to your site ever see the notes.

If you want to hide sensitive information, such as pricing structures or creative strategies, yet still be able to share it with other members of your development team, use Design Notes. Information saved as a Design Note in Dreamweaver can travel with any HTML file or image, even if the file transfers from one Web site to another or from Fireworks to Dreamweaver.

To activate the Design Notes feature, follow these steps:

1. **Choose Site⇨Manage Sites.**

   The Manage Sites dialog box opens.

2. **Select the site you want to work on and then click the Edit button.**

   The Site Definition dialog box opens.

3. **Select the Advanced tab.**

4. **In the Category list at the left, choose Design Notes.**

   The Design Notes page appears.

5. **Select the Maintain Design Notes option.**

   With this option selected, whenever you copy, move, rename, or delete a file, the associated Design Notes file is also copied, moved, renamed, or deleted with it.

6. **If you want your Design Notes to be sent with your files when they are uploaded to your server, select the Upload Design Notes for Sharing option.**

   If you're making notes only to yourself and don't want them to be associated with the page when you upload them to the server, deselect this option and Design Notes is maintained locally but not uploaded with your files.

7. **Click OK in the Site Definition dialog box; then click the Done button in the Manage Sites dialog box.**

   The Manage Sites dialog box closes.

To add Design Notes to a document, follow these steps:

1. **Open the file you want to add a Design Note to and choose File⇨ Design Notes.**

   The Design Notes dialog box opens (see Figure 4-8).

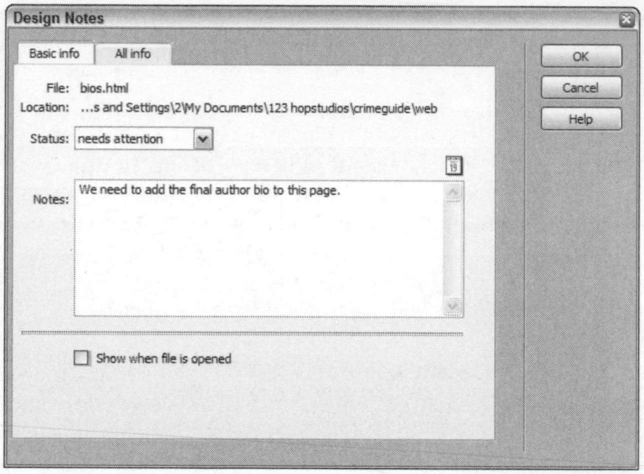

Figure 4-8:
Design
Notes make
associating
messages
with HTML
documents
for other
members
of your
develop-
ment team
easy.

2. **Choose the status of the document from the Status drop-down list box.**

   Your options are Draft, Revision 1, Revision 2, Revision 3, Alpha, Beta, Final, and Needs Attention. You can choose any status, and you should set a policy with your design team about what each status means and how you use these options to manage your development.

3. **Type your comments in the Notes text box.**

4. **Click the Insert Date icon (icon of a calendar page just above the Notes text box) if you want to insert the current local date.**

   The current date is inserted automatically.

   You can also select the Show When File Is Open check box. If this is selected, the Design Notes displays whenever the file is opened so that it can't be missed.

5. **Click the All Info tab in the Design Notes dialog box.**

   On the All Info tab, you can add other information that may be useful to developers of your site. For example, you can name a key designer (in the Name field) and define the value as the name of that person or the priority of the project (in the Value field). You also may define a field for a client or type of file that you commonly use.

6. **Click the plus (+) button to add a new information item; click the minus (–) button to remove a selected item.**

7. **Click OK to save the notes.**

   The notes you entered are saved to a subfolder named *notes* in the same location as the current file. The filename is the document's filename, plus the extension .mno. For example, if the filename is art.htm, the associated Design Notes file is named art.htm.mno. Design Notes are indicated in Site View by a small yellow icon that looks like a cartoon bubble.

Staying in Touch with Integrated E-Mail

Dreamweaver features integrated e-mail as another handy tool for collaborative Web design, when you use the Dreamweaver Check In/Out tool. (The Check In/Out feature is described fully in Chapter 2.) In conjunction with the e-mail program you already use, integrated e-mail gives you easy access to the e-mail addresses of other members of your team when you need them.

When you work on a site with a team of people, finding someone else has already checked out the page you want to work on is common, which makes doing the work you need to do on the page impossible. In the Dreamweaver Site Definition dialog box, each developer can type his or her e-mail address in the Check In/Check Out feature. Then when you find that someone else has the page you need, you can easily fire off an e-mail telling that person to check it back in so you can work on it. (Bribes can be more effective than threats, especially when you offer chocolate.)

Developers on your team can use the following steps to associate their e-mail addresses with their version of Dreamweaver as part of the Check In/Check Out set up:

1. **Choose Site⇨Manage Sites.**

   The Manage Sites dialog box opens.

2. **Select the site you want to work on and then click the Edit button.**

   The Site Definition dialog box opens.

3. **Click the Advanced tab.**

4. **In the Category list at the left, choose Remote Info.**

   The Remote Info page appears, shown in Figure 4-9.

5. **Select the Enable File Check In and Check Out check box.**

6. **Select the Check Out Files When Opening check box.**

7. **Enter your name in the Check Out Name text box.**

   Nicknames are okay as long as everyone on the team knows your silly name.

8. **Enter your e-mail address in the Email Address text box.**

9. **Click OK to save your changes. Click the Done button in the Manage Sites dialog box.**

   The Manage Sites dialog box closes.

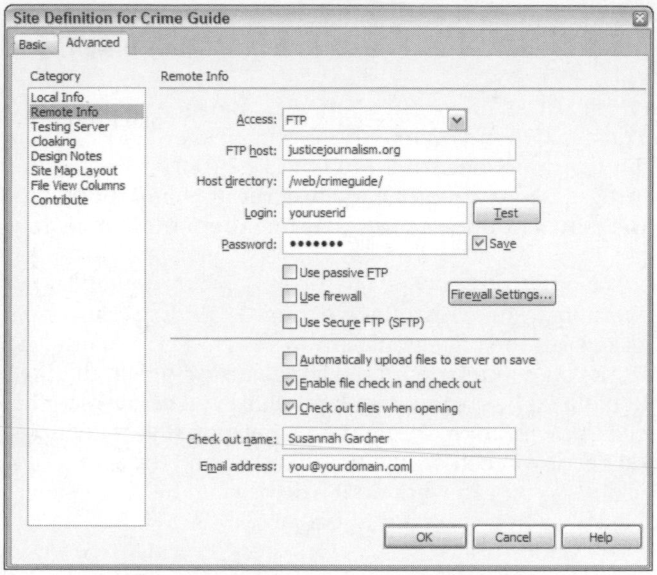

Figure 4-9:
You can
associate
your e-mail
address
with the
Check
In/Check
Out feature
to make
sending
messages
to team
members
easy.

Remembering Your History

You can keep track of what you're doing and even replay your steps with the History panel. The History panel also lets you undo one or more steps and create commands to automate repetitive tasks.

To open the History panel, shown in Figure 4-10, choose Window⇨History. As soon as you open a file, the History window starts automatically recording your actions as you do work in Dreamweaver. You can't rearrange the order of steps in the History panel, but you can copy them, replay them, and undo them. Don't think of the History panel as an arbitrary collection of commands; think of it as a way to view the steps you've performed, in the order in which you performed them. This is a great way to let Dreamweaver do your work for you if you have to repeat the same steps over and over again. It's also a lifesaver if you make a major mistake and want to go back one or more steps in your development work.

Here's a rundown of how you can put the History panel to use:

✔ **To copy steps you already executed:** Use the Copy Steps option as a quick way to automate steps you want to repeat. You can even select steps individually, in case you want to replay some, but not all, of your actions exactly as you did them.

✔ **To replay any or all the steps displayed in the History panel:** Highlight the steps you want to replay and click the Replay button in the bottom of the History panel.

✔ **To undo the results of the replayed steps:** Choose Edit➪Undo Replay Steps.

✔ **To apply steps to a specific element on a page:** Highlight that element in the Document window before selecting and replaying the steps. For example, if you want to apply bold and italic formatting to just a few words on a page, you can replay the steps that applied bold and italics to selected text.

You can also set the number of steps displayed in the History panel by choosing Edit➪Preferences and selecting General from the Category list on the left. The default is 50 steps, more than enough for most users. The higher the number, the more memory the History panel uses.

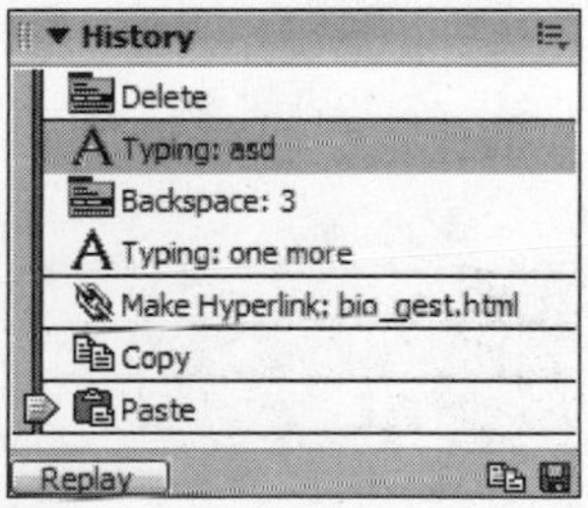

Figure 4-10:
The History
panel keeps
track of
what you
do, making
undoing and
repeating
any or all
your steps
easy.

▼ History	
🗒 Delete	
A Typing: asd	
🗒 Backspace: 3	
A Typing: one more	
🔗 Make Hyperlink: bio_gest.html	
🗐 Copy	
🗐 Paste	
Replay	🗐 💾

Using the Quick Tag Editor

If you're one of those developers who likes to work in the Dreamweaver WYSIWYG editing environment but still wants to look at the HTML tags once in a while, you'll love the Quick Tag Editor.

The Quick Tag Editor, as the name implies, lets you modify, add, or remove an HTML tag without opening the HTML Source Window. That means that while you're in the middle of working on a page, you can quickly bring up the tag you are working on without leaving the Document window. You can use the Quick Tag Editor to insert HTML, edit an existing tag, or wrap new tags around a selected text block or element.

Keeping the peace with version control

Version control systems enable you to better manage changes made by different team members and prevent them from overwriting each other's work. If you already use these programs, you'll be glad to know that you can now integrate both Visual SourceSafe and systems that use the Web DAV protocol with Dreamweaver. This way, you can take advantage of the Dreamweaver site management features and still protect your code development process. If you don't know about these programs, visit the Microsoft site (http://msdn.microsoft.com/ssafe/) to find out more about Visual SourceSafe, or visit www.ics.uci.edu/pub/ietf/webdav/ to discover more about WebDAV protocols.

The Quick Tag Editor opens in one of three modes — Edit, Insert, or Wrap — depending on what you selected on a page. Use the keyboard shortcut Ctrl+T (Windows) or ⌘+T (Macintosh) to change modes while the Quick Tag Editor is open.

You can enter or edit tags in the Quick Tag Editor, just as you would in the Document Source Window, without having to switch back and forth between the text editor and WYSIWYG environment.

To enter or edit tags in the Quick Tag Editor, follow these steps:

1. **With the document you want to edit open, select an element or text block.**

   If you want to add new code, simply click anywhere in the file without selecting text or an element.

2. **Choose Modify⇨Quick Tag Editor.**

   You can also press Ctrl+T (Windows) or ⌘+T (Macintosh).

   The Quick Tag Editor opens in the mode that is most appropriate for your selection, as shown in Figure 4-11. For example, if you click an image or formatted text, it displays the code so that you can edit it. If you don't select anything, or if you select unformatted text, the Quick Tag Editor opens with nothing in it, and you can enter the code you want to add. Press Ctrl+T to switch to another mode.

   If you want to edit an existing tag, go to Step 3. If you want to add a new tag, skip to Step 4.

3. **If you selected an element formatted with multiple HTML tags or a tag with multiple attributes, press Tab to move from one tag, attribute name, or attribute value to the next. Press Shift+Tab to move back to the previous one.**

If you aren't sure about a tag or attribute, pause for a couple of seconds and a drop-down list appears automatically, offering you a list of all the tags or attributes available for the element you are editing. If this "hints" list doesn't appear, choose Edit⇨Preferences⇨Quick Tag Editor Preferences and make sure that the Enable Tag Hints option is selected.

4. **To add a new tag or attribute, simply type the code into the Quick Tag Editor.**

   You can use the Tab and arrow keys to move the cursor where you want to add code. You can keep the Quick Tag Editor open and continue to edit and add attribute names and values as long as you like.

5. **To close the Quick Tag Editor and apply all your changes, press Enter (Windows) or Return (Mac).**

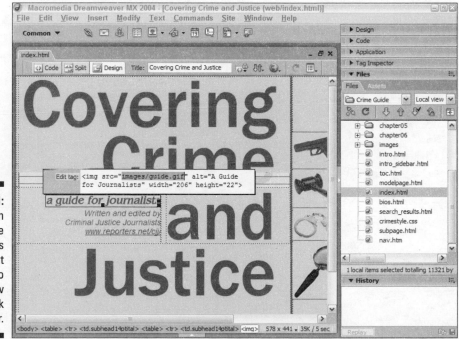

Figure 4-11:
You can
make
HTML edits
without
moving to
Code View
in the Quick
Tag Editor.

Chapter 5

Adding Graphics

• •

• •

*N*o matter how great the writing may be on your Web site, the graphics always get people's attention first. And the key to making a good first impression is to use images that look great, download quickly, and are appropriate to your Web site.

If you're familiar with using a graphics-editing program to create graphics, you're a step ahead. If not, you find pointers throughout this chapter and you discover how to find preexisting graphics to use on your Web site. You also find out how to bring graphics into Dreamweaver and how to edit them without leaving the Web design environment. To help you get the most out of the images for your site, you find information about choosing an image-editing program and keeping image file sizes small.

If your images are ready and you want to dive into placing them on your pages, jump ahead to the section, "Inserting Images on Your Pages" and find out how to place and align images, create image maps, and set a background image in Dreamweaver. You also discover some of Dreamweaver's newest features, which enable you to crop images and even adjust contrast and brightness without ever launching an external image-editing program.

Getting Great Graphics

You want your Web graphics to look good, but where do you get them? If you have some design talent, you can create your own images with Fireworks or any of the other image programs that you can find out in the section,

"Creating your own images," later in this chapter. If you're not an artist, you may be better off gathering images from *clip art collections* (libraries of ready-to-use image files) and using royalty-free or stock photography, as described in this section. If you have a scanner, you can also scan in existing photographs or logos to use.

Dreamweaver doesn't have any image-creation capabilities of its own, and only limited editing tools, so you probably want to use a different program to create or edit images. If you bought the Dreamweaver/Fireworks Studio, however, you're in luck; you have everything you need to create and edit images and photos for your Web site. Otherwise, you need a separate program to create and edit your images. Dreamweaver integrates well with almost any other image-editing program, and many designers use Photoshop or other programs to create images for the Web.

Buying royalty-free clip art and photographs

If you don't want the hassle of creating your own images (or if you lack the artistic talent), you may be happy to find many sources of clip art available. Royalty-free images, which include clip art and photographs, are generally sold for a one-time fee that grants you all or most of the rights to use the image. (Read the agreement that comes with any art you purchase to make sure that you don't miss any exclusions or exceptions.) You can find a wide range of CD-ROMs and Web sites full of clip art, photographs, and even animations that you can use on your Web site. (Speaking of animations, nowadays, you can even find Web sites that sell Flash files, animations, buttons, and other artistic elements that you can edit and integrate into your Web site. For more on creating a multimedia Web site, see Chapter 12.) Many professional designers buy clip art images and then alter them in an image program — such as Macromedia Fireworks, Adobe Illustrator, or Adobe Photoshop — to tailor them for a specific project or to make an image more distinct. Here are some clip art suppliers:

- ✔ **Getty Images, Inc.** (`www.gettyimages.com`): Getty Images is the largest supplier of royalty-free digital imagery on the Web, specializing in photographs and illustrations of a wide variety of subjects, including film footage. Pay for images and footage as you go.

- ✔ **Stockbyte** (`www.stockbyte.com`): Stockbyte is a great source for international royalty-free photos. You can purchase photographs at a variety of qualities, as you need them.

- ✔ **Photos.com** (`www.photos.com`): Photos.com is a subscription-based service for royalty-free stock photography and photo objects. A 1- to 12-month subscription gives you unlimited access and use of its collection.

✔ **Fonts.com (**www.fonts.com**):** You can preview and purchase a huge number of fonts at Fonts.com. You can search this site by font name or using descriptive keywords. They can also help if you need a specific font but don't know its name.

✔ **Web Promotion (**www.webpromotion.com**):** A great source for animated GIFs and other Web graphics. Artwork on this site is free provided you create a link back to Web Promotion on your Web site, or you can buy the artwork for a small fee.

Creating your own images

The best way to get original images is to create your own. If you're not graphically talented or inclined, consider hiring someone who can create images for you. If you want to create your own images for use in Dreamweaver, Fireworks is a good program to start with because of its tight integration with Dreamweaver and overall "dummy-proof" features — no pun intended! Fireworks is a perfect tool for making Web graphics and is easy to learn because it shares a common interface with Dreamweaver. However, you can use any other image-editing programs on the market either separately or in unison with Fireworks. You find some listed later in this section.

The last few years have seen a tremendous advancement in the features and capabilities of specialized Web graphics programs as well as increased competition between application vendors, especially the heavyweights like Adobe and Macromedia. Consequently, the current "best of the crop" graphics program is a toss-up between Macromedia's Fireworks and Adobe's Photoshop. Ask any good Web designer what graphics program they use, and it will be one of these. If you're serious about Web graphics, consider getting one of these two programs — they're the cream of the crop and can easily pay for themselves by giving you the most professional and efficient results on your Web projects. The biggest difference between the two, besides Fireworks' integration with Dreamweaver, is that Fireworks was specifically created to design Web graphics. Photoshop is also a favorite program for print designers and so has many features you won't need for Web graphics.

However, if you don't have the budget or the time to learn more complex programs, you may be better off with a more limited photo-editing program such as Adobe Photoshop Elements, which is a capable yet far less expensive option, costing only around $99. For creating buttons, banners, and other Web graphics on a budget, consider Jasc Paint Shop Pro or MicroFrontier Color It!

Unless otherwise indicated, all the following programs are available for both Mac and Windows. Also, most of these programs allow you to scan photographs and logos using a scanner.

- **Macromedia Fireworks** (www.macromedia.com/software/fireworks): Fireworks was one of the very first image-editing programs designed specifically to create and edit Web graphics. Fireworks gives you everything you need to create, edit, and output the best-looking Web graphics, all in one well-designed product. Besides sharing a common interface with Dreamweaver, Fireworks also integrates extremely well with Dreamweaver to speed up and simplify the process of building a Web site. In Chapter 11, you discover some of the special features of Fireworks and Dreamweaver that help you to work together with these two programs.

- **Adobe Photoshop** (www.adobe.com/products): Adobe calls Photoshop the "camera of the mind." This is unquestionably the most popular image-editing program on the market and a widely used standard among graphics professionals. With Photoshop, you can create original artwork, correct color in photographs, retouch photographs and scanned images, and do much more. Photoshop has a wealth of powerful painting and selection tools in addition to special effects and filters to create images that go beyond what you can capture on film or create with classic illustration programs. The latest versions of Photoshop also add a wealth of features for creating and editing Web graphics, putting it on par with Fireworks in this department.

- **Adobe Photoshop Elements** (www.adobe.com/products): For novices or users who don't need all the bells and whistles offered in the full-blown version of Photoshop, Adobe provides Photoshop Elements. This program often comes bundled with a scanner or printer. Adobe says that Elements is geared for Web graphics output and is very easy to learn and use.

- **Adobe Illustrator** (www.adobe.com/products): Illustrator is one of the industry standards for creating illustrations. You can drag and drop illustrations that you create in Illustrator right into other Adobe programs, such as Photoshop or PageMaker. Illustrator also comes with an export feature that enables you to export your illustrations in GIF or JPEG format with a browser-friendly palette of colors so that your illustrations look great on the Web.

- **CorelDRAW Essentials** (www.corel.com): Widely used, though definitely not an industry standard, CorelDRAW offers features and capabilities similar to those of Adobe Photoshop, for a fraction of the price. The Essentials package comes with CorelDRAW and CorelPHOTO-PAINT. Photo-Paint comes with a generous clip art and royalty-free photography collection. For about $180 less than the cost of Photoshop, you can get the complete CorelDRAW Graphics Suite, which includes CorelDRAW and the Essentials package. This is a great set for home users who want professional-grade graphics and page layout capabilities at a more affordable price.

- **Equilibrium DeBabelizer** (www.equilibrium.com/Internet/Equil/Products/DeBabelizer/): DeBabelizer, by Equilibrium Technologies, is a graphics-processing program capable of handling almost every image format ever used on a computer. This one probably isn't the best program to use for creating images from scratch, but it does excel at some of the highly specialized tasks of preparing and optimizing images for the Web. One of the best features of DeBabelizer is its capability to convert images from just about any format to just about any other. If you have a bunch of images to convert, you can use the DeBabelizer *batch convert* feature, which enables you to automatically convert hundreds of photographs into JPEGs or convert many graphics into GIFs all at once without having to open each file separately. Be aware, though, that DeBabelizer has a pretty steep learning curve and isn't recommended for someone just starting out in creating Web graphics. This program makes the best sense for someone who needs to process hundreds of images or who has to manage images in many different formats.

✔ **Jasc Paint Shop Pro** (www.jasc.com): Paint Shop Pro, by Jasc Software, is a fully featured painting and image-manipulation program available only for Windows. Paint Shop Pro is very similar to Photoshop, but on a more limited scale because it doesn't offer the same range of effects, tools, and filters. However, it costs less than Photoshop and may be a good starter program for novice image-makers. You can also download an evaluation version for free from the Jasc Web site.

✔ **Macromedia Freehand** (www.macromedia.com/software/freehand): Macromedia Freehand is an illustration program used widely both on the Web and in print. Freehand has many excellent Web features, including support for Web file formats such as GIF89a, PNG, and JPEG, as well as vector formats such as Flash (.SWF) and Shockwave FreeHand (.FHC). Thirty-day trial versions are available for free on the Macromedia Web site.

✔ **MicroFrontier Color It!** (www.microfrontier.com): This low-cost, easy-to-use graphics program is available only for the Macintosh and is a great tool for beginners, as well as those on a tight budget. Although it's much more limited than many of the other programs in this list, it provides enough features to create basic banners and buttons for a small business Web site. A demo version is available for free from the MicroFrontier Web site.

Understanding the Basics of Web Graphics

Because having a basic understanding of graphics formats and how they work on the Web is so important, the following sections give you an overview of what you need to know about graphics as you create them or place them on your pages.

The most important thing to keep in mind when placing images on a Web page is that you want to keep your file sizes as small as possible. You may ask, "How small is *small?*" In fact, this is one of the most common questions people ask about Web graphics. The answer is largely subjective — remember that the larger your graphics files are, the longer people have to wait for them to download before they can see them. You can have the most beautiful picture of Mount Fuji on the front page of your Web site, but if it takes forever to download, most people aren't going to be patient enough to wait to see it. Also remember that when you build pages with multiple graphics, you have to consider the cumulative download time of all the graphics on the page. So smaller is definitely better.

Most Web pros consider anything from about 40K to 60K a good maximum *cumulative* size for all the elements on a given page. With the increasing popularity of DSL and cable modems, many Web sites are starting to become a bit more graphics-heavy. However, anything over 100K is definitely a no-no if you expect people with dial-up modems (56K and under) to stick around long enough to view your pages.

To make determining the total file size of the images on your page easy, Dreamweaver includes this information in the status bar of the current Document window, as shown in Figure 5-1. This number indicates the total file size of all the images and HTML on your page as well as the expected download time at a given connection speed (you can set your own connection speed by choosing Edit⇨Preferences⇨Status Bar⇨Connection Speed).

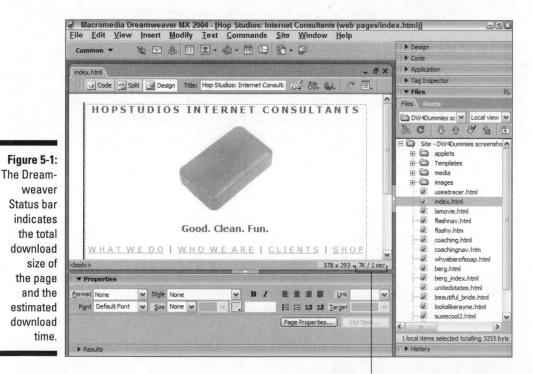

Figure 5-1:
The Dream-weaver Status bar indicates the total download size of the page and the estimated download time.

Total download size and estimated download time.

Achieving small file sizes requires using compression techniques and color reduction, tasks that you can achieve using any of the graphics programs mentioned in the preceding section. Whatever program you use, you should understand that you can reduce image sizes to varying degrees and that the challenge is to find the best balance between small file size and good image quality. If you really want to find out the best ways to create graphics for the Web, read *Web Design For Dummies* by Lisa Lopuck (Wiley Publishing, Inc.). It has a fantastic section on designing Web graphics.

One of the most common questions about images for the Web is when you use GIF and when you use JPEG. The simple answer:

Use	*For*
GIF	Line art (such as one- or two-color logos), simple drawings, and basically any image that has no gradients or blends
JPEG	Colorful, complex images (such as photographs), images containing gradients or color blends, and so on

That said, sometimes the best thing to do is just experiment with both formats and see which yields the best results. In time, you'll get a knack for which is the best format to use, depending on the type of image you're working with.

Inserting Images on Your Pages

Dreamweaver makes placing images on your Web pages easy.

Before inserting any images into your page, saving your page is important. After you save, Dreamweaver knows the directory location of the page and can then properly create the image links.

To place an image in a new file, follow these steps:

1. **Choose File⇨New to start a new page.**

2. **In the Category list, choose Basic Page. In the Basic Page list, choose HTML.**

3. **Click the Create button.**

4. **Choose File⇨Save to name and save the new HTML file in the folder of your choice.**

5. **If the Properties inspector isn't already visible, choose Window⇨ Properties to open it.**

More about GIFs

GIFs, aside from the poorly supported PNG format, is the only widely accepted file format that can have an invisible color to create a transparency effect. GIFs can also have multiple frames, so you can create small, animated loops with this format. Animated ads on the Web, generally referred to as *banners,* are sometimes made in GIF.

Designers frequently create a GIF that just consists of words because it lets you use non-standard fonts with perfect anti-aliasing and whatever colors and effects you want without worrying about whether the end user has the font. GIF is the ideal format for this because it offers transparency, where JPEG compression can make the small lines and curves in text fuzzy.

6. **Click the Insert Image icon in the Common Objects panel (the icon is of a small tree).**

 The Select Image Source dialog box appears, as shown in Figure 5-2.

7. **In the Select Image Source dialog box, browse your local drive in order to locate the image you want to place.**

 Alternatively, you can insert images simply by choosing Insert➪Image, which also brings up the Select Image Source dialog box, or by dragging and dropping image files from the Files panel right into your Dreamweaver document, provided that they are in a valid Web graphics file format, such as GIF or JPEG.

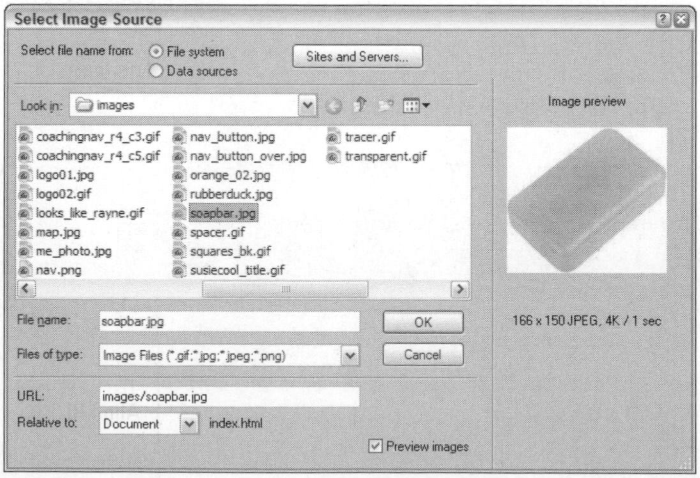

Figure 5-2:
You can locate and preview the image you want to place in the Select Image Source dialog box.

Select Image Source			
Select file name from: ● File system ○ Data sources		Sites and Servers...	Image preview
Look in: 📁 images			
coachingnav_r4_c3.gif	nav_button.jpg	tracer.gif	
coachingnav_r4_c5.gif	nav_button_over.jpg	transparent.gif	
logo01.jpg	orange_02.jpg		
logo02.gif	rubberduck.jpg		
looks_like_rayne.gif	soapbar.jpg		
map.jpg	spacer.gif		
me_photo.jpg	squares_bk.gif		
nav.png	susiecool_title.gif		
File name: soapbar.jpg		OK	166 x 150 JPEG, 4K / 1 sec
Files of type: Image Files (*.gif;*.jpg;*.jpeg;*.png)		Cancel	
URL: images/soapbar.jpg			
Relative to: Document ⌄ index.html			☑ Preview images

When you work with image files, maintaining the same directory structure on your local hard drive as you intend to use on your server when you upload your files is best. Mirroring the structure of your server on your local machine vastly simplifies uploading, tracking, and maintaining your site structure throughout the development cycle as well as later on when you want to update your site. (See Chapter 3 for details on creating a folder structure for your site's files.)

8. **Double-click the image to insert it or click once and then click OK.**

   The image automatically appears on your page.

Aligning Images on a Page

After you place an image on your Web page, you may want to center or align it so that text can wrap around it. In the following two sections — "Centering an image" and "Aligning an image with text wrapping" — you find out the steps to accomplish both of these goals.

Centering an image

To center an image on a page, follow these steps:

1. **Click to select the image that you want to center.**

   The Properties inspector changes to display the image properties.

2. **From the icons for alignment options in the Properties inspector, shown in Figure 5-3, click the Align Center icon.**

   The image automatically moves to the center of the page.

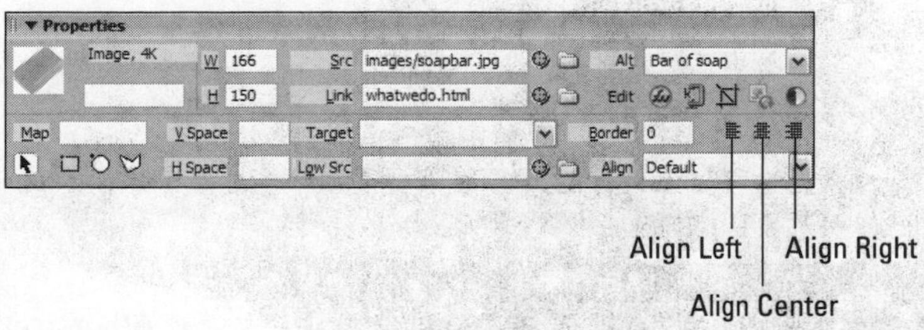

Figure 5-3:
Use the alignment icons in the Properties inspector to center an image.

▼ Properties						
	Image, 4K	W 166	Src images/soapbar.jpg	Alt Bar of soap		
		H 150	Link whatwedo.html	Edit		
Map		V Space	Target	Border 0		
		H Space	Low Src	Align Default		

Align Left   Align Right

Align Center

How an image appears on a Web page

The HTML tag that you use to place images on a Web page is similar to the link tag that you use to create hyperlinks between pages. Both tags instruct the browser where to find something. In the case of the link tag, the path to the linked page instructs the browser where to find another URL. In the case of an image tag, the path in the tag instructs the browser to find a GIF or JPEG image file. The path describes the location of the image in relation to the page on which it appears. For example, `images/baby.gif` is a path that instructs a browser to look for an image file called `baby.gif` in the images directory. This path also implies that the images directory is in the same directory as the HTML file containing the link. Whenever you see a forward slash in HTML, it signifies a directory (or folder) that contains other files or folders.

Trying to determine the path can get a little complicated. Fortunately, Dreamweaver sets the path for you, but you need to take care of two important steps before Dreamweaver can do this properly:

1. **Save your page.**

   When you save a page, Dreamweaver automatically remembers the exact location of the page in relation to the image. Saving the file is essential because the path always indicates the location of an image relative to the page containing the link (this is called a *relative link*). If you forget to save your file beforehand, Dreamweaver always prompts you to save the file before completing the link. If you don't save the file, Dreamweaver inserts an absolute link that references the image's location on your hard disk, but this link isn't valid on any other machine or when you upload your Web site. An *absolute link* to your hard drive works on your machine, but not on your Web server — or any other machine, for that matter.

2. **Make sure that your images and pages stay in the same relative locations when you're ready to go public with your site and move them all to a server.**

Aligning an image with text wrapping

To align an image to the right of a page and wrap text around it on the left, follow these steps:

1. **Insert the image immediately to the left of the first line of the text (see Figure 5-4).**

   The easiest way to do this is to place the cursor before the first letter of text; then choose Insert⇔Image.

   Don't put spaces or line breaks between the image and the text.

2. **Select the image.**

   The Properties inspector changes to display the image attribute options.

3. **In the Properties inspector, choose Left from the Align drop-down list.**

   The image aligns to the left and the text automatically wraps around it, as shown in Figure 5-5.

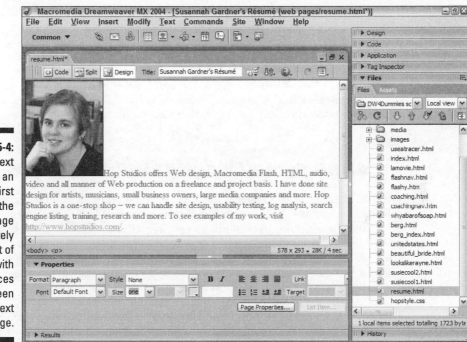

Figure 5-4:
To wrap text around an image, first place the image immediately to the left of the text with no spaces between the text and image.

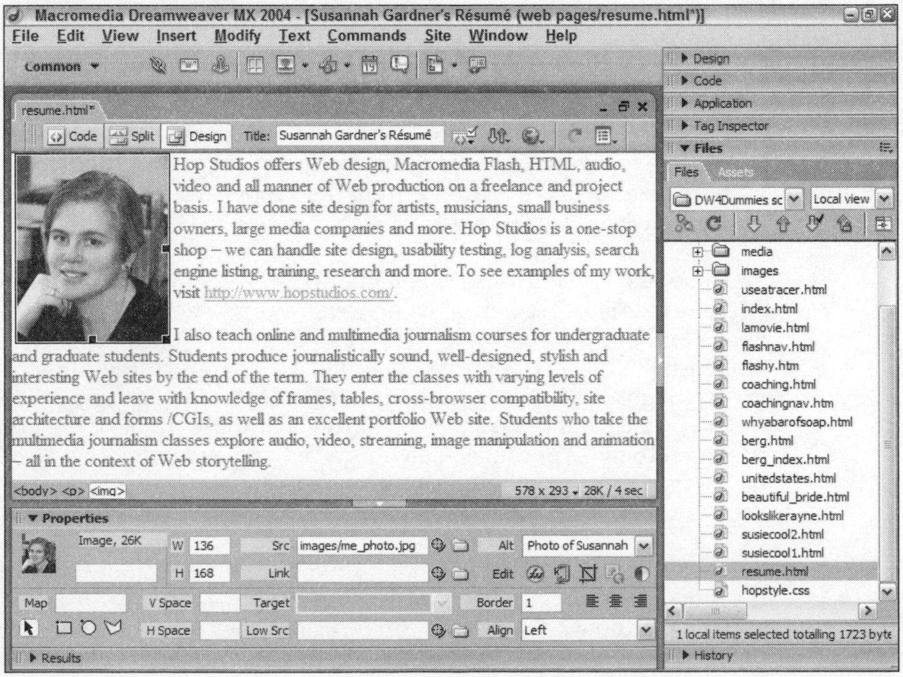

Figure 5-5:
The Align drop-down list in the Properties inspector aligns an image.

To align the image to the right of the page with text wrapping around on the left, follow Steps 1 and 2, and then in Step 3, choose Right from the Align drop-down list instead of Left.

To prevent text from running up against an image, click the image, find V and H spacing on the Properties inspector, and enter the amount of space you'd like (the space is measured in pixels). Ten pixels is typically a safe number. This adds space around the image preventing the text from hitting its edge.

Creating complex designs with images

The alignment options available in HTML enable you to align your images vertically or horizontally, but you can't do both at once. Also, the alignment options don't really enable you to position images in relation to one another or in relation to text with much precision. The way to get around this limitation is to create HTML tables and use the cells in the table to control positioning. See Chapter 6 to find out how to make tables. You can also use layers and Cascading Style Sheets to position elements on a page (Chapter 8).

This sounds complex at first, but with a little experimentation, you can create almost any page layout using tables. Chapter 9 shows how to use tables to create more complex Web page designs.

Image Editing in Dreamweaver

New features in Dreamweaver allow you to make minor image editing inside Dreamweaver, without opening Fireworks or any other graphics-editing program. These tools are available from the Properties inspector, when an image is selected (see Figure 5-6).

You also find two buttons that enable you to use Macromedia Fireworks to edit images. The Edit button launches Fireworks and opens the selected image in the main window of the program, which makes using all the Firework editing features easy. Macromedia's careful integration of these programs means that when you save changes to the image, they are reflected in the page in Dreamweaver. A new button, just to the right of the Edit button, is designed to make optimizing an image fast and easy, which makes downloading faster. Both the Edit and Optimize in Fireworks features are covered in greater detail in Chapter 10.

Before you get carried away editing your images, remember that Dreamweaver is primarily a Web page creation application and not really designed to edit graphics. Although these tools can be useful, they shouldn't take the place of doing serious work on your graphics in an actual graphics application, such as Fireworks or Photoshop.

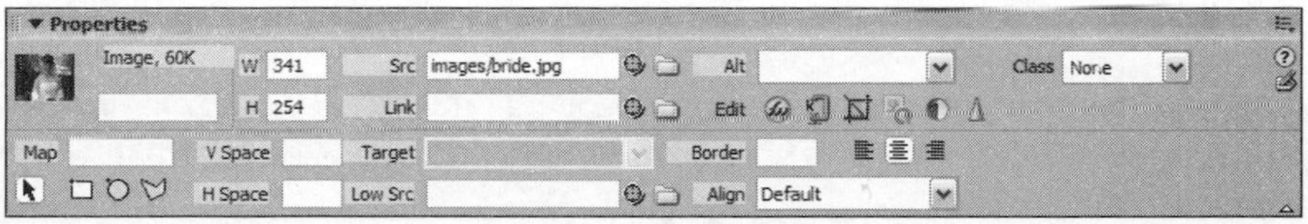

Figure 5-6:
The Crop,
Brightness
and
Contrast,
and
Sharpen
tools in the
Properties
inspector
edit an
image inside
Dream-
weaver.

When you do use the tools for cropping, adjusting brightness and contrast, and sharpening an image, beware that you are changing the actual image (not just a copy of it). Make sure you're happy with these changes before you save the page you're working on. You can use the undo feature in Dreamweaver to revert back several steps, but after you save the page, you can't undo changes to an image. To protect your original image, considering saving a copy before editing it.

Cropping an image

Essentially, cropping an image is trimming it. To crop a graphic or photo, follow these steps:

1. **In the Document window, select the image you'd like to crop by clicking it.**

   The Properties inspector changes to display the image's properties.

2. **From the Edit icons, click the Crop tool.**

   A dialog box appears warning you that cropping changes the original image.

   Don't make the change if you're concerned about needing to keep the entire image available. If you're concerned, the best thing to do may be to make a copy of the image and apply your cropping to the copy.

3. **Click OK.**

   A dotted line with handlebars appears in the image.

4. **Outline the area of the image you want to keep with the handlebars.**

   Any part of the image that is darkened, as shown in Figure 5-7, is deleted when the crop completes.

5. **Double click inside the box, or press Enter.**

   The image is cropped.

You can undo cropping by choosing Edit⇨Undo, but remember that, after you save the page, changes permanently apply to the image and cannot be undone.

Adjusting brightness and contrast

Adjusting an image's brightness allows you to change the overall amount of light in an image. Contrast controls the difference between the light and dark areas of an image. To adjust brightness and contrast, follow these steps:

1. **In the Document window, select the image you want to alter.**

   The Properties inspector shows the image properties.

2. **From the Edit tools, click the Brightness and Contrast icon (a circle with light and dark halves).**

   A dialog box appears, indicating that changes you make are made to the original file.

3. **Click OK.**

   The Brightness/Contrast dialog box appears.

4. **Adjust the brightness and contrast settings of the image with the sliders.**

   Make sure to select the Preview check box if you want to see the changes affect the image as you move the sliders around.

5. **Click OK.**

   The settings take effect permanently when you save the page.

Sharpening an image

When you apply sharpening to an image, you increase the distinction between areas of color. The effect can be one of increased definition to the shapes and lines in an image. To sharpen an image, follow these steps:

Dotted crop line

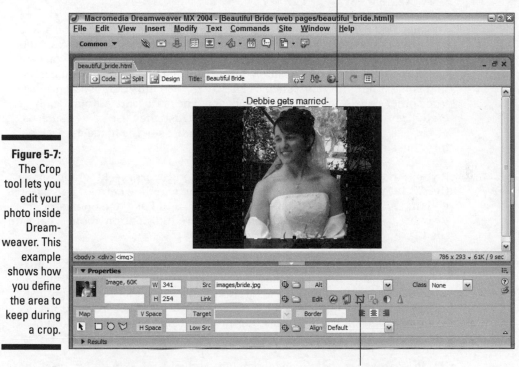

Figure 5-7:
The Crop tool lets you edit your photo inside Dream-weaver. This example shows how you define the area to keep during a crop.

Crop tool

1. **In the Document window, select the image you want to sharpen.**

   The Properties inspector shows the image properties.

2. **From the Edit tools, click the Sharpen icon (a blue cone).**

   A dialog box appears, indicating that your change is made to the original file.

3. **Click OK.**

   The Sharpen dialog box appears.

4. **Adjust the sharpness of the image with the slider.**

   Make sure you select the Preview check box if you want to see the changes affect the image as you move the slider.

5. **Click OK.**

   The image is sharpened and changes are made permanently when you save changes to the page.

Using the Transparent GIF Trick

You may find it strange that I suggest you place an invisible image on a Web page, but that's exactly what I show you how to do in this section. A small, transparent GIF is a powerful element in Web page design because you can use it to control the exact position of other elements on a page. You'll notice that some other programs, such as Fireworks, also utilize transparent GIFs to force other page elements into compliance. These GIFs are automatically generated, and you can often recognize them because they use names such as `shim.gif`, `clear.gif`, or `spacer.gif`. Regardless of the name, they all perform the same function.

If you're not sure how to make a clear GIF, don't worry — I include one on the CD-ROM that accompanies this book. You can do whatever you like with it. I always name this image `clear.gif`, and I use one on nearly every Web site I work on. See the appendix for more information about what's on the CD.

If you want to make your own transparent GIF, just create a small, solid-color image, save it as a GIF, and designate the color you use as transparent. You can make a color transparent in most good graphics programs, including Adobe Photoshop and Fireworks. You can find descriptions of a number of graphics programs that provide this feature earlier in this chapter.

HTML enables you to specify any height and width for an image, regardless of its actual size. Thus, you can use a small transparent GIF with a corresponding small file size (for quick download) and then alter the image attributes for height and width to create exact spaces between other visible elements on your page. Many Web designers recommend that you create a single-pixel graphic for this purpose, but I find that a 10 x 10-pixel image works best because it's easier to select after you place it on your page in Dreamweaver. Remember, even if the clear GIF is 10 x 10 pixels, you can still set the height and width to a smaller size.

Dreamweaver makes using the transparent GIF trick easy because you have easy access to the height and width attributes in the Properties inspector. You may also need to specify the alignment of the image to achieve the desired effect.

You can also use a transparent GIF to control spacing around text. This method is handy when you want more than just a break between lines of text or other elements, but not as much as you get with the paragraph tag. This is also an ideal way to create larger spaces between elements with down-to-the-pixel design control.

To use a transparent GIF between images, text, or other elements on a page, follow these steps:

1. **Insert the image in the space where you plan to use it, whether it is between two images or within text.**

2. **Click OK.**

   The transparent GIF is inserted on your page and automatically selected.

3. **With the `clear.gif` image still selected, type** 20 **in the W text box and type** 20 **in the H text box (both text boxes are in the Properties inspector).**

   This sets the height and width of the image to 20 pixels each.

   You can set the height and width to any values you want.

If you click `clear.gif`, you can see the outline of the image while it's selected. Notice that as soon as you deselect the image, it becomes invisible in Dreamweaver. You can always reselect it by clicking in the area until the cursor highlights it.

If you're working with a very small GIF, say one that's only 1 pixel high by 1 pixel wide, you may have difficulty selecting it by clicking after it's been deselected. For this reason, I recommend resizing the GIF as soon as it's been placed on the page and is still highlighted.

Creating a Background

Background images can bring life to a Web page by adding color and fullness. Used cleverly, a background image helps create the illusion that the entire page is one large image while still downloading quickly and efficiently. The trick is to use a small background image that creates a dramatic effect when it *tiles* (repeats) across and down the page (see Figure 5-8).

Background images are often called *tiles,* because they repeat like tiles across a kitchen floor. However, if you use a long, narrow image as a background or a large image that's small in file size, you can create many effects beyond a repeating tile.

Beware that certain backgrounds can make reading text that's placed on top of them hard (such as the one shown in Figure 5-9). Choose your background images carefully and make sure there is plenty of contrast between your background and your text — reading on a computer screen is hard enough.

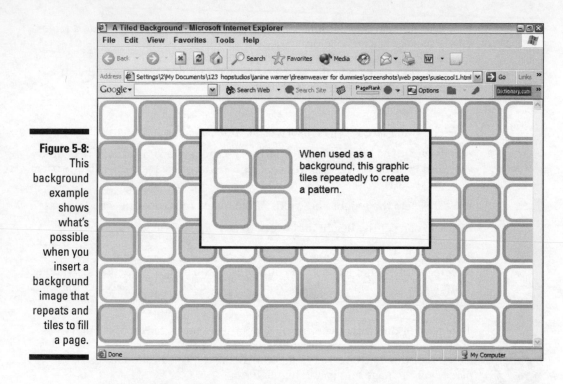

When used as a background, this graphic tiles repeatedly to create a pattern.

Figure 5-8:
This background example shows what's possible when you insert a background image that repeats and tiles to fill a page.

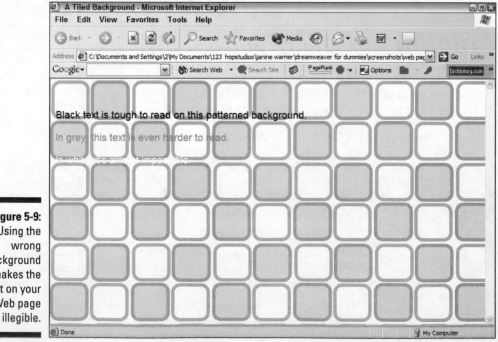

Black text is tough to read on this patterned background.

In grey, this text is even harder to read.

Figure 5-9:
Using the wrong background makes the text on your Web page illegible.

As you work with backgrounds, you may find another use for a transparent GIF. If you place a graphic on top of a patterned background, you end up with a rectangular area around the graphic that obscures the patterned background, as in Figure 5-10. To allow the background to be visible around, say, a headline, you can create your headline graphic on top of a color similar to the dominant color used in the background. When you save the GIF, set that color to be transparent. Placed on the page, the headline looks like it's floating on top of the pattern (see Figure 5-11).

In the event that you don't want a background image to tile, your only option is to use an image that is larger than the maximum size of the largest monitor you expect people to view your site with. That way, they never see the next tile because it's always out of view. Sometimes, I create a background image that is something like 1200 x 1600 pixels in size. The key here is that you must be careful to keep your image file size very small. Background images of these dimensions work well only if you use GIFs with very limited numbers of colors in them, never with JPEG images. Because GIFs can use only a couple of colors, their file sizes stay small even though their physical dimensions are huge. A GIF that size with no more than eight solid colors takes up only a few kilobytes of space. Use fewer colors, and it takes up even less space.

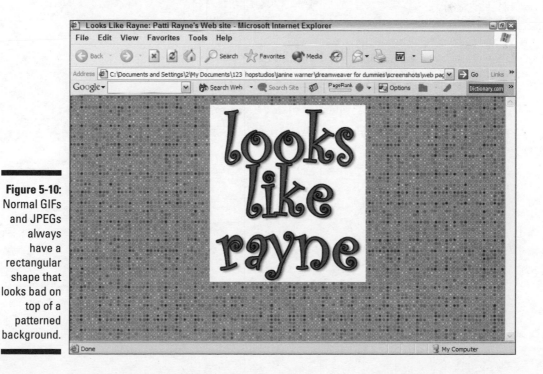

Figure 5-10:
Normal GIFs and JPEGs always have a rectangular shape that looks bad on top of a patterned background.

Figure 5-11:
After the
white
around
the title is
set to be
transparent,
it floats on
top of the
background.

To set a background on a Web page, follow these steps:

1. **Choose Modify➪Page Properties.**

   The Page Properties dialog box appears, as shown in Figure 5-12.

2. **Click Appearance from the Category list on the left.**

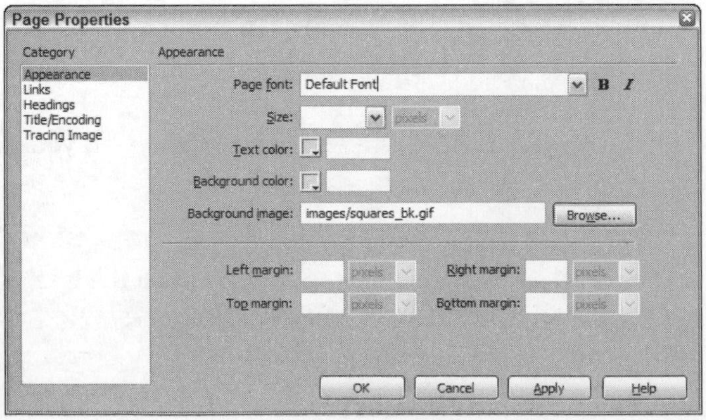

Figure 5-12:
The Page
Properties
dialog box
enables you
to set a
background
image, as
well as a
background
color,
among
other things.

Page Properties

Category
- Appearance
- Links
- Headings
- Title/Encoding
- Tracing Image

Appearance

Page font: Default Font   **B** *I*

Size: pixels

Text color:

Background color:

Background image: images/squares_bk.gif   Browse...

Left margin: pixels   Right margin: pixels

Top margin: pixels   Bottom margin: pixels

OK   Cancel   Apply   Help

3. **Click the Browse button to the right of the Background Image text box.**

   The Select Image Source dialog box opens.

4. **Browse to find the image that you want to use as your background image.**

   When you insert an image in your Web site, you want to make sure that the image is in the same relative location on your hard drive as it is on your server. If you plan to use your background tile throughout your site, you may want to store it in a common images folder where you can easily link the image from any page in your site. See Chapter 3 for details on organizing image files.

5. **Double-click the filename of your background image to select it.**

   The Select Image Source dialog box disappears.

6. **Click OK in the Page Properties dialog box to finish.**

   Note that if you click the Apply button, you see the effect of the background tile being applied to the page, but the Page Properties dialog box stays open.

Creating Image Maps

Image maps are popular on the Web because they enable you to create hot spots in an image and link them to different URLs. A common use of an image map is a geographic map, such as a map of the United States, that links to different locations, depending on the section of the map selected. For example, if you have a national bank and want customers to find a local branch or ATM machine easily, you can create hot spots on an image map of the United States and then link each hot spot to a page listing banks in that geographic location. Dreamweaver makes creating image maps easy by providing a set of simple drawing tools that enable you to create hot spots and set their corresponding links.

To create an image map, follow these steps:

1. **Place the image you want to use as an image map on your page.**

2. **Select the image.**

   The image properties display in the Properties inspector.

3. **To draw your hot spot, choose a shape tool from the Image Map tools in the lower-left of the Properties inspector (see Figure 5-13).**

   The shape tools include a rectangle, an oval, and an irregular polygon that allow you to draw regions on your images, called *hot spots,* each with a specific link.

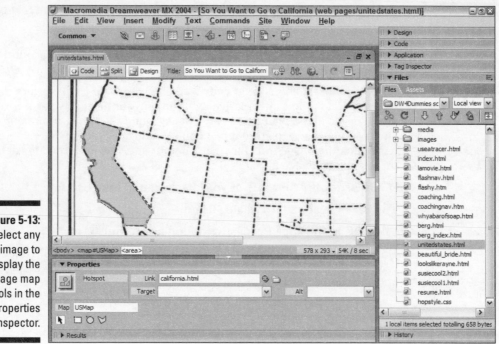

Figure 5-13:
Select any
image to
display the
image map
tools in the
Properties
inspector.

4. **With the shape tool selected, click and drag over an area of the image that you want to make** *hot* **(link to another page). Here's how the different hot spot tools work:**

   • **Rectangle:** As you click and drag, a light blue highlight appears around the region that you're making hot; this highlighted area indicates the active region. If you need to reposition the hot area, select the Pointer Hotspot Tool (black arrow) from the lower-left corner of the Properties inspector and then select and move the region to the location you want. You can also resize it by clicking and dragging any of the corners.

   • **Oval:** The oval tool works much like the rectangle tool — just click and drag. To resize an oval hot spot, select the Pointer Hotspot Tool, and click and drag one of the small square boxes on its edges.

   • **Polygon:** The polygon tool functions a little bit differently; to make a polygon selection (such as one of the state of California in a U.S. map), you click the tool once for each point of the polygon shape you want to draw. Then, to close the shape, click again on the first point you drew after you finish drawing all the other points. You can change the size of the polygon or move any of its points by using the Pointer Hotspot Tool.

5. **To link a selected hot area, click the Folder icon next to the Link text box (at the top of the Properties inspector).**

   The Select File dialog box opens.

6. **Browse to find the HTML file that you want to link to the hot spot on your image.**

7. **Double-click the file to which you want to link.**

   The hot spot links to the selected page and the Select File dialog box automatically closes. You can also type the path directly into the link field if you know it, so you don't have to find it on your hard drive.

8. **To add more hot spots, choose a shape tool and repeat Steps 4 through 7.**

9. **To give your image map a name, type a name in the Map text field, just above the shape tools.**

   Giving your map (and all the hot spots it includes) a name helps to distinguish it in the event that you have multiple image maps on the same page. You can call the map anything you want, with the exception of spaces or special punctuation.

   When you finish, you see all your image-map hot spots indicated by a light blue highlight.

At any time, you can go back and edit the image map by clicking and highlighting the blue region on your image and dragging the edges to resize the hot spot or by entering a new URL to change the link.

Part III
Advancing Your Site

The 5th Wave   By Rich Tennant

VISUAL WEB DEVELOPMENT TEAM

"Give him air! Give him air! He'll be okay. He's just been exposed to some raw HTML code. It must have accidently flashed across his screen from the server."

In this part . . .

If you want to create compelling designs within the confines of the rules of HTML, you need to use HTML tables, frames, and Cascading Style Sheets (CSS). This part walks you through the maze of nested tables and merged cells, split pages framed with links, and the power and design control that you can achieve only with CSS. As CSS becomes increasingly important and well supported for Web design, Macromedia is working hard to make sure that Dreamweaver MX 2004 handles these advanced features.

Chapter 6

Coming to the HTML Table

Designers often get frustrated when they move from print to the Web and discover that they don't have the design control they're used to in print — they can't put an image wherever they want on a page just by dragging the image into place, and they don't have line spacing control in text and many other design features that are common in print.

Although more recent developments in HTML provide better design control, HTML tables have long been the most common way to work around these limitations because designers have found that using tables provides more complex design control on their pages. The downside of tables is that they're complicated to create because you have to merge and split cells to position elements where you want them. Fortunately, Dreamweaver has lots of tools to help you create tables.

This chapter is designed to show you how to create HTML tables for everything from columnar data to complex page designs. You explore a wide range of uses for HTML tables and find out how to create a variety of designs for your Web pages.

Choosing between Tables and CSS Layers for Design Control

With the release of the HTML 4.0 specification, layers were added as part of the HTML code options. Layers are much easier to create than tables, especially in Dreamweaver where you can just click and drag to place them wherever you want on a page. And you can put any element in a layer, including images, text, and multimedia files. You can even stack layers on top of each other. That means you really get down-to-the pixel design control, which is much better than what you get with tables.

So why doesn't everyone use layers? Because older browsers don't support layers, and even the newer ones aren't always consistent in the way they display layers and their contents. (By older browsers, I mean Netscape 4.0 and earlier and Internet Explorer 4.0 and earlier. The 4.0 versions were the first to support layers; they just don't do it very consistently.) So, what you gain in easy design control with layers, you may lose with the risk that someone using an old browser may not be able to view your work as you intended it. And with a really old browser, they may not see your work at all because the layers and their contents won't display. In many cases, designers still prefer not to take this risk, and tables continue to be an important design tool on the Web.

But because layers are so much easier to use than tables that many designers are anxious to make the shift from tables to layers. Expect to see more and more pages on the Web designed with layers because support for HTML layers increases as Internet users upgrade to versions 5.0 and later of Netscape and Internet Explorer.

You really have to base your decision on using layers on your audience. Check the log statistics from your server to see what versions of browsers your visitors use (your service provider or system administrator can give you these). On many major sites, less than 5 percent of the users are still using browsers in versions 4.0 or earlier and many designers think less than 5 percent of their visitors not seeing their sites is okay. But your audience may be different, and you have to decide what percentage of audience you are willing to give up to gain the advantage of using layers.

If your goal is to have design control and the *most* universally recognized Web pages, tables are still the way to go.

If you have ever used a desktop publishing program, such as QuarkXPress or Adobe PageMaker, you have probably used text and image boxes to lay out pages. Layers work similarly, and tables achieve a similar effect. You use the table cells (the "boxes" created at the intersection of each row and column in a table) to control the placement of text and images. Because you can make the borders of the table invisible, your viewers don't see the underlying structure of your table when they look at your Web page in a browser. For example, you can use a table to align elements side by side on a page and create columns of text. You still don't get the design control you're used to in a desktop publishing program, but with a little ingenuity, you can create the same effects.

You have one other option in Dreamweaver. You can create your design using layers and then use the Dreamweaver automated Layers to Tables conversion option to create a page with tables. But be careful if you choose this option. Conversion is not a perfect process because you can do things with layers, such as overlap them, that you can't do with tables.

For details about using layers, see Chapter 9.

Creating Simple Tables in Layout Mode

Tables are made up of three basic elements: rows, columns, and cells. If you have ever worked with a spreadsheet program, you're probably familiar with what tables are all about. Tables in HTML differ from spreadsheet tables mainly in that they're used for more complex alignment of data, which requires lots of merging and splitting cells. Back in the days when you had to design Web pages in raw HTML code by hand, even simple tables were difficult to create. The code behind an HTML table is a complex series of <TR> and <TD> tags that indicate table rows and table data cells. Figuring out how to type those tags so that they create a series of little boxes on a Web page was never an intuitive process. If you wanted to merge or split cells to create uneven numbers of rows or columns, you faced a true challenge.

Thank the cybergods that you have Dreamweaver to make this process easy. If you have ever written HTML code manually, you can appreciate how much Dreamweaver simplifies this work. Using Dreamweaver, you can modify both the appearance and the structure of a table by simply clicking and dragging. You can add any type of content to a cell, such as images, text, and multimedia files. You can also add color to the background or border and change the alignment of elements within a cell. And, you can even get around one of the great pitfalls of table design: changing your mind about how you want the table to look after you have built it.

The easiest way to work with tables in Dreamweaver is to switch to Layout mode and use the special Layout Cell and Layout Table tools (see the following steps). With these tools, available only in Layout mode, Dreamweaver makes table creation much more intuitive. You can even switch between the two modes: Standard and Layout. You're already used to working in Standard mode in Dreamweaver because that's the default for working on documents. Layout mode provides a special view mode designed to assist in the constructing and editing of tables. In this mode, you can draw cells anywhere on a page and drag the edges of a table to change its size. Figures 6-1 and 6-2 show the same table in Layout mode and Standard mode. You can tell the difference in modes by the way the table displays in Dreamweaver or by checking the Layout Mode and Standard Mode icons in the Layout bar.

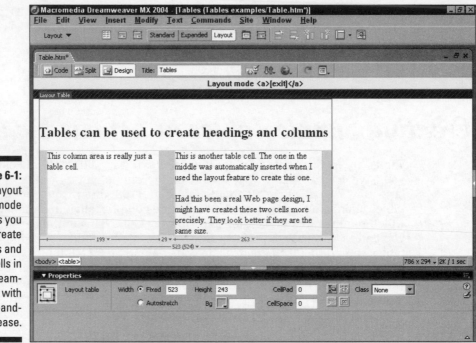

Figure 6-1:
Table Layout
mode
enables you
to create
tables and
cells in
Dream-
weaver with
drag-and-
drop ease.

These steps show how to create a table in Layout mode with a long cell across the top and two smaller cells below it (like the table shown in Figures 6-1 and 6-2):

1. **Create a new HTML page.**

   To create a new page, choose File⇨New and then select Blank Page from the Category list and HTML from the Basic Page list.

2. **Switch to Layout mode by clicking the Layout Mode button, which is a little to the left of the Title text box.**

   You can also switch to Layout mode by choosing View⇨Table Mode⇨ Layout Mode.

   You may see a message describing how to use the Layout Table and Layout Cell buttons when you first select this option. The message has some useful tips, but if you click the Don't Show Me This Message Again check box, you can avoid seeing it the next time. Click OK to close it.

3. **Select Layout from the Insert bar at the top of the screen (refer to Figures 6-1 and 6-2).**

   The Table and Frame layout options become visible on the Insert bar, as shown in Figures 6-1 and 6-2.

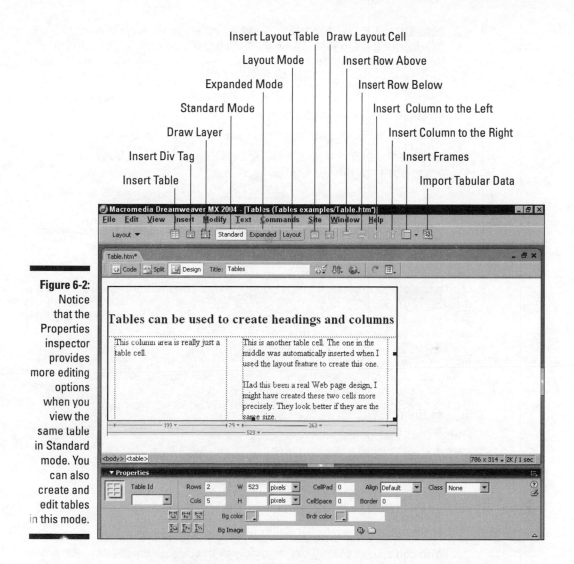

Insert Layout Table Draw Layout Cell
Layout Mode Insert Row Above
Expanded Mode Insert Row Below
Standard Mode Insert Column to the Left
Draw Layer Insert Column to the Right
Insert Div Tag Insert Frames
Insert Table Import Tabular Data

Figure 6-2:
Notice that the Properties inspector provides more editing options when you view the same table in Standard mode. You can also create and edit tables in this mode.

4. **Click the Draw Layout Cell button, located in the Layout bar.**

   The cursor changes to a crosshair when you move the mouse over the document area, indicating that you're ready to draw a table cell.

5. **With the mouse pointer on the document, click and drag to draw a rectangular shape across the top of the page for your first table cell (refer to Figure 6-1).**

   The cell is drawn, and its surrounding table structure is automatically generated. A grid representing the table structure appears with the current cell shown in white.

6. **Below the cell you just drew, draw another cell of approximately half the size of the top cell. To do this, click the same Draw Layout Cell button again and then click and drag under the first cell to create the new cell.**

   As you draw, notice that the cell "snaps" into place along the guidelines in the table grid. Use the grid as a guide in lining up your cells.

7. **Draw a third cell to the right of the second one you created.**

8. **Click in the first cell you drew and type some text; then repeat that action for the other two cells.**

   You can type any text you want. This step just shows you that you can enter text into a cell as easily as you can anywhere else on the page.

9. **Switch to Standard mode by selecting Layout mode again or choosing View⇨Table Mode⇨Standard Mode to see how your table looks.**

Depending on where you started drawing table cells, Dreamweaver may create table cells around the cells you created to maintain their position on the page. For example, in the table shown in Figures 6-1 and 6-2, although I have created three new cells, Dreamweaver has filled in the gaps by automatically creating more cells, so this final table has seven cells. A table's default position is normally in the upper-left corner of a page, so the first cells in the table are close to the upper-left margin. However, using Layout mode, you can draw cells wherever you want them on a page, and Dreamweaver automatically generates the other cells needed to keep the positioning you created in Layout mode. *Remember:* TML doesn't allow you to place things anywhere on a page unless you use table cells to control their placement. Empty cells that Dreamweaver creates to fill space in a table merely act as *spacer cells* and don't show up in the browser, giving the illusion that various page elements are positioned independently on any part of the page.

Designers often wonder how wide they should make their tables. My best advice is to design your pages for an 800 x 600 screen resolution because that's the most common size now in use on the Web. If you're creating a table that you want to cover the entire display area, a safe bet is to make your table 760 pixels wide and center it in the middle of the page because that leaves a little room on each side to prevent sideways scrollbars from appearing.

Editing Tables in Layout Mode

One wonderful advantage of working with tables in Layout mode is that you can use the layout grid to edit, move, and resize any of the rows, columns, and cells in the table. This capability allows you to use the grid as a true design guide for creating any kind of layout you want.

Tables are much easier to edit in Layout mode because you can click and drag to create cells wherever you want on the page and Dreamweaver automatically fills in the rest of the table needed to position the cells for you. That means you don't have to manually create spacer cells or do lots of merging or splitting to get cells where you want them on a page. This feature is still not as precise as layers, but it comes close.

You also have the flexibility to create *nested* tables (tables drawn within tables) for even more control over your layout. To create a nested table, simply click the Draw Layout Table button and begin drawing a new table inside an existing table cell. For more information on nested tables, see the section "Using nested tables: Tables within tables," later in this chapter.

Using Expanded Table Mode

A third option for table editing is Expanded Table mode. To access this view, choose View➪Table Mode➪Expanded Tables Mode. This design view makes selecting inside and around tables easier (without this option, it can be tricky to select elements of a table, especially if you're not really adept with your mouse). If you're in a hurry or working on lots of cells, this design view makes tedious work on a table much easier to handle.

Beware, however: To make this task possible, Dreamweaver zooms the size of the table in the viewing area, making the table display much larger than it really is. As a result, the page looks very different in a browser; make sure that you preview your work in the standard Design view or better yet, preview it in a browser, to ensure that it's displayed well on the Web.

Understanding Table Options

Layout mode works best for creating and editing the overall *structure* of your table. When you're ready to start editing the *contents* of the table and its individual cells, you should work in Standard mode or in the new Expanded mode, as covered in the preceding section. Using Layout mode, you can change some table attributes, but by using Standard mode, you can change all HTML table attributes, including the number of rows and columns as well as height, width, border size, and spacing.

When you select a table or cell, the attributes are displayed in the Properties inspector, at the bottom of the work area. Click the border of any table to select it, and the Properties inspector displays the table options shown in Figure 6-3. To view all the options, click the expander arrow in the lower-right corner of the Properties inspector.

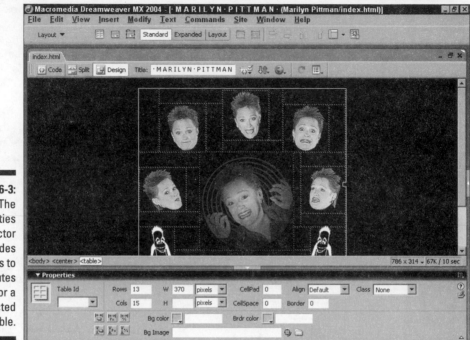

Figure 6-3:
The
Properties
inspector
provides
access to
attributes
for a
selected
table.

You can also insert elements such as text, images, and multimedia files into cells. First, click to place the cursor in the cell, and then type text or use the Insert Common Objects bar options to insert images, multimedia files, and other elements.

Sometimes, selecting a table with the mouse can be a bit tricky. Here are a couple of tips for selecting a table more easily:

✔ **Select a simple table:** In Standard mode, you can access table proper- ties by clicking directly on top of the border of the table, which works best for simple tables.

✔ **Select a nested table:** Nested tables contain many confusing borders touching each other. Try clicking inside any cell that belongs to the table you want to select and then right-clicking and choosing Table⇨ Select Table.

✔ **Select an entire table:** Use the HTML tag selector on the document's Status bar at the lower-left edge of the work area to select an entire table easily. You can click your mouse anywhere in your table to display the HTML tags on the Status bar; then click the <TABLE> tag in the tag selec- tor to select the entire table.

The Properties inspector gives you access to these table options for customizing the appearance of your table:

✔ **Table Id:** Provides a text area where you can enter a name or table.

✔ **Rows:** Displays the number of rows in the table. You can alter the size of the table by changing the number. Be careful, though: If you enter a smaller number, Dreamweaver deletes the bottom rows — contents and all.

✔ **Columns:** Displays the number of columns in the table. You can alter the size of the table by changing the number. Again, if you enter a smaller number, Dreamweaver deletes the columns on the right side of the table — contents and all.

✔ **W (Width):** Displays the width of the table. You can alter the width by changing the number. The width can be specified as a percentage or a value in pixels. Values expressed as a percentage increase or decrease the table's size relative to the size of the user's browser window.

✔ **H (Height):** Displays the height of the table. You can alter the height by changing the number. The height can be specified as a percentage or a value in pixels. Values expressed as a percentage increase or decrease the table's size relative to the size of the user's browser window. This table attribute is recognized by only version 4.0 browsers and above.

✔ **CellPad:** Specifies the space between the contents of a cell and its border.

✔ **CellSpace:** Specifies the space between table cells.

✔ **Align:** Controls the alignment of the table. Options are left, right, and center.

✔ **Border:** Controls the size of the border around the table. The larger the number, the thicker the border. If you want the border to be invisible, set the border to 0.

✔ **Class:** Provides easy access to style sheet options. (See Chapter 9 for more on CSS.)

✔ **Clear and Convert:** The icons in the lower-left area of the Properties inspector (click the expander arrow in the lower-right corner to view them) provide these formatting options:

  • **Clear Row Heights** and **Clear Column Widths** enable you to remove all height and width values at one time, leaving the table to adjust to the table size.

  • **Convert Table Heights to Pixels** and **Convert Table Heights to Percents**, and **Convert Table Widths to Pixels** and **Convert Table Widths to Percents** enable you to automatically change Height and Width settings from percentage to pixels. Pixels specify a fixed width; a percent setting means the browser automatically adjusts to the specified percentage of the browser display area.

Table dimensions expressed as a percentage enable you to create a table that changes in size as the browser window is resized. If you want a table to always take up 75 percent of the browser window, no matter how big the user's monitor or display area, percentages are a good way to specify table size. If you want a table to always occupy a specific number of pixels — that is, to remain the same size regardless of the browser window size — choose pixels rather than percentages for your table dimensions.

Your table contents will always fit into the table cells. Table cells automatically adjust to accommodate the elements you insert into them. For example, if you create a cell that is 100 pixels wide and then insert a 300-pixel-wide image, the table cell automatically adjusts to fit the image.

✔ **Bg Color:** Controls the background color. Click the color square next to this label and select a color from the box that appears. When you click the color square, the cursor changes to an eyedropper, enabling you to pick up a color from anywhere on the page by clicking the color. You can apply this option to a single cell by placing your cursor in a particular cell before specifying the color.

✔ **Bg Image:** Enables you to select a background image. Specify the filename or click the folder icon to locate the image. You can apply this option to a single cell or to the entire table. Note that because many older browsers don't support background images in single cells, the image isn't displayed for all viewers.

✔ **Brdr Color:** Controls the border color. Click the color square next to this label and select a color from the box that appears. When you click the color square, the cursor changes to an eyedropper, enabling you to pick up a color from anywhere on the page by clicking the color. You can apply this option to a single cell or to the entire table.

Dreamweaver limits the colors to those best supported on the Web. As a result, if you sample a color from a 16-bit color (or higher) image, you may not get exactly the color you want. (I have had light greens replaced as grays, for example.) If this happens, you can, after using the eyedropper tool, tweak the color with the System Color Picker button within the Properties box.

For diehard designers who dream in Pantone: If you insist on a 100 percent match from your design, you can create a small (10 x 10 pixel), one-color GIF with an image editor and use a background image to ensure an exact color match. Because background images are tiled by default, the cell appears filled in with the GIF's color even if the cell is bigger than the GIF.

Controlling Cell Options

In Standard mode, you can control options for individual cells within the table. When you select a cell, which you do by clicking the cursor anywhere inside the cell area, the Properties inspector changes to display the individual properties for that cell (see Figure 6-4). With the cell selected, you can change the attributes for a specific cell in the Properties inspector.

You can also change multiple cells at the same time. Suppose that you want to have some, but not all, of the cells in your table take on a certain color background and style of text. You can apply the same properties to multiple cells at the same time by holding down the Shift key while clicking adjacent cells to select multiple cells at one time. To select multiple cells that are not adjacent, hold down the Ctrl key (the ⌘ key on the Mac) and click each cell you want to select. Any properties you change in the Properties inspector are applied to all selected cells.

If you're having trouble selecting an individual cell because it contains an image, click the image and then use either the ← or → key on your keyboard to move the cursor and deselect the image, which activates the Properties inspector and displays the options for that cell.

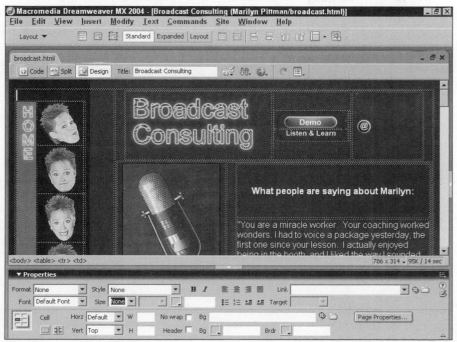

Figure 6-4: When you select an individual cell, the Properties inspector provides access to attributes for the selected cell within a table.

When one or more cells are selected (they have to be adjacent for this to work), the top half of the Properties inspector controls the formatting of text and URLs within the table cells. The lower half of the Properties inspector provides these table cell attribute options (refer to Figure 6-4):

- ✔ **Merge Cells:** Merges two or more cells. To merge cells, you must first select two or more cells by clicking and dragging or by holding down either the Shift or Ctrl key while selecting multiple cells.

- ✔ **Split Cells:** Splits one cell into two. When you select this option, a dialog box lets you specify whether you want to split the row (you split the cell horizontally) or the column (you split the cell vertically). You can then specify the number of columns or rows, which controls how many times the cell is divided. Note that you can apply the Split Cell option to only one cell at a time.

- ✔ **Horz:** Controls the horizontal alignment of the cell contents.

- ✔ **Vert:** Controls the vertical alignment of the cell contents.

- ✔ **W:** Controls the width of the cell.

- ✔ **H:** Controls the height of the cell.

- ✔ **No Wrap:** Prevents word wrapping within the cell. The cell widens to accommodate all text as you type or paste it into a cell. (Normally, the text would just move down to the next line and increase the height of the cell.)

- ✔ **Header:** Formats a cell's contents by using a Header style, which makes the text bold and centered.

- ✔ **Bg (Image):** Allows you to specify a background image for the cell.

- ✔ **Bg (Color):** Allows you to specify a background color for the cell.

- ✔ **Brdr (Color):** Allows you to change the border color of the cell.

Using the Format Table Feature

One of the best reasons for using tables is to present lots of data in a clear and structured way. Tables accomplish this task because the use of rows and columns allows the reader to follow along easily when lots of data is represented. One way to make your data even more presentable and attractive is to colorize the rows and columns in the table. In the preceding section, you find out how to change the attributes of individual cells. This section explains how to use the Format Table feature, an excellent Dreamweaver feature that allows you to select predefined table formats with fantastic color schemes to enhance your presentation.

Professional designers created these color schemes, so you can be sure that they will look good on your Web page.

To use the Format Table feature, open an existing document or create a new HTML page, insert a simple table of any size, and follow these steps:

1. **Select an existing table in the document.**

2. **Make sure that you're in Standard mode. (Choose View⇨Table Mode⇨ Standard Mode.)**

3. **Choose Commands⇨Format Table.**

   The Format Table dialog box appears, as shown in Figure 6-5.

4. **Select one of the schemes by scrolling the list or modify any of the parameters to create your own scheme.**

5. **Click OK.**

   The color scheme is applied to the table.

You can also modify any of the attributes in the Format Table dialog box and create your own color schemes.

Using low-contrast color schemes in tables is considered the most effective way to present content. (Just look at the Intuit Quicken software, E-Trade, and Amazon for examples of real-life illustrations.) High-contrast colors in tables are usually reserved for site menus and submenus or other elements you want to call more attention to.

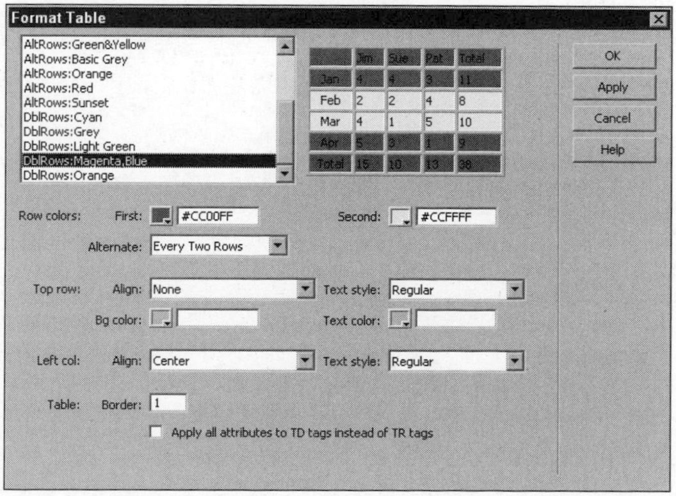

Figure 6-5: The Dreamweaver Format Table feature provides a variety of previously created color schemes to enhance the look of your tables.

Format Table

AltRows:Green&Yellow		Jim	Sue	Pat	Total
AltRows:Basic Grey					
AltRows:Orange	Jan	4	4	3	11
AltRows:Red					
AltRows:Sunset	Feb	2	2	4	8
DblRows:Cyan					
DblRows:Grey	Mar	4	1	5	10
DblRows:Light Green					
DblRows:Magenta,Blue	Apr	5	3	1	9
DblRows:Orange	Total	15	10	13	38

OK
Apply
Cancel
Help

Row colors: First: #CC00FF   Second: #CCFFFF

Alternate: Every Two Rows

Top row: Align: None   Text style: Regular

Bg color: Text color:

Left col: Align: Center   Text style: Regular

Table: Border: 1

☐ Apply all attributes to TD tags instead of TR tags

Formatting Multiple Columns in a Table

When you're working with lots of cells in a table, you may want to format multiple cells in the same way. Dreamweaver makes that task easy, whether you want to align numbers, make the headings bold, or change the color scheme. But before you start planning how to line up all your numbers perfectly, be aware that you don't have as much control in HTML as you have in a program such as Excel, where you can align numbers to the decimal point. You can, however, align the content of columns to the left, right, or center. Thus, if you use the same number of digits after the decimal point in all your numbers, you can get them to line up. For example, if one price is $12.99 and another is $14, express it as $14.00; then, when you right-align, the numbers line up properly. (If your columns are still not lining up the way you want them to, consider using a monospace font, which lines up better.)

The steps in this section explain how to create a table of financial data in Standard mode and align all the data cells on the right so that the numbers align. You can also use these steps to align the contents of table cells to the left, center, or top, or to apply other formatting options, such as bold or italic. In these steps, I insert the data into the table after I create the table in Dreamweaver.

If you want to import data from a table you have created in a program such as Word or Excel, see the section, "Importing Table Data from Other Programs," later in this chapter. If you're working with a table that already has data in it and just want to format or align the cells, go directly to Step 7.

If you're starting from scratch, create a new, blank HTML page and follow these steps from the beginning:

1. **Make sure that you're in Standard mode. (Choose View⇨Table Mode⇨ Standard Mode.)**

2. **Click to place the cursor where you want to create a table.**

3. **Click the Insert Table icon on the Insert bar.**

   Alternatively, you can choose Insert⇨Table. The Insert Table dialog box appears.

4. **In the appropriate boxes, type the number of columns and rows you want to include in your table.**

5. **Specify the width, border, cell padding, and cell spacing; then click OK.**

   The table automatically appears on the page.

6. **Click to place the cursor in a cell, and then type the data you want in each cell.**

7. **Select the column or row for which you want to change the alignment.**

   Place the cursor in the first cell in the column or row you want to align; then click and drag your mouse to highlight the other columns or rows that need to be changed.

8. **Right-click (Windows) or Ctrl+click (Mac) in any cell in the high-lighted column or row.**

   A pop-up menu appears, as shown in Figure 6-6. Alternatively, you can use the Properties inspector to change selected items.

9. **From the pop-up menu, choose Align and then choose Left, Center, Right, or Justify from the submenu.**

   This option enables you to change the alignment of all highlighted cells in the column or row at one time. If you're working with financial data, choose Align⇨Right, which produces the best alignment for numbers. You can also apply other formatting options, such as bold or italic, to selected cells and their contents by choosing the option from the pop-up menu or the Properties inspector.

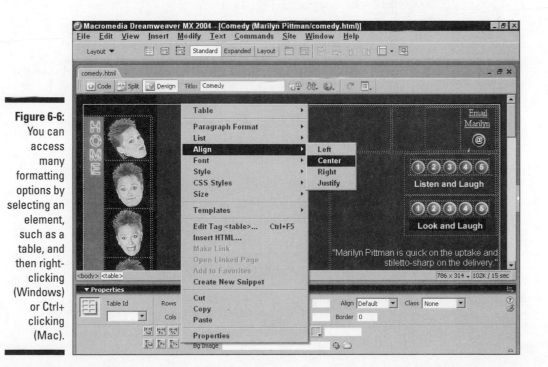

Figure 6-6: You can access many formatting options by selecting an element, such as a table, and then right-clicking (Windows) or Ctrl+ clicking (Mac).

If you want to format one cell in a column or row differently from the others, click to place the cursor in just that cell and then click one of the formatting options in the Properties inspector. You can also choose to align multiple cells that aren't *contiguous* (they don't touch each other) by pressing and holding down the Ctrl key in Windows while you click the cells you want to select. On the Mac, you press and hold down the Command key (⌘) while you click to select particular cells. Any options you change on the pop-up menu or in the Table Properties inspector are applied to all selected cells.

Using the Sort Table Feature

When you're working with lots of columnar data, you want to be able to sort that data, like you do in a spreadsheet program, such as Excel. In this newest version of Dreamweaver, you can now sort data even after it's formatted in HTML (something that wasn't easily done before).

To use the Sort Table Data feature, create a new, blank HTML page, add a table with several rows and columns, and add some content (I explain how in the preceding section). You may want to use an existing table with columnar data so that you have some content to sort. Then, follow these steps:

1. **Select two or more cells.**

   Place the cursor in the first cell in the column or row you want to align; then, click and drag your mouse to highlight the other columns or rows that need to be changed.

2. **Make sure that you're in Standard mode. (Choose View⇨Table Mode⇨ Standard Mode.)**

3. **Choose Commands⇨Sort Table.**

   The Sort Table dialog box appears, as shown in Figure 6-7.

4. **Specify which column you want to sort by; then, choose Alphabetically or Numerically, and Ascending or Descending.**

   You can set up one or two sorts to happen simultaneously and opt whether to include the first row and whether to keep the TR (Table Row) attributes with a sorted Row.

5. **Click OK.**

   The selected cells are sorted, just like they are in a program like Microsoft Excel. (Pretty cool, huh?)

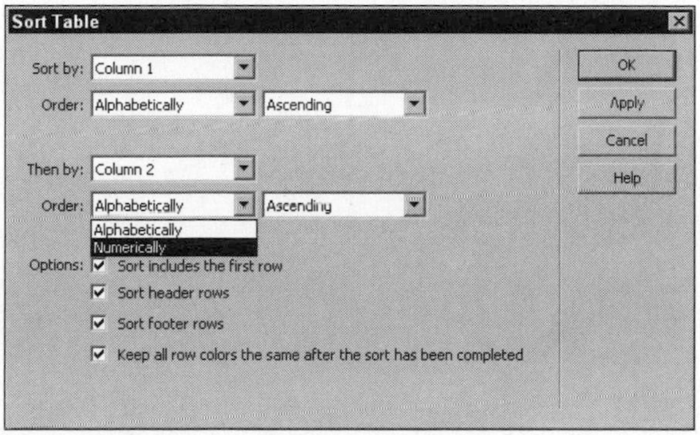

Figure 6-7:
You can
use the
Dream-
weaver Sort
Table Data
feature to
sort cell
contents
alphabet-
ically or
numerically,
even after
they're
formatted in
HTML.

Importing Table Data from Other Programs

Manually converting financial data or other spreadsheet information can be tedious. Fortunately, Dreamweaver includes a special feature that enables you to insert table data created in other applications, such as Microsoft Word or Excel. To use this feature, the table data must be saved from the other program in a *delimited* format, which means that the columns of data are separated by either tabs, commas, colons, semicolons, or another type of delimiter. Most spreadsheet and database applications, as well as Microsoft Word, enable you to save data in a delimited format, often called CSV because that's the file extension they're given. Consult the documentation for the application you're using to find out how. After the data is saved in a delimited format, you can import it into Dreamweaver.

To import table data into Dreamweaver after it has been saved in a delimited format in its native application, create a new, blank HTML page and follow these steps:

1. **Choose File⇨Import⇨Tabular Data or choose Insert⇨Table Objects⇨Import Tabular Data.**

   The Import Tabular Data dialog box appears (see Figure 6-8).

2. **In the Import Tabular Data text box, type the name of the file you want to import or use the Browse button to locate the file.**

Import Tabular Data

Data file: [ ] Browse...

Delimiter: Tab

Table width: ⦿ Fit to data

○ Set: [ ] Percent

Cell padding: [ ]   Format top row: [No Formatting]

Cell spacing: [ ]   Border: 1

OK | Cancel | Help

3. **From the Delimiter drop-down list, select the delimiter format you used when you saved your file in the other application.**

   The delimiter options are Tab, Comma, Semicolon, Colon, and Other. You should have made this choice when you exported the data from the original program in which you created it, such as Excel. If you don't remember what you chose, you can always go back and do it again. You must select the correct option in order for your data to be imported correctly.

4. **Select the table width.**

   If you choose Fit to Data, Dreamweaver automatically creates the table to fit the data being imported. If you choose Set, you must specify a Percent or Pixel size.

5. **Specify the cell padding and cell spacing only if you want extra space around the data in the table to be created.**

6. **Choose an option from the Format Top Row option only if you want to format the data in the top row of the table. Your options are bold, italic, or bold italic.**

7. **Specify the border size. The default is 1, which puts a small border around the table. Choose 0 if you don't want the border to be visible. Choose a larger number if you want a thicker border.**

8. **Click OK to automatically create a table with the imported data.**

Dreamweaver also enables you to export data from a table into a delimited format. This capability is useful if you want to export data from a Web page so that you can import it into another program, such as Word or Excel, or into a database program, such as FileMaker or Access. To export data from Dreamweaver, place the cursor anywhere in the table and choose File⇨Export⇨Table. In the Export Table dialog box, choose from the options on the Delimiter pull-down menu (you can choose Tab, Space, Comma, Semicolon, or Colon). From the Line Breaks pull-down menu, specify the operating system (you can choose Windows, Mac, or Unix).

Using Tables for Spacing and Alignment

As you get more adept at creating Web pages, you may find that HTML tables are a crucial part of creating almost any design that requires more than basic alignment of elements on a page. Using tables, you can get around many of the limitations of basic HTML and accomplish some of these design feats:

- ✔ Evenly spaced graphical bullets (little GIF files that can take the place of bullets) next to text
- ✔ Text boxes and fields properly aligned in a form
- ✔ Images placed wherever you want them on a page
- ✔ Columns of text that don't span an entire page
- ✔ Myriad intricate layouts that are impossible to accomplish without using tables or layers (for more on layers, see Chapter 9.)

In the rest of this chapter, I show you how to use tables to create a variety of page designs, including a few of the ones I just listed.

 When you use a table for design control, turn off the border so that it's not visible in the design. You do that by typing **0** (zero) in the Border text box in the Table Properties inspector with the table selected.

Using tables to design forms

Creating text boxes and pull-down menus for HTML forms is easy in Dreamweaver, but you need to use tables to make them look good. You can find in Chapter 12 lots of information about creating forms; for now, I assume that you have already created a form and want to align the text boxes evenly. I use a guest book form — a common, yet simple, form — as an example, but you can use this technique to align other form elements.

To use a table to align text boxes evenly on your form, create a new blank HTML page and follow these steps:

1. **Open a page that has an HTML form on it (or create an HTML form).**

   See Chapter 13 to find out how to create an HTML form.

2. **Click to place the cursor where you want to start formatting your form.**

3. **Choose Insert⇨Table.**

   The Insert Table dialog box appears.

4. **Type the number of columns and rows you want in your table.**

   I set the table to three rows and two columns.

5. **Set the width to whatever is most appropriate for your design and click OK.**

   I set the width to 763 pixels because that's a good width if you are designing for an 800 by 600 screen resolution, which many designers consider the best size to reach the most users.

6. **Enter 0 for the border.**

   When you set the border to 0, the edges of your table change from solid lines to dotted lines so that you can still see where the borders are while you're working in Dreamweaver. When you view the page in a browser, as shown in Figure 6-9, the border of the table is invisible.

7. **Click OK.**

8. **You need to copy the data from your form into the table. Using the Copy and Paste commands from the Edit menu, copy the text preceding the form's first text field and paste it into the cell in the upper-left corner of the table.**

   Alternatively, you can click and drag the text and form elements into each table cell.

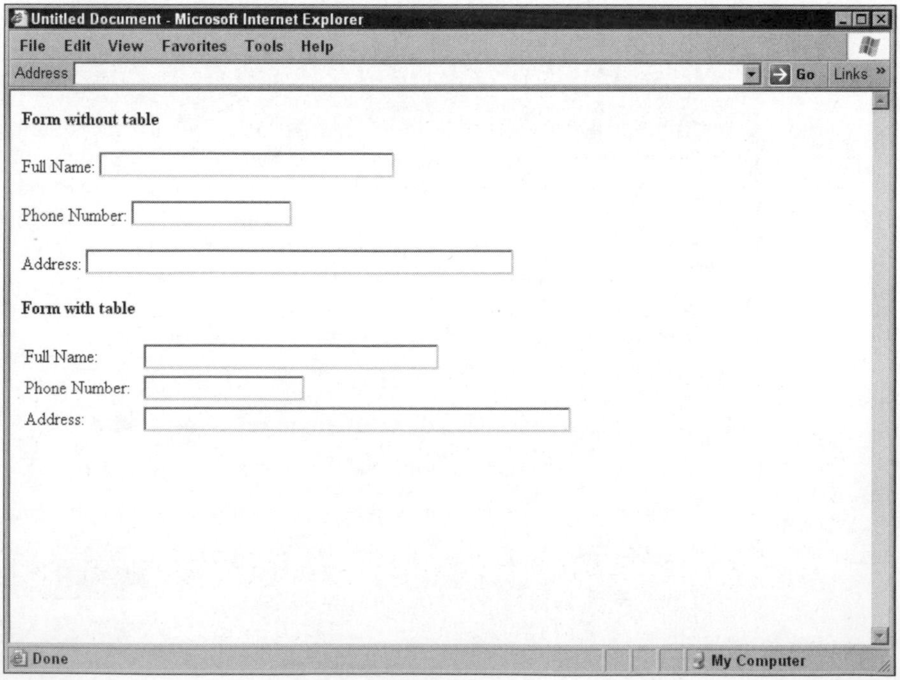

Figure 6-9:
When the form fields in the table display in the browser, they line up evenly with no visible border.

Untitled Document - Microsoft Internet Explorer

File   Edit   View   Favorites   Tools   Help

Address [   ] Go   Links »

Form without table

Full Name: [   ]

Phone Number: [   ]

Address: [   ]

Form with table

Full Name: [   ]
Phone Number: [   ]
Address: [   ]

Done   My Computer

In my example in Figure 6-10, you copy the words *Full Name* and paste them into the first table cell.

9. **Select the first text field (the empty box where users type their names) and copy and paste (or click and drag) it into the upper-right cell of the table.**

10. **Repeat Steps 6 and 7 for the rest of the form until you have moved all form elements into table cells.**

11. **Click the vertical column divider line between the first and second columns and drag it to the left or right to create the alignment you want for your form.**

Aligning a navigation bar

A common element on Web pages is a *navigation bar,* a row of images or text with links to the main sections of a Web site. Navigation bars are usually placed at the top, bottom, or side of a page, where users can easily access them but where they're out of the way of the main part of the page design. Designers often use HTML frames (see Chapter 7) to insert a navigation bar, but you can effectively place a navigation bar on a page by using tables.

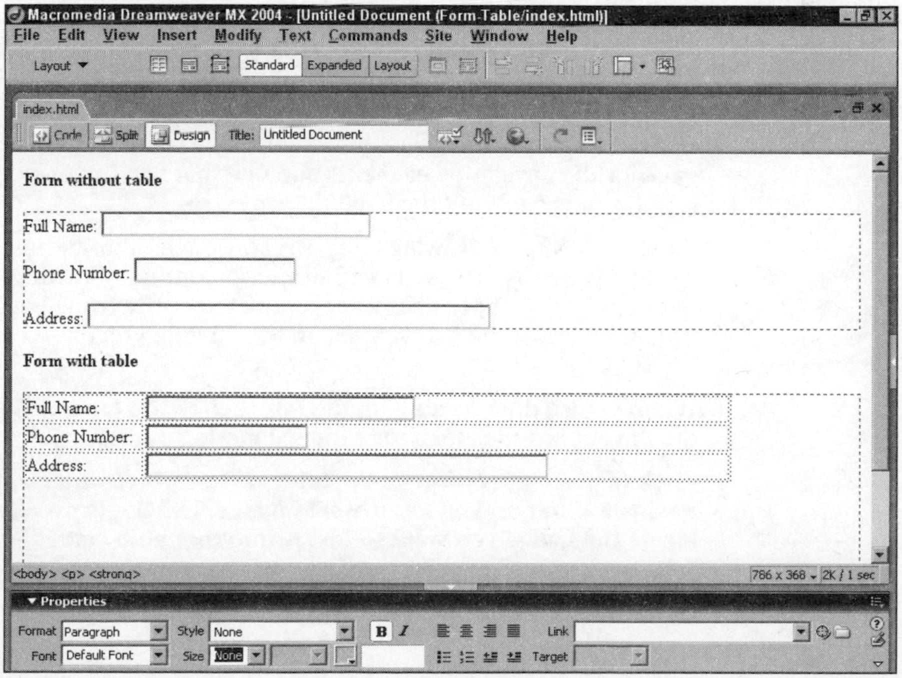

Figure 6-10:
You can use a table to better align form data and elements.

In the last example in the preceding section, you see how to create a table in Standard mode by using the regular table tools. In this example, you discover how to use the table tools in Layout mode to build a table, similar to the way you do at the beginning of this chapter. You can use either view mode for creating a table, but you may find that Layout mode is easier to use because you can create the table by dragging the cells into place rather than having to calculate where to merge and split cells to create a complex design. To use Layout mode to create a table that positions a navigation bar on the left side of a Web page, create a new, blank HTML page and follow these steps:

1. **Switch to Layout mode by choosing Layout from the pull-down list on the Insert bar and clicking the Layout icon, or choose View⇨Table Mode⇨Layout Mode.**

2. **Select the Draw Layout Table button from the Layout bar, and create a table by clicking in the upper-left region of the display area and dragging to fill the entire page.**

3. **Click the Draw Layout Cell button in the Layout bar to select the tool for drawing table cells.**

   Visualize how you want your table to be structured as you begin drawing cells in the next step. The structure is dictated by the shape and size of your navigation bar and other elements that need to be on the page. (Figure 6-11 shows an example of the kind of design you create in this exercise.)

4. **Click and drag your mouse on the page to draw the size and shape of cells you need to contain your navigation bar and other page elements.**

   Figure 6-11 shows a table with two cells, one down the left side of the page for the navigation elements and one that fills the rest of the display area for the content of the page.

   Even while you're drawing cells, Dreamweaver automatically creates a table to enclose the cells you draw. To continue drawing cells without having to go back each time and reselect the Draw Layout Cell tool, hold down the Ctrl key (⌘ on Mac) while you draw cells to retain the tool.

5. **When you're done setting up the table, click the Layout Mode icon in the Layout bar to return to Standard mode.**

6. **Click to place the cursor in the table cell in which you want to insert a navigation bar and choose Insert⇨Image. Use the Browse button to locate the image you want to insert into the table cell.**

7. **Double-click the filename of the image.**

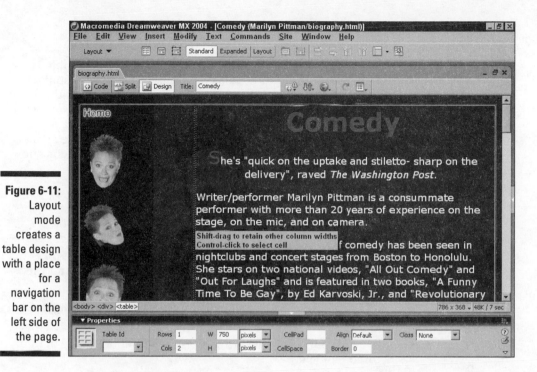

Figure 6-11:
Layout
mode
creates a
table design
with a place
for a
navigation
bar on the
left side of
the page.

The image automatically appears in the table cell. Repeat this step to insert multiple images.

As you can see in Figure 6-11, you can insert a series of images one beneath the other, separated by breaks, to create a row of buttons that runs down the left side of the page. You can also use text by simply typing in the table cell the names of each element on the navigation bar.

Make sure that you put paragraph returns or breaks between each image, or else you risk their lining up end to end if the cell is ever displays wider than the images. A little more work is involved, but you have greater design control if you place each image in a separate table cell because you can better adjust the spacing between images that way.

8. **Select the table and make sure that the Border option is set to 0 in the Properties inspector.**

    This step makes your table invisible so that the border isn't displayed in a browser.

Merging and splitting table cells

Sometimes, the easiest way to modify the number of cells in a table is to *merge* cells (combine two or more cells into one) or *split* cells (split one cell into two or more rows or columns). Using this technique, you can vary the space in table sections and customize their structure. For example, you may want a long cell space across the top of your table for a banner and then multiple cells underneath it so that you can control the spacing between columns of text or images. The following two sets of steps show you how to merge and split cells in a table.

You can merge and split cells only in Standard mode.

To merge cells, create a new HTML page and follow these steps:

1. **Choose Insert⇨Table and create a table with four rows and four columns, a 75 percent width, and a border of 1. Click OK, and the table appears on the page.**

2. **Highlight two or more adjacent cells by clicking and dragging the mouse from the first cell to the last.**

    You can merge only cells that are adjacent to one another and in the same row or column.

3. **Click the Merge Selected Cells icon in the lower-left region of the Properties inspector to merge the selected cells into a single cell.**

    The cells are merged into a single cell by using the Colspan or Rowspan attributes. These HTML attributes make a single cell merge with adjacent cells by spanning extra rows or columns in the table.

To split a cell, follow these steps:

1. **Click to place the cursor inside the cell you want to split.**

2. **Click the Split Selected Cell icon in the lower-left region of the Properties inspector.**

    The Split Cell dialog box appears.

3. **Select Rows or Columns in the dialog box, depending on how you want the cell to be divided.**

    A cell can be split into however many new rows or columns you want.

4. **Type the number of rows or columns you want to create.**

    The selected cell is split into the number of rows or columns you entered.

Using nested tables: Tables within tables

Placing tables within tables, called *nested tables,* can help you create extremely complex designs. You create nested tables by inserting a table within a cell of another table. In the days when you had to write your own code, this task was daunting. Dreamweaver now makes nesting tables easy, enabling you to create complex designs without ever looking at the HTML code.

The best Web designs communicate the information to your audience in the most elegant and understandable way and are easy to download. To make sure that your designs don't get too messy, remember these guidelines:

✔ A table within a table within a table is nested three levels deep. Anything more than that gets hairy.

✔ Pages that use nested tables take longer to download because browsers have to interpret each table individually before rendering the page. For some designs, the slightly longer download time is worth it, but in most cases you're better off adding or merging cells in one table, as I explain in the section "Merging and splitting table cells," earlier in this chapter. One situation that makes a nested table worth the added download time is when you want to place a table of financial or other data in the midst of a complex page design.

To place a table inside another table, follow these steps:

1. **Click to place the cursor where you want to create the first table.**

2. **Choose Insert⇨Table.**

   The Insert Table dialog box appears.

3. **Type the number of columns and rows you need for your design.**

4. **Set the Width option to whatever is appropriate for your design and click OK.**

   The table is automatically sized to the width you set.

5. **Click to place the cursor in the cell in which you want to place the second table.**

6. **Repeat Steps 2 through 4, specifying the number of columns and rows you want and the width of the table.**

   The new table appears inside the cell of the first table.

7. **Type the information that you want in the nested table cells as you would enter content in any other table.**

Chapter 7

Framing Your Pages

· ·

· ·

*N*o one wants to be "framed," whether that means being falsely accused of a crime or trapped in the HTML frameset of a Web site with no escape. Appreciating not only the best way to create frames, but also the best way to use them to enhance site navigation and not leave viewers feeling stuck in your pages is important.

Many experienced Web designers say you should never use frames. I take a more open approach — I don't *recommend* frames, but I think you should decide for yourself. Besides, I can think of a few instances when frames come in quite handy.

To help you make the most of this HTML design feature, this chapter not only covers how to build HTML framesets in Dreamweaver, but also discusses when frames are most useful and when you should avoid them. Frames add a wide range of design possibilities, but they can also create confusing navigation systems and can be very frustrating to viewers. As you go through this chapter, consider not only how to create frames, but also whether they are really the best solution for your Web site project.

Appreciating HTML Frames

Frames add innovative navigation control because they enable you to display multiple HTML pages in one browser window and control the contents of each framed area individually. Designers commonly use frames to create a page with two or more sections and then place links in one section that, when selected, displays information in another section of the same browser window.

Web pages that use frames, such as the one shown in Figure 7-1, are split into separate sections — or individual *frames*. All the frames together make up a *frameset*. Behind the scenes, each frame of the frameset is a separate HTML file, which makes a page with frames a little complicated to create, even with Dreamweaver. If you choose to create your frame files in a text editor, you have to juggle multiple pages, working on each frame one at a time, and you can see what you create only when you preview your work in a browser. The visual editor in Dreamweaver makes creating frames a lot easier because you can view all the HTML files that make up the frameset at the same time and can edit them while they display in the way in which they appear in a browser.

As a navigational feature, frames enable you to keep some information constant, while changing other information on the same page. For example, you can keep a list of links visible in one frame and display the information each link brings up in another frame, as the site shown in Figure 7-1 does.

You can create as many frames as you want within a browser window. Unfortunately, some people overuse them and create designs that are so complex and broken up that they're neither aesthetically appealing nor easily navigable. Putting too many frames on one page can also make a site hard to read because the individual windows are too small. This has led many Web surfers to passionately hate frames. And some sites that rushed to implement frames when they were first introduced have either abandoned frames or minimized their use.

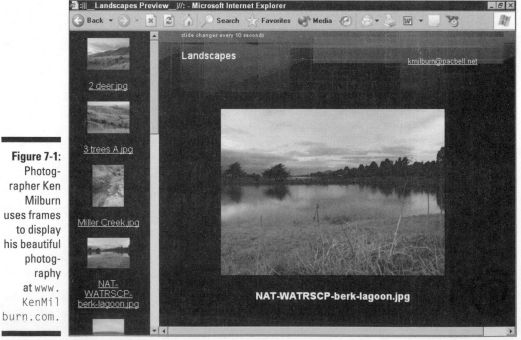

Figure 7-1:
Photographer Ken Milburn uses frames to display his beautiful photography at www. KenMil burn.com.

A more problematic aspect of frames is that they're not backward compatible for very old or purely text-based browsers, which means that if visitors use an older browser (older than Netscape 2.0 or Internet Explorer 3.0) that doesn't support frames, they won't see anything. That's right, they get a blank page — unless you use a special tag called the <NOFRAMES> tag to create an alternative page to supplement your framed page. Fortunately, Dreamweaver automatically inserts a <NOFRAMES> tag in all frameset pages so you can add the alternative content for viewers with browsers that don't support frames. You find out how to do this in the "Creating Alternative Designs for Older Browsers" section at the end of this chapter. If you don't use the <NOFRAMES> tag, you exclude an estimated 2 to 3 percent of the Web's population. Just remember, those few people won't see anything on your Web pages.

If you want to see some good examples of frames on the Web, visit www. Lynda.com, follow the link to Inspiration, and look at the frames she features on her site.

Here's a list of guidelines to follow when using frames:

- **Don't use frames just for the sake of using frames.** If you have a compelling reason to use frames, then create an elegant and easy-to-follow frameset. But don't do it just because Dreamweaver makes creating them relatively easy.

- **Limit the use of frames and keep files small.** Remember that each frame you create represents another HTML file. Thus, a frameset with three frames requires a browser to display four Web pages, and that dramatically increases download time.

- **Turn off frame borders.** Newer browsers support the capability to turn off the border that divides frames in a frameset. If the section is scrollable, the border is visible no matter what. But if you turn the borders off, your pages look cleaner. Frame borders, shown in Figure 7-1, are thick and an ugly gray in color, and they can break up a nice design. You can change the color in the Properties inspector, but I still recommend that you only use them when you feel that they're absolutely necessary. I show you how to turn off frame borders in the "Changing Frame Properties" section toward the end of this chapter.

- **Don't use frames when you can use CSS or tables instead.** Tables are easier to create than frames and provide a more elegant solution to your design needs because they're less intrusive to the design. I include lots of information on creating tables in Chapter 6, and you find coverage of CSS — an increasingly popular design option — in Chapter 8.

- **Don't place frames within frames.** The windows get too darned small to be useful for much of anything, and the screen looks horribly complicated. You can also run into problems when your framed site links to another site that's displayed in your frameset. The sidebar "Resist using frames when you link to other people's Web sites" later in this chapter provides many more reasons to limit using frames inside of frames.

✔ **Put in alternate** <NOFRAMES> **content.** The number of users surfing the Web with browsers that don't support frames becomes smaller every day. Still, showing them *something* other than a blank page is a good idea. I usually put in a line that says, "This site uses frames and requires a frames-capable browser to view."

Understanding How Frames Work

Frames are a bit complicated, but Dreamweaver helps to make the whole process somewhat easier. When you create a Web page with frames in Dreamweaver, you need to remember that each frame area is a separate HTML file, and you need to save each frame area as a separate page. You also want to keep track of which file displays in each section of the frame so that you can set links.

Figure 7-2 shows a simple frameset example with three frames, each containing a different HTML page and different text *(Page 1, Page 2,* and *Page 3)* so that I can clearly refer to them in the following numbered steps.

Figure 7-2:
This three-
frame
frameset
comprises
of four
different
HTML files:
`frameset`
`.html,`
`page1.`
`html,`
`page2.`
`html, and`
`page3.`
`html.`

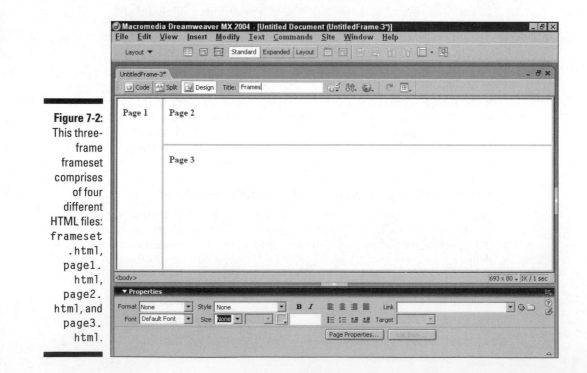

In addition to the files that display in each frame, you need to create a separate HTML file to generate the frameset. This page isn't visible in the browser, but it describes the frames and instructs the browser how and where to display them. This gets a little complicated, but don't worry: Dreamweaver creates the frameset HTML file for you. I just want to give you a general understanding of all the files that you're creating so that the following steps make more sense.

To help you understand how this works, take a look at the example in Figure 7-2. In this document, you see three frames, each displaying a different HTML page. The fourth HTML file that makes up the frame page *contains* the other frames but doesn't show up in the browser. This file is the frameset file, and it describes how the frames display, whether they are on the left or the right side of the page, the top or bottom, and how large they are. The frameset file also contains other information, such as the <NOFRAMES> tag I mention earlier and the names you assign to each frame section. The name of each frame sets links that specify which frame a new HTML file *targets,* or opens into. You find out more about linking frames in the "Setting Targets and Links in Frames" section later in this chapter.

Creating a frame in Dreamweaver

When you create a frame page in Dreamweaver, realizing that the file you are starting with is the *frameset* file is important — the file doesn't show up in the browser but merely instructs the browser how to display the rest of the frames and which pages to use as content for each frame. When you edit the *content* of any of the frames in the frameset, you do not actually edit the frameset file, but the files that populate the framed regions within the frameset. Normally you have to edit the files separately, but Dreamweaver makes designing with frames easier by letting you edit the content of each frame in the *context* of the frameset as it looks in a browser. If you can grasp this concept, you come a long way in understanding how frames work and how to use Dreamweaver to create and edit them. If it hasn't sunk in yet, read on, and it will.

Creating a frame by using the Split Frame command

You can create frames in two ways in Dreamweaver. The first way is achieved by splitting a single HTML file into two sections, which then become individual frames. When you do that, Dreamweaver automatically generates an untitled page with the <FRAMESET> tag and then additional untitled pages display in each of the frames within the frameset. Suddenly, you're managing several pages, not just one. This is important to understand because you have to save and name each of these pages as a separate file, even though Dreamweaver makes you think you're working on only one page that's broken into sections.

Always save your HTML files first before inserting anything into them; however, the opposite is true when you work with frame files in Dreamweaver. Wait until after you created all the frames in your frameset and *then* save them; otherwise, tracking your files gets a bit too complicated and confusing. I explain more in the section, "Saving files in a frameset," later in this chapter, but first, you create a simple framed page.

To create a simple frameset in Dreamweaver, such as the one shown in Figure 7-2, follow these steps:

1. **Choose File⇨New.**

   The New Document window opens, as shown in Figure 7-3.

2. **Choose Framesets from the General list, and then select the Fixed Top, Nested Left option from the Framesets list on the right.**

3. **Click the Create button.**

   The frameset automatically appears.

4. **Click and drag any of the bars dividing the frames to adjust the size of the frame area.**

5. **To edit each section of the frameset, click inside the frame that you want to work on and edit it like any other HTML page.**

   Remember, always save your files before setting links or inserting images and other files.

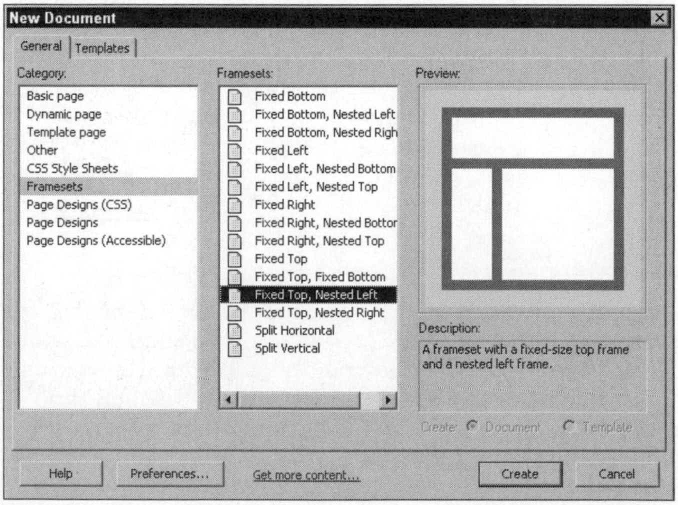

Figure 7-3:
Dream-
weaver
includes a
long list of
predefined
framesets
to make
creating
new frames
easier.

New Document

General | Templates

Category:
- Basic page
- Dynamic page
- Template page
- Other
- CSS Style Sheets
- Framesets
- Page Designs (CSS)
- Page Designs
- Page Designs (Accessible)

Framesets:
- Fixed Bottom
- Fixed Bottom, Nested Left
- Fixed Bottom, Nested Right
- Fixed Left
- Fixed Left, Nested Bottom
- Fixed Left, Nested Top
- Fixed Right
- Fixed Right, Nested Bottom
- Fixed Right, Nested Top
- Fixed Top
- Fixed Top, Fixed Bottom
- Fixed Top, Nested Left
- Fixed Top, Nested Right
- Split Horizontal
- Split Vertical

Preview:

Description:
A frameset with a fixed-size top frame and a nested left frame.

Create: ● Document ○ Template

Help | Preferences... | Get more content... | Create | Cancel

You can type text, insert images, create tables, and add any other features just as you do to any other page.

To save your files, continue with the instructions in the section "Saving files in a frameset," later in this chapter.

Creating a frame by using the Frames icon in the Layout bar

Another way to create frames is with the Frames icon (which has a drop-down menu), shown at the top of Figure 7-4. The Layout bar (available by selecting Layout Bar from the pull-down list at the top of the work area) includes the Frames icon, which displays several predefined frames sets from a drop-down menu. You can create a frameset in Dreamweaver simply by selecting any of these options from the Frames drop-down menu. Figure 7-4 shows the Layout bar with the Frames icon selected and an option applied to a new document from the pull-down list.

To create a framed page using the Frames icon in the Layout bar, follow these steps:

1. **Choose File⇨New⇨Basic Page to create a new page.**

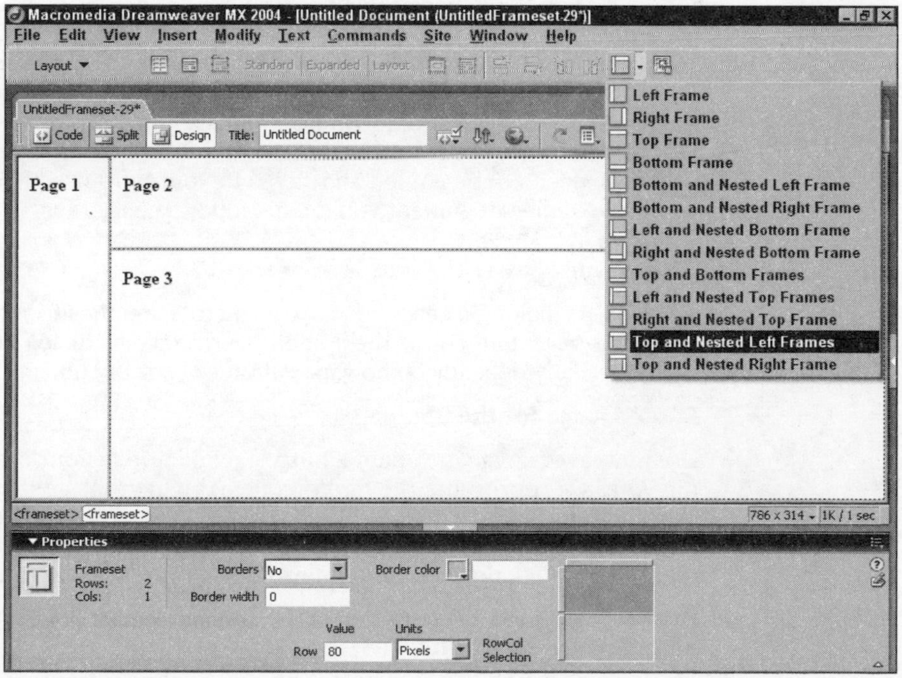

Figure 7-4: The Layout bar contains predefined framesets that you select from the drop-down menu by clicking on the Frames icon.

2. **From the Layout bar, click the Frames icon and select the design that most closely approximates the type of frameset you want to build from the pull-down list (refer to Figure 7-4).**

Don't worry if it isn't exactly the design you want; you can alter it later.

3. **Modify the frameset as needed.**

You can further modify your frameset by clicking and dragging the borders of the frames to resize them.

You can also split frames by choosing Modify➪Frameset and then choosing to split the frame left, right, up, or down.

To save your files, continue with the instructions in the next section "Saving files in a frameset."

Saving files in a frameset

As I mention earlier, you shouldn't save your frameset file until *after* you add all your frames; otherwise, keeping track of your files gets very complicated. Remember, frames in HTML consist of at least two or more HTML files, even if it appears as if you are only working on one file.

When you are ready to save, Dreamweaver gives you multiple save options for saving all the files. You can either save everything all at once, or you can save each frame and frameset individually. The example in the previous section, "Creating a frame in Dreamweaver," is composed of four separate HTML files, and each needs to be named and saved to your hard drive. To save all the files in the frames document you create, follow these steps:

1. **Choose File➪Save All.**

The Save As dialog box appears, asking you to name the file and designate a folder to save it in. This is the first of several Save As dialog boxes you see (how many depends on how many frames your document contains).

2. **Enter a name for the file.**

Dreamweaver suggests a name, but you can choose your own. The first file you save represents the *frameset* file (the file that holds all the other frames in place). You can tell this by looking at the Dreamweaver Document window behind the Save As dialog box: The entire document has a thick dotted highlight around it representing the frameset.

3. **Browse your hard drive to locate the desired folder for the HTML files and click the Save button.**

The first frameset file saves, and a new Save As dialog box appears for the next one. For each frameset file, you need a distinct name. I like names such as `frame1.html`, `frame2.html`, or `leftframe.html`, `rightframe.html`. It doesn't matter, but such names can help you distinguish the frame files later. After you save all the frames, the Save As dialog box disappears.

Carefully name the files that you save in a way that helps you keep them in order and know which is which. Notice that as you are prompted to save each file, Dreamweaver indicates which frame area it is by highlighting it with a dark border on-screen behind the dialog box. You may find choosing filenames that make sense and help you to identify which area they represent makes setting links in the frames a much easier task.

After you save and name your documents the first time, choosing Save All saves any and all of the files in your frameset without prompting you separately for each frame. Choosing Save All is a good way to make sure that all the pages in your frameset save whenever you edit a frames-based document.

Sometimes, you may not want to save all the files at once. To save an individual frame displayed in a frameset without saving all the other frames, place your cursor in any of the frames and choose File⇨Save Frame just as you save any other individual page. Dreamweaver saves only the file for the frame in which your cursor is located.

To save only the page that defines the frameset, make sure the entire frameset is selected (you can do this by clicking in the upper-most left corner of the Workspace), and then choose File⇨Save Frameset. If you have not selected the entire frameset, the Save Frameset option will not appear in the File menu. *Remember:* This page doesn't display in any of the frames; it simply defines the entire display area, specifying which of the other pages displays in each frame, as well as the position and size of the frames.

As you continue to work on your frame page, remember that whenever you make a change in one of the content frames, you edit content in a *different* file from the one you started with (the frameset file). You may get confused as to which file you need to save when working in this manner. Don't worry — this is what confuses a lot of people about using frames in Dreamweaver. When you edit the content in one of the frames, make sure that your cursor is still in that frame when you choose File⇨Save Frame so that you save the page that corresponds to the frame you are working on. To be safe, you can always choose File⇨Save All Frames in order to save all changes to all files in the frameset, including the frameset file itself. The Save All command is also useful when you make changes to several of the frames and want to save all the changes with just one command.

Resist using frames when you link to other people's Web sites

I understand that most people don't want to lose viewers to another site when they set a link, but that's the nature of the Web. If your site is designed well, you shouldn't have to worry about losing people. Instead, you should guide them around your informative site and then politely help them to other resources that they may find of interest — and let them go. Frames keep users captive and usually leave them annoyed with you for taking up part of their browser area with your site. By displaying content from other sites within one or more of the frames in your site, you do yourself more harm than good in trying to keep them.

If you insist on using frames when you link to another site, do so discreetly by placing a small, narrow frame across the bottom of the screen or the left side — not a wide band across the top, and certainly not more than one frame that still contains information from your site. Not only is this rude and ugly, but some people have sued Web site designers because the designers made it look like their content belonged to the site using frames.

An additional reason not to use frames when you link to another site is that many other sites use frames, too. You can quickly create a mass of frames within frames that makes users trying to find their way through information hard. Not everyone realizes that you can get out of frames. If you haven't figured it out yet as a user, within the browser, you can always right-click the link in Windows or click and hold the link on a Mac to open the frame in a separate window. Now that you know this trick, you can get out of a framed situation — but don't count on your users knowing how to do this if they get annoyed.

Setting Targets and Links in Frames

One of the best features of frames is that you can change the contents of each frame separately within the Web browser. This feature opens a wide range of design possibilities that improves navigation for your site. One very common way to use a frameset is to create a frame that displays a list of links to various pages of your site and then open those links into another frame on the same page. This technique makes keeping a list of links constantly visible possible and makes navigation a lot simpler and more intuitive.

Setting links from a file in one frame so that the pages they link to open in another frame is like linking from one page to another, and that's essentially what you're doing. What makes linking a frameset distinctive is that, in addition to indicating which page you want to open with the link, you have to specify which frame section it *targets* (opens into).

But before you can set those links, you need to do a few things: First, you need to create some other pages that you can link to (if you haven't done so already). Creating new pages is easy. Choose File⇨New ⇨HTML Page to create additional pages and then save them individually. If your pages already exist, you're more than halfway there; it's just a matter of linking to those pages.

The other thing you have to do before you can set links is to name each frame so that you can specify where the linked file loads. If you don't, the page just replaces the frameset altogether when someone clicks the link and defeats the purpose of using frames in the first place.

Naming frames

Naming a *frame* is different from naming the *file* that the frame represents. You find out how to name the files in the previous section "Saving files in a frameset;" you do that just as you name any other file you save. The *frame name* is like a nickname that allows you to distinguish your frames from one another on a page and refer to them individually — this becomes important when you set links and want to target a link to open in a particular area of the frameset. The *filename* is the actual name of the HTML file for the frame. The *frame name* is the nickname that you refer to when you want to set links.

Trust me, this makes more sense after you see how it works in these next sections. To specify the names of the frames in your frameset, follow these steps:

1. **Open an existing frameset or create a new one.**

   See the "Creating a frame in Dreamweaver" section, earlier in this chapter, if you don't know how to create a frame.

2. **Choose Window⇨Frames to open the Frames panel at the right of the work area.**

   The Frames panel opens, as shown in Figure 7-5.

   The Frames panel is a miniature representation of the frames on your page that enables you to select different frames by clicking within the panel.

3. **Click to place your cursor in the area of the Frames panel that corresponds to the frame that you want to name.**

   As displayed in Figure 7-5, you can see that I selected the left frame. You can click to select any of the frames in the panel.

   The Properties inspector displays the properties for that particular frame. You can make any changes to the frame's properties by altering the properties in the Properties inspector after selecting the frame. You can also select the entire frameset by clicking the border around all the frames in the Frames panel. The Frames panel allows you to select only one frame or frameset at a time.

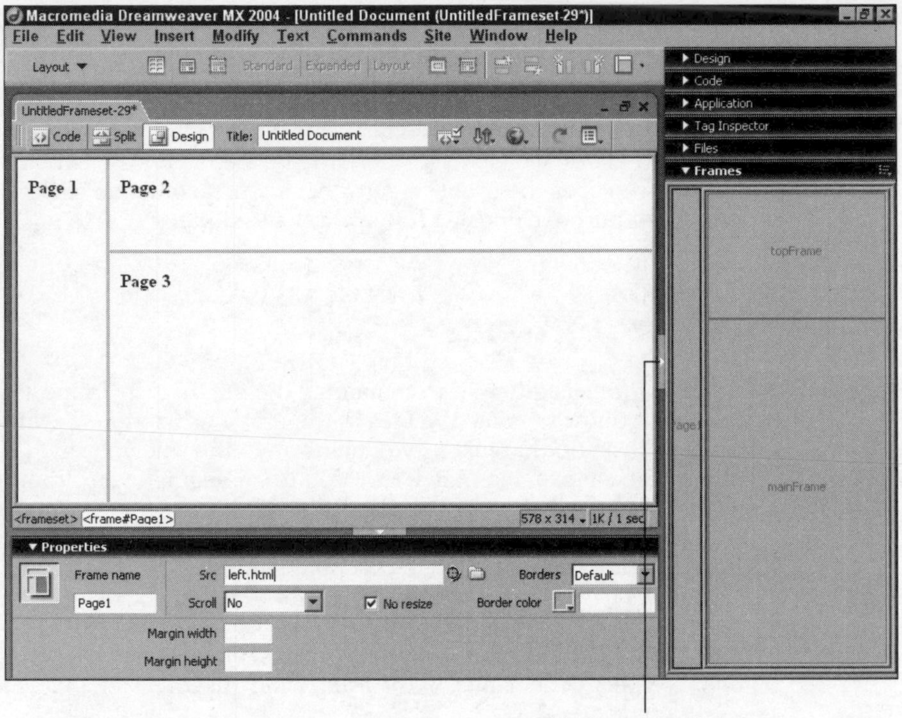

Figure 7-5:
The Frames
panel is a
miniature
representa-
tion of the
framed
page that
provides
access to
Frame
properties.

This frame is selected.

**4. In the Frame Name text box on the left side of the Properties inspec-
tor, type a name for the frame.**

Dreamweaver assigns names automatically when you save the files in a
frameset. In the example shown in Figure 7-5, Dreamweaver assigns the
names topFrame, mainFrame, and leftFrame. You can leave these
names as is or change them to something else in the Properties inspector. I recommend naming frames with something that makes sense to
you. For example, in the Properties inspector in Figure 7-5, you can see
that I rename the leftFrame frame and call it Page1.

5. Save the frameset page after changing all of the names.

You can either save each frame individually or choose the Save All
Frames command. Refer to the "Saving files in a frameset" section earlier
in this chapter for more information on saving frames.

Now that you identified or changed the names of your frames, you're ready to
start setting links that target frames. Don't close these files yet — you want to
use them to follow the steps in the next section to set links.

I like to save my work on a regular basis so that I never lose more than a few minutes of work if my system crashes or the power goes out. Beware, however, that when you work with frames, you need to save all your pages to save your work. You can save each page separately by choosing File➪Save Frame to save only the frame that the cursor is currently located in. To save all your pages at once, simply choose File➪Save All to save all the pages in the frameset.

Setting links to a target frame

Setting links in a frameset requires some preliminary work. If you jumped to this section without creating a frameset or naming your frames, you may want to refer to the sections earlier in this chapter. If you already have a frameset, have named the frames, and just want to find out how to set links, this section is where you want to be.

Setting links in a frameset is like setting any other links between pages, except that you need to specify the target frame, meaning the frame where the link displays. For example, if you want a link in the right frame to display in the main frame, you need to specify the main frame as the target in the link. If you don't specify a target, the link opens in the same frame the link is in. Because the most common reason to use frames is to keep navigation links in one frame and open them in another, you probably want to know how to target a frame when you set a link.

For the purposes of this exercise, I walk you through creating three text links in the right frame that open in the main frame, the left area of the frameset you created in the last exercise. If you work on your own frameset, refer to Figures 7-5 and 7-6 to follow along and set the links as they correspond to your frameset.

If this seems confusing, don't fret. After you try the following steps, you'll understand frames easier:

1. **Click to place the cursor inside the left frame, type** Cool Link 1, **and press Enter. Then type** Cool Link 2 **and press Enter; then type** Cool Link 3.

   See Figure 7-6 to see how this looks.

2. **Highlight the text link.**

   Highlight the words *Cool Link 1*. Note that this works the same way if you want to link an image.

3. **In the Properties inspector, type the URL** http://www.wiley.com **in the Link text box.**

   This creates a link to the Wiley Web site. If you want to create a link to another page in your Web site, select the file icon next to the Link box and browse to find the link, just like you set any other link in your site.

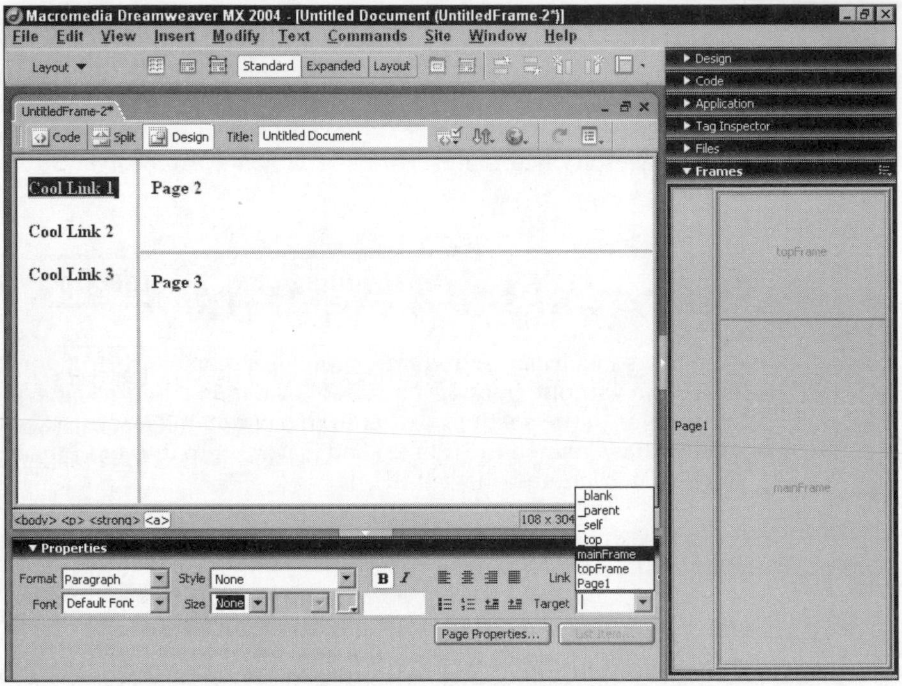

Figure 7-6:
Use targets
to specify
where a link
opens in a
frameset.

4. **From the Target drop-down list in the Properties inspector, choose the name of the frame that you want the link to open into.**

   Select *mainFrame*. If you changed the names, choose the name that corresponds to the main frame on the page. Notice that Dreamweaver conveniently lists all the frames you named in your document in this drop-down list.

   The result, as shown in Figure 7-7, is that when you click the linked text Cool Link 1 in the left frame, the Wiley Web site displays in the main frame area. *Note:* You have to save your work before you preview it in a browser. Press F12 as a shortcut to save all files and open them in a browser automatically. Also note that I set this link as an example because you see how linking works. In general, I do not recommend that you use frames when linking to a page on another Web site. (See the sidebar, "Resist using frames when you link to other people's Web sites," in this chapter.)

Comparing target options

You have many options when you target links in a frameset. As shown in the preceding section, "Setting links to a target frame," you can specify that a linked page open in another frame within your frameset. In addition, you can set linked pages to open in the same frame as the page with the link, to open a completely new page, and even to open a second browser window. Table 7-1 provides a list of target options and what they mean. You can find all these options in the Target drop-down list of the Properties inspector.

TIP

The Target drop-down list in the Properties inspector is activated only when you select a linked image or section of text and specify the link in the page you want to link to in the link text box.

Table 7-1	Understanding Frame Target Options
Target Name	*Action*
_blank	Opens the linked document into a new browser window.
_parent	Opens the linked document into the parent frameset of the page that has the link. (The *parent* is the browser window that contains the frameset.)
_self	Opens the linked document in the same frame as the original link, replacing the current content of the frame. This is the default option and does not need to be selected
_top	Opens the linked document into the outermost frameset, replacing the entire contents of the browser window.

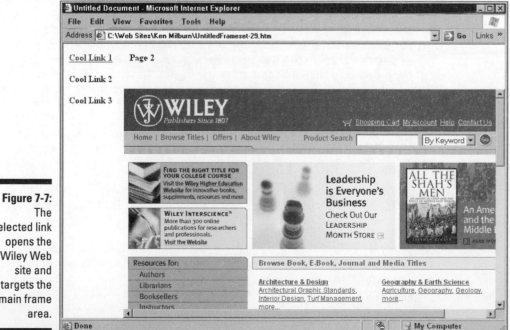

Figure 7-7:
The selected link opens the Wiley Web site and targets the main frame area.

Changing Frame Properties

As you get more sophisticated in using frames, you may want to further refine your frames by changing properties, which enables you to turn off frame borders, change the frame or border colors, limit scrolling, and so on. To access these options in Dreamweaver, choose Window⇨Frames, click inside the Frames panel in the area that corresponds to the frame that you want to change, and then use the Properties inspector to access the options I describe in the following four sections. Figure 7-8 shows the Properties inspector, as it appears when you select a frameset in the Frames panel.

If you don't see the margin height and width options, make sure that you click the expander arrow in the bottom-right corner of the Properties inspector. Clicking this arrow causes all available properties to display for the selected item.

Changing frame borders

I think the best thing that you can do with a frame border is to turn it off. You can turn the borders off for your site by choosing No from the Borders drop-down list in the Properties inspector for either the frameset or any of the individual frames in the frameset. Your other options include Yes, which forces the borders to be visible, and Default, which usually means Yes. In case of individual frames, however, the Default option defaults to the settings for the parent frameset.

You can make global border settings by using the Properties inspector and applying the settings to the frameset. To select the frameset so that its properties are visible in the inspector, click the border that encloses the frameset in the Frames panel. Figure 7-8 shows a frameset selected in the Frames panel and its corresponding properties displayed in the Properties inspector.

If you choose to keep your borders visible, you may want to customize the color by clicking the Border Color square in the Properties inspector and then choosing a color from the Dreamweaver palette.

If you select a specific border, the Properties inspector also enables you to specify the border width. Simply enter a value in pixels in the Border Width text field to change the width of the selected border.

Frame border colors are not well supported by all browsers and may not display as you intend. Most designers simply turn off frame borders, but if you do keep them make sure that your design will still look okay if the borders are thick and grey, which is the default. Many browsers, including recent ones, don't display a different border color.

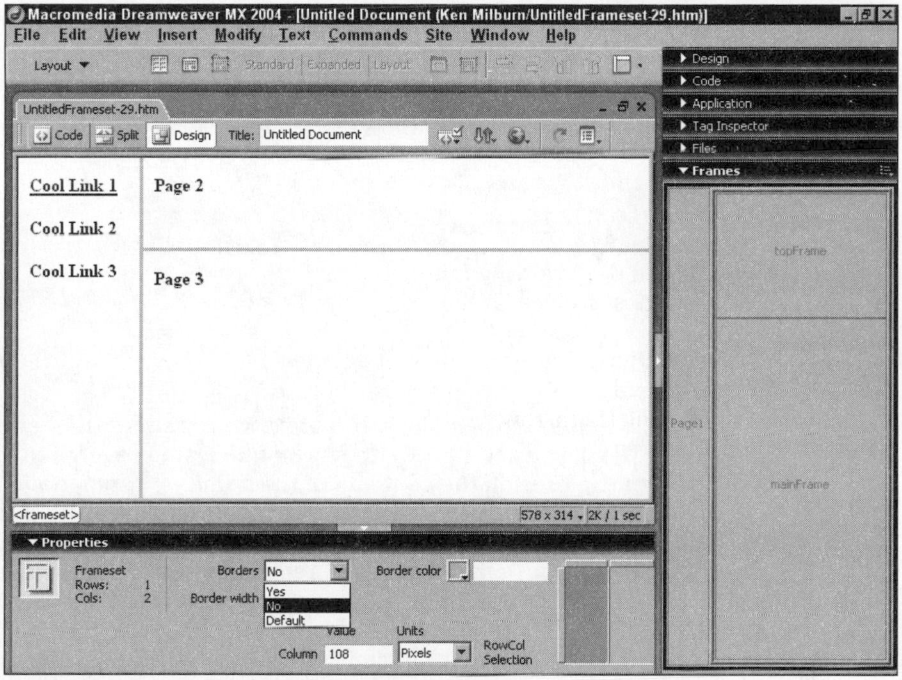

Figure 7-8:
The selected frames or framesets and their properties are visible in the Properties inspector.

Changing frame sizes

The easiest way to change the size of a frame is to select the border and drag it until the frame is the size that you want. When you select the border, the Properties inspector displays the size of the frame, enabling you to change the size in pixels or as a percentage of the display area by entering a number in the Row or Column text area boxes. If you specify 0 width for your frame borders, you may not see them on the page in order to drag and resize them. If this is the case, you can view the borders by choosing View➪Visual Aids➪ Frame Borders, and Dreamweaver indicates the borders with a thin gray line that you can easily select.

Changing scrolling and resizing options

Scrolling options control whether a viewer can scroll up and down or left and right in a frame area. As shown in Figure 7-9, the scrolling options for frames are Yes, No, Auto, and Default. As a general rule, I recommend leaving the Scroll option set to Auto because a visitor's browser can then turn scrolling on if necessary. That is, if the viewer's display area is too small to see all the contents of the frame, the frame becomes scrollable. If all the contents are visible, the scroll arrows aren't visible.

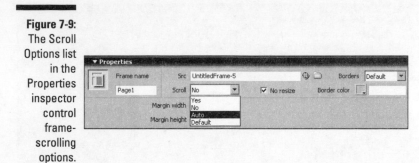

Figure 7-9:
The Scroll
Options list
in the
Properties
inspector
control
frame-
scrolling
options.

If you set this option to Yes, the scroll arrows are visible whether they're needed or not. If you set it to No, they won't be visible, even if that means your viewer can't see all the contents of the frame — a sometimes dangerous proposition because there's no way to scroll. Default leaves it up to the browser. In most browsers, the Default option results in the same display as the Auto option, but Default yields unpredictable results. As a general rule, using Auto is best so the scroll bar is visible only if needed.

Also notice the No Resize option in Figure 7-9. If you place a check mark in this box, a visitor to your site can't change the size of the frames. If you leave this box unchecked, your user can select the border and drag it to make the frame area smaller or larger, just as you can when you develop your frames in Dreamweaver. Generally, I like to give viewers control, but I often check the No Resize option because I want to ensure that my viewers don't alter the design, especially because some viewers may do so accidentally.

Setting margin height and width

The Margin Width and Margin Height options enable you to specify the amount of margin space around a frame. Normally in a browser window, a small margin is visible between the edge of the window and any content, such as images or text. That's why you can't normally place an image on your page flush against the edge of the browser. With frames, though, you can actually control the size of the margin or even eliminate the margin altogether.

I generally recommend that you set the margin to at least two pixels and make the margin larger if you want to create more space around your content. If you want to get rid of the margin altogether, set it to zero and any images or text in the frame appear flush against the edge of the frame or browser window if the frame touches the edge of the browser. If the frame touches another frame, you can use this technique to create the impression of seamless images across frames.

TECHNICAL STUFF Note that the margin settings for frames do not override the margin settings in the page itself if the margins are set in the `<BODY>` tag. If you use Dreamweaver, this shouldn't matter because Dreamweaver MX 2004 now sets the margins with CSS. If margins are set in CSS, then that setting overrides the settings in the individual page.

Creating Alternative Designs for Older Browsers

Frames provide some great navigational options, but they also provide the worst possible navigation nightmare. Navigation problems exist because very old or text-only browsers do not support frames. For example, if you create a frameset on your site and visitors try to access your page with an old browser that doesn't support frames, they won't see the contents of any of your frames. In fact, if you don't provide an alternative, they won't see anything at all.

So what's the alternative? It's called the `<NOFRAMES>` tag, and Dreamweaver makes creating this option for low-end users easy. The `<NOFRAMES>` tag enables you to create an alternative page that displays in browsers that don't support frames. The contents of the `<NOFRAMES>` tag are stored in the frameset file — that invisible file that describes how your frames look, but never shows up in the browser. A browser that supports frames ignores the contents of the alternative page because it knows not to display anything that appears in the `<NOFRAMES>` tag. A browser that doesn't support frames ignores the contents of the frameset because it doesn't understand the pointers within the `<FRAMES>` tag and displays all the content contained within the `<NOFRAMES>` tag instead.

If this all sounds a bit complicated, don't worry; it works like a charm. Fortunately, you don't have to know much about how it works; you just need to know that you can add the alternative content in Dreamweaver if you want to ensure that your pages look okay to people with older browsers.

To create an alternative page for older browsers by using the `<NOFRAMES>` tag, open any document that uses frames and follow these steps:

1. **Choose Modify⇨Frameset⇨Edit NoFrames Content.**

   A new Document window opens with `NoFrames Content` displayed at the top.

2. **Edit this page as you do any other page in Dreamweaver by inserting images, typing text, creating tables, and adding any other features that you want (except frames, of course).**

   Your goal is to create an alternative page that is viewed by people using older browsers. The alternative page can be as simple as instructions for how viewers can get a newer copy of Microsoft Internet Explorer or Netscape Navigator or as complex as a copy of the page you created in frames that you re-created as well as you can without frames.

   Your best bet is to keep your NoFrames page as simple as possible, using only text to ensure it displays well for the broadest possible audience.

3. **To close the window and return to your frameset, choose Modify↔ Frameset↔Edit NoFrames Content again.**

   The check box next to the Edit NoFrames Content option disappears, and the frames page replaces the NoFrames Content page in the Document window.

If you create an alternative page, don't forget to update it when you make changes to your frameset.

Chapter 8

Cascading Style Sheets

• •

• •

*T*ext is at the heart of nearly every Web page. In fact, HTML was originally developed as a way to exchange text-only files between scientists and researchers, not to design attractive, well-laid-out pages. Graphics didn't come along until a few years after HTML appeared on the scene. Before graphical HTML editors, like Dreamweaver, even formatting text for attributes like bold and italics required a thorough knowledge of HTML tags, and designers had to memorize lots of tags.

After you figure out how to work with text in Dreamweaver, you may conclude that HTML doesn't give you much typographic control. Welcome to the world of Web design with HTML. Fortunately, the situation in the HTML world has progressed a great deal since the early days of the Web, and thanks to a constant stream of new technologies, Web designers now have much more control over type than they did even a few years ago.

The biggest boon for Web designers has been the advent of *Cascading Style Sheets (CSS),* a kind of extended HTML that enables greater style control and the ability to specify formatting features for frequently used elements, such as headlines and subheads. For example, if you want all main headlines to be font face Arial, bold, and centered, you can create a style with those options and apply all options at one time. You can even create style sheets that work across multiple pages or your entire site.

Cascading Style Sheets also enable you to design your pages — and they're much easier to use than tables to control layout. CSS and CSS-P (which enable you to position elements, such as layers on a page) are rapidly becoming the preferred method of designing pages. Many forward-looking designers consider CSS and layers to be the ultimate solutions to the limitations of text formatting and page layout with plain HTML.

If you haven't jumped on the CSS bandwagon yet, this chapter is designed to help you appreciate the benefits and introduce you to the timesaving CSS features so that you can begin using CSS in your page designs right away. Macromedia believes strongly in CSS and has designed this newest version of Dreamweaver to make working with style sheets even easier.

In this chapter, you see how CSS works and how it's implemented in Dreamweaver. You're also introduced to the most advanced CSS capabilities, and you gain a glimpse into the future of Web design. In Chapter 9, you find more detailed instructions about using CSS-P and layers to control page layout.

Checking Browser Compatibility

Although CSS has been around for a while, many designers have resisted using it because it wasn't well supported by early browsers, such as Netscape 4. That's all changing, now that most modern browsers do a better job of rendering CSS pages. The newest versions of Netscape, Internet Explorer, Safari, and Opera all offer very good (though at times inconsistent) support for CSS. To help you watch out for inconsistencies, Dreamweaver offers several features designed to help manage browser differences (these features are covered at the end of Chapter 9).

Unless you need to reach the widest possible audience and expect that some viewers may be using ancient browsers, like Netscape 4 and earlier, you shouldn't have to worry much about browsers that can't render CSS. Even in cases where you do need to reach those archaic holdouts, CSS is designed to degrade gracefully: You may lose your fancy formatting, but at least viewers can still see your content. (The exception is layers, as described in Chapter 9, which aren't always displayed in older browsers.)

Appreciating Cascading Style Sheets

The concept of style sheets has been around since long before the Web. Word processing programs, such as Microsoft Word, have long used style sheets to control text formatting. Using style sheets in a word processor, for example, you could create specific style definitions — such as Heading, Body, and Footer — and apply those styles to regions of a page. The timesaving benefits of this approach are enormous because you need to define your styles only once and then apply them with a single click anywhere in your document. The concept is exactly the same with Web documents and Cascading Style Sheets.

The most powerful aspect of CSS, as you see in the section "Using External Style Sheets," is its ability to make global style changes across an entire Web site. Suppose that one fine day you decide that all your headlines should be purple rather than blue. You can change the style definition for Headline, and all the text on your page or site that you formatted with the Headline style can be automatically changed from blue to purple. And, you have the option to apply the style change to all Headlines that use that style or to only some of them. If you ever have to redesign your site (and believe me, every good site goes through periodic redesigns), you can save hours, or even days, of work if you have created your design with CSS.

Looking at the code behind CSS

A *Cascading Style Sheet* is basically a list of rules defined in an HTML document. HTML already contains a bunch of rules about the behavior of different tags, but you can't alter those rules — they're kind of like the grammar rules in a language.

CSS, however, enables you to create your own rules and override the rules of HTML, which are quite limited in terms of page design. These new rules determine how a browser renders certain page elements. Imagine if you could invent a bunch of new words and grammar rules for the English language. Now imagine that everyone else could do that too. Communication could get confusing pretty quickly, right?

What keeps the communication from breaking down with CSS is that every time you invent new rules, you include the equivalent of a dictionary entry and grammar guide that goes along with each document.

CSS styles reside in the <HEAD> area of an HTML page if they apply to only that page, or in a separate file if you create an external CSS that applies to multiple pages. CSS consists of lines of code that describe the attributes of the style, such as the color, font, and alignment. A style can contain any number of rules, and each rule contains a declaration composed of one or more properties and a corresponding property value. If this stuff is starting to sound a little confusing, don't worry. You find step-by-step directions in the second half of this chapter, and Dreamweaver hides most of the technical stuff behind the scenes (unless you like to look at the code.)

To give you an idea of what CSS looks like, Figure 8-1 illustrates the various components of a style sheet.

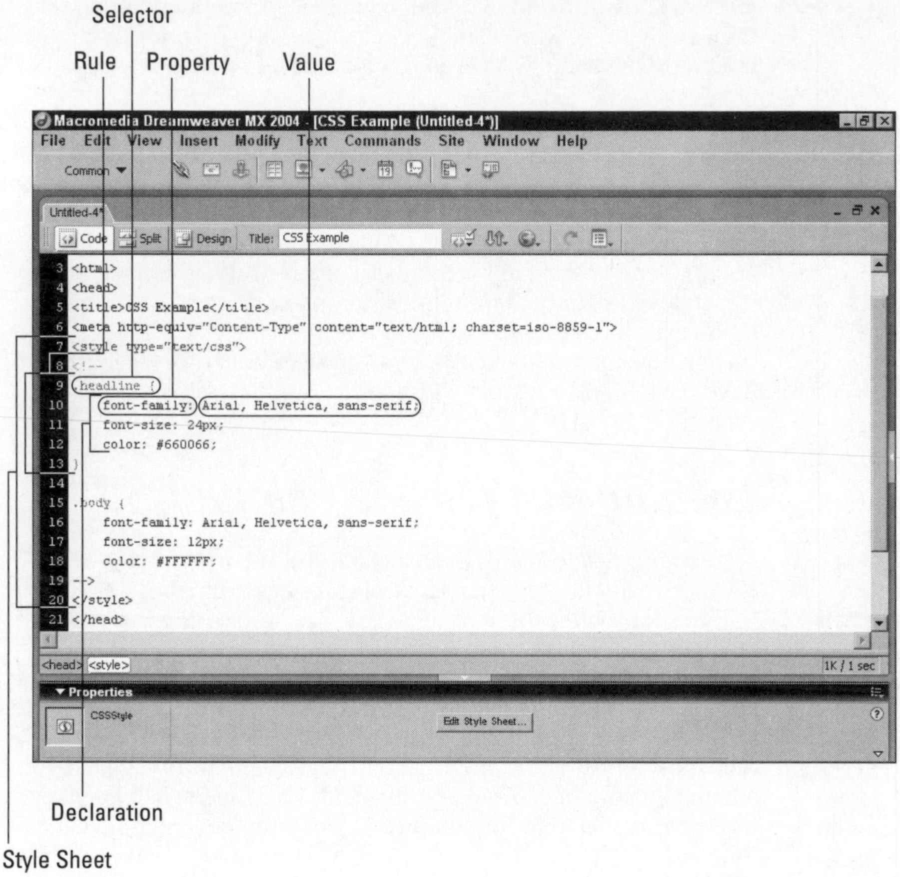

Selector

Rule Property Value

Figure 8-1:
A style sheet
embedded
in an HTML
document.

Declaration

Style Sheet

After looking over Figure 8-1, you may be thinking that CSS looks kind of complicated. Well, to be perfectly honest, it is. But the beauty of Dreamweaver is that it hides the complicated code necessary to create CSS behind an easy-to-use interface. You can do in Dreamweaver pretty much anything you can do with CSS without ever seeing or touching a line of code!

Dreamweaver MX 2004 takes this benefit even further by enabling you to preview many CSS effects directly from within the application. You don't even have to preview your work in a browser to see how CSS will work. The folks at Macromedia believe so much in the power and future of CSS that they have even done away with the older and less powerful feature HTML Styles. If you have used HTML Styles, you will find CSS similar — and much better. CSS is clearly the way of the future.

What is the Document Object Model?

If you want to impress your geek friends, start talking about the DOM (rhymes with "mom"). But first, you may want to know a bit more about what it means. The Document Object Model (DOM), part of the World Wide Web Consortium's HTML 4.0 specification, strives to make every element on a page an identifiable object. Because the properties of that object are then readable and writeable, you can use a scripting language such as JavaScript to change, hide, or move the object's attributes. For example, if object #2 is an image, you can say "Move object #2 over here" and cause an image to move across a Web page. The DOM is way cool — it provides the method to refer to and control objects.

By defining a standard DOM, a consistent method for interacting with page elements can be achieved across platforms and browsers. This capability makes possible most DHTML effects, such as dynamically changing text and images.

Unfortunately, as with many standards in the world of HTML, a great divergence still exists in the way the major browsers implement the DOM. This inconsistency has limited the practical usefulness of DHTML in recent years. Although the latest browsers are getting better and better in their support of the World Wide Web Consortium (W3C) standards, cross browser issues still exist. If you choose to use these advanced options, make sure that you use the built-in Dreamweaver features for testing your pages in different browsers. I describe these features at the end of Chapter 9.

If you happen to know some CSS already, and you're advanced enough to be able to hand-code CSS, Dreamweaver includes a cool feature named Code Hints. Code Hints offer autocomplete options for filling in code that speed up the manual coding process. Code Hints work only in Code view and are activated as you type new CSS declarations. You can also force the list of Code Hints to appear by pressing Ctrl+spacebar (or ⌘+spacebar on the Mac).

"So what's all this about cascading?"

The term *cascading* refers to the way in which conflicts in CSS rules are resolved. Because cascading style sheets involve a hierarchy of formatting options, the browser interprets these options in a certain order. This hierarchical order works in kind of a vertical fashion, in much the same way as water cascades over rocks as it flows down a stream.

The benefits of this cascading process become apparent when you define multiple style choices in your style sheet. Cascading style sheets enable you to define a variety of presentation possibilities that are rendered in the browser and help you compensate for variables that change the way the page looks — like the differences among computer platforms, screen resolution, and browser versions. When you define your presentation choices by creating your CSS rules, items higher in the list receive greater priority. As items "cascade" down the list, they receive less priority. This concept becomes clearer as you read more and become more familiar with how CSS operates. You also find out what happens when you apply conflicting styles in the section "Conflicting styles," later in this chapter.

Advanced capabilities of CSS

Besides helping you to format your text, CSS also encompasses a host of other geeky technologies that enable you to control the layout and appearance of page elements. CSS forms the basis of layers (which you can read more about in Chapter 9), even though you wouldn't know it without looking closely at the code on your page. *Layers* are an advanced CSS implementation that enable you to precisely position objects on your page, stack them one on top of the other, and even add interactivity to elements. Interactive effects with layers can be programmed by using DHTML (Dynamic HTML) and JavaScript to create complex animations and transitions on your pages.

Cascading Style Sheets and Dynamic HTML are covered in greater detail in Chapter 9. Dynamic HTML is made possible through scripting languages that use the Document Object Model to create dynamic effects and global styles. Think of Cascading Style Sheets as HTML on steroids. For more on the Document Object model, see the nearby sidebar, "What is the Document Object Model?"

Benefits of CSS

CSS is a continually developing technology, and not all its capabilities are included in Dreamweaver MX 2004. Those I don't mention here simply aren't well supported across platforms and browsers — they aren't safe to use, so Macromedia didn't bother to include them.

Nonetheless, you gain many, many advantages by using CSS in Dreamweaver. The following partial list shows what you can do:

- ✔ Designate specific fonts.
- ✔ Define font sizes based on percentages, pixels, picas, points, inches, millimeters, and other precise measurements.
- ✔ Set bold, italic, and underline and properties.

✔ Set text color and background color for text blocks and other objects.

✔ Change link colors and remove link underlining.

✔ Create mouseover effects on links.

✔ Indent and justify text.

✔ Use upper-, lower-, and mixed-case text.

✔ Create customized bullets.

✔ Control margins and borders around text.

✔ Redefine how specific HTML tags are displayed.

✔ Precisely position elements on a page.

✔ Flow text around images and other text.

Using CSS in Dreamweaver

When you start creating and using Cascading Style Sheets, you use one of the most complex and advanced Dreamweaver features. Consequently, creating style sheets takes a little more time to grasp than applying basic HTML tags and modifying their attributes. Still, Dreamweaver makes defining style sheets much easier than writing them by hand — a task much closer to writing programming code than to creating HTML tags (refer to Figure 8-1).

To help you get the hang of using Dreamweaver to create style sheets, this section walks you through the panels and dialog boxes that define CSS rules and gives you an overview of your options as you create new style definitions. After the sections on each aspect of style sheet creation, you find specific numbered steps that walk you through the process of creating and applying your own CSS styles.

Understanding style types in CSS

You can create two types of style sheets with CSS and Dreamweaver: internal and external. An *internal style sheet* stores its data within the HTML code of a page and applies styles to only that page. An *external style* is a text file you create and store outside your HTML page. You can then reference it as a link, much like you do any other HTML page on the Web. In this way, you can apply style sheets to an entire Web site or to any page that links to the external style sheet, which also means that you can have many different pages referencing the same style sheet. You create these two kinds of style sheets in much the same way, as you see later in this chapter.

You can also define three different kinds of CSS styles to use in either an internal or external style sheet:

- **Custom styles:** A *custom style* is a completely new set of formatting attributes you can apply to any text selection. Custom styles in CSS are referred to as *classes.* Don't worry much about the technical terms because I get into them in more detail as you read on. For now, just know that when you define a custom style, you give it a class name, and then you use that name to apply the style to any text block or other element on the page. Creating a custom style is a little like making up your own HTML tag, with formatting rules you can define yourself.

- **Redefined HTML tags:** You create redefined HTML tag styles by redefining how *existing* HTML tags are rendered by the browser; in this case, you're changing existing rules rather than creating new ones. You change the way common HTML tags format text throughout your page — or throughout your Web site, if you want to define it that way.

- **Selectors:** The third kind of style, called a selector, relates to specific, preexisting attributes of tags that can be modified with CSS. For example, selector styles are often used to change attributes of the <A> tag and allow you to alter the appearance of links on your page. This kind of style is also referred to as a *pseudoclass* because it's a combination of the two preceding styles.

Creating a new style sheet

To create a new style sheet, open any HTML document or create a new document in Dreamweaver and choose Window⇨CSS Styles to open the CSS Styles panel in the Design panel group. The CSS Styles panel lists all styles associated within your document and also enables you to easily add, edit, and remove existing styles (see Figure 8-2). When you first open this panel, you need to click the plus sign (+) (or triangle on the Mac) that is next to the <STYLE> tag in the CSS Styles panel to see any styles associated with the page. If you don't see a style tag or any styles, no styles are associated with the page.

In the lower-right corner of this panel, you can see four small (really small) icons. From left to right, these icons represent Attach Style Sheet, New CSS Style, Edit Style Sheet, and Delete CSS Style (resembles a trash can). Click the second button (New CSS Style) to create a new style sheet. When you do so, the New CSS Style dialog box opens, as shown in Figure 8-3.

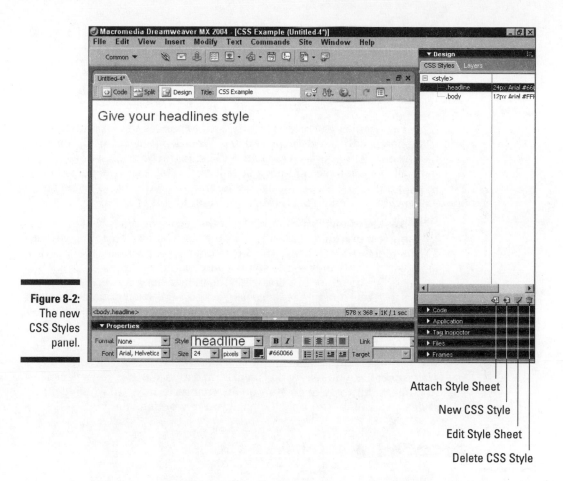

Figure 8-2:
The new
CSS Styles
panel.

Attach Style Sheet

New CSS Style

Edit Style Sheet

Delete CSS Style

You have the following options:

- **Name:** Although the first field in this box is Name, when you first bring it up, its title *changes,* depending on which of the CSS types you select by using the three radio buttons in the Selector Type area, beneath it. Read the description for each of the CSS types in the following three bullets under Selector Type o see how to fill out this field.

- **Selector Type:** These three radio button options allow you to define the type of style you want to create:

   - **Class** enables you to define a new style that you can apply to any section of text on a page by using the Class attribute. When you select this option, you must also fill in the name of the class in the Name field above it. All custom style names must begin with a period, which Dreamweaver automatically inserts as you name the style. If you choose this option, after clicking OK another dialog box appears, in which you define the different rules for the style, which I explain in the section "Creating a new style," later in this chapter.

- **Tag** enables you to create a style that changes the formatting associated with an existing HTML tag. When you select this option, the Name field asks for a tag name. Clicking the Name pull-down menu allows you to select from a huge list of HTML tags (the default one is the <BODY> tag). For more information on this option, see the section, "Redefining HTML tags," later in this chapter.

- **Advanced** enables you to define other types of styles, which usually consist of a kind of pseudoclass that combines a custom style with a redefined HTML tag. The most common of these are the a: styles, which apply only to the <A> tag and enable you to do tasks such as change the color of a link when the mouse hovers over it. When you select this option, the Name field asks for the selector name. Choices in the pop-up list are a:active, a:hover, a:link, and a:visited. Find out more about these options toward the end of this chapter.

✔ **Define In:** This option lets you choose whether your style sheet exists within the current document or in a separate file. When you select a new style sheet file, you're creating an external style sheet. If you select This Document Only, you're creating an internal style sheet, in which defined styles are available for only the page you're working on.

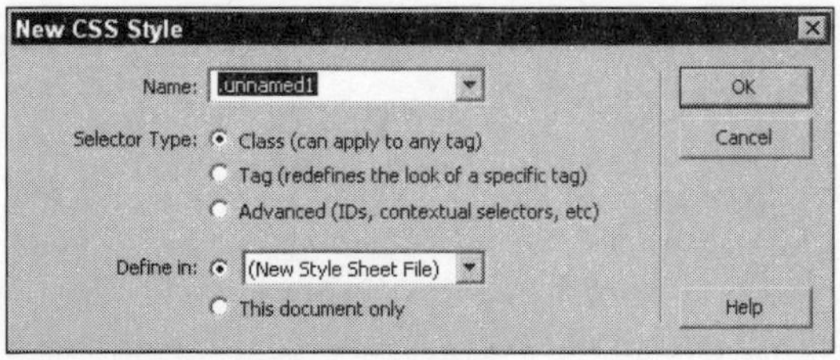

Figure 8-3:
The New
CSS Style
dialog box.

Defining rules

When you choose to make a new style and select one of the three style options in the New CSS Style dialog box, the CSS Style Definition dialog box opens. It's where you decide how you want your style to look by selecting the attribute options, which in CSS are referred to as *rules*. This dialog box includes eight categories, each with multiple options you can use to define various rules to apply as part of your CSS declaration. In this section, I discuss each of these eight categories.

You don't have to make selections for all options in each category. Any options you leave blank remain as the browser's default. For example, if you don't specify a text color, the text is displayed as black or whatever the page's default color is.

Note: Many options in the CSS Style Definition dialog box aren't supported by all current browsers and are included only for future compatibility. Don't be frustrated by options in these categories that Dreamweaver doesn't display. If they aren't displayed in Dreamweaver, they almost certainly don't work in any of the current browsers. The good news is that Macromedia is looking ahead and building these options into Dreamweaver so that they're ready whenever these features are supported. Keep an eye on the Macromedia Web site, at www.macromedia.com, and the Macromedia DHTML information site, at www.dhtmlzone.com, for changes and updates to Dreamweaver, as well as for news about changing standards and support for these CSS features. When in doubt, always preview your work in your target browser to see whether the feature is indeed supported.

The Type category

After you name your style and specify the fields described in the "Using CSS in Dreamweaver" section, earlier in this chapter, click OK and the CSS Style Definition dialog box appears (see Figure 8-4).

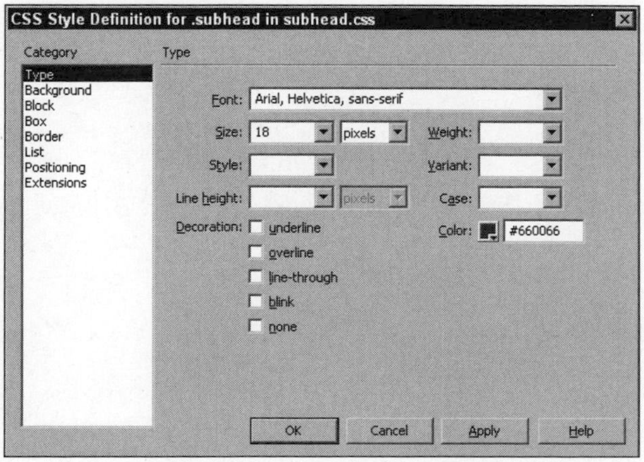

Figure 8-4:
The Type
page in the
CSS Style
Definition
dialog box.

When you choose Type from the Category panel on the left, the Type options are visible, and you have these formatting options:

- **Font:** Specifies a font, font family, or series of families. You can add fonts to the list by choosing Edit Font List from the drop-down list.

- **Size:** Defines the size of the text. You can choose a specific numeric size, and the pop-up menu to the right of this field allows you to choose the unit of measurement.

- **Style:** Enables you to choose whether the text appears as normal, italic, or oblique.

- **Line Height:** Enables you to specify the height of a line on which the text is placed (graphics designers usually call it *leading*).

- **Decoration:** Enables you to specify whether text is underlined, overlined (the line appears over the text rather than under it), or displayed with a strikethrough. You can also choose Blink, which makes the text flash on and off, or None, which removes all decorative effects.

  Use the Decoration options sparingly, if at all. Links are automatically underlined, so if you underline text that isn't a link, you risk confusing viewers. Overlined and strikethrough text can be hard to read. Use these options only if they enhance your design. And, by all means, resist the blink option; it's distracting and can make the screen difficult to read. (Overline and blink weren't displayed in Dreamweaver at the time this book was written.)

- **Weight:** Enables you to control how bold the text is displayed by using a specific or relative boldness option.

- **Variant:** Enables you to select a variation of the font, such as small caps. Unfortunately, this attribute isn't yet supportedby most browsers; for example, if you specify small caps the text simply displays in all caps.

- **Case:** Enables you to globally change the case of selected words, making them all uppercase or lowercase or with initial caps.

- **Color:** Defines the color of the text. You can use the color well (the square icon) to open a Web-safe color palette in which you can select predefined colors or create custom colors.

After you select the Type options for your style sheet, click OK to save the settings.

The Background category

The Background category in the CSS Style Definition dialog box (see Figure 8-5) enables you to specify a background color or image for a style.

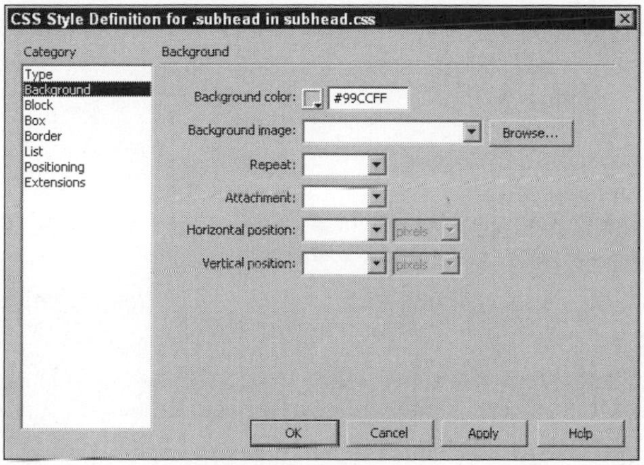

Figure 8-5:
The
Background
page in the
CSS Style
Definition
dialog box.

You can choose from these options:

- **Background Color:** Specifies the background color of an element, such as a table.

- **Background Image:** Enables you to select a background image as part of the style definition. Click the Browse button to select the image.

- **Repeat:** Determines how and whether the background image tiles across and down the page. In all cases, the image is cropped if it doesn't fit behind the element.

  The Repeat options are shown in this list:

  - **No repeat:** The background is displayed once at the beginning of the element.

  - **Repeat:** The background tiles repeat vertically and horizontally behind the element.

  - **Repeat-x:** The background repeats horizontally, but not vertically, behind the element.

  - **Repeat-y:** The background repeats vertically, but not horizontally, behind the element.

- **Attachment:** Controls the alignment and positioning of the background image.

  - **Horizontal Position** aligns the image from left to right.

  - **Vertical Position** aligns the image from top to bottom

The Block category

The Block category (see Figure 8-6) defines spacing and alignment settings for tags and attributes.

You can choose from these options:

- ✔ **Word Spacing:** Can be specified in points, millimeters (mm), centimeters (cm), picas, inches, pixels, ems, and exs.

- ✔ **Letter Spacing:** Can be specified in points, millimeters (mm), centimeters (cm), picas, inches, pixels, ems, and exs.

- ✔ **Vertical Alignment:** Works with only the <IMAGE> tag in Dreamweaver. It specifies the vertical alignment of an image, usually in relation to its parent.

- ✔ **Text Align:** Specifies how text aligns within an element.

- ✔ **Text Indent:** Specifies how far the first line of text is indented.

- ✔ **Whitespace:** Options are Normal, Pre (for preformatted), and Nowrap.

- ✔ **Display:** Indicates how an element should be rendered. An element can be hidden by choosing None.

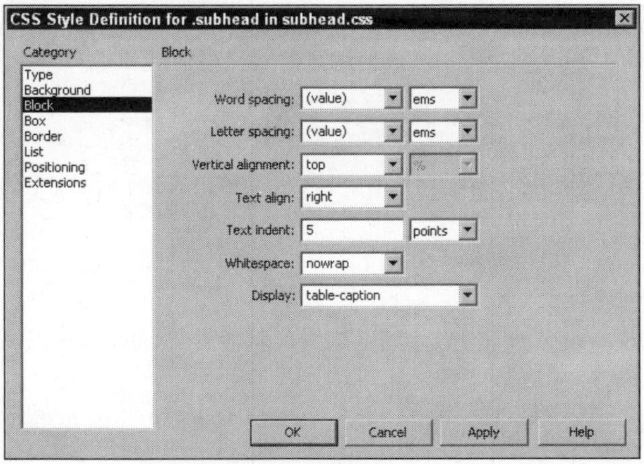

Figure 8-6:
The Block page in the CSS Style Definition dialog box.

The Box category

The Box category (see Figure 8-7) defines settings for tags and attributes that control the placement and appearance of elements on the page.

You can think of all HTML elements (tags such as <A> and <P></P>) as boxes in terms of CSS layout. These boxes are invisible by default because their attributes don't contain any values. By changing their values, you can change the appearance of these boxes. These options are available:

✔ **Width, Height:** Enable you to specify a width and height that you can use in styles you apply to images, layers, or any other element that can have its dimensions specified.

✔ **Float:** Enables you to align an image or other element to the left or right so that other elements, such as text, wrap around it.

✔ **Clear:** Sets the side (left or right) on which layers aren't allowed to be displayed next to the element. The element drops behind the layer if the layer intersects the selected side. (This option doesn't currently display in Dreamweaver.)

✔ **Padding:** Sets the amount of space between the element and its border or margin.

✔ **Margin:** Enables you to define the amount of space between the border of the element and other elements on the page.

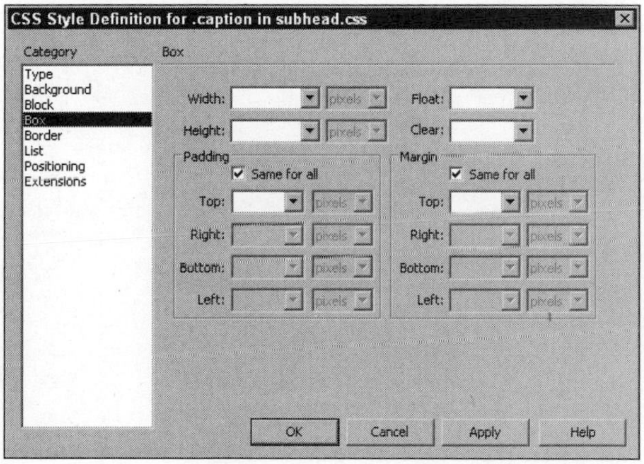

Figure 8-7:
The Box page in the CSS Style Definition dialog box.

For more on using the Box category for layout, see the section, "The Box model," later in this chapter.

The Border category

The Border category defines settings — such as width, color, and style — for the borders of box elements on a page. Your options are Style, Width, and Color (see Figure 8-8).

The List category

The List category defines settings, such as bullet size and type, for list tags. You can specify whether bullets are disc, circle, square, decimal, lower-roman, upper-roman, upper alpha, lower alpha, or none. If you want to use a custom bullet, you can use the Browse button to locate an image to be used as the bullet. You can also specify an inside or outside location to control positioning (see Figure 8-9).

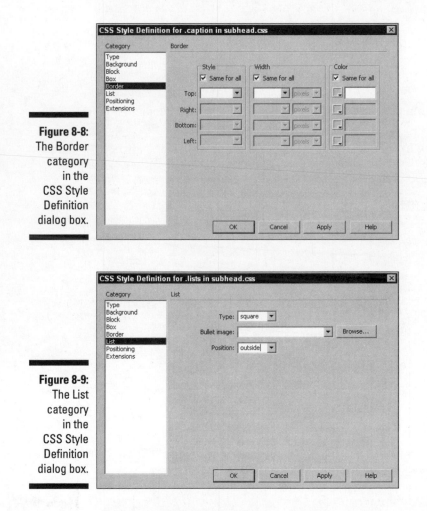

Figure 8-8:
The Border
category
in the
CSS Style
Definition
dialog box.

Figure 8-9:
The List
category
in the
CSS Style
Definition
dialog box.

The Positioning category

The Positioning category (see Figure 8-10) enables you to precisely position elements on a page, much like you can with layers. When this style is applied, it uses the tag specified for defining layers in the Layer preferences. The default in Dreamweaver for layers is the <DIV> tag. You can change it by editing the Layer preferences. The <DIV> tag is the most commonly supported, however, so you should try to stick with it. See Chapter 9 for more on layer preferences.

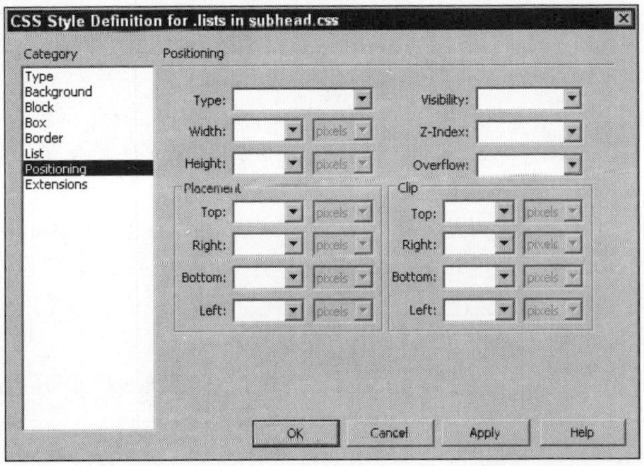

Figure 8-10:
The
Positioning
page in the
CSS Style
Definition
dialog box.

After you define the position as either absolute or relative, the element appears like a layer object in Layout mode, enabling you to position it anywhere on the page by clicking and dragging. The Positioning options are shown in this list:

✔ **Type:** Enables you to specify the position of a layer as absolute, relative, or static:

 • **Absolute:** This positioning uses the top and left coordinates entered in the Placement text boxes on this screen to control the position of the layer relative to the upper-left corner of the Web page.

 • **Relative:** This positioning uses a position relative to the current position of the layer rather than the upper-left corner of the page.

 • **Static:** This positioning keeps the layer in the place where you insert it on the page. With this selection active, the element cannot be moved by clicking and dragging in Layout mode.

✔ **Visibility:** Enables you to control whether the browser displays the layer. You can use this feature, combined with a scripting language, such as JavaScript, to dynamically change the display of layers. Visibility is used to create a number of effects on a page because you can control when something is seen or not seen. For example, you can cause an element to appear on a page only when a user clicks a button, and then make it disappear when they click the button again.

The default on most browsers is to inherit the original layer's visibility value:

 • **Inherit:** The layer has the visibility of its parent.

 • **Visible:** The layer is displayed.

 • **Hidden:** The layer isn't displayed.

✔ **Z-Index:** Controls the position of the layer on the *Z* coordinate, which is how it stacks in relation to other elements on the page. Higher-numbered layers overlap lower-numbered layers.

✔ **Overflow:** Tells the browser how to display the contents of a layer if it exceeds its size. (This option does not currently display in the Dreamweaver Workspace.)

  • **Visible:** Forces the layer to increase in size to display all its contents. The layer expands downward and to the right.

  • **Hidden:** Cuts off the contents of the layer that don't fit and doesn't provide any scroll bars.

  • **Scroll:** Adds scroll bars to the layer regardless of whether the contents exceed the layer's size.

  • **Auto:** Makes scroll bars appear only when the layer's contents exceed its boundaries. (This feature does not currently display in the Dreamweaver Workspace.)

✔ **Placement:** Defines the size and location of a layer, in keeping with the Type setting. The default values are measured in pixels, but you can also use pc (picas), pt (points), in (inches), mm (millimeters), cm (centimeters), or % (percentage of the parent's value).

✔ **Clip:** Enables you to specify which part of the layer is visible by controlling which part of the layer is cropped if it doesn't fit in the display area.

The Extensions category

Extensions (see Figure 8-11) include filters and cursor options.

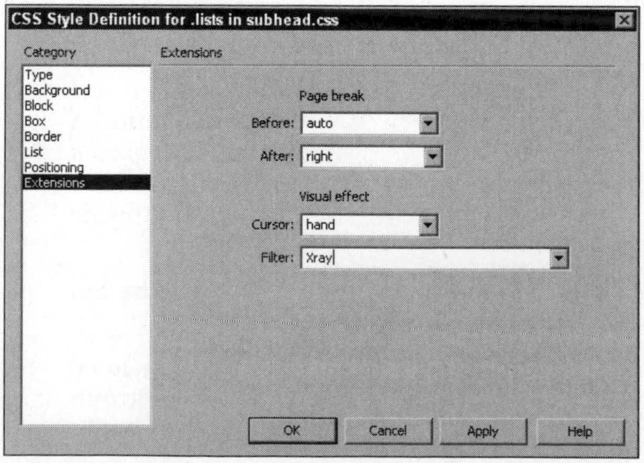

Figure 8-11:
The Extensions page in the CSS Style Definition dialog box.

Most of them are supported in only the latest versions of Internet Explorer:

✔ **Pagebreak:** Inserts a point in a page where a printer sees a page break. This option allows you to control the way the document is printed.

✔ **Cursor:** Defines the type of cursor that appears when a user moves the cursor over an element.

✔ **Filter:** Enables you to apply to elements special effects such as drop shadows, motion blurs, and many others.

Creating a new style

The preceding section describes different ways to define rules for your style sheet. You gain practical experience in this section by using Dreamweaver to create a new style from scratch. In this example, you define a style for headlines using CSS. If you want to create a style for another element, follow these same steps and change the specific attributes as needed.

You can leave attributes unspecified if you don't want to use them. If you don't specify them, the browser uses its own default. For example, if you don't specify a font, the browser uses the font specified in the page's HTML definition.

To define a new style, open a new or existing HTML document and follow these steps:

1. **Choose Text⇨CSS Styles⇨New.**

   The New CSS Style dialog box appears. The new style is automatically named `.unnamed1`.

2. **In the Name text box, type a new name for the style.**

   Dreamweaver gives you a default name that begins with a period (.) because class names must *always* begin with a period. You can name the style anything you want as long as you don't use spaces or punctuation. Dreamweaver adds the initial period to the class name if you omit it. Because you're creating a headline style, naming this new style *.headline* makes sense.

3. **In the Selector Type category, make sure that the button next to Class is selected.**

4. **In the Define In area, select This Document Only to create an internal style sheet (one that affects only the page, not a group of HTML pages — you can find more details later in this chapter).**

5. **Click OK.**

   The CSS Style Definition dialog box opens.

6. **For the Font choice, select a font set from the drop-down list or enter the name of a font in the Font field.**

   To use fonts that aren't in the pop-up list, choose the Edit Font List option from the drop-down list to create new font options.

   You generally should use a font set that specifies three or more fonts rather than just specify a single font in the font choices. The reason is that viewers need to have installed on their system the font you specify in order to correctly view it. If they don't have the font, their browser searches for the next font you have specified in your font set, or if none has been specified, the browser's default font is used for displaying the text. By specifying multiple fonts, though, you maintain at least some control and predictability over how the text appears.

7. **From the Size drop-down list, choose the size you want for your headline.**

   Large headlines may appear at 24 or 36 points. Notice that you can also specify sizes in pixels, picas, mm, and several other measurements.

   Using precise CSS measurement units, such as pixels and points, for text is much more consistent across computer platforms than using HTML sizes, such as 1, 2, and 3, for example. Still, because of the different screen resolutions between Macs and PCs, you don't achieve perfect size consistency between the two platforms, although you get much closer than by using HTML size formatting. Always check your designs on multiple platforms and multiple browsers if exact text formatting and appearance are critical. (See Chapter 9 for more on the Dreamweaver features for checking browser compatibility.)

8. **From the Style drop-down list, choose a font style.**

   Either italic or oblique is good for making text stand out on a page.

9. **From the Weight drop-down list, choose Bold to make your headline thicker and darker.**

10. **Ignore Variant and Case because these attributes aren't well supported by current browsers.**

11. **Click the Color well and choose a color for the headline.**

    Sticking to the default color swatches in the color well is your best strategy because it ensures that you use a Web-safe color. You can also create a custom colors by clicking the icon that looks like a rainbow-colored globe in the upper-right corner of the color well and selecting a color from the color picker.

12. **Click OK when you're finished.**

    Notice in Figure 8-12 that your new headline style is added to the list of styles in the CSS Styles panel. If the style doesn't appear, click the plus sign (+) (or triangle on the Mac) next to the <STYLE> tag to reveal the rules in the current style.

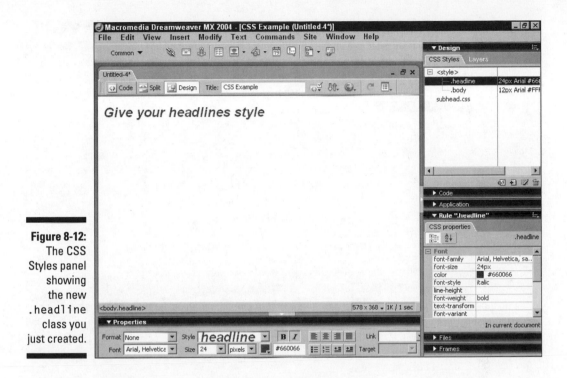

Figure 8-12:
The CSS
Styles panel
showing
the new
.headline
class you
just created.

After you create a Style Sheet and add rules to it, you can apply the styles to any Web page or selected text block using several different methods. See the next section for details.

Applying styles in Dreamweaver

Defining custom styles in Dreamweaver is the time-consuming part. Applying them after you have defined them is the timesaving part. Applying them is easy: You simply select the text you want to affect and choose the predefined style you want to apply to it.

To apply a style in Dreamweaver, follow these steps:

1. **Highlight the text in an open document for which you want to apply a style.**

2. **In the Properties inspector, click the Style pop-up menu to reveal the list of styles associated with the document and select the one you want.**

   Notice that Dreamweaver allows you to preview the style when you select it with this method, as shown in Figure 8-13. After you choose a style, the selected text changes in the Document window (see Figure 8-14).

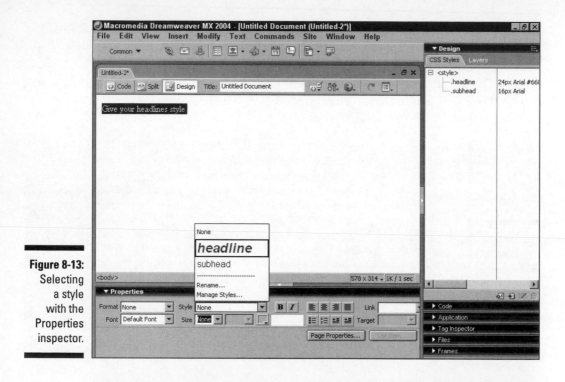

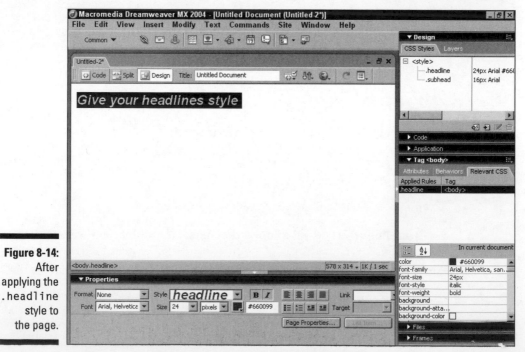

Another way to apply a style to a highlighted text selection is by choosing the name of the style from the menu you see when you choose Text⇨CSS Styles or right-click (Control+click on the Mac) the selected text and then choose the style from the resulting pop-up menu. Dreamweaver gives you several different ways of applying styles. The one you choose depends on your own personal preferences. I like to use the Properties inspector because it's the only method that allows you to preview the way the style appears before applying it.

At the code level when you apply a style, Dreamweaver generally adds a class attribute to the tag surrounding the text to which you apply the style. This class attribute is tied to the style you defined and causes the selected text to inherit the properties of the style. For example, if you have a section of text that looks like this in Code view before attaching a style:

```
<P>This is my headline</p>
```

Dreamweaver adds a class attribute to the <P> tag, which associates it to the .headline class. The resulting code would look like this:

```
<P class="headline">This is my headline</P>
```

In cases where no tags enclose the text, Dreamweaver adds the <SPAN> tag, which acts as a container for the style. A selection of text that starts out like this in Code view:

```
This is my headline
```

would end up like this after the style is applied:

```
<SPAN class="headline">This is my headline</SPAN>
```

Removing styles in Dreamweaver

To remove a style from a selected text block, choose the None option from the Style pop-up menu in the Properties inspector or by choosing Text⇨CSS Styles, as shown in Figure 8-15. It's really that simple.

Redefining HTML tags

When you create a custom style, as I explain in the preceding section, you start a completely new style with its own, unique name, containing various rules that you define by using the CSS Style Definitions options covered in the "Creating a new style sheet" section, earlier in this chapter. When you redefine an HTML tag, however, you begin with an existing HTML tag — such as <B> (bold), <HR> (horizontal rule), or <TABLE> (table) — and change the attributes associated with this specific tag. In this case, you don't need to apply the style like you did previously because *all* content that falls inside the tag you redefine automatically takes on the attributes you define for it. This distinction between creating a new class and redefining an existing tag is an important one.

You may ask "Why would I need such a feature?" or "What's the best scenario in which to use it?" In the preceding section, you find out how to create a new style class that you can *selectively* apply to any block of text on your page. In the case of redefined HTML tags, the new attributes apply to *all* instances of that tag. This feature can be quite powerful if used correctly, but it does require a little knowledge about HTML tags and how they work.

For example, every HTML page has a <BODY> tag. If you know that you want all the text on your page to appear in a specific font, you can redefine the <BODY> tag to inherit a specific font, and that would save you the time of having to apply a class to all body text. Because of the cascading nature of style sheets, you can still apply class styles to individual selections of text falling within the body tag that can further modify or even override the attributes initially defined for this tag.

Figure 8-15:
Removing
a style in
Dream-
weaver.

To redefine an HTML tag, follow these steps:

1. **Create a new CSS Style.**

   You have several ways to call up the New CSS Style dialog box. This time, try clicking the New CSS Style button in the CSS Styles panel to call it up.

2. **In the Selector Type category in the New CSS Style dialog box, click the Tag button.**

   Notice that when you select the Tag option, the name of the Name text box at the top of the window changes to Tag.

3. **Click the Tag pop-up menu to reveal a comprehensive list of HTML tags and choose the tag you want from this list (see Figure 8-16).**

   Select the This Document Only option in the Define In field to create an internal style sheet. If you're unsure of the meaning of any of these HTML tags, consult the Reference panel, available by choosing Window⇨ Reference.

4. **Click the OK button, and then use the CSS style definition categories to define the new tag style.**

   Be aware that when you redefine an existing HTML tag, any text you have already formatted with that tag changes to reflect the new definition.

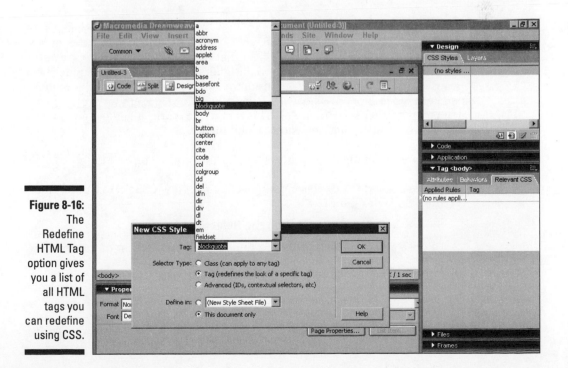

Figure 8-16: The Redefine HTML Tag option gives you a list of all HTML tags you can redefine using CSS.

A good use of the Redefine HTML tag feature is to create style definitions for HTML header tags, such as H1, H2, and H3. This way, you can exercise greater control over the appearance of these headers and easily apply them by choosing the Text⇨Paragraph Format command. Using header tags also has an added benefit because search engines often give higher priority to keywords that appear in the H1 to H6 header tags.

Working with CSS Selectors

The third type of style you explore is the CSS Selector. Dreamweaver refers to it as an *advanced selector,* and it's also referred to as a *pseudoclass.* This style is kind of a combination of the two other styles you may have read about. The CSS Selector allows you to affect various predefined attributes of a given HTML element. The most common use of this type of style is in conjunction with the ⟨A⟩ anchor tag: You can use it to change the appearance of links on your page. The ⟨A⟩ tag already has certain attributes associated with it — such as link, visited, active, and hover — that affect the appearance of hypertext links in the document. Using a CSS Selector style allows you to access these attributes and change their qualities. For example, you can remove underlines from links and create mouseover effects using Selector styles, as you can see in the next two sections.

Eliminating underlines from links

One of the most commonly used CSS techniques involves disabling the underline attribute of the anchor tag, ⟨A⟩, so that hypertext links are no longer underlined in the browser. Many Web designers like to remove the underline because they think that it detracts from the design and they consider underlined links old-fashioned. Instead, they use other, more modern ways of displaying links using CSS Selector styles. This technique works in almost all modern Web browsers, including Netscape 4.0 and higher.

To disable underlining for hypertext links, follow these steps:

1. **Choose Text⇨CSS Styles⇨New (or click the New CSS Style button in the CSS Styles panel).**

2. **Select the Advanced option in the Selector Type area.**

3. **Choose a:link from the Selector pop-up menu at the top of the window.**

4. **In the Define In area, select This Document Only.**

5. **Click OK.**

   The CSS Style Definition dialog box opens.

6. **Make sure that the Type category is selected; then, check the None option in the Decoration area, as shown in Figure 8-17.**

7. **Click OK to apply the changes.**

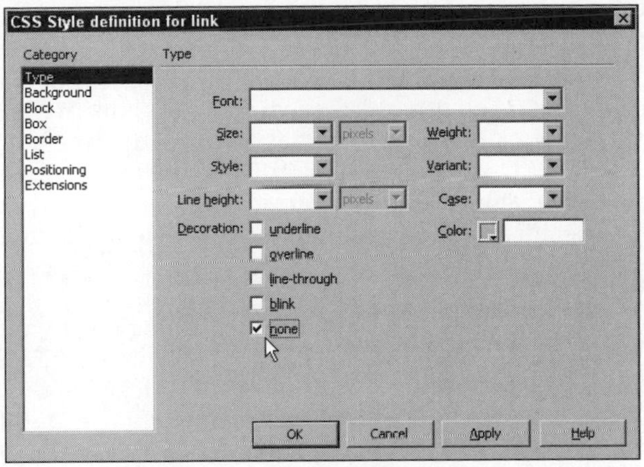

CSS Style definition for link

Category	Type

Category:
Type
Background
Block
Box
Border
List
Positioning
Extensions

Font: [▾]

Size: [▾] [pixels ▾]   Weight: [▾]

Style: [▾]   Variant: [▾]

Line height: [▾] [pixels ▾]   Case: [▾]

Decoration: ☐ underline   Color: [☐] [   ]
☐ overline
☐ line-through
☐ blink
☑ none

[OK] [Cancel] [Apply] [Help]

Figure 8-17:
Using CSS
to disable
the under-
lining of
hypertext
links.

After you click OK, active links are no longer underlined on the page when they're displayed in a browser (as long as it's 4.0 or higher). Try creating a link on the page in Design mode, and you see that the link is no longer underlined. The link takes on the default blue color for hyperlinks, however, so that you know that it's still a link. If you want to change the blue color, you can use the CSS style definitions to change the color for the a:link selector.

Adding a little interactivity

To make your links interactive, you can further modify the <A> tag by adding an effect that underlines the link only when viewers hover the mouse over it. That way, they instantly receive feedback that the link is indeed a hyperlink.

To display an underline when users mouseover a link:

1. **Choose Text⇨CSS Styles⇨New (or click the New CSS Style button in the CSS Styles panel).**

2. **Select the Advanced option in the Selector Type area.**

3. **Choose a:hover from the Selector pop-up menu at the top of the window.**

4. **In the Define In area, select This Document Only.**

5. **Click OK.**

6. **Make sure that the Type category is selected and check the Underline option in the Decoration section.**

7. **Click OK to apply the changes and then save your document.**

To preview the effects of the style changes you just made, you need to view the page in a Web browser because some interactive effects don't show up in Dreamweaver Design view. Take a look at how your links now appear and how they interact with the user. This cool effect was much simpler to create than by using a rollover behavior. Try experimenting with different style sheet rules on the different anchor selectors to achieve different results. You can also make the link, when it's moused over, turn bold rather than underlined, or change color, and you can apply any other CSS effect you can think of to enhance the appearance of your links. You can also modify a:visited to change the attributes of visited links and a:active to change the attributes of links while they're being clicked. Remember that any styles you create in this way affect *all* links on your page unless you specifically apply a different class style to the individual link that overrides the selector style.

In Dreamweaver, you can use the Page Properties dialog box to automatically generate the correct CSS code for <A> selectors (see Figure 8-18). You don't gain as much control over your link appearance, but for quickly modifying link behavior via CSS, this shortcut is a good one. Simply choose Modify⇨Page Properties and make your changes in the Links category.

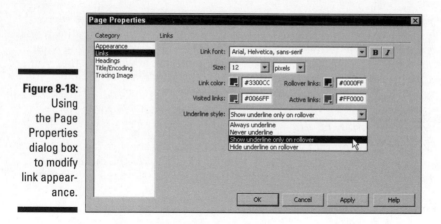

Figure 8-18:
Using
the Page
Properties
dialog box
to modify
link appear-
ance.

Conflicting styles

Be careful when you apply more than one style to the same text (something that's easier to do than you may realize). This advice holds true for CSS styles as well as styling attributes applied via HTML, such as font-styling properties. The styles may conflict, and because browsers aren't all consistent in the way in which they display styles, the results can be inconsistent and unexpected.

For the most part, Netscape and Internet Explorer display all attributes applied to an element, even if they're from different styles, as long as the styles don't conflict. If they do conflict, browsers prioritize styles depending on how the styles have been defined and the order in which they appear. The method for determining this priority is what cascading is all about

Here's an example to help you get the idea. You define a custom style named `.headline` with red text that's not bolded, and you apply it to a block of text on the page. Then you decide that you want that text to be bold, so you apply the bold tag independently by selecting it from the Properties inspector. You have now used two different types of styles. Because they don't conflict, all of them take effect and your text becomes bold and red. If, however, you apply another color to the same block of text — blue, for example — using the Properties inspector, you have a conflict.

Understanding how browsers handle these conflicts is important. The basic guideline is that CSS rules get the highest priority, followed by HTML presentation attributes (for example, align, color, face, and bgcolor), followed by the browser default settings (font type and font size, for example). CSS rules always get the highest priority in any scenario, and internal style sheets get priority over external style sheets.

When two CSS styles conflict, priority is determined through *order of cascade*. Although this concept can get complex, one guideline to follow is that the style that was listed most recently usually has priority. You generally should avoid creating styles that conflict. Either go back and redefine an existing style, apply regular HTML tags individually, or create a new style. Remember that you can use the Duplicate option from the Edit Style Sheet dialog box to create a new duplicate style and then make minor alterations. (For more on the Edit Style Sheet dialog box, see the following section.)

In cases where you do end up with conflicting styles, the best practice is to view your page in a Web browser to see how the style looks to the user. Although Dreamweaver MX 2004 has greatly improved its rendering of CSS, Dreamweaver still doesn't always replicate the browser display perfectly.

Editing an Existing Style

You can change the attributes of any style after you have created it by editing its style definitions. This capability is a major advantage of Cascading Style Sheets: You can make global changes to a page or even to an entire Web site by changing a style you applied to multiple elements through the use of an external style sheet. Be aware, however, that everything you defined with that style changes when you do.

Remember that you can also create new styles by duplicating an existing style and then altering it. Then, you can apply that new style without affecting elements that are already formatted on your pages with the original version of the style.

To edit an existing style, follow these steps:

1. **Click the Edit Style Sheet button in the Properties inspector.**

   This step brings up the <style> dialog box, as shown in Figure 8-19.

Alternatively, on the PC you can select the style name in the CSS Styles panel, right-click and select Edit. On the Mac, choose Text➪ CSS Styles➪Edit.

2. **Select from the list of styles the style you want to change and click the Edit button.**

   The CSS Style Definition dialog box for that style appears.

3. **Choose from the Category panel a category you want to change, such as Type or Background; then specify the style changes you want to make.**

   You can find descriptions of all style options in the section, "Creating a new style sheet" section earlier in this chapter.

4. **When you have made all the changes you want, click OK.**

   The style is automatically redefined to reflect your changes. At the same time, all elements you defined with that style automatically change.

Duplicating a style with a new name and deleting the old one is a quick way to disable an unwanted style without losing the code. This way, you don't have to re-create it if you ever want it back.

The Undo feature doesn't work with the Remove option from the <style> dialog box. If you delete a style by mistake, close the dialog box by clicking Done and then choose Edit➪Undo Remove CSS Style from the main menu before doing anything else.

Another way to edit an existing style sheet is to select the style in the CSS Styles panel and click the Edit Style button in the lower-right area of the panel (the third icon from the left). This action also brings up the CSS Style Definition dialog box, where you can change the properties of the style as needed.

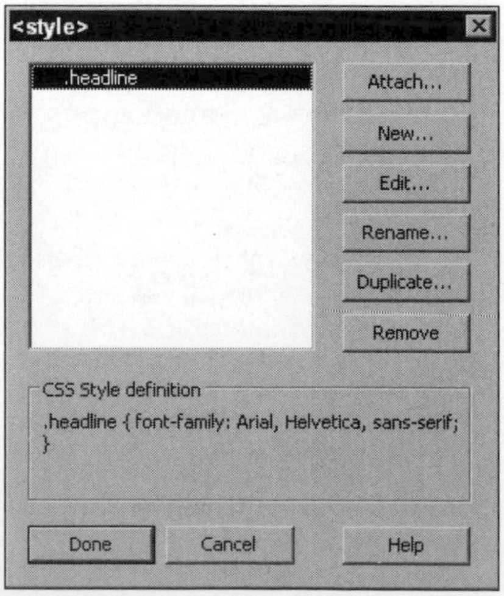

Figure 8-19:
The <style>
dialog box.

A new feature in Dreamweaver MX 2004 is the CSS Properties panel (see Figure 8-20), also referred to as the CSS Rule Inspector. Whenever you select a style in the CSS Styles panel, its properties are also displayed in the CSS Properties panel, where you can edit each attribute directly. The panel is divided into two columns: The first lists the style property; the second, its value. Click inside the value column and directly edit any property. Using the CSS Styles panel offers a quick way to alter style sheet rules without having to maneuver through several dialog boxes.

Notice that the CSS Styles panel organizes by default the CSS properties by category (Font, Background, and Block, for example). Clicking the Show List View button in the upper-left area of the panel changes the panel to display all properties alphabetically by name.

Using External Style Sheets

The first part of this chapter focuses on using CSS only in the context of internal style sheets. Internal style sheet information is stored in the HTML code of the document you're working on and applies to only the current document. If you want to create styles you can share among documents, you need to use external style sheets. External style sheets enable you to create styles you can apply to pages throughout a Web site by storing the style sheet information on a separate text page that can be linked to from any HTML document.

External style sheets (also called *linked style sheets*) are where you can realize the greatest timesavings with CSS. You can define styles for common formatting options used throughout an entire site, such as headlines, captions, and even images, which makes applying multiple formatting options to elements fast and easy. Big news- and magazine-type Web sites often use external style sheets because they need to follow a consistent look and feel throughout the site, even when many people are working on the same site. Using external style sheets also makes global changes easier because when you change the external style sheet, you globally change every element to which you applied the style throughout the site.

Creating an external style sheet

You create external style sheets almost exactly the same way you create internal style sheets, except that external style sheets need to be saved as separate text files. When you use Dreamweaver to create an external style sheet, Dreamweaver automatically links the style sheet to the page you're working on. You can then link it to any other Web page in which you want to apply the style definitions.

Figure 8-20:
You can edit rules for any style directly in the CSS Properties panel.

To create an external style sheet, follow these steps:

1. **Choose Text➪CSS Styles➪New.**

   The New CSS Style dialog box appears.

2. **Select from the Selector Type category the type of style you want to create.**

   Remember that you have three options: Class, Tag, or Advanced.

3. **In the Define In area, select New Style Sheet File.**

4. **Click OK.**

   This step brings up the Save Style Sheet File As dialog box.

5. **Select a location in which to save the Style Sheet file and click Save. Be sure to use a** `.css` **extension to identify your file as a style sheet.**

Your style sheet is now saved as an external file. The next step is to link to it from the page where you want to apply the styles.

Linking to an external style sheet

To link an existing external style sheet to the current document, follow these steps:

1. **Choose Window⇨CSS Styles.**

   The CSS Styles panel appears.

2. **Click the Attach Style Sheet icon in the CSS Styles panel (the first button in the lower-right area).**

   The Select Style Sheet dialog box appears, prompting you to select the location of the external style sheet. You can either type the URL if it's a remote file on the Web — for example, type this line: **http://www.my company.com/mystyle.css**, or use the Browse button to locate a file inside your site folder.

   Notice that two options are available for linking to an external style sheet: Link and Import. Both options achieve the same effect, but the Link method is better supported by older browsers, such as Netscape 4. This method is also the default that Dreamweaver uses.

3. **After you select the external filename, click the OK button.**

   The dialog box disappears, and the external CSS file is automatically linked to your page. Any styles you have defined in the external style sheet now appear in the CSS Styles panel, and any redefined HTML styles or CSS Selectors are automatically applied to the page. Because you have established a link on this page to the external style sheet, the styles in the external style sheet always appear in the CSS Styles panel whenever you open this file (see Figure 8-21).

4. **To apply a style on your page, select the text to which you want to apply the style and apply the style in the same way you would with an internal style sheet (see the section "Applying styles in Dreamweaver," earlier in this chapter).**

Editing an external style sheet

You edit linked external style sheets exactly the same way as you edit internal style sheets using the CSS Styles panel, which lists all styles in the document, whether they're internal or external. You can use either the Style Sheet definition categories or the CSS Properties panel to directly edit the rules for each style. With either method, any changes you make to the external style sheet

are automatically made in the external file, even though it's a separate document (as long as the style sheet exists locally on the computer). If you try to
edit a remote CSS file from a linked page in Dreamweaver, you can't because
Dreamweaver doesn't have edit privileges for the file.

If you need to edit a remote CSS file, you have to copy the remote file to your
local computer and open it in Dreamweaver. In Dreamweaver, you can open
.css files by either double-clicking them or choosing File⇨Open, both of which
open the style sheet in Code view. Code view is the only view available for CSS
files because they're text files and have no layout components. When you
view an external style sheet this way, you can still use the CSS Panel and CSS
Properties panel to edit the style sheet, even if the style sheet isn't linked to
any HTML page. Of course, if you prefer, you can also edit the code by hand
directly in Code view. Figure 8-22 shows an example of a style sheet opened
directly in Dreamweaver. Notice that the CSS Styles panel and CSS Properties
panel display all relevant style information and give you access to the visual
CSS editing tools.

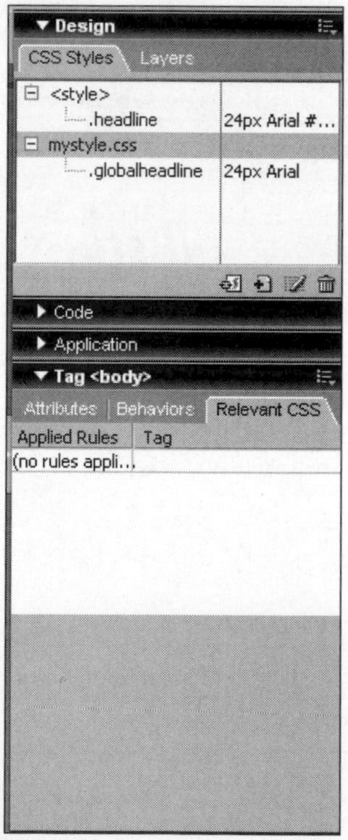

Figure 8-21:
External
style sheets
linked to
the current
document
appear in
the CSS
Styles panel.

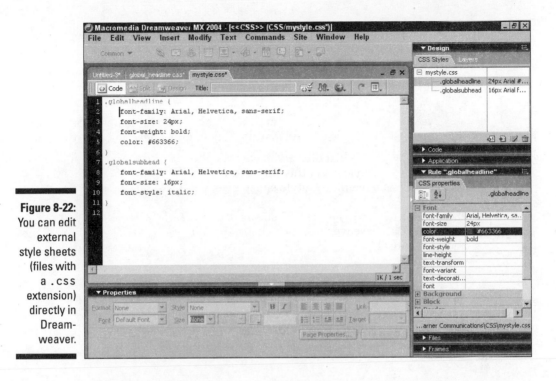

Figure 8-22:
You can edit
external
style sheets
(files with
a .css
extension)
directly in
Dream-
weaver.

Applying ready-made external style sheets

Macromedia includes a bunch of sample style sheets for you to use as part of the default Dreamweaver installation. These come in the form of external styles sheets that have been created with some popular styles in mind to help you get better acquainted with working with style sheets and give you a jump-start in designing with them. You can either use these styles as is or modify them to suit your needs.

To access the sample style sheets provided by Macromedia, follow these steps:

1. **Choose File⇨New.**

   This step brings up the New Document dialog box (see Figure 8-23).

2. **Click the CSS Style Sheets category on the left to display the list of CSS files, and try clicking any of the sample styles that are listed.**

   Notice that you can preview how the style appears when you click any of the sample styles.

3. **Select a style you like and click Create.**

   This step opens a new, untitled style sheet in Code view.

4. **To save the style sheet, choose File⟹Save (or Save As) and save it in the site directory where you plan to use it.**

   You can also modify the rules before saving the file if you want to customize your style sheet in which case you should choose Save As, because you leave the original style sheet unchanged in case you want to use it again.

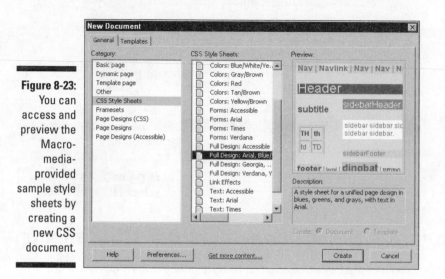

Figure 8-23:
You can access and preview the Macro-media-provided sample style sheets by creating a new CSS document.

Using Design Time Style Sheets

After you become savvy in using style sheets, you find that working with external style sheets affords the most power because you can link to them from multiple pages in your site. Rather than have to create a new internal style sheet for each page in your site, you're far more sensible to have a single external file you can easily alter when needed. Even better, you can also create multiple external style sheets as part of the design process and use a Dreamweaver feature named Design Time Style Sheets to switch back and forth between them as you work on your document.

One benefit of the Design Time Style Sheets feature is that you can view how different external style sheets affect your page without having to link to them. This feature is a great way to quickly switch back and forth between style sheets in a document and explore various what-if scenarios with the style sheets you create. You may begin to like this feature because you can play around with and explore the full power of CSS.

After you decide that you like a particular style sheet, you can apply it to your page as you do any other style sheet. (See the section, "Applying Styles in Dreamweaver," earlier in this chapter for how to apply a style.)

Design Time Style Sheets affect only the appearance of styles in Dreamweaver. Because they're not real links, they show up only at runtime when a Dreamweaver document is open. Design Time Style Sheet info is also stored in a Design Note file. If you want to preserve your Design Time Style Sheet info, be sure that you don't delete the corresponding Design Note file.

To set up Design Time Style sheets, follow these steps:

1. **Choose Text⇨CSS Styles⇨Design-Time.**

   The Design Time Style Sheets dialog box appears (see Figure 8-24).

2. **To work with a specific style sheet, click the Add Item (+) button above the Show Only at Design Time field.**

   The Select File dialog box appears, and you can select a CSS file. Remember that CSS files usually end with a .css extension. You can also add multiple CSS files by clicking the Add button again to add a new CSS file.

3. **To hide a specific style sheet, click the Add Item (+) button above the Hide at Design Time field and select from the Select File dialog box the style to hide.**

4. **To delete a listed style sheet from either category, select the style sheet and click the Remove Item (-) button to delete it.**

Figure 8-24: Design Time Style Sheets let you view or hide multiple style sheets at runtime.

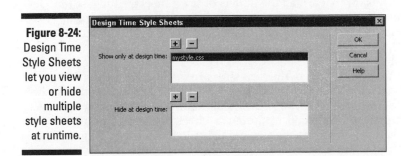

Using CSS with Templates

Templates, as described in Chapter 4, are ideally suited for use with CSS because they're geared toward a collaborative work environment. With

Dreamweaver, you can use both internal and external styles sheets in a template. In fact, using external style sheets makes a great deal of sense when using templates because the formatting of the page is separated from its content. To save a page with CSS info as a style sheet, just choose File⇨Save As Template. Any template you create that contains internal styles or links to external styles are automatically updated whenever its style sheet changes.

With templates, both the link code at the head of the page and any internal styles are locked regions by default. Users are then prevented from editing the style sheet definitions, and they have an ideal way to manage the look and feel of a site via formatting specifications that cannot be modified from a document that uses a template.

Using CSS for Page Layout

Besides using CSS to format text, you can control visual formatting and lay out pages using the positioning features of CSS. This advanced CSS application is becoming a more popular alternative to using tables to lay out pages. Many strong advocates of CSS are recommending that designers even abandon table layouts in favor of CSS. Although I don't argue with them — because it's definitely the wave of the future for Web design — I do still recommend some caution if you are designing for the broadest possible audience. If you venture into this route, be sure to read Chapter 9, too, because layers and CSS are often used in combination.

This chapter gives you the introduction you need to use style sheets effectively, but if you really want to learn all the details of style sheets, I suggest that you explore some other, more complete resources on CSS, such as *Cascading Style Sheets For Dummies,* by Damon Dean (published by Wiley Publishing, Inc.).

Take a look at examples of CSS-designed Web pages as you begin to explore the world of CSS for layout. Two of the best sites are maintained by the CSS gurus Eric Meyer (www.meyerweb.com/eric/css/edge) and Jeffrey Zeldman (www.zeldman.com). You find on these sites lots of examples of CSS-designed pages and general tips about using CSS. In particular, check out Zeldman's use of type, color, and link rollover effects. He's one of the true pioneers of using CSS for page layout.

To use CSS for page layout, explore the Box, Border, and Positioning categories in the CSS Style Definition dialog box, as I describe in the "Using CSS in Dreamweaver" section, earlier in this chapter. These categories allow you to move and modify page elements in the same way that layers can be moved and modified on the page.

The Box model

The key to understanding the way CSS works with page layout is to think in terms of the Box model. The *Box model* asserts that any element tag in an HTML document is handled by CSS as a container box. When you define a CSS style and apply it to your page, you're creating a box on the page, not too unlike a cell in a table. This box acts as a container for your content and has attributes such as margin, border, and padding, for example. Because all these attributes are set to zero by default, you can't see them when you first create a CSS style.

Layers are CSS boxes that have had positioning attributes applied to them (you can find more about this topic in Chapter 9). The basic component of a CSS "layer" is the <DIV> tag, which stands for *div*ision. <DIV> tags are used as containers to hold other content — in other words, to make a division on the page. Any content on a page that is surrounded by an opening and closing <DIV> tag becomes an object (also referred to as a box or layer) with properties such as border, margin, and size, for example, that you can manipulate using CSS. Because all these properties are set to zero by default, you don't see a box around content that has been surrounded with a <DIV> tag until you change these properties in your CSS declarations.

If you have been following along closely in this chapter, you may have noticed that both <DIV> and <SPAN> tags can be used to apply style sheets. In both cases, an attribute is added to the tag that references the style in question (for example, <span class="mystyle"> and <div class="mystyle">) and causes the contents of the tag to inherit the style's properties. So, what's the difference between <SPAN> and <DIV>? For one thing, <SPAN> is considered an *inline* element and <DIV> is considered a *block* element.

Inline elements flow with the text and don't contain begin and end lines. For example, the <B> and <IMG> tags are inline elements. You can place these elements one after the other, and a new line break doesn't appear between each element. They simply flow with the text.

In contrast, the <DIV> tag is a block element used to identify a distinct block of content. A new line is created after the beginning and ending of each <DIV> tag, in much the same way as a new line is created before and after a <P> tag, which is also a block element.

As you also see in this section, <DIV> tags are used to create layers. The <SPAN> tag doesn't create a layer and is used only to apply a style to a specific region of text. Whenever you utilize layers or any of the CSS positioning capabilities, you're utilizing the <DIV> tag.

The <DIV> tag

In the steps in this section, you find out how to create a style for an element such as a sidebar and then apply the style to create a stand-alone sidebar. You work with the <DIV> tag to create the layer and find how to make it a fully draggable object that you can easily position anywhere on the page. After you begin to master this technique, you're well on your way to designing page layouts with layers.

To insert a <DIV> element with style information, follow these steps:

1. **Create a new class style by choose Text⇨CSS Styles⇨New and name the style** .sidebar.

2. **Save the style as an internal style sheet in the current document (you can also save the style sheet externally, if you prefer).**

3. **In the CSS Style definitions for your sidebar style, set the text size to 12 pixels and the font to Arial, Helvetica, Sans Serif. Click OK.**

4. **Place your cursor anywhere on the page in Design view and choose Insert⇨Layout Objects⇨Div Tag.**

   The Insert Div Tag dialog box appears (see Figure 8-25).

5. **In the Class pop-up menu that appears, choose the sidebar style you just created and click OK.**

   Dreamweaver inserts filler text as a placeholder for your content. Notice that the filler text reflects the styling attributes of the sidebar style you created earlier.

6. **Change the placeholder text as necessary by typing the content you want to use.**

   For this exercise, you can just type **This is text for my sidebar**.

   At this point, you should see your styled text positioned on the page where you first inserted the <DIV> tag (see Figure 8-26). Notice that when you mouseover the block of text, a red outline appears around it. Dreamweaver makes working with <DIV> tags easy in Design mode through visual cues like these.

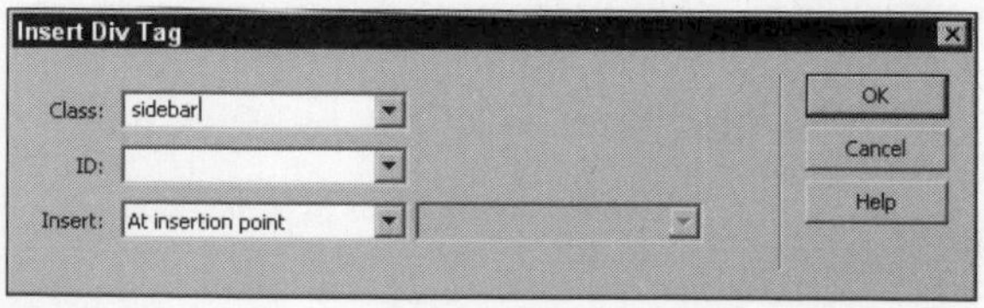

Figure 8-25:
The Insert
Div Tag
dialog box.

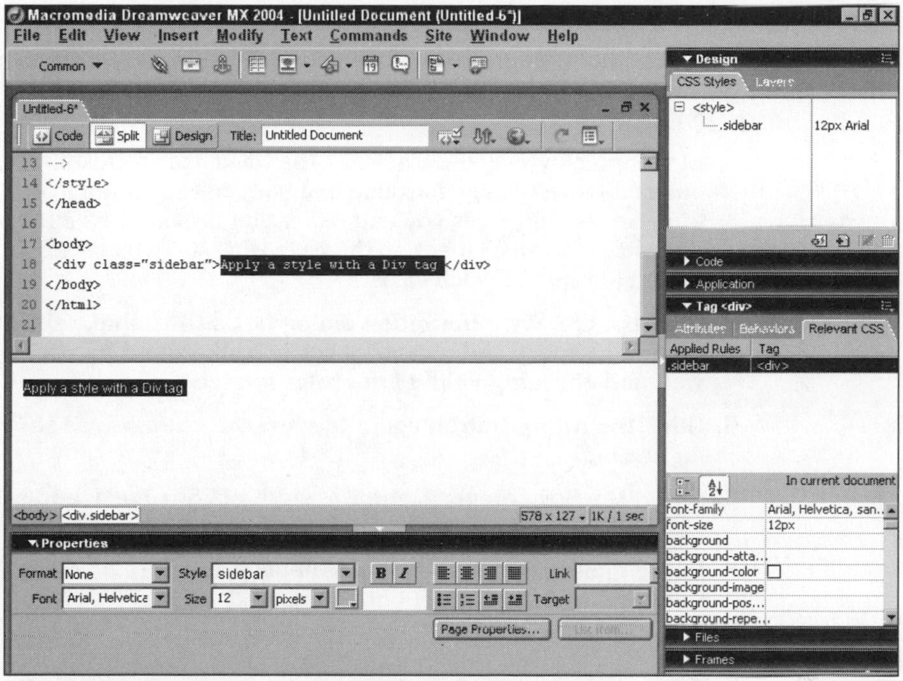

Figure 8-26:
A `<DIV>`
tag inserted
with styled
text.

In the following steps, you see how to make the `<DIV>` block visible as a layer and format it as a usable sidebar element that can be positioned anywhere on your page by simply dragging it around in the document.

To make the layer visible and modify its visible box properties, follow these steps:

1. **Select the sidebar style in the CSS Styles panel, right-click and select Edit. (On the Mac, click the Edit Style button.)**

   The CSS Style Definition dialog box appears.

2. **Select the Positioning category, and in the Type field choose Absolute from the pull-down menu.**

   Setting the type to either Absolute or Relative gives the layer visible handles in Design view.

3. **In the Placement section, enter** 100 px **in the Top field and** 100 px **in the Left field.**

   This step creates a layer positioned 100 pixels from the top and left edges of the page.

4. **Click the Apply button.**

   Notice that the selected text on your page (when viewed in Design mode) now appears as a layer with handles that allow you to drag it anywhere on the page.

   At this point, you could also click the OK button to dismiss the dialog box and move the layer around manually to reposition it. If you do this, the positioning values you entered earlier are updated automatically. Repositioning an element on the page where you can see it in relation to other elements is much easier!

5. **With the CSS Style Definition dialog box still visible, select the Background category and pick a light gray background by clicking the color well and choosing a light gray color swatch.**

6. **Click the Apply button again to view the changes, as shown in Figure 8-27.**

7. **Select the Box category, enter a width of** 250 **pixels, and set the Height to** Auto. **Click the Apply button again.**

8. **In the Padding area of the Box category, enter** 10 **pixels in the Top field and click the Apply button again.**

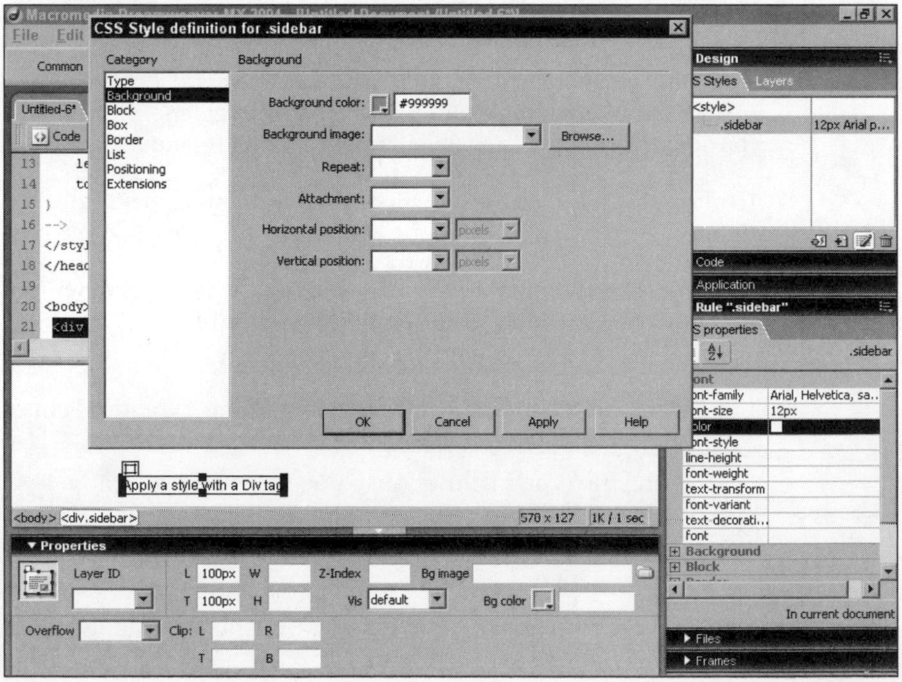

Figure 8-27: Adding a background color to the CSS box.

Because the Same for All option is checked, Dreamweaver applies a padding of 10 pixels to the upper, right, lower, and left regions of the box (see Figure 8-28).

9. **Select the border category and set the Style to Dashed and the color to dark gray. Click the OK button to apply the changes and dismiss the CSS Style Definition dialog box.**

Figure 8-29 shows the final appearance of the sidebar layer. You can also play around with other settings in the CSS Style Definition dialog box to customize the appearance of the sidebar. Clicking the Apply button allows you to preview the changes without dismissing the dialog box.

What you have done in this section is create a layer with style information added to it that you can easily position anywhere on the page. From this point, you can just click and drag the layer around or enter positioning values into the Properties inspector for the layer. As long as you select either Absolute or Relative as values in the Type field of the Positioning category for the class in question, the CSS element appears as a layer in Dreamweaver. To remove the layer handles, just choose Static rather than Absolute or Relative in the Positioning options.

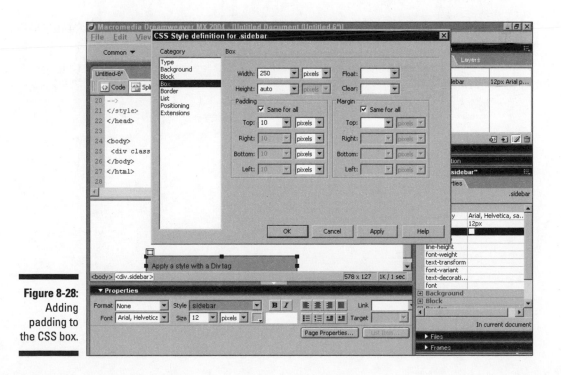

Figure 8-28: Adding padding to the CSS box.

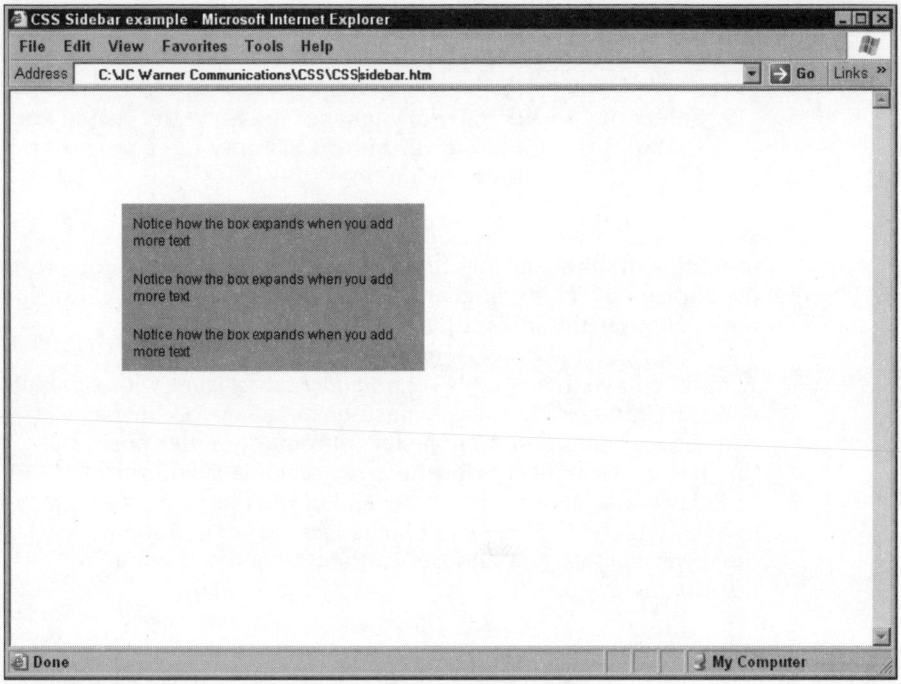

Figure 8-29:
A completed sidebar as viewed in a browser.

In Chapter 9, you find out much more about layers and how to use them as positioning devices. You also find out how to manipulate many more layer properties and attributes.

Part IV
Making It Cool

The 5th Wave   By Rich Tennant

Rothman
Paint Drying Equip.
TV Test Pattern Design
Sap Buckets

"Maybe it would help our Web site if we showed our products in action."

In this part . . .

As you develop your Web site, don't forget that one of the most important elements of the Internet is the ability to interact directly with visitors to your site. In this part, you find a chapter dedicated to interactivity and Dynamic HTML. You discover how Macromedia has integrated its image design program, Fireworks, to work with Dreamweaver to make image creation and editing seamless. This is also the part where you find out how to add all those great multimedia elements, such as Flash animations, to your Web pages.

Chapter 9

Layers, DHTML, and Behaviors

● ●

● ●

*T*wo powerful Dreamweaver features make creating advanced HTML and DHTML features possible: layers and behaviors. Before you start working with these, a little background information is helpful (you're getting into some of the most complex Dreamweaver Web design features). This chapter starts off by explaining what each feature accomplishes and how they can work together to create dramatic effects. You then find out about using layers to position elements precisely on your page with better reliability than HTML tables. The rest of this chapter explains how to implement DHTML in your Web pages by applying behaviors to add powerful, preset actions and interactivity.

Working with Layers

Layers permit precise positioning of elements on an HTML page. Think of a layer as a container for other elements, such as images, text, tables, and even other layers. You can put this container anywhere on an HTML page, and even stack those containers on top of each other.

Using layers, you can position text blocks and images exactly where you want them on a page by specifying their distance from the top and left sides of a page — something sorely missing in HTML. One of the greatest limitations of HTML is its inability to stack elements on top of each other. With layers, a positioning option called the Z coordinate adds this capability, making it possible to layer text, images, and other elements.

Because a layer is a container, everything in it can be manipulated as a unit: You can move a layer on top of another layer or make the entire layer visible or invisible.

Remember that pre-algebra teacher who was addicted to transparencies and the overhead projector? Layers work similarly to those transparencies: You can move layers around to position elements exactly where you want them, use the layers to overlap elements on a page, or turn the layers on and off to control visibility. If you're new to layers, you may want to use the following steps to experiment a little with creating layers, adding images and other elements, and moving layers around.

Creating layers

To create a layer, follow these steps:

1. **Choose Insert➪Layout Objects➪Layer.**

   A box representing an empty layer appears at the top of the page.

   Alternatively, you can click the Draw Layer button in the Layout Insert bar and then click and drag to create a new layer anywhere in the work area (see Figure 9-1).

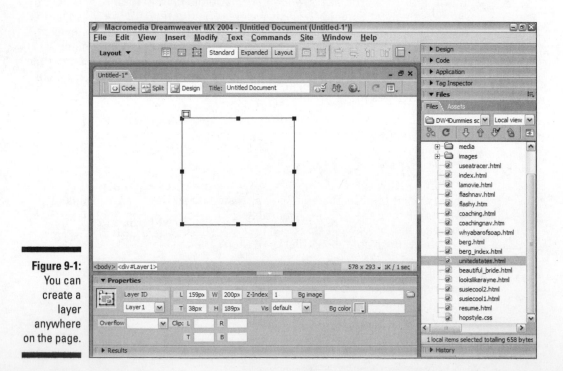

Figure 9-1:
You can create a layer anywhere on the page.

2. **Click anywhere along the outline of the layer box to select it.**

   When you hold the mouse over the outline of the layer, the cursor turns to a four-pointed arrow (or a hand on the Macintosh) and the layer is outlined; clicking with the cursor selects the layer. When the layer is selected, eight tiny, black, square handles appear around the perimeter of the box, indicating that it has been selected.

3. **Click and drag any of the handles to resize the layer.**

Adding elements, resizing, and repositioning layers

To make a layer useful, you have to put something inside it. You can place within a layer pretty much anything you can place in a document. To add images or text to a layer, follow these steps:

1. **Click to insert your cursor inside the layer.**

   A blinking cursor appears inside the layer box.

2. **Choose Insert⇨Image.**

   The Select Image Source dialog box appears.

3. **Click the filename of the image you want to insert.**

4. **Click OK.**

   The image appears inside the layer.

5. **Select the image and use the Properties inspector to make any formatting changes to it.**

   Formatting images inside layers works the same way as on a regular HTML page. For example, using the Align Center icon centers the image in the layer. Find more information about formatting images in Chapter 5.

6. **Click inside the layer again to insert your cursor and enter some text (see Figure 9-2).**

7. **Highlight the text and format it by using the text-formatting options in the Properties inspector or by choosing formatting options from the Text menu.**

   Formatting text inside layers is just like formatting text inside a regular Dreamweaver document. You can read more about formatting text in Chapter 2.

Click the tab to select the layer.

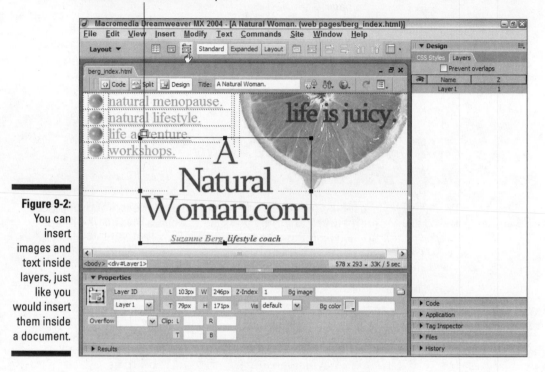

8. **Click the tab that appears in the upper-left area of the layer or any-where along the border to select the layer.**

   You know that you have successfully selected the layer when you see the selection *handles,* the little black squares that appear at the corners and in the middle of each side.

9. **Click any handle and drag to resize the layer.**

   As a general rule, always size a layer so that its contents *just* fit within its boundaries. Positioning the layer on the page is then easier.

   If you look again at Figure 9-2, you can see that the Properties inspector displays the height (H) and width (W) of the layer in pixels. Rather than drag to resize, you can type new measurements for the width and height directly into the Properties inspector. The Properties inspector displays these options only when the layer is selected.

10. **To move a layer, click and drag the little tab (which appears in the upper-left area of the layer when it's selected) to move the layer any-where on the page.**

Because layers use exact positioning, you can move them to any precise location on a page, and they're displayed in that exact location in browsers that support layers, such as Netscape Navigator 4 and Internet Explorer 4 and later.

The Properties inspector also displays the Layer coordinates when the layer is selected: L (for left), T (for top). In addition to using the click-and-drag method to move a layer, you can change a layer's position by entering a number in the position boxes, L (number of pixels from the left edge of the page), and T (number of pixels from the top of the page).

11. **Name your layer by typing a name in the Layer ID text box in the upper-left corner of the Properties inspector.**

When you create a new layer, Dreamweaver automatically names your layers for you, starting with Layer1, Layer2, and so on. You should change the name to something more descriptive, especially if you're working with lots of layers on a page. Keeping track of them by name makes them much easier to manage. Remember that you must select the layer first in order for its properties to appear in the Properties inspector.

Stacking layers and changing visibility

A powerful feature of layers is their maneuverability: You can stack them on top of each other and make them visible or invisible. Later in this chapter, in the "Working with Behaviors" section, you find out how to use these features in combination with behaviors to create rollovers and other effects. To stack layers, simply drag one layer on top of another. Unlike images, layers give you complete layout control on the page by including the ability to overlap one another. To overlap images, simply place each image within a separate layer and then move one layer so that it overlaps the other. To let you control which layer is on top, Dreamweaver provides two ways of changing the order of stacking: the Z index, available in the Properties inspector, and the Layers panel (see Figure 9-3), which you can access by choosing Window⇨Layers.

To stack layers and change their order and visibility, follow these steps:

1. **Open a page that has two or more layers on it.**

2. **Select the layer by clicking anywhere on the border outline of the layer.**

3. **Choose Window⇨Layers to open the Layers panel.**

The Layers panel lists any layers that appear on your page. If you're familiar with layers in Adobe Photoshop or Macromedia Fireworks, you may find some similarities here, such as the eye icon to control layer visibility and the ability to drag layers around in the panel to reposition them.

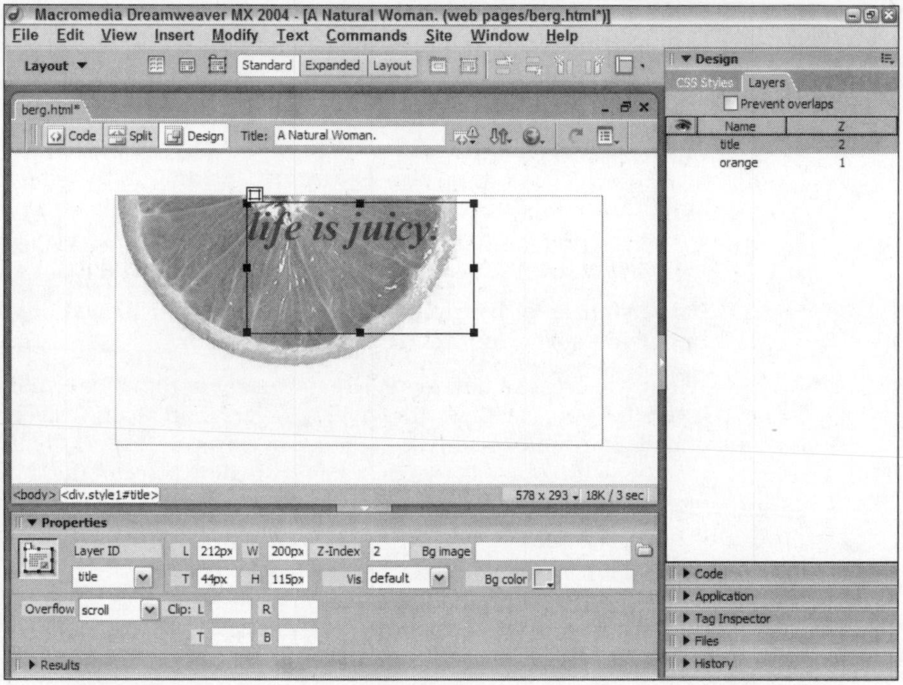

Figure 9-3:
The Layers
panel
changes the
visibility and
stacking
order of
your
document's
layers.

4. **Reorder the stacking of the layers by clicking the layer name in the Layers panel and dragging it up or down.**

   The layer order changes in the Layers panel. The panel also indicates the Z number of the layer. The lowest number is the bottommost layer.

   You can rename a layer by double-clicking the name in the Layers panel to select it and then typing a new name.

5. **Click the eye icon to the left of any layer in the Layers panel to turn the layer visibility on or off (refer to Figure 9-3).**

   If no eye appears, the visibility is set to default, which usually means on, except in the case of nested layers. (You can find out about nested layers in the next section.) If the eye is open, the layer is visible on the screen and in the browser. If the eye is closed, the layer is invisible; it's still there — it just isn't displayed on-screen or in the browser.

Nesting layers: One happy family

Another way to position layers on a page is by nesting them. A *nested layer* is essentially a layer that's invisibly tied to another layer and maintains a kind of parent-child relationship with the first layer. The child layer uses the upper-left corner of the parent layer as its orientation point for positioning rather than use the upper-left corner of the document because it's nested *within* the parent layer. Even if the layers are on different areas of the page, they still retain this parent-child relationship. When you move the first layer around on the page, the nested layer moves along with it. You can also think of this scenario as an owner walking his dog on a leash — where the owner goes, the dog has to follow, even though the dog can still move independently of its owner within the confines of the length of the leash.

If you were to nest another layer into the child layer, that would then make the child layer both a parent and a child. The new layer then uses the upper-left corner of its parent layer as its orientation point. The first layer in the nested chain still retains control over all the child layers, so they all move when the parent moves.

Nested layers can be a great way to keep chunks of your layout working together as you move them around the page. Rather than try to keep track of loads of different layers and move each one individually, you can group them into more easily manageable "family units." Furthermore, you can make a whole family visible or invisible by clicking the eye icon of the parent layer in the Layers panel if the child layer's visibility has been set to default (no eye icon in the Layers panel). When the child layer's visibility is set to default, it inherits the visibility of its parent layer. As you experiment with layers and start using lots of them on your page, understanding inheritance becomes essential. Be aware, though, that when a child layer is set to either visible (eye icon on) or invisible (eye icon off) in the Layers panel, it's unaffected by the visibility setting of its parent layer.

To create a nested layer, follow these steps:

1. **Choose Insert➪Layout Objects➪Layer.**

   A box representing the layer appears at the top of the page. Dreamweaver automatically names the layer Layer1.

2. **Place the cursor inside the first layer, and choose Insert➪Layout Objects➪Layer to create a second layer inside the first.**

3. **Position the second layer anywhere on the page by dragging the small tab in the upper-left corner of the layer box or clicking and dragging anywhere on the layer's border.**

   Visually, nested layers don't need to reside inside their parent layers; they can be placed anywhere else on the page or be stacked on top of each other.

4. **Choose Window➪Layers to open the Layers panel, if it isn't already open.**

   The Layers panel opens.

   In the Layers panel, you see that a nested layer is displayed underneath and slightly indented from its parent, and a line shows their relationship (see Figure 9-4).

Figure 9-4:
The Layers
panel lets
you set
visibility
and stack
order, and
indicates
parent-child
relation-
ships
between
layers.

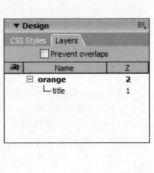

Setting layer options

Like other HTML elements, layers have many attributes you can set.
Dreamweaver makes these options available in the Properties inspector
whenever you select a layer.

This list describes the layer options and what they control:

✔ **Layer ID:** You can type your own descriptive name on this pull-down
menu in the upper-left corner of the Properties inspector. If you don't
name a layer, Dreamweaver names it for you. Use only standard alpha-
numeric characters for a layer name (don't use special characters, like
spaces, hyphens, slashes, or periods).

✔ **L (Left):** This value specifies the distance of the layer from the left side
of the page or parent layer. Dreamweaver automatically enters a pixel
value when you create or move a layer with drag-and-drop. You can also
enter a numeric value (positive or negative) to control the positioning.

✔ **T (Top):** This value specifies the distance of the layer from the top of the
page or parent layer. Dreamweaver automatically enters a pixel value
when you create or move a layer with drag-and-drop. You can also enter
a numeric value (positive or negative) to control the positioning.

✔ **W (Width):** Dreamweaver automatically specifies the width when you
create a layer on a page. You also have the option of entering a numeric
value to specify the width. You can change the px (pixels) default measurement to any of the following: pc (picas), pt (points), in (inches), mm
(millimeters), cm (centimeters), or % (percentage of the page or parent
layer's width). Don't put any spaces between the number and the measurement abbreviation.

✔ **H (Height):** Dreamweaver automatically specifies the height when you create a layer on a page. You also have the option of entering a numeric value to specify the height. You can change the default measurement of px (pixels) to any of the following: pc (picas), pt (points), in (inches), mm (millimeters), cm (centimeters), or % (percentage of the page or parent layer's height). Don't put any spaces between the number and the measurement abbreviation.

✔ **Z-Index:** This option determines the position of a layer in relation to other layers when layers are stacked. Higher-numbered layers appear on top of lower-numbered layers, and values can be positive or negative.

Changing the stacking order of layers is easier to do in the Layers panel than by entering specific Z-index values.

✔ **Vis:** This visibility setting controls whether a layer is visible or invisible. You can use this setting with a scripting language, such as JavaScript, to dynamically change the display of layers.

You can choose from these visibility options:

• **Default:** The default option in most browsers is the same visibility property as the parent's value. If there is no parent layer, the default state is visible.

• **Inherit:** This option always uses the visibility property of the layer's parent.

• **Visible:** This option always displays the layer, regardless of the parent's value.

✔ **Hidden:** This option always makes the layer transparent (invisible), regardless of the parent's value. Even when it is hidden, all the content on a layer will be downloaded when the page is viewed in the browser. You can dynamically control visibility by using the JavaScript behaviors covered in "Attaching a behavior" later in this chapter.

✔ **Bg Image:** With this option, you can select a background image for the layer in the same way that you would select a background image for a Web page. Click the folder icon to select an image or enter the name and path in the text box.

✔ **Bg Color:** Use this option to set a background color for a layer. Clicking the color square opens the color palette. If you want the layer background to be transparent, leave it blank.

✔ **Tag:** This enables you to choose between using CSS layers (<DIV> or <SPAN> tags). The <DIV> tag is generally considered the better choice.

✔ **Overflow:** These options determine how the contents of a layer are displayed if they exceed the size of the layer. (Note that this option applies to only CSS layers.)

You can choose from these Overflow options:

- **Visible:** Forces the layer size to increase so that all its contents are visible. The layer expands down and to the right.

- **Hidden:** Clips off the edges of content that doesn't fit within the specified size of a layer. Be careful with this option; it doesn't provide any scroll bars.

- **Scroll:** Adds scroll bars to the sides of a layer regardless of whether its contents exceed the layer's size.

- **Auto:** Displays scroll bars only if the layer's contents don't fit within the layer's boundaries.

✔ **Clip:** This option controls which sections of the contents of a layer are cropped if the layer isn't large enough to display all its contents. You should specify the distance from the L (Left), T (Top), R (Right), and B (Bottom). You can enter values in px (pixels), pc (picas), pt (points), in (inches), mm (millimeters), cm (centimeters), or % (a percentage of the parent's value). Don't add any spaces between the number and the measurement abbreviation.

Converting layers to tables: Precise positioning for older browsers

If you want to achieve precise pixel-perfect positioning of elements on a Web page, layers are the easiest way to do it. You can achieve precision at a level impossible to obtain using regular HTML. Unfortunately, layers work only in browser versions 4.0 and later.

What if you want to use the precision layout features allowed by layers and also want to support a wider audience of pre-4.0 browser users? These days, not many of those browsers are used, but if you find that you have to support one of them, you're sure to be pleased to find that Dreamweaver has a tool for you. Using this feature, you can convert a layout you created by using layers into an HTML page that uses tables. By building a layout using layers and then converting it to tables, you can (with a single command) create a version of your page that works in older browsers.

To convert a page that uses layers to a page that uses tables and maintains the same page layout, choose Modify➪Convert➪Layers to Table. Dreamweaver rebuilds the page with a table structure that mimics the layers' layout and uses table cells to control positioning. (*Note:* If you haven't saved your page already, Dreamweaver prompts you to do so before it completes this task because it can dramatically alter the original page design.)

Netscape layers versus CSS layers

Netscape was the first browser to bring layers to the Web. However, it pushed the limits on its own and didn't wait for a standard. Unfortunately for Netscape (and for those of us sorting out DHTML), the result is that you now have two different ways to create layers: the Netscape layer tag, which consists of the <LAYER> and <ILAYER> tags, and the CSS positioning option *(CSS-P)*. This version of Dreamweaver lets you create layers using only CSS positioning, although you can still edit preexisting pages that use the Netscape layer tag.

Netscape now supports CSS positioning, but Internet Explorer doesn't support the Netscape layer tag. Spend the time to update any pages you have already created using the <LAYER> or <ILAYER> tags because they're on their way to becoming obsolete.

You can go in the other direction too, and convert a table into layers. Choose Modify➪Convert➪Tables to Layers and the table layout converts to a layers layout where you can easily reposition elements with pixel-level precision. After you're done, convert to tables again and — voilà! — you have achieved exact positioning without requiring a 4.0 or later browser.

The Dreamweaver Layers to Table conversion feature isn't perfect because you can do things with layers that you can't do with tables. For example, you can't convert a page that contains nested layers. Some designers use the Layers to Table conversion feature to create multiple pages and then direct visitors to the best design, even if they have to alter the tables version to make it look okay without all the DHTML features. Just make sure to use the Save As feature to save your converted page under a new name so that you have both versions.

All About DHTML

Dynamic HTML *(DHTML)* has received so much hype and attention that you would think you could do anything with it, including your laundry. Well, DHTML isn't quite powerful enough to take over your domestic duties, but it does add a range of functionality to a Web page that has been impossible with HTML alone. In fact, DHTML is kind of like HTML on steroids. DHTML is really about using advanced scripting techniques to create dynamic content, which is impossible with HTML alone. *Dynamic content* means that you can create and alter page content *after* the page has been loaded in a browser. JavaScript has been used by designers to add dynamic effects to Web pages for a while, but with DHTML you can affect the attributes of HTML tags, which means that you can create many more kinds of effects and make them happen more quickly.

The biggest drawback of DHTML is the same as you find with any new Web technology: Because browsers aren't consistent about support, some cool things you can do with DHTML don't work in all browsers and therefore aren't widely used on the Internet. Dreamweaver includes features to make it easier than ever to design pages that work in various browsers.

DHTML is, however, much more complicated to write than regular old HTML. Even HTML frames, which are complex by many Web design standards, look relatively simple when compared to JavaScript and the kind of code you have to write in order to create DHTML. This area is where Dreamweaver shines: Macromedia has implemented a series of tools that let you create DHTML effects without having to be a JavaScript programmer.

Working with Behaviors

Some of the coolest features used on the Web today are created by using Dreamweaver behaviors, which use a scripting language called JavaScript. These behaviors are really just built-in scripts — some of which use DHTML and some of which don't — that provide an easy way to add interactivity to your Web pages. You can apply behaviors to many elements on an HTML page, and even to the entire page itself. Writing JavaScript is more complex than writing HTML code, but not as difficult as writing in a programming language such as C, C++, or Java. (No, Java and JavaScript are not the same. Read Chapter 11 for more on Java applets and how they differ from JavaScript.) Dreamweaver takes all the difficulty out of writing JavaScript behaviors by giving you an easy and intuitive interface that doesn't require you to ever touch the complicated code behind the scenes.

Using the behaviors options, you can make images change when viewers pass their cursors over them (a rollover), or make a layer draggable by the person viewing the Web page. Combining the power of behaviors with layers opens up a range of tricks that look great on a page and load quickly.

Consider this slightly corny example: If you tickle someone, that person laughs. Dreamweaver would call the tickling an *event* and the laughter an *action*. The combination is a Dreamweaver *behavior*.

You may already be familiar with the rollover behavior, when one image is switched for another. In a rollover, putting your mouse over an image is the event. The action is the switching of the original image for another. Rollovers are especially common in navigation; mousing over a navigation button causes it to be highlighted. You can use behaviors to affect text, images, and — you guessed it — layers.

Attaching a behavior

If you have always wanted to add cool interactive features, such as making something flash or pop up when users move their cursors over an image or click a link, you're going to love the *behavior* feature in Dreamweaver. To fully appreciate what Dreamweaver can do for you, you may want to switch to Code view after attaching a behavior, just to see the complex code required to create behaviors. If you don't like what you see, don't worry: Go back to Design view and just let Dreamweaver take care of the code for you.

When you use behaviors in Dreamweaver, you use dialog boxes to set up interactive effects. You can attach behaviors to a page, a link, an image, or almost any other element on a page by simply selecting the element and specifying the behavior you want from the Behaviors tab in the Tag panel.

The following steps show you how to apply a behavior to an image. At least 20 behaviors are built into Dreamweaver, so it's worth spending a little time finding out what they are so that you can make the best use of them.

To add a behavior to an image on a page, follow these steps:

1. **Select an image on a page by clicking it.**

    You can select any image, text, or layer on a page and apply a behavior to it.

    To attach a behavior to the entire page, click the <BODY> tag in the tag selector on the far left side of the Status bar, at the bottom of the Document window.

2. **Choose Window⇨Behaviors to open the Behaviors panel.**

3. **Click the plus sign (+) and choose the Open Browser Window behavior from the pop-up menu (see Figure 9-5).**

    The Open Browser Window dialog box appears, enabling you to specify the parameters for the new browser window.

    You can choose any behavior listed on the pop-up menu.

    You should know that Dreamweaver behaviors almost always must be implemented inside an anchor (<A>) tag, which is created by filling in the Link box in the Properties inspector. If you open the Events drop-down list and see quite a short list, the reason may be that the image you selected doesn't link to anything. This problem has a quick solution. Select the image and type **javascript:;** in the Link box in the Properties inspector. This code makes the image a link, but means that the browser doesn't open a new Web page when the image is clicked. Take another look at the Events pull-down menu in the Behaviors panel, and you now see many more events you can use to open the new window.

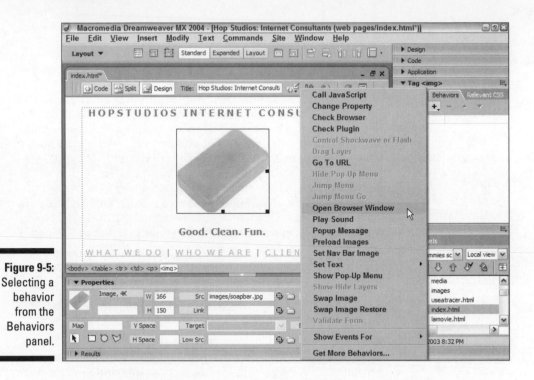

Figure 9-5:
Selecting a
behavior
from the
Behaviors
panel.

If an action is grayed out in the list on the pop-up menu, it's also possible that the action doesn't work with the file or element you selected. The Control Shockwave action, for example, works only if you select a Shockwave file.

After selecting the behavior, a dialog box specific to the behavior always appears, enabling you to specify the parameters for each behavior.

4. **Specify the parameter options to control how you want the behavior to work.**

The Open Browser Window behavior means that when someone clicks the image to which you applied this behavior, a new browser window opens. This dialog box allows you to set the properties of how that browser window is displayed (see Figure 9-6). You don't have to set any of these parameters except for the URL to Display box. Setting a window width and height gives you the ability to open much smaller windows if you choose. You can also decide which attributes that window should have: navigation toolbar, location toolbar, status bar, menu bar, scrollbars as needed, and resize handles. Finally, you can name the new window, which is important if you plan to target that window and load new pages into it.

5. **After you have specified the parameters for the behavior, click OK.**

The dialog box closes, and the Open Browser Window behavior now appears in the Behaviors panel.

Figure 9-6:
Select an
action
from the
Behaviors
panel, and a
dialog box
offers you
different
options for
control-
ling the
behavior.

Open Browser Window		
URL to display: whyabarofsoap.html Browse...		OK
Window width: 200 Window height: 200		Cancel
Attributes: ☐ Navigation toolbar ☐ Menu bar		Help
☐ Location toolbar ☑ Scrollbars as needed		
☐ Status bar ☐ Resize handles		
Window name: hopstudiospopup		

6. **To change the event that triggers your behavior, select the current event from the left side of the Behaviors panel.**

   This step opens the Events drop-down list, from which you can select various events to trigger the behavior.

   The most commonly used event is the `onClick` event, which causes the new browser window to open when a user clicks the image. For more information about events and what each one accomplishes, see the section "About events" later in this chapter.

7. **To test the action, choose File⇨Preview in Browser, and then select the browser in which you want to test your work.**

   This step opens the page in whatever browser you choose so that you can see how it really looks in that browser. Click the image to test whether a new browser window opens (see Figure 9-7).

If you're using behaviors, try to avoid starting your filenames with a number or using a slash mark, which is never a good idea for a filename but is particularly problematic when applying behaviors (more so with JavaScript than with Dreamweaver). Your safest option is to avoid using slashes anywhere in the name or numbers at the beginning of a filename (you can use numbers anywhere else in the name).

Many event options, such as `onMouseDown`, `onMouseOver`, and `onMouseOut`, are available only if the element is linked, as described in the preceding steps. Another clue that you need to create a link is that the majority of the behaviors are grayed out when you try to select one from the Behaviors panel. If that happens, add **javascript:;** to the Link box in the Properties inspector for the text, image, or layer you're trying to work with. You can also make that item link to another Web page, if you prefer. Using the number sign means that the current Web page stays open.

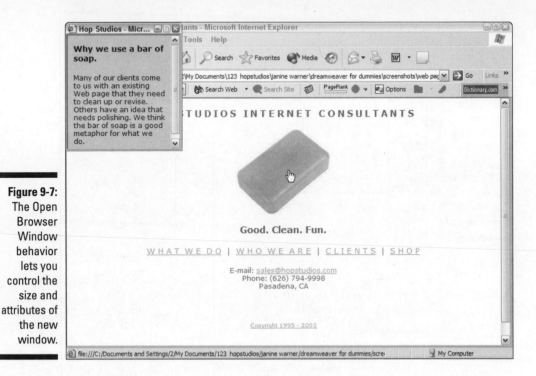

Figure 9-7:
The Open Browser Window behavior lets you control the size and attributes of the new window.

About events

Events, in interactive Web-speak, are things a user does to interact with your Web page. Clicking an image is an event, as is loading a page in the browser or pressing a key on the keyboard. You can probably think of many more. Different browser versions support different events (the more recent the browser version, the more events are available), and you can select the types of browsers you want to support. To see the list of available events for specific browsers, click the plus (+) sign in the Behaviors panel, choose Show Events For, and select the type of browser your users should use. You should always provide support for as many browsers and browser versions as possible.

As well, some events are available only for certain kinds of objects in your page. This list describes some of the more commonly used events, ones that the majority of Web users can experience (using Netscape Navigator and Internet Explorer 4.0 and later):

✔ onAbort: Triggered when the user stops the browser from completely loading an image (for example, when the user clicks the browser's Stop button while an image is loading).

- onBlur: Triggered when the specified element stops being the focus of user interaction. For example, when a user clicks outside a text field after clicking in the text field, the browser generates an onBlur event for the text field. onBlur is the opposite of onFocus.

- onChange: Triggered when the user changes a value on the page, such as choosing an option from a pop-up menu, or when the user changes the value of a text field and then clicks elsewhere on the page.

- onClick: Triggered when the user clicks an element, such as a link, button, or image.

- onDblClick: Triggered when the user double-clicks the specified element.

- onError: Triggered when a browser error occurs while a page or image is loading. This event can be caused, for example, when an image or URL can't be found on the server.

- onFocus: Triggered when the specified element becomes the focus of user interaction. For example, clicking in a text field of a form generates an onFocus event.

- onKeyDown: Triggered as soon as the user presses any key on the keyboard. (The user doesn't have to release the key for this event to be generated.)

- onKeyPress: Triggered when the user presses and releases any key on the keyboard; this event is like a combination of the onKeyDown and onKeyUp events.

- onKeyUp: Triggered when the user releases a key on the keyboard after pressing it.

- onLoad: Triggered when an image or page finishes loading.

Adding new behaviors to Dreamweaver

If you know how to write JavaScript, you can add your own behaviors to the list of choices in Dreamweaver. You can also find new behaviors created by Macromedia, and by other developers, many that you can download for free and then add to Dreamweaver. There is also a range of extensions that can be purchased. You can find instructions for creating and adding new actions in the Dreamweaver Exchange section of the Macromedia site, at www.macromedia.com/exchange/dreamweaver.

To go to this site automatically to get new behaviors, click the plus sign (+) in the Behaviors panel and choose the Get More Behaviors option at the bottom of the pull-down menu. This action launches your default Web browser and connects you to the Dreamweaver Exchange section of the Macromedia Web site if you're online.

✔ onMouseDown: Triggered when the user presses the mouse button. (The user doesn't have to release the mouse button to generate this event.)

✔ onMouseMove: Triggered when the user moves the mouse while pointing to the specified element and the pointer doesn't move away from element (stays within its boundaries).

✔ onMouseOut: Triggered when the pointer moves off the specified element (usually, a link).

✔ onMouseOver: Triggered when the mouse pointer moves over the specified element.

✔ onMouseUp: Triggered when a mouse button that has been pressed is released.

✔ onMove: Triggered when a window or frame is moved.

✔ onReset: Triggered when a form is reset to its default values, usually by clicking the Reset button.

✔ onResize: Triggered when the user resizes the browser window or a frame.

✔ onScroll: Triggered when the user scrolls up or down in the browser.

✔ onSelect: Triggered when the user selects text in a text field by highlighting it with the cursor.

✔ onSubmit: Triggered when the user submits a form, usually by clicking the Submit button.

✔ onUnload: Triggered when the user leaves the page, either by closing it or focusing on another browser window.

Adding a rollover image behavior to swap images

Rollover images are now some of the most commonly used interactive elements on Web sites. With rollovers, you can swap one image with another one when the mouse passes over it, giving users visible feedback as they interact with your site. You have seen this effect on Web site navigation menus in which moving your mouse over a menu choice makes it appear highlighted. To create a rollover (swapping) image in Dreamweaver, follow these steps:

1. **Click to place your cursor on the page where you want the rollover to appear.**

   Rollover effects require at least two images: one for the initial state and one for the rollover state. You probably should make a special set of images to use with your rollover behavior. They both should be the same dimensions, or else you get some strange scaling effects.

2. **Choose Insert⇨Image Objects⇨Rollover Image to open the Insert Rollover Image dialog box.**

   The Insert Rollover Image dialog box appears, as shown in Figure 9-8.

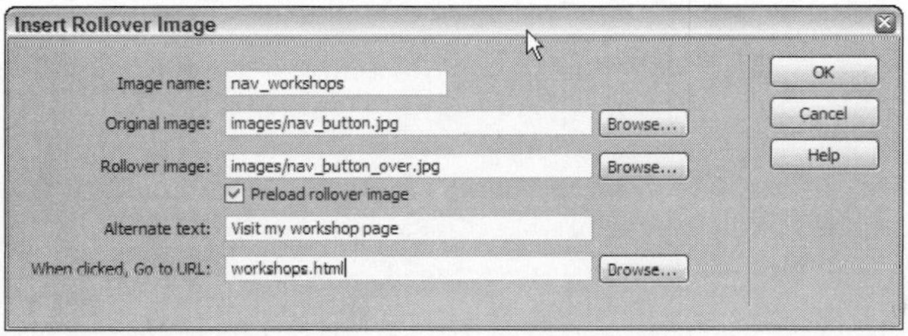

Figure 9-8:
In the Insert
Rollover
Image
dialog box,
you can
specify the
original and
rollover
images.

3. **Name your image in the Image Name field of the dialog box.**

   For you to be able to apply a behavior to an element, such as an image, the element must have a name so that the behavior script can reference it. Names also enable you to swap images in other locations on the page by using their names as a reference ID. The name can be the same as the filename, but can also simply be descriptive.

4. **Specify the first image you want visible in the Original Image text file. (Use the Browse button to easily locate the image.)**

5. **Specify the Rollover image, the one you want to have visible when visitors move their cursors over the first image. (Use the Browse button to easily locate the image.)**

6. **Check the Preload Rollover Image check box if you want the image to be loaded into the browser's cache even before it becomes visible to a visitor.**

   If you don't choose to do this step, the image has to be downloaded when a visitor puts the mouse over the original image. This option should almost always be turned on.

7. **In the When Clicked, Go To URL section, enter a URL or browse to locate another page on your site that you want to link to.**

   If you don't specify a URL, Dreamweaver automatically inserts the # (anchor tag reference).

8. **Click OK.**

   The images are automatically set up as a rollover.

9. **Preview your work in a browser to make sure that the rollover works.**

   You can discover more about previewing your pages in the browser in Chapter 2.

Attaching multiple behaviors

You can attach multiple behaviors to the same element on a page (as long as they don't conflict, of course). For example, you can attach one action that is triggered when users click an image and another when they move their cursor over the image. You can also trigger the same action by using multiple events. For example, you can play the same sound when a user triggers any number of events.

To attach additional behaviors to an element, follow the same steps in the section "Attaching a behavior," earlier in this chapter, and then click the plus sign again in the Behaviors panel and select another option from the pop-up menu. Repeat this process as many times as you want.

Editing a behavior

You can always go back and edit a behavior after you create it. You can choose a different event to trigger the behavior, choose a different action, and add or remove behaviors. You can also change parameters you have specified.

To edit a behavior, follow these steps:

1. **Select an object with a behavior attached.**

2. **Choose Window⇨Behaviors to open the Behaviors panel.**

   Here are some options you can choose from in the Behaviors panel:

   - To change an event, choose a different one from the Events pull-down menu in the Behaviors panel.

   - To remove a behavior, click the action in the Behaviors panel to select it and then click the minus sign at the top of the pane. The behavior disappears.

   - To change parameters for an action, double-click the gear icon next to the action and change the parameters in the dialog box that opens.

   - To change the order of actions when multiple actions have been set, select an action and then click the Move Event Value Up or Move Event Value Down buttons to move it to a different position in the list of actions.

Ensuring That Your Pages Work in Older Browsers

You may love all the Dreamweaver features described in this chapter because they make creating dynamic, interactive elements for your Web pages easy. However, don't forget that older browsers may have trouble handling some of the more advanced features you can create. Every day, older browsers (pre-4.0) are less of an issue because fewer people are using them, although browser support is certainly still a problem. Even newer browsers don't support all DHTML in quite the same way.

Figuring out which browser to target when you start working with behaviors can be frustrating. One solution (besides not using behaviors) is creating two versions of pages that use behaviors and adding a Check Browser behavior that can redirect visitors to the page that works best for them.

The Check Browser action is implemented from the Behaviors panel. This action automatically sends users to different URLs depending on the version of browser they're using, so you can create a fancy version of your site for new browsers and a simpler version for older browsers. Because this action even allows you to send Netscape and Internet Explorer users to different URLs, you can design different pages for each browser's capabilities, as shown in Figure 9-9. Here's the best way to use this action: Select the <BODY> tag by using the HTML tag selector on the document's status bar, and then choose the Check Browser action in the Behaviors panel (click the plus sign to access the list of actions).

Applying this behavior to your page causes a browser-detect script to determine the type of browser your visitor uses when the page first loads. After the page is loaded, the visitor is either directed to a different URL based on that detection or kept on the same page. For example, you can send all visitors using Netscape 4.0 and older to one page in your site and users of Internet Explorer 5.0 to another page. To ensure that users of the oldest browsers see the simple page rather than try to interpret fancy code that they don't understand, you should insert this behavior in the basic version of the page and then redirect newer browsers to the alternative fancy pages. The only problem with this solution, of course, is that you have to create more than one site — one for older browsers and one or more for the newer browsers, and that can turn into lots more work.

If you have an audience that is using some of the less common browsers — like Safari or Opera — this solution may not work for you. Remember that testing your pages in the browser you think your site visitors use is the only way to be sure you have created pages that will work for them.

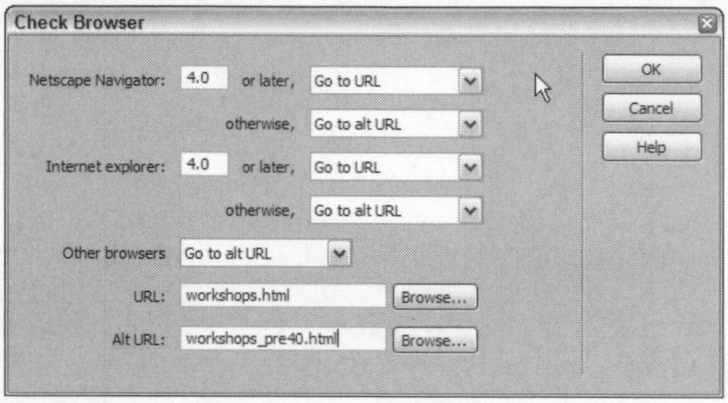

Figure 9-9:
The Check
Browser
dialog box
lets you
direct users
to different
URLs based
on which
browser
they're
using.

Using Extensions and the Extension Manager

Extensions let you easily add new features to Dreamweaver by simply down-loading them from a Web site or creating your own new extensions, which you can share with others. Extensions are similar to behaviors except that they're even more powerful: You can alter the menu system in Dreamweaver, adding new features by adding new menu items. With extensions, you can do things like change background colors, add a list of state zip codes or country codes, instantly embed QuickTime movies, or connect to back-end databases with a simple menu command. The idea behind extensions is that anyone with a little bit of scripting ability can create new ways to customize Dreamweaver and share their creations with the Dreamweaver community. The place to find out more about extensions and to download them (mostly for free) is the Macromedia Exchange for Dreamweaver site, at `www.macromedia.com/exchange/dreamweaver`.

After you log into Macromedia Exchange (membership is free), you're wel-come to download and install any of the scores of extensions — they grow every day as developers continually create new ones. You can search for extensions by category or simply browse the ever-growing list.

To install an extension, download it first from the Macromedia Exchange site or any other source (many sites now have free extensions on the Web) and then use the Extension Manager, a utility included in Dreamweaver, to install the new extension. Extensions you download from the site are saved as files on your computer with an `.mxp` extension. The Extension Manager makes installing and removing these files in Dreamweaver a breeze.

To run the Extension Manager and install an extension, follow these steps:

1. **Choose Commands⊏⊐Manage Extensions.**

   The utility launches.

2. **Choose File⊏⊐Install Extension in the Extension Manager; then browse your drive to select the new extension.**

   After the installation is complete, you see brief instructions on how to use the extension.

3. **Unless the instructions require you to restart Dreamweaver, simply switch to Dreamweaver, and you're ready to use your new extension.**

Converting to XHTML

The Dreamweaver Convert feature enables you to convert an HTML page into XHTML. The eXtensible Markup Language is increasingly important on the Web, and if you work with XML, you may appreciate that Dreamweaver is starting to support XML development.

XML isn't a markup language — it's a meta-markup language you can use to store and organize data so that it can be tailored to meet a broad range of needs. XML is a subset of SGML, but it retains much more of the power of SGML than HTML did, while still being streamlined enough to be efficient on the Web. Because XML doesn't have a fixed set of tags and elements, XML enables developers to define the elements they need and apply those elements where they need them. That's what the X in XML is all about: It's *eXtensible*. You can adapt it to fit your content, whether you're a stockbroker, publisher, or astronomer.

XML is built on a solid foundation of rules and standards, and it's officially endorsed by the W3C, so it has the potential to solve many of the problems caused by conflicting standards in other formatting options now available. The rules dictate such crucial issues as where tags appear, which names are legal, and which attributes can be attached to which elements. These strict standards make it possible to develop XML parsers that can handle any XML document without limiting the ultimate flexibility of the kind of content or how it's displayed. The XML standards also feature rules for syntax and link checking, comparing document models, and datatyping, as well as checking to see whether a document is well formed and valid. And, XML uses Unicode as its standard character set, so it supports the broadest range of languages, special characters, and symbols, including Arabic, Chinese, and Russian.

One of the most significant differences between XHTML and HTML is that XHTML can be used to describe the type of content, not just specific formatting. That enables content to be stored and shared in a way that makes publishing in multiple formatting styles easy. For example, rather than describe a headline as font size 5, Helvetica, bold, you can simply describe the headline as a headline. XML then allows you to apply a style sheet (or multiple style sheets) to that content so that the headline and body can be formatted on the fly. You do this with Cascading Style Sheets and the XML Extensible Style Sheets. The separation of the formatting from the content description is what enables the same content to be sent efficiently to a wide range of partners who can each apply their own formatting or to a broad range of viewing devices, such as Web browsers, Palm handheld devices, and cell phones, which require different formatting.

If you want to know more about XML, consider reading *XML For Dummies,* 3rd Edition, by Ed Tittel (published by Wiley Publishing, Inc.).

Chapter 10

Roundtrip Integration: Fireworks and Dreamweaver

*I*n this chapter, you discover some of the special features that make Dreamweaver work so well with Fireworks, the Macromedia image-creation and -editing program. Fireworks, specially designed for developing images for the Web, is a great complement to Dreamweaver. Much of the information in this chapter also applies, however, to other image-editing programs, such as Adobe Photoshop.

If you don't have Fireworks, you can download the free, 30-day trial from this URL: www.macromedia.com/software/fireworks/trial. Because Dreamweaver offers only basic graphics capabilities, you want to use Fireworks (or programs like it — see the list of options in Chapter 5) to create images from scratch or to edit existing images and prepare them for use on the Web.

Fireworks goes much further than most graphics programs because it's one of the first image-editing programs designed specifically for the special needs of the Web. Using Fireworks, you can automate your workflow, *optimize* graphics (compress and prepare them for Web use), and create sophisticated animations, fancy *rollovers* (images that change when you hover the mouse pointer over them), and special effects in a fraction of the time these tasks used to take. Fireworks can even generate HTML and create Web pages all by itself! More importantly for you, Fireworks integrates especially well with Dreamweaver, enabling roundtrip graphics editing back and forth between the two programs. Normally, when you work with Dreamweaver and another graphics editor, it takes many steps between creating images and getting them into a Web page — one of the most time-consuming parts of building and maintaining a Web site. *Roundtrip graphics editing* gives you lots of shortcuts, making the trips back and forth between the two programs much quicker and easier.

Dreamweaver to Fireworks: Image Editing

Suppose that a client suddenly wants the logo on a Web page to be a different color. Normally, you have to launch an image-editing program, track down the logo, open it, edit it, save it, switch back to Dreamweaver, and then import the logo again to your page. Using the special integration features between Dreamweaver and Fireworks, though, greatly simplifies the entire process — a few clicks of the mouse can replace all those other time-consuming tasks.

The following steps show you how to select an image in Dreamweaver, automatically open the image in Fireworks, edit the image, and update it back in Dreamweaver with just a few mouse clicks.

To launch Fireworks directly from Dreamweaver and edit an existing image, follow these steps:

1. **In an open document, select a GIF or JPG image you want to edit.**

2. **In the Properties inspector, click the Edit button, as shown in Figure 10-1.**

   The Find Source dialog box appears, asking whether you want to use an existing document as the source of the file you selected.

Figure 10-1:
The Properties inspector displays an Edit button when an image is selected.

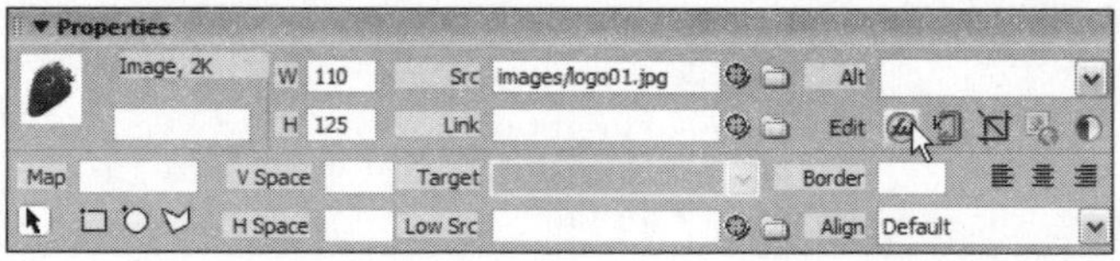

3. **Click one of the options in the Find Source dialog box.**

   Clicking the Yes button lets you select a different file from the optimized image file on your page. For example, you can select the original file from which you exported the optimized Web version of the graphical image on your page. It may be a PNG file or a Photoshop file, for example. (For more on PNG files, see the "PNG: Portable Network Graphics files" sidebar, later in this chapter.)

   Clicking the No button opens the GIF or JPEG that you selected in Dreamweaver and are using on the Web page.

Because the GIF or JPEG image used on your Web page was probably optimized earlier, editing it often doesn't give you the best image-quality results. Going back to the original, pre-optimized version of the graphical image gives you the option to start again from scratch. Keep in mind that when a GIF or JPEG is created, it gets compressed and loses some data and quality. Then you can understand more easily that if you need to make a serious edit, using the original image and saving a new GIF or JPEG produces a better-looking file.

After clicking the Yes or No button, the image document opens in Fireworks.

4. **Make the edits you need to make to the image within Fireworks.**

   You can edit the image by using any of the tools in Fireworks, or change the optimization settings for the file in the Optimize panel.

5. **When you're finished editing the image, click the Done button in the upper-left corner of the Fireworks Document window (see Figure 10-2).**

   Dreamweaver becomes the active window and the image is automatically updated on the page, reflecting recent edits without requiring any other action on your part, other than saving the document.

After you click the Done button in Fireworks, you can't undo any changes you make to the image files by choosing the Undo command. The changes are permanent.

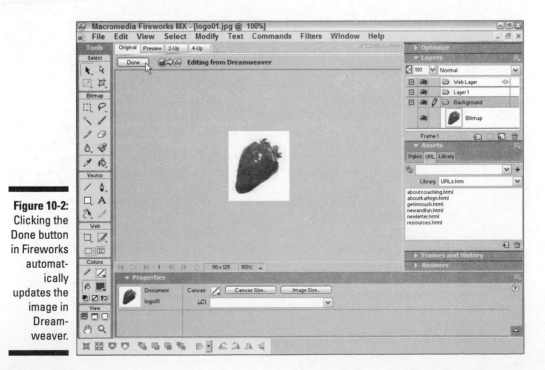

Figure 10-2: Clicking the Done button in Fireworks automatically updates the image in Dreamweaver.

PNG: Portable Network Graphics files

Fireworks uses the PNG *(Portable Network Graphics)* format as its native file format. PNG is similar to the PSD format, used by Adobe Photoshop, in that it retains the highest possible quality for the graphical image without suffering any of the degradation in image quality that usually occurs when a GIF or JPEG is generated. The Portable Network Graphics format was created long before Fireworks was. The PNG format is one of the few formats, in addition to GIF and JPEG, that can be viewed from within a Web browser. Because the PNG format allows for the many extra features that Fireworks offers, Macromedia chose it as the native format for Fireworks.

The PNG file format was originally created as a potential replacement for the GIF format because PNGs offered far greater image quality, compression levels, and numerous other features lacking in GIFs. PNG files offer a multitude of improvements over GIFs, including resolution up to 48 bits (as opposed to 8 bits in GIF), better compression, built-in *gamma correction* (the capability to adjust to the different brightness levels between PC and Mac monitors), and greater levels of transparency.

So, why are we all still using the GIF format? Although PNG files represent a marked improvement over GIF files, many of its most useful features simply aren't well supported by some browsers.

For more information about PNG files, take a look at the PNG home page at www.libpng.org/pub/png/, or the W3C PNG page at www.w3.org/Graphics/PNG.

Using an Image Editor Other Than Fireworks

When you click the Edit button in the Properties inspector (see Step 2 in the preceding section), Dreamweaver tries to launch Fireworks as its default editing application. But what if you don't use Fireworks or don't own a copy? Fear not: You can achieve a somewhat less-automated workflow with almost any other graphics editor. You just need to change your preferences in Dreamweaver to specify which program you prefer to use instead of Fireworks.

To designate a different application as the Dreamweaver external image editor, follow these steps:

1. **On the Dreamweaver menu bar, choose Edit⇨Preferences and select the File Types/Editors category.**

   The Preferences dialog box for File Types/Editors appears, as shown in Figure 10-3.

2. **Select an image format from the Extensions list.**

   For each file format, you can specify one or more external editors, in addition to a primary editor.

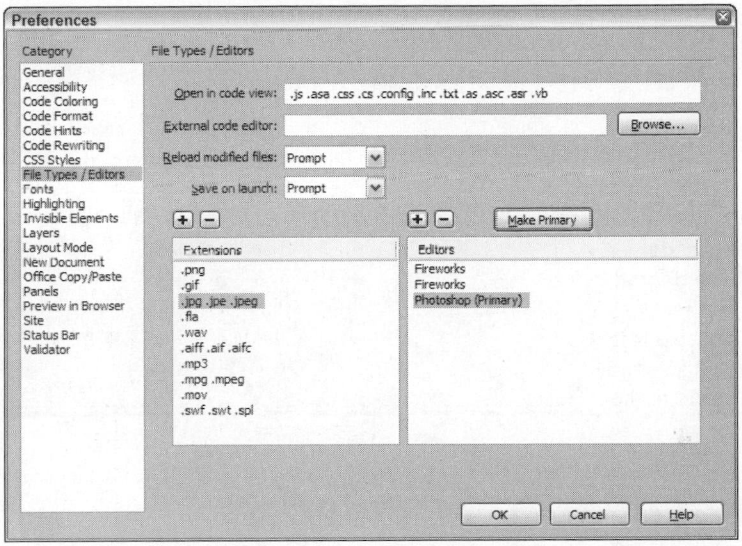

Preferences

Category | File Types / Editors

General
Accessibility
Code Coloring
Code Format
Code Hints
Code Rewriting
CSS Styles
File Types / Editors
Fonts
Highlighting
Invisible Elements
Layers
Layout Mode
New Document
Office Copy/Paste
Panels
Preview in Browser
Site
Status Bar
Validator

Open in code view: .js .asa .css .cs .config .inc .txt .as .asc .asr .vb

External code editor: _____ Browse...

Reload modified files: Prompt

Save on launch: Prompt

[+] [-]   [+] [-]   Make Primary

Extensions | Editors
.png
.gif
.jpg .jpe .jpeg
.fla
.wav
.aiff .aif .aifc
.mp3
.mpg .mpeg
.mov
.swf .swt .spl

Editors
Fireworks
Fireworks
Photoshop (Primary)

OK   Cancel   Help

Figure 10-3:
You can specify other image editors besides Fireworks.

3. **In the Editors list on the right, click the plus sign (+) to add an editor for all your GIF files.**

   The Select External Editor dialog box appears, asking you to find the program to assign as the editor for this file type.

4. **Browse your drive until you locate the graphics application you want to assign; then click the Open button.**

   After you click the Open button, the application appears in the list of image editors on the right.

5. **Click the Make Primary button to make it your primary editor. You can add as many editors to the list as you want, but you can assign only one primary editor for each file type.**

6. **Repeat Steps 2 through 5 for any other graphics extensions you want to assign to other graphics editors.**

7. **Click OK.**

   Clicking the Edit button opens the assigned application for the image format you changed. You can also select an alternative image-editing application when you right-click the image and open the Edit With menu.

Although you can use graphics applications other than Fireworks, none except Fireworks includes the Done button, which updates the image in Dreamweaver. If you use another application, you need to save the edited graphical image and import the image into Dreamweaver again manually.

Adobe Photoshop and ImageReady

Although Fireworks does the whole roundtrip thing with Dreamweaver and using Fireworks rather than another image editor makes more sense, many Web designers use Adobe Photoshop and its integrated Web application, Adobe ImageReady.

Because Photoshop and ImageReady can do many of the same functions as Fireworks (image slicing, optimization, rollovers, and animation), many designers reason: "Why spend time finding out how to use a new program and figuring out how to do what I already know how to do (and perhaps, do *well*) in another program?" Seamless integration with Dreamweaver is certainly a big benefit, and Fireworks is less expensive than Photoshop. However, both are excellent programs, and the choice is up to you.

Dreamweaver to Fireworks: Optimizing an Image

Suppose that the logo on your page looks fine, but is taking too long to download and needs to be compressed a bit more. The latest version of Dreamweaver puts immediate access to the Fireworks optimization window into the Properties inspector.

To optimize an image in Fireworks from within Dreamweaver, follow these steps:

1. **Select the image in Dreamweaver.**

2. **Click the Optimize in Fireworks button in the Properties inspector (see Figure 10-4).**

   The Find Source dialog box appears, asking whether you want to use an existing document as the source of the file you selected.

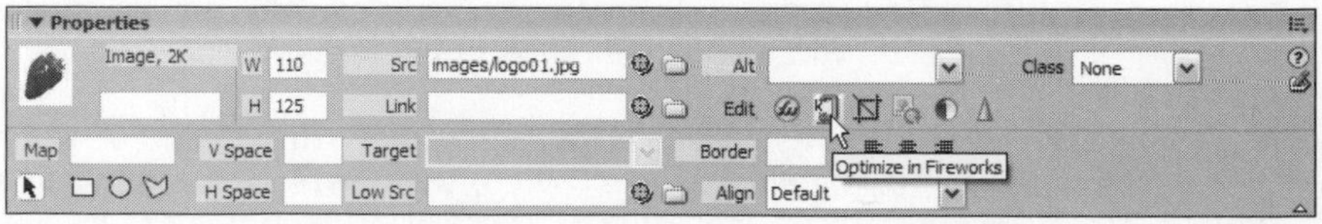

Figure 10-4:
The Optimize with Fireworks button is in the Properties inspector.

The default setting for this command is for Dreamweaver to ask about source files each time you launch Fireworks. You can change this setting by choosing Always Use Source PNG or Never Use Source PNG from the Fireworks Source Files pull-down menu in the same dialog box.

3. Click the Yes or No button in the Find Source dialog box.

Clicking the Yes button enables you to select a different file from the optimized image file on your page, such as the original file from which you exported the optimized Web version of the graphical image used on your page.

Clicking the No button opens the file used on your Web page and displays the optimization dialog box within Fireworks.

Whichever option you click, the image opens in the Fireworks Optimize dialog box.

4. Apply new optimization settings in the Options tab of the Fireworks Optimize dialog box (see Figure 10-5).

You can change the number of colors in the file or change its quality settings to achieve a smaller file size and then preview the changes within the Fireworks preview panel. You can also crop the image, but you can't make any other image edits in this window.

5. Click the Update button.

The file automatically updates in Dreamweaver with the changes you just applied. If you selected a PNG file to edit (you clicked the Yes button in the Find Source dialog box), the original PNG file isn't altered — only the optimized GIF or JPEG file is. If you cropped your image first, click the Reset Size button.

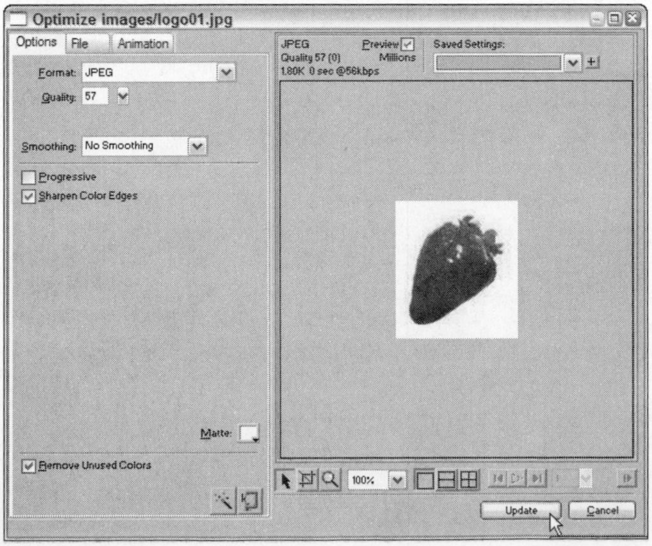

Figure 10-5:
You can optimize an image with the Fireworks Optimize tool without leaving Dreamweaver.

After you click the Update button in Fireworks, you cannot undo any changes you make to the image files by choosing the Undo command. The changes are permanent.

The coolest Fireworks optimization feature by far has to be the Optimize to Size Wizard. Click the button with a vise icon on it at the bottom of the Options tab and type the target file size. Then the wizard tries to compress the file enough to achieve the size you specify; this usually means a decrease in quality or in the number of colors used. Although the settings usually require a bit more tweaking after you run this command, the wizard does a great job of doing the groundwork.

Inserting Fireworks HTML

One of the niftiest Fireworks features is that you can automatically generate HTML files when you're cutting up images for your Web designs. This feature works well for slicing large graphics into pieces and generating tables to hold the pieces together. For example, you can use Fireworks to create a navigation bar, and then slice that bar to create a separate graphic for each navigation item. The only question is, after you generate this HTML code from Fireworks, how do you get it to your Dreamweaver page? Because Fireworks generates an HTML page, you can simply open that page in Dreamweaver, of course. But if you want to put that HTML directly into an existing Web page, you can easily insert the HTML and its associated images with just the click of a button.

To insert a Fireworks-generated table with sliced images into a Dreamweaver document, follow these steps (I assume in this example that you know how to use Fireworks to slice up images and generate HTML tables and that you have already exported an HTML file from within Fireworks):

1. **With a document open and the cursor placed at the point where you want the HTML to be placed, choose Insert⇨Image Objects⇨ Fireworks HTML.**

   The Insert Fireworks HTML dialog box appears (see Figure 10-6).

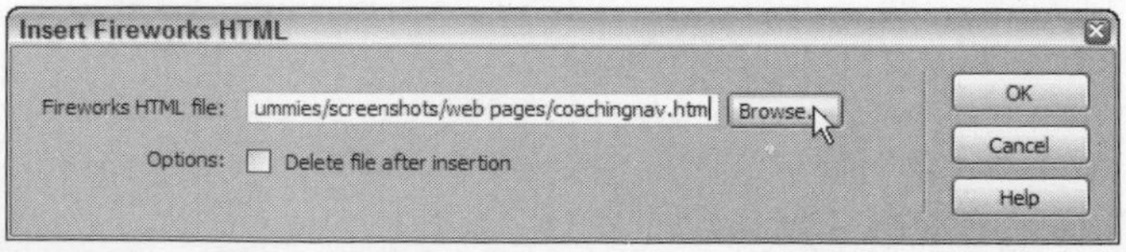

Figure 10-6:
You can insert Fireworks HTML directly into Dreamweaver.

Insert Fireworks HTML

Fireworks HTML file: ummies/screenshots/web pages/coachingnav.htm [Browse...]

Options: ☐ Delete file after insertion

OK
Cancel
Help

2. **Click the Browse button to select the HTML file to import; click OK when you have located it.**

   Dreamweaver inserts the table and its associated images from the Fireworks document into Dreamweaver (see Figure 10-7).

If you're interested in finding out more about Macromedia Fireworks, check out *Fireworks 4 For Dummies,* by Doug Sahlin, or the *Fireworks MX Bible,* by Joseph W. Lowery and Derren Whiteman, both published by Wiley Publishing, Inc.

Editing Fireworks HTML

After you insert Fireworks HTML into Dreamweaver, some special options become available in the Properties inspector, allowing you to easily edit the images and their associated code back in Fireworks. In Figure 10-7, you see that the Properties inspector adds a few items that appear only when you insert a Fireworks HTML table. One item is an indicator of the source PNG file for the images, and the other is an Edit button, which lets you edit the table in Fireworks.

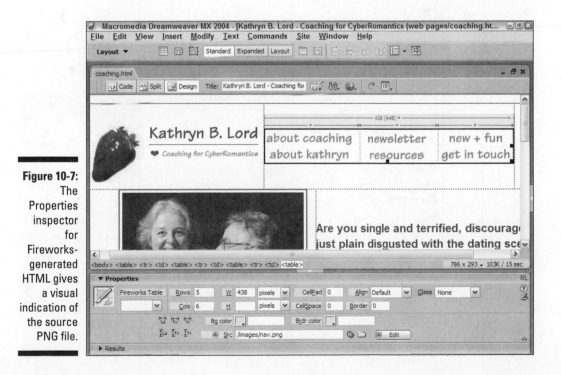

Figure 10-7: The Properties inspector for Fireworks-generated HTML gives a visual indication of the source PNG file.

To edit an existing Fireworks table in Dreamweaver, follow these steps:

1. **Select the table in the Dreamweaver document.**

   Fireworks-generated HTML imported into Dreamweaver becomes an "object" with special attributes that display in the Properties inspector when the object is selected (refer to Figure 10-7).

2. **Click the Edit button in the Properties inspector to launch Fireworks.**

   You're asked to find the original PNG file corresponding to the inserted HTML and images if Fireworks can't find it automatically. After you locate the PNG file, the image appears within a Fireworks document window.

3. **Make any edits or adjustments to the Fireworks document.**

4. **Click the Done button in the upper-left corner of the Fireworks Document window (see Figure 10-8).**

   The HTML code and graphics are regenerated and automatically updated in Dreamweaver!

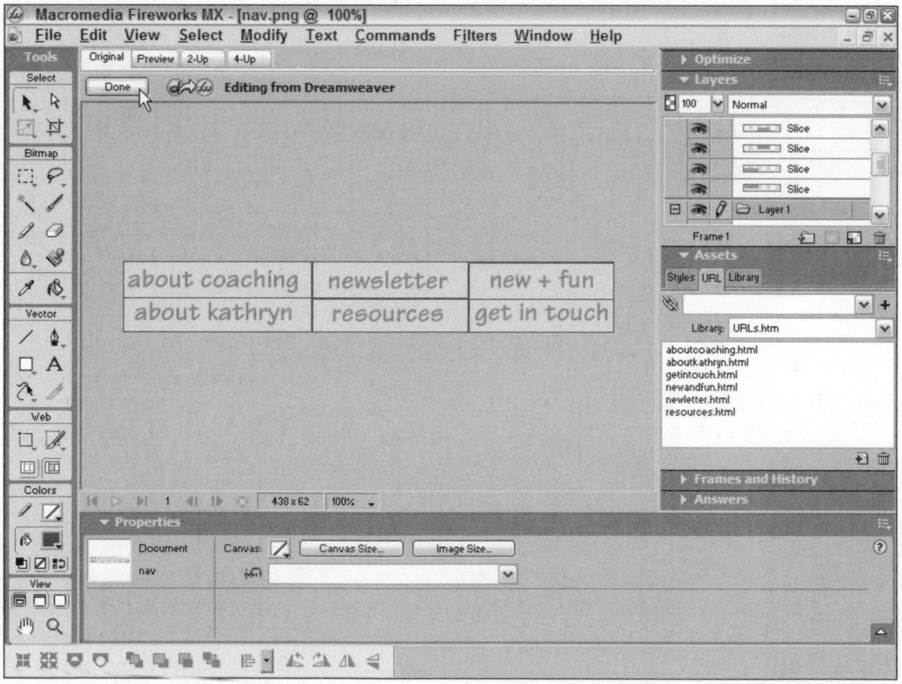

Figure 10-8: Clicking the Done button in Fireworks automatically updates the code in Dreamweaver without any further work.

Chapter 11

Showing Off with Multimedia

. . . .

. . . .

*T*hose who live in this multimedia world, spoiled by CD-ROMs and music videos, are far from satisfied with flat, text-based Web sites. Most Web designers want the rich, interactive features that they know are possible, even with the limits of bandwidth. They want animation, sound, video — the features that bring life to other media. But HTML, even with the addition of Dynamic HTML features, just doesn't fulfill those desires.

That's where plug-ins come in.

Plug-ins are small programs that work in cooperation with a Web browser to add support for non-browser functionalities, such as sound, video, and animation. These programs are called plug-ins because they're basically small applications that plug into the browser and extend its capabilities. Any company can create plug-ins, and some plug-ins have become so popular that Netscape and Microsoft have built them into their latest browsers. Plug-ins that aren't so well known require viewers to download and install them on their computers to run with the browsers.

Well-known multimedia and plug-in technologies include the Macromedia Shockwave and Flash players, the Real Networks RealPlayer, Apple QuickTime, and the Adobe Acrobat Reader, to name a few. In this chapter, you read about several types of multimedia and how to use Dreamweaver to place multimedia files in your Web pages. You also find out about making sure that your multimedia pages work in multiple browsers. Of course, many more plug-ins are available than I can cover in this book, but you find the most important ones here and general information that can help you with other formats in the section "Working with Other Plug-In Technologies," later in this chapter.

Working with Macromedia Shockwave and Flash Files

Flash and Shockwave are now among the most widely used plug-in technologies on the Web. Although the two have similarities, Macromedia provides a different plug-in for Shockwave and Flash media types. Anyone can download these plug-ins separately or get them all in one large plug-in package from the Macromedia Web site. The software that plays Shockwave and Flash is available as both a Netscape plug-in and an ActiveX control for Internet Explorer.

Dreamweaver can handle both Shockwave and Flash media types as well as most other media types that use the Netscape plug-in architecture.

What is Shockwave?

Macromedia Shockwave for Director enables you to display multimedia files created in Macromedia Director on a Web page. Director is the most popular program around for creating CD-ROMs and other types of multimedia titles, which means that the program has a large following and many people know how to use it. You can recognize a Shockwave file because it uses the extension `.dcr`. Shockwave is one of the best formats available for creating complex multimedia files — such as games — that include animation, sound, video, and other intensive interactive features, like the capability to shoot a target or drive a car. Shockwave has some powerful capabilities, such as the Lingo programming language, which enables complex interactive features, but it can also be a difficult program to study, and an even harder one to master.

Although Shockwave for Director is one of the most popular plug-ins on the Web, it still has a problem with file size. Most files created for CD-ROMs are huge, by Web standards. Developers who create Shockwave files for use on the Web face serious bandwidth limitations. Even though the process of converting Director files to Shockwave somewhat reduces file sizes, most developers stick to small, simple files that download quickly. Still, a few developers create large, complex Shockwave files and hope that their users have the bandwidth, or patience, to enjoy them. As always, when creating high-bandwidth multimedia files, you need to consider the audience you're targeting and the type of Internet connections visitors are likely to be using when you decide on file sizes. For more information on creating Shockwave for Director files, visit `www.macromedia.com/software/director`.

Using the <OBJECT> and <EMBED> tags together for best results in multiple browsers

HTML supports plug-in file formats, such as Macromedia Shockwave and Flash, through either the <OBJECT> or <EMBED> tag. Both tags accomplish the same task, yet each one is designed for only one particular browser. If you're designing Web pages for the broader audience of the World Wide Web, your best option is to use both tags in your HTML because, unfortunately, Netscape and Microsoft have never agreed on a standard. You see, some time ago, the two largest browser makers went off in different directions: Netscape created the <EMBED> tag, and Microsoft introduced the <OBJECT> tag. Both tags are used for the same task: to display plug-in media. Until the browser companies can agree on a standard, though, the best way to handle the situation is to use both tags when you insert plug-in files.

You can use these HTML tags together because browsers ignore HTML tags that they don't recognize. Because Navigator doesn't support the <OBJECT> tag, for example, Navigator doesn't display any file that is embedded using that tag. Internet Explorer understands the <EMBED> tag, but has better support for the <OBJECT> tag. You may wonder, if Internet Explorer understands both tags, why your media file isn't displayed twice. The reason is that the <EMBED> tag is contained within the <OBJECT> tag. You can, in fact, use the <EMBED> tag to link an alternative GIF or JPEG image that's displayed in place of the plug-in file if the browser doesn't support plug-ins or lacks the appropriate plug-in. Don't spend time trying to figure out whether you can get away with using only one of the tags; using both ensures that your pages are displayed properly for most people.

If you're writing the code yourself and want to design for optimal results in both browsers, make sure that you nest the <EMBED> tag within the <OBJECT> tag. Here's an example of what the HTML code looks like when you use both tags in combination to embed a Macromedia Flash file:

```
<object
    classid="clsid:D27CDB6E-
    AE6D-11cf-
    96B8-444553540000"
    codebase="http://download.m
    acromedia.com/pub/shock-
    wave/cabs/flash/swflash.cab
    #version=5,0,0,0"
    width="250" height="350"
    vspace="0" hspace="0">
<param name=movie value="flash-
    presentation.swf">
<param name=quality
    value="high">
<embed src="flash-presenta-
    tion.swf" quality=high plu-
    ginspage="http://www.macrom
    edia.com/shockwave/down-
    load/index.cgi?P1_Prod_Vers
    ion=ShockwaveFlash"
    type="application/x-shock-
    wave-flash" width="250"
    height="350" vspace="0"
    hspace="0">
</embed>
</object>
```

Before you get too worried about how complex the code is, let me reassure you: Dreamweaver creates the code for you. This example just shows you what's happening behind the scenes and provides an example in case you like to code these things by hand.

What is Flash?

You have probably heard a great deal about Flash but may be wondering what exactly it is and how it differs from Shockwave. Flash utilizes *vector graphics,* a technology in which the graphics in Flash are based on mathematical descriptions that take up far less space than bitmapped graphics, like the kind Shockwave uses. Because vector graphics are a description, they can be scaled up or down to fill a browser window of any size without affecting the image quality or the size of the file that's downloaded. Because of this ability to scale, Flash is perfectly suited for use on the Web. Flash files can be recognized by their file extension, .swf. Although Shockwave now supports vector graphics and Flash files can now incorporate bitmap files, Flash was specifically created to make Web files, and is still better suited to creating files that download faster.

As a format designed specifically for the Web, Flash continues to win acclaim and widespread adoption because it enables users to create animations that download really fast. You can also produce scalable, interactive animations with synchronized sound. All that, and you still get smaller file sizes than with any other animation technology on the Web. For more on why Flash files download more quickly than other file types, see the nearby sidebar, "Download Flash files in a flash."

With such great performance on the Web, why would anybody choose Shockwave over Flash? Well, Director is still a far more robust multimedia programming environment than Flash, allowing for much more complicated applications, particularly for games. However, if you don't have a need for a high degree of interactive content and don't relish the steep learning curve of Director, Flash is a better bet.

Like Director, Flash has an integrated programming language. It's called ActionScript, and although it isn't as robust as Lingo, it's powerful enough to interact with database-driven Web pages and can be used to create fairly complex games. If you want to see an example, try out the Banja game, at www.banja.com, which was built in Flash with a database backend.

Inserting Shockwave and Flash movies

Unless you have already created a Shockwave or Flash movie file to use, you can find a sample Flash file on the CD-ROM accompanying this book — just look for files with the .swf extension. In this section, you find out how to create Flash buttons and text directly within Dreamweaver.

Download Flash files in a flash

Flash files are dramatically faster to download because Flash images are *vector-based*. This term means that the images are made up of coded instructions to draw specific geometric shapes, filled with specific colors. As a result, Flash files often have a distinctive look that is similar to cartoons. These solid shapes and colors occupy much less space than the individual pixel data needed for bitmapped images, such as those used in animated GIFs. As a result, Flash files may be significantly smaller than other types of images and animation files. A 200K animated GIF that takes a minute to download on a 33 Kbps modem may be only 20K when it's re-created as a Flash animation and take only a few seconds to download. In fact, you can watch in Flash, over a regular 56 Kbps modem, entire animated cartoon movies that are 10 minutes or longer. You can find lots more information about creating Flash files at www.macromedia.com/software/flash.

If you need help using Shockwave or Flash, check out these books: *Shockwave For Dummies,* 2nd Edition, by Greg Harvey, and *Macromedia Flash MX 2004 For Dummies,* by Gurdy Leete and Ellen Finkelstein (both published by Wiley Publishing, Inc.).

To add an existing Shockwave or Flash movie file to a Web page by using Dreamweaver, follow these steps:

1. **Click to insert the cursor where you want the Shockwave or Flash movie to display on your Web page.**

2. **Select Common from the Insert bar, if it isn't already selected.**

3. **From the Media pull-down menu on the Common Insert bar, choose either Shockwave or Flash (see Figure 11-1).**

   You can also choose Insert➪Media➪Shockwave or Insert➪Media➪Flash. The Select File dialog box appears in either case.

4. **Browse your drive to locate the appropriate movie file that you want inserted into your page. Click to select the file.**

5. **Click OK.**

   After you click OK, the dialog box closes and the code is inserted into your document.

   Dreamweaver doesn't display plug-in media files in the Document window unless they're playing. Instead, you see a gray box that represents the Shockwave or Flash movie. To play the file, click to select it and then click the green Play button on the right side of the Properties inspector. Or, you can preview the page in a browser to see the file in context.

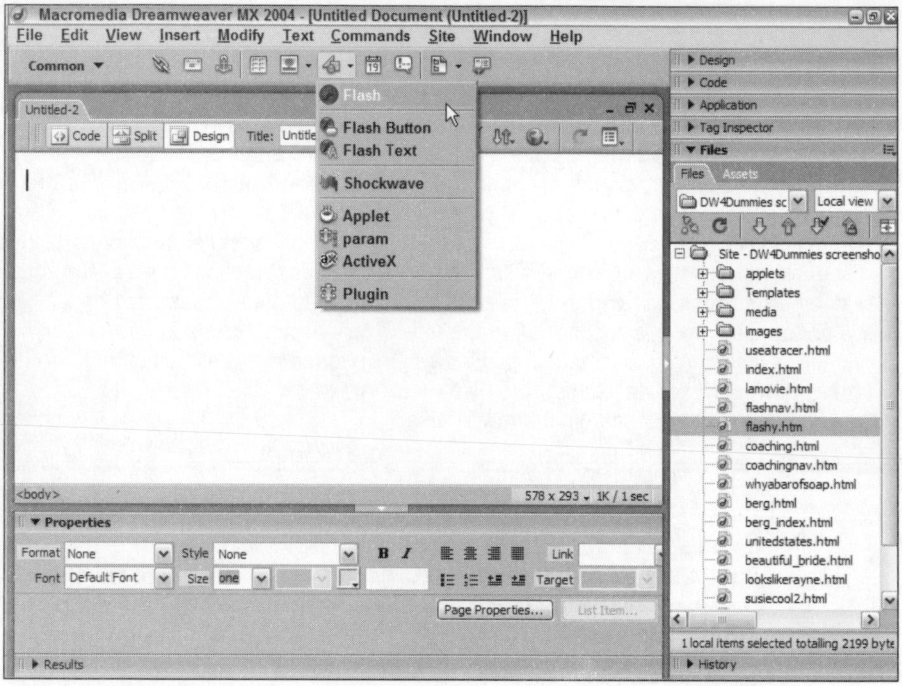

Figure 11-1:
You can
insert many
different
multimedia
file types
into your
documents
by click-
ing the
appropriate
icon on the
Insert bar.

Setting parameters and other options for Shockwave and Flash

Like most HTML tags, the tags that link Shockwave, Flash, and other plug-in files to Web pages have *attributes* (they're called *parameters* when used with the <OBJECT> tag). These parameters are even more important for plug-in files because you must set some of them — such as the height and width — for the file to work properly in a browser. Dreamweaver takes care of setting the height and width, but you may want to change some other settings. This section provides a list of attributes and parameters that you can change in the Properties inspector and describes what those attributes affect.

Don't worry about making sure that you specify property settings for both the <EMBED> and <OBJECT> tags. Dreamweaver automatically inserts both tags for you. If you want to see the code yourself, click the Code View button at the top left of the Document window.

If you don't see all the options in the Properties inspector, click the expander arrow in the lower-right corner to display the more advanced options.

This list describes the Flash options in the Properties inspector, as shown in Figure 11-2:

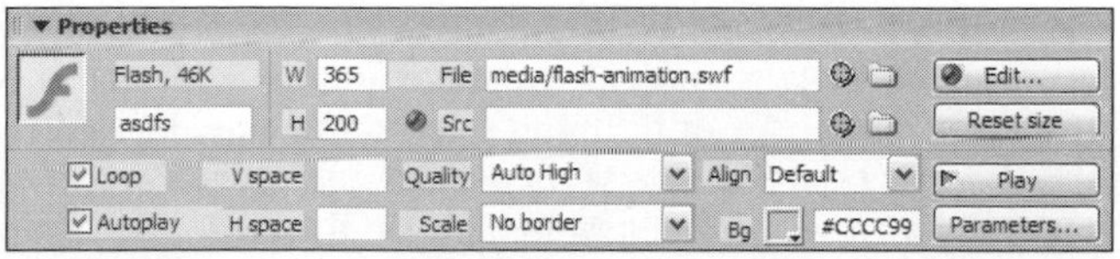

Figure 11-2:
The Flash options in the Properties inspector.

▼ Properties							
Flash, 46K	W	365	File	media/flash-animation.swf		Edit...	
asdfs	H	200	Src			Reset size	
☑ Loop	V space		Quality	Auto High	Align	Default	▶ Play
☑ Autoplay	H space		Scale	No border	Bg	#CCCC99	Parameters...

- **Name field:** Use the text field in the upper-left corner of the Properties inspector, just to the right of the F icon, if you want to type a name for your file. You can leave this field blank or name the file whatever you want. Dreamweaver doesn't apply a name if you leave the field blank. You only have to provide a name for scripting.

- **W (Width):** Use this option to specify the width of the file. The file is measured in pixels, but you can also set the file to be a percentage of the browser window's width by using a percent (%) sign immediately following the number.

- **H (Height):** Use this option to specify the height of the file. The file is measured in pixels, but you can also set the file to be a percentage of the browser window's height by using a percent (%) sign immediately following the number.

  Although the height and width pull-down lists in Dreamweaver include picas as a measurement, this feature doesn't work properly in the program and is not used commonly on the Web so we have not included it in the list of options in this book.

- **File:** Use this text field to enter the name and path to the file. You can change the name by typing a new name or path or by clicking the folder icon to browse for a file.

- **Edit:** You can launch the multimedia file in another program, such as Flash, where you can edit it and then return to Dreamweaver. Remember that in order to edit the file, you need the source Flash file. After Flash files are generated for Web use (.swf), they can't be edited.

- **Src (Source):** This text field allows you to identify the source file you used to create the .swf file for the Web. After this option is set, clicking the Edit button automatically opens the source file in Flash and provides a Done button to integrate changes back into Dreamweaver.

- **Reset Size:** Because Flash files can be scaled without losing any image quality, a Flash file is commonly scaled on a Web page to a different size from the size at which it was created. Clicking this button reverts the Flash file to its original size.

✔ **Loop:** Checking this box causes the Flash file to repeat (or *loop*). If you don't check this box, the Flash movie stops after it reaches the last frame.

✔ **Autoplay:** This option controls the Play parameter, enabling you to determine whether a Flash movie starts as soon as it downloads to the viewer's computer or whether a user must click a button or take another action to start the Flash movie. A check mark in this box causes the movie to automatically start to play as soon as the page finishes loading. If you don't check this box, whatever option you have set in the Flash file (such as onMouseOver or onMouseDown) is required to start the movie, or you can use a behavior with another element on the page to start play.

✔ **V Space (Vertical Space):** If you want blank space above or below the file, enter the number of pixels here.

✔ **H Space (Horizontal Space):** If you want blank space on either side of the file, enter the number of pixels here.

✔ **Quality:** This option enables you to prioritize the antialiasing options of your images versus the speed of playback. *Antialiasing,* which makes your files appear smoother, can slow down the rendering of each frame because the computer must first smooth the edges. The Quality parameter enables you to regulate how much the process is slowed down by letting you set priorities based on the importance of appearance versus playback speed.

You can choose from these Quality options:

• **Low:** Antialiasing is never used. Playback speed has priority over appearance.

• **High:** Antialiasing is always used. Appearance has priority over playback speed.

• **Auto High:** With this somewhat more sophisticated option, playback is set to begin with antialiasing turned on. However, if the frame rate supported by the user's computer drops too low, antialiasing automatically turns off to improve playback speed. This option emphasizes playback speed and appearance equally at first but sacrifices appearance for the sake of playback speed, if necessary.

• **Auto Low:** Playback begins with antialiasing turned off. If the Flash player detects that the processor can handle it, antialiasing is turned on. Use this option to emphasize speed at first but improve appearance whenever possible.

✔ **Scale:** Specify this option only if you change the file's original Height and Width size settings. The Scale parameter enables you to define how the Flash movie displays within those settings.

The following options in the Scale drop-down list enable you to set preferences for how a scaled Flash movie displays within the window:

- **Default (Show all):** This option enables the entire movie to display in the specified area. The width and height proportions of the original movie are maintained and no distortion occurs, but borders may appear on two sides of the movie to fill the space.

- **No border:** This option enables you to scale a Flash movie to fill a specified area. No borders show up, and the original aspect ratio is maintained.

- **Exact fit:** The Flash movie is exactly the width and height that are set, but the original aspect ratio may not be maintained.

✔ **Align:** This option controls the alignment of the file on the page. This setting works the same for plug-in files as for images.

✔ **BgColor:** This option sets a background color that fills the area of the file. This color displays if the specified height and width are larger than the file and during periods when the movie isn't playing, either because it's loading or has finished playing.

✔ **Play button:** Click the green Play button to preview the Shockwave or Flash file directly in Dreamweaver.

✔ **Parameters:** This button provides access to a dialog box where you can enter additional parameters for the Shockwave movie.

Creating Flash Files from within Dreamweaver

Dreamweaver features the ability to create and edit simple Flash files from within Dreamweaver. For simple Flash elements, therefore, you don't have to buy Flash or figure out how to use it — a huge savings. Though you can't create any fancy Flash animations, this feature still allows you to create graphical text objects and cool Flash buttons by using the familiar Dreamweaver interface. Dreamweaver has a large library of existing Flash objects that you can use. Even better, because the Macromedia Flash Objects architecture is extensible, you can download new Flash styles from the Web or work with Flash developers to create new Flash objects for Dreamweaver.Creating Flash text

With the Flash text object, you can create and insert a Flash (.swf) text movie into your document. Flash text movies allow you to utilize a vector-based text graphic in the font of your choice. (*Vector-based* means that the images are made up of coded instructions to draw specific geometric shapes.) The great advantage to using Flash text is that you can use any fonts you want without worrying about whether your audience has the same font on their computers. You can also set a rollover effect without the need to create separate images, and the size of the text can scale up or down without any effect on image quality or file size.

To insert a Flash text object, follow these steps:

1. **Save your Dreamweaver document.**

   The document must be saved before you can insert a Flash text object.

2. **Select Common from the Insert bar, if it isn't already selected.**

3. **From the Media pull-down menu on the Common Insert bar, choose Flash Text.**

   Or you can choose Insert⇨Media⇨Flash Text.

   The Insert Flash Text dialog box appears, as shown in Figure 11-3.

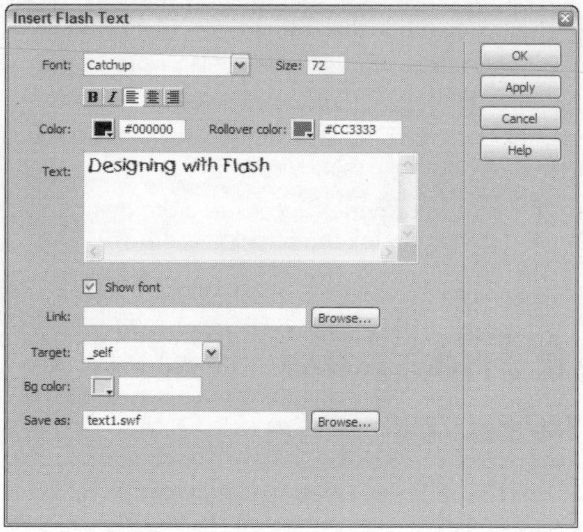

Figure 11-3:
The Insert Flash Text dialog box lets you create and edit interactive Flash text within Dream- weaver.

4. **Select the Text box options, including font, style, size, color, and alignment.**

   To see the text previewed in your font of choice, check the Show Font box. The other options are defined in this list:

   - **Rollover Color:** This option indicates the color that the text changes to when the user rolls the mouse over the text. If you don't want a rollover effect, make the rollover color the same color as the text color.

   - **Link, Target:** You can set these options for the text by using the appropriate fields. The link is activated when the user clicks the text.

   - **Bg Color (background color):** Make this option the same as the background color of the Web page on which you're placing the text.

• **Save As:** Always save the file with the .swf extension because you're creating a Flash file. Browse your drive to indicate where you want to save the Flash file.

5. **Click OK.**

You can also click the Apply button to see the effects in your Dreamweaver document before clicking OK.

The dialog box closes and the Flash text is inserted on the page. To edit the text again or change any of the options, double-click the Flash text to open the dialog box.

If you're interested in creating WYSIWYG (what-you-see-is-what-you-get) Flash movies, but don't want to spend the money for the program or don't have the time to figure out how to use it, check out Swish, a great little program that's reasonably priced. To find out more, visit www.swishzone.com.

Creating Flash buttons

Even more exciting than Flash text are Flash buttons. *Flash buttons* are precreated graphics that you can customize and use as interactive buttons on your Web sites. Like Flash text, Flash buttons are made up of vector graphics and can be scaled and resized without any degradation in quality. Dreamweaver ships with a library of more than 50 button styles for you to use. You can also add styles by downloading them from the Web or creating your own in Flash.

To insert a Flash button, follow these steps:

1. **Save your Dreamweaver document.**

The document must be saved before you can insert a Flash button object.

2. **Select Common from the Insert bar, if it isn't already selected.**

3. **From the Media pull-down menu on the Common Insert bar, choose Flash Button.**

Or choose Insert⇨Media⇨Flash Button.

The Insert Flash Button dialog box appears, as shown in Figure 11-4.

4. **In the Style field, scroll to select the type of button you want to use.**

You can view the selected choice in the Sample field.

5. **Select the appropriate options to customize your button.**

Enter the text you want to use in the Button Text field or leave it blank if you don't want any text on the button. Select the other text options, including font, style, size, color, and alignment.

Select the link, target, and background colors in the appropriate fields, if applicable.

Always save the file with the `.swf` extension because you're creating a Flash file. Browse your drive to indicate where you want to save the Flash file.

6. When you're done setting the options, click OK to insert the button.

You can also click the Apply button to see the effects in your Dreamweaver document before clicking OK.

The dialog box closes and the button is inserted on the page. To edit the button again or change any of the options, double-click the button to open the dialog box.

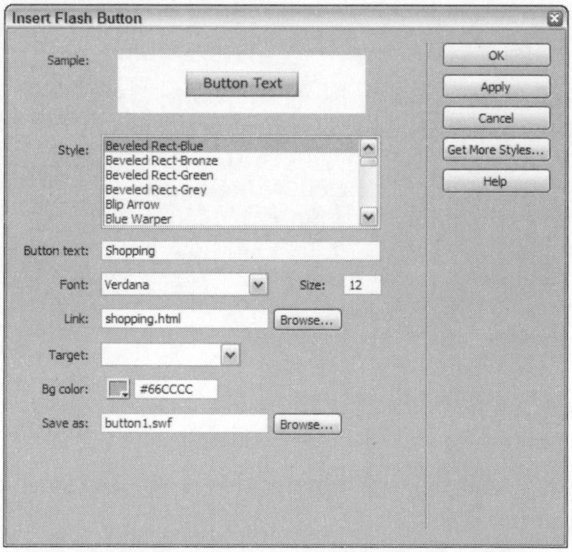

Figure 11-4:
The Insert
Flash Button
dialog box
lets you
create
and edit
interactive
Flash button
graphics
within
Dream-
weaver.

Adding new button styles

Because the Macromedia Flash Objects architecture is extensible, you can download new Flash styles from the Web or work with Flash developers to create new Flash objects to use in Dreamweaver. To get more styles from the Macromedia Exchange Web site, click the Get More Styles button in the Insert Flash Button dialog box. Clicking this button launches your Web browser and connects you to the Macromedia Exchange site, where you can download more buttons (you must have a live Internet connection).

Because Macromedia developed Flash as open source, you can create Flash files with a variety of programs, including Adobe Illustrator, which has an Export to SWF option. A great site for reading more about the latest in Flash development is www.openswf.org.

Working with Java

Java is a programming language, like Pascal, Basic, C, or C++, that you can use to create programs that run on a computer. What makes Java special is that it can run on any computer system and can be displayed in your browser. If you create a program in a computer language, you usually have to create one version for the Macintosh, another for the PC, and a third for Unix. But Java, created by Sun Microsystems, is platform-independent so that developers can use it to create almost any kind of program — even complex programs, like word processors or spreadsheets — that work on any type of computer without having to customize the code for each platform. Normally, programs also run independently of each other. But with Java, the programs (also called *applets*) can run within a Web browser, allowing the program to interact with different elements of the page or with other pages on the Web. This capability has made Java quite popular because it provides a way to add more sophisticated capabilities to Web browsers regardless of which operating system the Web browser is running on. You can embed Java applets in Web pages, you can use Java to generate entire Web pages, or you can run Java applications separately after they're downloaded.

Inserting Java applets

To insert a Java applet in your Web page, follow these steps:

1. **Click to insert the cursor where you want the applet to be displayed on your Web page.**

2. **Select Common from the Insert bar, if it isn't already selected.**

3. **From the Media pull-down menu on the Common Insert bar, choose Applet (the icon looks like a little coffee cup).**

   Alternatively, you can choose Insert➪Media➪Applet.

   The Select File dialog box appears.

4. **Use the Browse button to locate the Java applet file you want inserted on the page.**

5. **Click to highlight the filename, and then click OK to close the dialog box.**

   Dreamweaver doesn't display applets in the Dreamweaver work area. Instead, you see an icon that represents the applet. To view the applet on your Web page (the only way to see the applet in action), preview the page in a browser, such as Navigator 4.0 and later or Internet Explorer 4.0 and later, that supports applets.

6. **Select the Applet icon to open the Properties inspector.**

   You can set many options in the Properties inspector. If you want to know more about these options, read on.

TECHNICAL STUFF If you're having trouble viewing Java applets, the reason may be that you're using an older version of Internet Explorer. Microsoft and Sun have fought long and hard about Java standards, and as a result, native Java support was stripped from earlier versions of Internet Explorer. To view Java applets in older Microsoft browsers, you have to download Microsoft Virtual Machine or Sun Java Runtime. If your visitors are using an old version of Internet Explorer, you should prompt them to go to the Windows Update site to get a newer version.

Setting Java parameters and other options

Like other file formats that require plug-ins or advanced browser support, Java applets come with the following options (see Figure 11-5):

- **Applet Name:** Use this field in the upper-left corner if you want to type a name for your applet. Dreamweaver doesn't apply a name if you leave this field blank. This name identifies the applet for scripting.

- **W (Width):** This option specifies the width of the applet. You can set the measurement in pixels or as a percentage (%) of the browser window's width.

- **H (Height):** This option specifies the height of the applet. You can set the measurement in pixels or as a percentage (%) of the browser window's height.

- **Code:** Dreamweaver automatically enters the code when you insert the file. Code specifies the content file of the applet. You can type your own filename or click the folder icon to choose a file.

- **Base:** Automatically entered when you insert the file, Base identifies the folder that contains the applet. Most browsers aren't set up for automatic install, so you can type your own directory name.

- **Align:** This option determines how the object is aligned on the page. Alignment works just as it does for images.

✔ **Alt:** This option enables you to specify an alternative file, such as an image, that's displayed if the viewer's browser doesn't support Java. That way, the user doesn't see just a broken file icon. If you type text in this field, the viewer sees this text; Dreamweaver writes it into the code by using the Alt attribute of the Applet tag. If you use the folder icon to select an image, the viewer sees an image; Dreamweaver automatically inserts an <IMG> tag within the <OPEN> and <CLOSE> tags of the applet.

✔ **V Space (Vertical Space):** If you want blank space above or below the applet, enter the number of pixels you want.

✔ **H Space (Horizontal Space):** If you want blank space on either side of the applet, enter the number of pixels you want.

✔ **Parameters:** Click this button to access a dialog box in which you can enter additional parameters for the applet.

You can find lots more information in *Java 2 For Dummies,* by Barry Burd (published by Wiley Publishing, Inc.).

Figure 11-5:
The Properties inspector lets you specify options for Java applets.

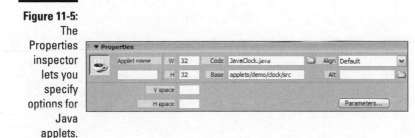

Using ActiveX Objects and Controls

Microsoft ActiveX objects and controls are reusable components similar to miniature applications that can act like browser plug-ins. Because they work only in Internet Explorer on the Windows platform, they're useful for only certain audiences. As a result, no clear standard for identifying ActiveX objects and controls exists. Still, Dreamweaver supports using ActiveX and provides some flexibility so that you can set the parameters for the ActiveX control you use, if you decide to use them.

The ActiveX Properties inspector provides the following options (see Figure 11-6):

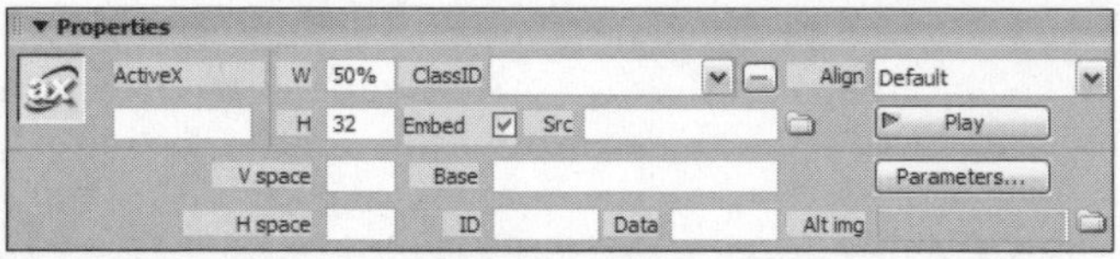

Figure 11-6:
The
Properties
inspector
lets you
specify
options for
ActiveX
objects and
controls.

✔ **Name text field:** Use the text field in the upper-left corner of the Properties inspector, just to the right of the ActiveX icon, if you want to type a name for your ActiveX object. You can leave this field blank or name it whatever you want. Dreamweaver doesn't provide a name if you leave it blank. This name identifies the ActiveX object only for scripting purposes.

✔ **W (Width):** You can specify the measurement of an ActiveX object in pixels or as a percentage (%) of the browser window's width.

✔ **H (Height):** You can specify the measurement of an ActiveX object in pixels or as a percentage (%) of the browser window's height.

✔ **ClassID:** The browser uses the ClassID to identify the ActiveX control. You can type any value or choose any of these options from the drop-down list: RealPlayer, Shockwave for Director, and Shockwave for Flash.

✔ **Embed:** Checking this box tells Dreamweaver to add an <EMBED> tag within the <OBJECT> tag. The <EMBED> tag activates a Netscape plug-in equivalent, if available, and makes your pages more accessible to Navigator users. Dreamweaver automatically sets the values you have entered for ActiveX properties to the <EMBED> tag for any equivalent Netscape plug-in.

✔ **Source:** This option identifies the file to be associated with the <EMBED> tag and used by a Netscape plug-in.

✔ **Align:** This option specifies how the object is aligned on the page. Alignment works just as it does for images.

✔ **Parameters:** Click this button to access a dialog box in which you can enter additional parameters for the ActiveX controls.

✔ **V Space (Vertical Space):** If you want blank space above or below the object, enter the number of pixels you want.

✔ **H Space (Horizontal Space):** If you want blank space on either side of the object, enter the number of pixels you want.

✔ **Base:** This option enables you to specify a URL for the ActiveX control so that Internet Explorer can automatically download the control if it's not installed on the user's system.

✔ **ID:** This option identifies an optional ActiveX ID parameter. Consult the documentation for the ActiveX control you're using to find out which parameters to use.

✔ **Data:** This option enables you to specify a data file for the ActiveX control to load.

✔ **Alt Img:** This option enables you to link an image that's displayed if the browser doesn't support the <OBJECT> tag.

Working with Other Plug-In Technologies

So many plug-ins, so little bandwidth. You can find literally hundreds of plug-ins available for Web pages. Some of them give you fabulous results, such as sound, video, a variety of image formats, and even three-dimensional worlds and animations. But with plug-ins — perhaps more than with any other technology on the Web — you have to be careful. Web page visitors aren't usually excited about having to download a new plug-in, even if you as a Web site creator are excited about deploying it. Indeed, many visitors are scared off by the idea, others are just plain annoyed, and others lack the hardware or software requirements to run them. Don't risk doing that to your viewers unless you have a compelling reason.

If you visit a site that sends you off to get a plug-in just so that you can see a logo spinning around in all its three-dimensional splendor, you may not be happy with all the work it takes to get just a little reward. On the other hand, if the site features interactive games or a three-dimensional environment with chat capability targeted for users with those interests, you may be quite happy to get a plug-in. Make sure that you let your users know what they're in for before you send them off on a plug-in adventure. You're also wise to stick to the better-known plug-in technologies — such as QuickTime, RealPlayer, and the Shockwave/Flash suite — because users are more likely to already have them or appreciate the benefit of getting them because they know that they can use them at other sites.

Inserting Netscape Navigator plug-ins

Because Netscape invented the idea of browser plug-ins, most plug-ins use the Netscape specifications to create new browser plug-ins. In most cases, Netscape Navigator plug-ins also function in Internet Explorer. Some of the more popular plug-ins are RealPlayer, QuickTime, and Flash and Shockwave, which are also considered Navigator plug-ins.

JavaScript is not Java

JavaScript, a scripting language that many people often confuse with Java, has little in common with Java other than its name and some syntactic similarities in the way the language works. To be more accurate, think of JavaScript as a much-simplified relative of Java's with far fewer capabilities. Unlike Java, though, you can write JavaScript directly into HTML code to create interactive features. You can't use it, however, to create stand-alone applets and programs, as you can in Java. You don't get the complex functionality of Java, but JavaScript is much easier to use and doesn't require a plug-in.

JavaScript is often used in combination with other multimedia elements on a page, such as images or sound files, to add greater levels of interactivity. Dynamic HTML also uses JavaScript and is covered in Chapters 8 and 9. In those chapters, you can read about how to use Dreamweaver to apply behaviors and other features created by using JavaScript with HTML.

To use Dreamweaver to insert a Netscape-compatible plug-in file other than Flash or Shockwave in your Web page, follow these steps:

1. **Click to insert the cursor where you want the file to be displayed on your Web page.**

2. **Select Common from the Insert bar, if it isn't already selected.**

3. **From the Media pull-down menu on the Common Insert bar, choose Plugin. (The icon looks like a puzzle piece.)**

   You can also choose Insert➪Media➪Plugin.

   The Select File dialog box appears.

4. **Browse your drive to locate the plug-in file you want inserted in your page and click to select it.**

5. **Click OK.**

   The dialog box closes and the file is automatically inserted on the page. You see a small icon that represents the file (the icon looks like a puzzle piece).

6. **Click the plug-in icon to open the Properties inspector.**

   You can set many options in the Properties inspector. If you want to know more about these options, continue reading the next section.

7. **Preview the plug-in (see Figure 11-7).**

   Dreamweaver doesn't display plug-in files in the editor unless the plug-in is installed on your computer, and you click the green Play button in the Properties inspector.

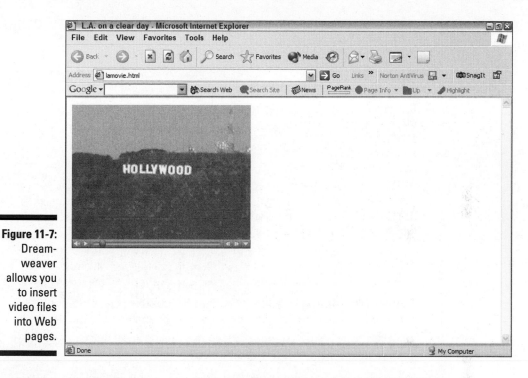

Figure 11-7:
Dream-
weaver
allows you
to insert
video files
into Web
pages.

Many people like to have multimedia files, such as video, pop up in a new or smaller browser window. To do this, simply create an HTML file with a multimedia clip in it, as I describe here. Then use the Open Browser Window behavior in Dreamweaver to create a pop-up window that displays your multimedia page. For more on how to work with Dreamweaver behaviors, see Chapter 9.

Setting Netscape plug-in parameters and other options

You can specify these settings in the Plug-In Properties inspector (see Figure 11-8):

✓ **Name text field:** Use the text field in the upper-left corner of the Properties inspector, just to the right of the plug-in icon, if you want to type a name for your plug-in file. You can leave this field blank or provide any name you want. Dreamweaver doesn't provide a name if you leave this field blank. This name identifies the file only for scripting purposes.

✓ **W (Width):** You can specify the measurement of any Netscape plug-in in pixels or as a percentage (%) of the browser window's width.

Figure 11-8:
The
Properties
inspector
lets you
specify
options for
Netscape
plug-ins.

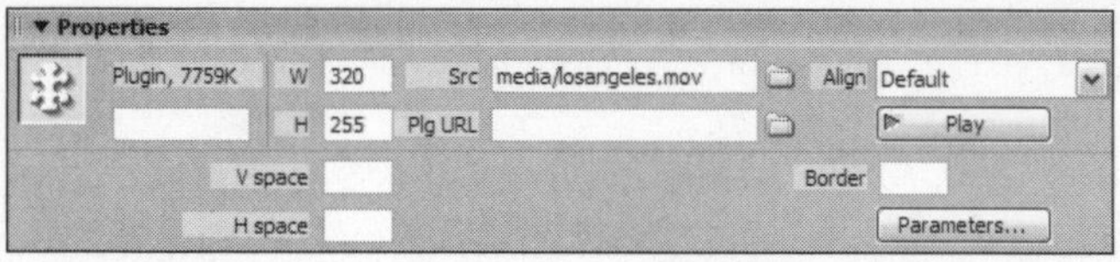

✔ **H (Height):** You can specify the measurement of any Netscape plug-in in pixels or as a percentage (%) of the browser window's height.

For most plug-ins, the height and width tags are required. However, in some cases — such as sound files that aren't displayed on a page — you can't specify height and width. In those cases, simply leave the fields blank.

✔ **Source:** This option specifies the name and path to the plug-in file. You can type a filename or click the folder icon to browse for the file.

✔ **Plg URL:** This option enables you to provide a URL where viewers can download the plug-in if they don't already have it.

✔ **Align:** This option enables you to specify how the element is aligned on the page. Alignment works just as it does for images.

✔ **Alt:** You can provide alternative content that's displayed if the viewer's browser doesn't support the <EMBED> tag. You can link an image as an alternative or simply type text that's displayed in place of the plug-in file. You can use this to provide information that displays if the browser does not support the plug-in.

✔ **Play button:** Click the green Play button to preview the media file. The media plug-in must be installed in either Dreamweaver (in the Configuration/Plugins folder) or one of the browsers on your computer for it to preview in Dreamweaver.

✔ **V Space (Vertical Space):** If you want blank space above and below the plug-in, enter the number of pixels you want.

✔ **H Space (Horizontal Space):** If you want blank space on either side of the plug-in, enter the number of pixels you want.

✔ **Border:** This option specifies the width of the border around the file.

✔ **Parameters:** Click this button to access a dialog box in which you can enter additional parameters for the plug-in file. See the documentation for the plug-in media type you're using for information on the parameters it utilizes.

If you want to add multimedia files to your site, but you don't know how to create them yourself, these two excellent sites provide ready-to-use, premade Flash files:

- **Flash Kit** (www.flashkit.com): Flash Kit is mainly an open source Web site where you can download premade, fully editable Flash source files to enhance your existing Flash animations or to use as a starting point for new animations.

- **We're Here** (www.were-here.com): We're Here also provides Flash source files for download and use. This site also offers sound loops and links to other Flash resources.

Chapter 12

Forms Follow Function

● ●

● ●

*T*he most powerful and interactive Web sites rely on HTML forms to collect data from users. Whether HTML forms are simple text boxes that
provide the interface to search engines or are long registration forms that
collect valuable consumer information from visitors, forms are a crucial
element of interactivity.

The HTML tags used to create forms — from radio buttons to drop-down
lists — are relatively simple to create, but they're designed to work in conjunction with more complex programming on your server. In the past, forms were
created almost exclusively with *Common Gateway Interface (CGI)* scripts. CGI
has been largely replaced now with a more direct way to interface with a
server, made possible by technologies such as ASP, PHP, JSP, and ColdFusion.
These programs are now generally referred to as *server-side applications,* or
ASPs, if they're big applications (not to be confused with the programming
language ASP). To find out more about CGI, visit www.pcwebopedia.com/
TERM/C/CGI.html.

To better understand how Web forms work, think of the elements that make
up a job application on paper. You can fill in your address in little boxes and
check off items. You can create these traditional elements from paper forms
in HTML with tags that enable site visitors to submit information to your Web
server and receive information back from the server. You can instantly create
elements such as check boxes, radio buttons, and editable text boxes with
different types of tags.

To collect the information from a Web form after a visitor fills it out, a program needs to reside on your server. The program requires programming that
goes beyond HTML. Technologies, such as CGI, and programming languages,
such as ASP, are most commonly used to create the programs that process
the data collected by forms.

Whether you want to create a simple guest book or a complicated online shopping cart system, you need to know how to set up the text areas, radio buttons, and drop-down lists that make up an HTML form. Fortunately, Dreamweaver makes creating forms easy by including a special Forms Insert bar at the top of the screen to provide quick access to common form elements.

In this chapter, you discover the kinds of forms commonly used on the Web and find out how to create them in Dreamweaver. You also find out a little about the CGI scripts, ASPs, and database systems that you can use to process forms. Forms are a key element in the most interactive, database-driven sites. You find information in Chapters 13, 14, and 15 about creating dynamic sites using the Dreamweaver features, but you need the information in this chapter to create the HTML forms that go with those high-end features.

Appreciating What HTML Forms Can Do for You

Forms follow function, to paraphrase the old saying. On the Web, functions require forms because forms are an integral part of interactive features. By using forms, Web designers can collect information from users — information that they can then use in a variety of ways. Forms are commonly used to create shopping cart systems, guest books, contact forms, search engines, chat rooms, and discussion areas.

Creating HTML Forms

The basic elements of HTML forms — radio buttons, check boxes, and text areas, for example — are easy to create with Dreamweaver, as I demonstrate in this main section. Remember that your form doesn't work unless it links to a script. Although Dreamweaver doesn't provide any scripts, it does make linking your HTML forms to a script or database easy. You need to know where the script resides on the server to set this link. The name and location of the script depend on your server, but for the purposes of showing you how to link to a script with Dreamweaver, assume that the script you need to link to is named `guestbook.pl` (the `.pl` indicates that the script was written in Perl) and that the script is on the server in a folder named `cgi-bin` (a common name for the folder that holds these kinds of scripts).

Understanding how CGI scripts work

Common Gateway Interface (CGI) scripts are programs usually written in a programming language, such as Perl, Java, C, or C++. Think of CGI scripts as the engine behind an HTML form and many other automated features on a Web site. These scripts are much more complex to create than HTML pages, and these languages take much longer to figure out than HTML. CGI scripts reside and run on the server and are usually triggered by an action a user makes, such as clicking the Submit button on an HTML form.

A common scenario with a script may go like this:

1. A user loads a page, such as a guest book, fills out the HTML form, and clicks the Submit button.

2. That action triggers the CGI script on the server to gather the data entered on the form, format the data, place the data in an e-mail message, and send the message to a specified e-mail address.

In Dreamweaver, you can easily create HTML forms and the Submit buttons that go with them (you can even use the new code editor in Dreamweaver MX 2004 to write CGI and other scripts), but you have to know a programming language in order to do so. If you know Perl, Java, C, or C++, writing most simple CGI scripts isn't that hard. But if you don't know one of these programming languages, you're probably better off hiring someone else to do it for you or

downloading ready-made scripts from the Web. If you search the Web for CGI scripts, you can find that many programmers write them and give them away for free. Be aware, however, that when you download a program, you run the risk of getting a virus with it (so look for trustworthy sites with good reviews). You also have to install any scripts you get on your server and almost always have to alter the programming code at least a little to tailor them to work with your unique system. You may also need to contact your Internet Service Provider (ISP) to help you load the script on the server because many commercial service providers don't give you access to do it yourself.

Many ISPs make basic CGI scripts (such as guest-book forms and simple shopping-cart systems) available to their customers as part of membership. That's an easy way to get scripts for your Web site that may even be worth the hassle of changing ISPs if your ISP doesn't now offer the scripts you want. Most ISPs that offer CGI scripts provide instructions for using them on their Web sites. These instructions include the location of the script on the server. You must include this information in your HTML form so that the Submit button triggers the proper script. You can find more information about setting your HTML form to work with a script in the section, "Creating HTML Forms," later in this chapter.

The following steps walk you through linking any form to this sample script. To use these steps with a different script, simply change the name of the script and the name of the directory location to reflect your system. Start with an open page — either a new page or one to which you want to add a form:

1. **Choose Insert⇨Form⇨Form.**

   You can also select the Form icon from the Forms Insert bar, as shown at the top of Figure 12-1. This handy option reveals all the form elements you may want to add as you create your form.

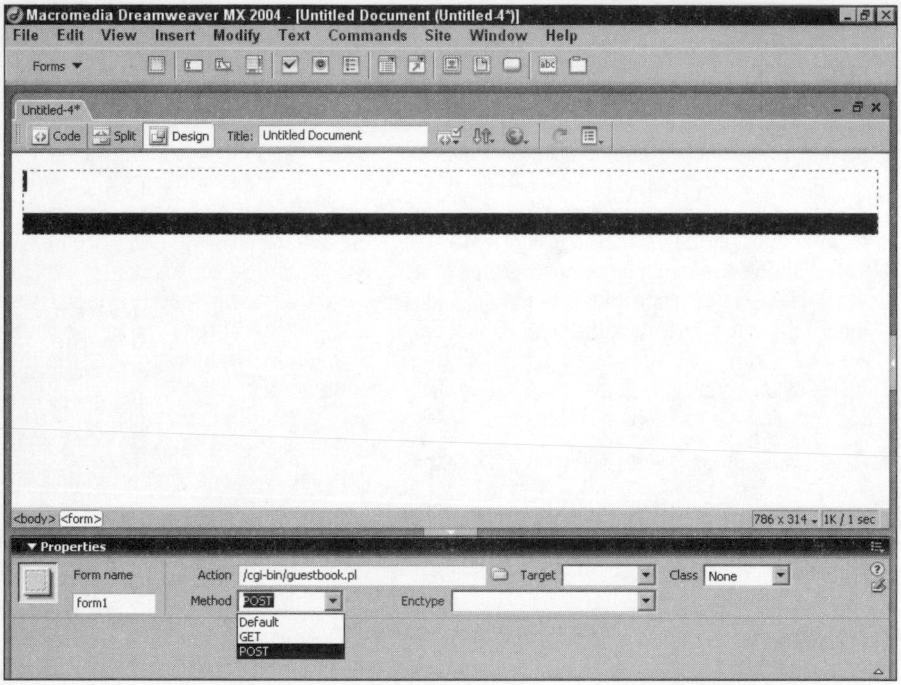

Figure 12-1:
The Forms
Insert bar
provides
easy access
to all
common
form
elements.

A blank form in Dreamweaver shows up as a rectangle outlined by a red dotted line, like the one shown in the main page area of the figure. This dotted line is used by Dreamweaver to indicate that an area is defined as a form in the HTML code.

2. **Click the red outline to select the form and display the form options in the Properties inspector (refer to the bottom of Figure 12-1).**

3. **Type a name in the Form Name text box.**

   You can choose any name for this field. Scripting languages, such as JavaScript, use the name to identify the form.

4. **Type the directory name and the name of the script in the Action text box.**

   Using the sample script I describe earlier, you can type **/cgi-bin/guest-book.pl** to specify the path to the Perl script in the cgi-bin directory. You can use the folder icon in the Properties inspector to set this link only if you have a copy of the script on your computer in the same relative location in which it resides on the server. If you're not the programmer, or you don't know much about the script, you probably have to ask your system administrator or Internet Service Provider for this information. (ISPs that offer scripts for their Web clients often include instructions with this information on their Web sites.)

Notice that the path to the script I include in the example starts with a forward slash, indicating the CGI-bin resides at the root level on the site.

5. **In the Properties inspector, use the Method drop-down list box to choose Default, Get, or Post (refer to Figure 12-1).**

   The Get and Post options control how the form works. The option you use depends on the kind of CGI script you use on your server. Get this information from your system administrator, programmer, or Internet Service Provider.

These are just the preliminary steps you need to take to create a form. When you establish the boundaries of a form, as represented by the dotted red line that appears after Step 1, Dreamweaver creates the code that goes in the background of your form and enables it to interact with a script on your server. The rest of this chapter shows you how to add various form elements, such as text boxes, radio buttons, and drop-down list boxes.

Comparing radio buttons and check boxes

Radio buttons and check boxes make filling in a form easy for viewers of your site. Rather than make users type a word, such as *yes* or *no,* you can provide radio buttons and check boxes so that users can simply click boxes or buttons.

Setting up secure commerce systems

Shopping-cart systems use HTML forms to collect data from visitors, such as the number of widgets they want to buy and the address where they should be delivered. You can sell millions of widgets over the Internet, but if you want to do it safely, you have to set up a secure transaction system to process the orders and confirm payment information.

Most shopping-cart systems on the Internet are linked to a secure transaction system. These systems use encryption technology to encode sensitive data (such as credit card numbers and customer addresses) that's entered into a form, which makes stealing the information difficult as it travels over the Internet. These systems are usually connected to a financial verification system that can immediately verify a credit card to approve or deny a charge and transfer funds to the appropriate bank account (yes, that should be *your* bank account) for the amount of the transaction. To make this process easier for businesses, many ISPs now offer complete e-commerce solutions, designed to help you coordinate all these requirements. Check the Web site of your Internet Service Provider to find out more. E-commerce systems are available also at Yahoo! (http://store.yahoo.com/) and at Costco (www.costco.com), in the Business Services section. To find out more about how secure transactions work and how to set up your own system, visit www.verisign.com.

What's the difference between radio buttons and check boxes? *Radio buttons* enable users to select only one option from a group. Thus, radio buttons are good for yes/no options or options in which you want users to make only one choice. *Check boxes,* on the other hand, enable users to make multiple choices, so they're good for "choose all that apply" situations when users can make multiple choices.

Creating radio buttons

To create radio buttons on a form, follow these steps:

1. **Click your form to select it.**

   If you haven't yet created a form, follow the steps in the section "Creating HTML Forms," earlier in this chapter.

2. **Click the Radio Button icon on the Forms Insert bar.**

   You can also choose Insert⇨Form⇨Radio Button. Either way, a radio button appears inside the form's perimeter.

3. **Repeat Step 2 until you have the number of radio buttons you want.**

4. **Select one of the radio buttons on the form to reveal the radio button's properties in the Properties inspector, as shown in Figure 12-2.**

5. **Type a name in the Radio Button text box.**

   All radio buttons in a group should have the same name so that the script associates them with one another and prevents users from being able to select more than one. If you want users to be able to choose more than one item from a list, use check boxes, as described in the following section.

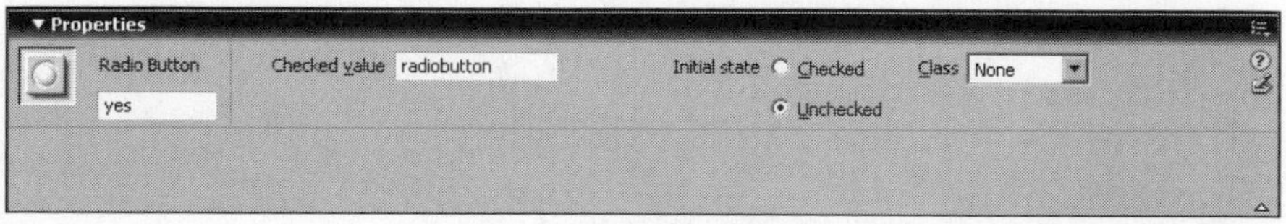

Figure 12-2:
Radio buttons are best for multiple-choice options when you want to restrict users to only one choice.

6. Type a name in the Checked Value text box.

Each radio button in a group should have a different Checked Value name so that the CGI script can distinguish them. Naming them for the thing they represent is usually best — "yes" when the choice is yes and "no" when it's no. If you're asking users about their favorite ice cream flavors, for example, use the names of the flavor the button represents. This name is usually included in the data you get back when the form is processed and returned to you (it can be returned in an e-mail message or sent directly to a database). How the data is returned depends on the CGI script or other programming used to process the form. If you're looking at the data later, interpreting it is easier if the name means something that makes sense to you.

7. Choose Checked or Unchecked next to Initial State.

These two buttons determine whether the radio button on your form appears already selected when the Web page loads. Choose Checked if you want to preselect a choice. A user can always override this preselection by choosing another radio button.

8. Select the other radio buttons (from the Forms Insert bar) one by one and repeat Steps 5 through 7 to specify the properties in the Properties inspector for each one.

Creating check boxes

To create check boxes, follow these steps:

1. Click your form to select it.

If you haven't yet created a form, follow the steps in the section "Creating HTML Forms," earlier in this chapter.

2. Click the Check Box icon on the Forms Insert bar.

You can also choose Insert➪Form➪Check Box.

3. Repeat Step 2 to place as many check boxes as you want.

4. Select one of the check boxes on your form to reveal the check box properties in the Properties inspector, as shown in Figure 12-3.

5. Type a name in the CheckBox text box.

You should use a distinct name for each check box because users can select more than one check box and you want to ensure that the information submitted is separated and can be associated with each individual check box.

6. Type a name in the Checked Value text box.

Each check box in a group should have a different Checked Value name so that the CGI script can distinguish them. Naming them for the thing they represent is usually best. As with radio buttons, the Checked Value is usually included in the data you get back when the form is processed and returned to you. If you're looking at the data later, interpreting it is easier if the name means something that makes sense to you.

7. Choose Checked or Unchecked next to Initial State.

This option determines whether the check box appears already selected when the Web page loads. Choose Checked if you want to preselect a choice. A user can always override this preselection by clicking the text box again to deselect it.

8. Select the other check boxes (from the Forms Insert bar) one by one and repeat Steps 5 through 7 to set the properties in the Properties inspector for each one.

9. After you have completed all other elements on your form, choose Insert⇨Form⇨Button.

Use this step to insert Submit, Refresh, and Clear buttons needed to complete the task.

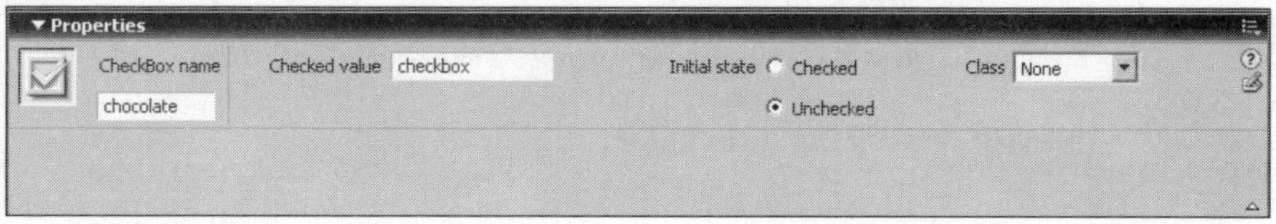

Figure 12-3:
Check boxes are best for multiple-choice options that enable users to select more than one option.

Adding text fields

When you want users to enter text, such as a name, e-mail address, or comment, use a text field. To insert text fields, follow these steps:

1. Click the form to select it.

If you haven't yet created a form, follow the steps in the section, "Creating HTML Forms," earlier in this chapter.

2. **Click the Text Field icon from the Forms Insert bar.**

   You can also choose Insert⇨Form⇨Text Field. A text field box appears.

3. **On the form, click to place your cursor next to the first text field and type a question or other text prompt.**

   For example, you may want to type `Address:` next to a text box where you want a user to enter an address.

4. **Select the text field on your form to reveal the Text Field properties in the Properties inspector, as shown in Figure 12-4.**

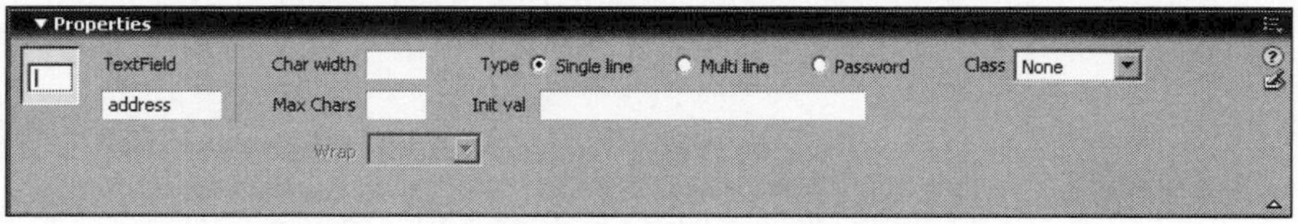

Figure 12-4:
Use the Text
Field option
to create
form fields
in which
users can
enter one or
more lines
of text.

5. **Type a name in the TextField text box.**

   Each text area on a form should have a different text field name so that the CGI script can distinguish them. Naming them for the thing they represent is usually best. In Figure 12-4, you can see that I named the Address option `Address`. Many scripts return this name next to the contents of the text field a visitor enters at your Web site. If you're looking at the data later, you can more easily interpret it if the name corresponds to the choice.

6. **In the Char Width box, type the number of characters you want to be visible in the field.**

   This setting determines the width of the text field that appears on the page. The size should be determined by the amount of information you expect users to enter.

7. **Type the maximum number of characters you want to allow in the Max Chars box.**

   If you leave this field blank, users can type as many characters as they choose. I usually limit the number of characters only if I want to maintain consistency in the data. For example, I like to limit the State field to a two-character abbreviation. Again, the size you make it should be determined by the amount of information you expect users to enter.

You can set the Char Width field to be longer or shorter than the Max Chars field. You can choose to make them different if you want to maintain a certain display area because it looks better in the design, but you want to enable users to add more information if they choose to. That way, if users type more characters than can be displayed in the area, the text scrolls so that users can still see the end of the text they're typing.

8. **Next to Type, click to select the button next to Single Line, Multi Line, or Password.**

   • Choose **Single Line** if you want to create a one-line text box, such as the kind I created for the Name and Address fields shown in Figure 12-4.

   • Choose **Multi Line** if you want to give users space to enter text. (Note that if you choose Multi Line, you also need to specify the number of lines you want the text area to cover by typing a number in the Num Lines field, which appears as an option when you choose Multi Line.)

   • Choose **Password** if the line is a text line in which you ask a user to enter data that you don't want displayed on the screen. This setting causes entered data to appear as asterisks.

9. **In the Init Val text box, type any text you want displayed when the form loads.**

   For example, you can include the words Add comments here on the form in the text field under Comments. These words were typed in the Init Val field of the Properties inspector for the Comments text field. Users can delete the Init Value text or leave it and add more text to it.

10. **Select the other text areas one by one and repeat Steps 5 through 9 to set the properties in the Properties inspector for each one.**

Netscape Navigator and Microsoft Internet Explorer don't support text fields in forms equally. The differences vary depending on the version of the browser, but the general result is that a text field is displayed wider in Navigator than in Internet Explorer. Unfortunately, this problem has no perfect solution, but you should test all your forms in both browsers and create designs that look okay even when the text fields are displayed differently.

Creating drop-down lists

When you want to give users a multiple-choice option but don't want to take up lots of space on the page, drop-down lists are an ideal solution. To create a drop-down list using Dreamweaver, follow these steps:

1. **Click your form to select it.**

   If you haven't yet created a form, follow the steps in the section "Creating HTML Forms," earlier in this chapter.

2. **Choose the List/Menu icon from the Forms Insert bar.**

   You can also choose Insert⇨Form⇨List/Menu. A drop-down list appears.

3. **Click to place your cursor next to the List field and enter a question or other text prompt.**

   In Figure 12-5, I use the example `What is your favorite sport?.`

4. **Select the field that represents the list on your page to reveal the List/Menu properties in the Properties inspector, as shown at the bottom of Figure 12-5.**

5. **Type a name in the List/Menu text box.**

   Each list or menu on a form should have a different name so that you can differentiate the lists when you sort out the data.

6. **Next to Type, choose Menu or List.**

   This step determines whether this form element is a pull-down menu or a scrollable list. If you choose List, you can specify the height and control how many items are shown at a time. You can also specify whether a user can select more than one item. If you choose Menu, these options aren't available.

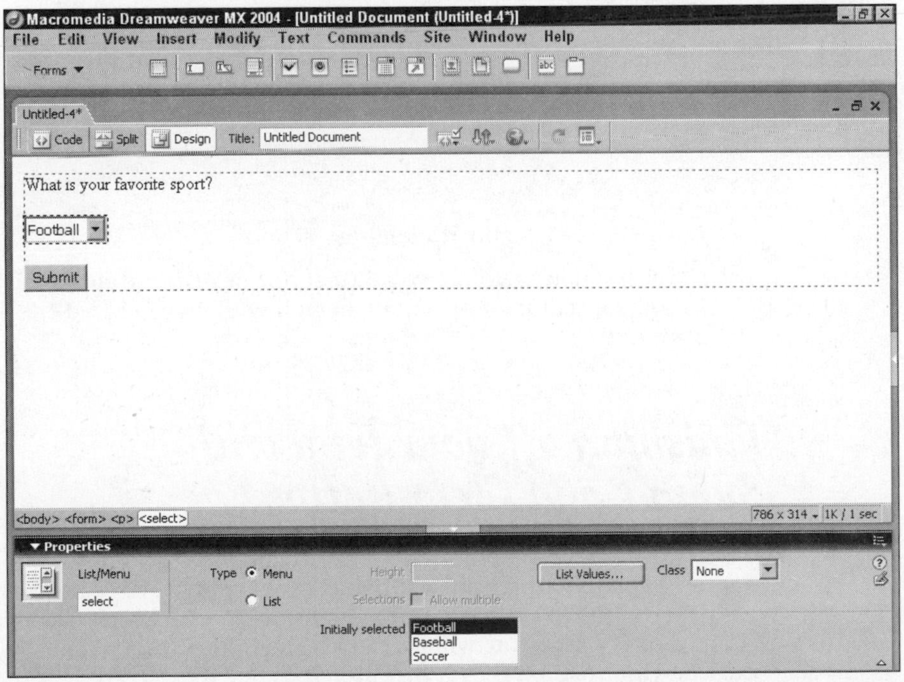

Figure 12-5: The List/Menu option enables you to create a drop-down list of options that don't take up lots of room on your page.

7. Click the List Values button in the upper-right of the Properties inspector.

The List Values dialog box opens (see Figure 12-6), and you can enter the choices you want to make available. Click the plus sign (+) to add an item label; then type the label text you want in the text box that appears in the dialog box. Item labels are displayed on the menu or list on the Web page in the order in which you enter them. Use the minus sign (–) to delete a selected option. Press the Tab key to move the cursor to the Value side of the dialog box, where you can enter a value. Values are sent to the server and provide a way of including information that you don't want displayed on the pull-down menu. For example, if you enter football as a label on the left, you can enter American as a value on the right to distinguish American football from soccer, which is often called football in other parts of the world. If you don't enter a value, the label is used as the only identifier when the data is collected.

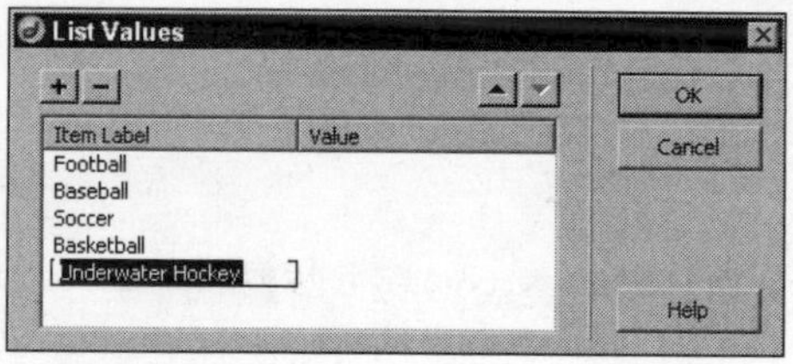

Figure 12-6:
Use the List
Values
dialog box
to create
the options
in a List
form field.

8. Click OK to close the dialog box.

Note that unless you have a CGI script or other program connected to this form, it isn't executed, even if you have created the form itself correctly.

Finishing off your form with Submit and Clear buttons

For your users to be able to send their completed forms to you, you need to create a Submit button, which, when clicked, tells the user's browser to send the form to the CGI script that processes the form. You may also want to add a Cancel or Clear button, which enables users to either not send the form or erase any information they have entered if they want to start over.

These buttons are easy to create in Dreamweaver. To create a button, follow these steps:

1. **Click your form to select it.**

   If you haven't yet created a form, check out the steps in the section "Creating HTML Forms," earlier in this chapter. I suggest that you also enter a few fields, such as radio buttons or text fields. There's not much point in having a Submit button if you don't collect any data that needs to be submitted.

2. **Click the Button icon from the Forms Insert bar.**

   You can also choose Insert⇨Form⇨Button.

   A Submit button appears, and the Form Properties inspector changes to reveal button properties. You can change it to a Reset button or other kind of button by altering the attributes in the Properties inspector, as shown in the remaining steps.

3. **Select the button you just added to display the button properties in the Properties inspector, as shown in Figure 12-7.**

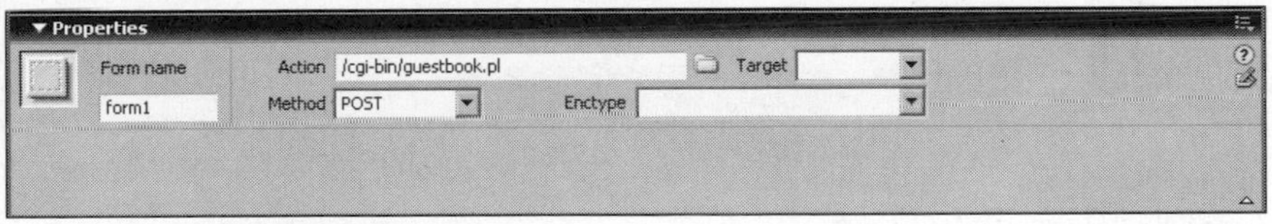

Figure 12-7:
Submit and Reset buttons enable users to submit their information or clear forms.

4. **Click either the Submit Form or Reset Form button, next to Action.**

   A Submit button invokes an action, such as sending user information to an e-mail address. A Reset button clears all user input.

5. **In the Label text box, type the text you want to display on the button.**

   You can type any text you want for the label, such as Search, Go, Clear, or Delete.

There you have it! Now that you know how to use Dreamweaver to create the basic elements of HTML forms, you can develop more intricate forms for your Web site. *Remember:* None of these forms works without a CGI script or other program behind it to execute when the information is entered.

Using jump menus

Many designers use jump menus as navigational elements because they can provide a list of links in a drop-down list without taking up lots of room on a Web page. You can also use a jump menu to launch an application or start an animation sequence.

To create a jump menu, follow these steps:

1. **Click your form to select it.**

   If you haven't yet created a form, follow the steps in the section "Creating HTML Forms," earlier in this chapter. Note that you don't need a Submit button to make a jump menu work, although adding one may make the action step clear to users.

2. **Click the Jump Menu icon from the Forms Insert bar.**

   You can also choose Insert⇨Form⇨Jump Menu.

   The Insert Jump Menu dialog box opens.

3. **In the Text area, under Menu Items, type the name you want to display in the drop-down list.**

   Click the plus sign (+) to add more items. As you type items in the Text field, they're displayed in the Menu Items list, as shown in Figure 12-8.

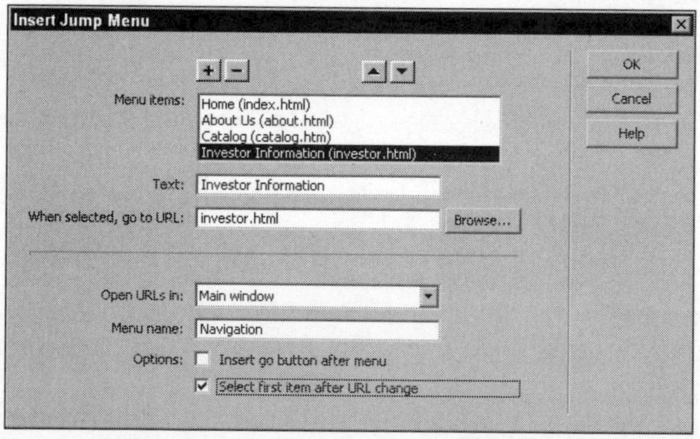

Figure 12-8:
When you create a jump list, items you type in the Text box are displayed in the Menu Items drop-down list.

4. **Use the Browse button to locate the page you want to link to or enter the URL for the page in the When Selected, Go to URL text area.**

   You can link to a local file or enter any URL to link to a page on another Web site and you can use the Browse button to specify the URL you want to link to.

5. **Use the Open URLs In field to specify a target if you're using frames.**

   If you're not using frames, the default is Main Window. Then, when the user selects an option, the new page replaces the page he is viewing.

6. **Use the Menu Name field if you want to enter a unique identifier for this menu.**

   This option can be useful if you have multiple jump menus on a page. You can use any name you want.

7. **Use the Insert Go Button After Menu option if you want to force users to click a button to activate the selection.**

   If you don't add a Go button, the linked page loads automatically as soon as the user makes a selection. The Go button is really just a Submit button — it's just usually labeled a Go button on a Jump menu.

   If you don't use a Go button, a user has no way to return to the same option, even by going back to that page or if the drop-down list is still visible because it's in a frame. The Go button lets you get around this situation and keeps all options available.

Choosing other form options in Dreamweaver

As though all the features I describe earlier in this chapter aren't enough, Dreamweaver includes a few specialized form options for facilitating interactivity, adding images, and even adding hidden fields. This list explains how you can use each of these options:

- **File Field icon:** Enables you to add a Browse option to a form so that users can upload files from their local computers to your server. The button enables users to upload images or text files, but it works only if your server is set up to handle this kind of upload from a browser. Check with your system administrator if you're not sure.

- **File Field feature:** Enables users to contribute their own materials to your Web site. For example, *The Miami Herald* has a "Build your own Web site" system that enables readers to create their own, individual sites. Many Web sites now provide this service to users. The sites are generally template-based systems that walk readers through a series of forms where they choose designs and enter text that they want to appear on their Web pages. Most people want to be able to add more than just text to their sites — they want to add their own images, such as logos and photos. That's where a File field becomes necessary. By using this form option, you can enable readers to browse their own hard drives for a file and then automatically upload it to your server, where it can be linked to their pages.

The complex File Field feature requires a sophisticated CGI script and special server access to work. If you aren't a programmer, you may need assistance to use this option on your site.

✔ **Image Field icon:** Makes adding an image to your form simple and easy.

✔ **Hidden Field icon:** Inserts text that isn't displayed to users but can be used by a script or other application that processes the form.

Making your forms look good

The best way to get your form fields to line up nicely is to use an HTML table. You may want to use a table to align a form by putting all your text in one row of cells and all your text fields in an adjacent row. You may also want to place all your radio buttons in the cells on the left and the text they correspond to in the cells on the right. (Chapter 6 shows you how to create HTML tables and how to use them to align information in your forms.) You can also use images and table border to make tables look better.

Part V
Working with Dynamic Content

The 5th Wave   By Rich Tennant

"See? I created a little felon figure that runs around our Web site hiding behind banner ads. On the last page, our logo puts him in a non lethal choke hold and brings him back to the home page."

In this part . . .

The most sophisticated and technically complicated Web sites are created using complex databases and often generate Web pages on the fly and make adding and managing data much more flexible and robust. The Macromedia creation tools for dynamic, database-driven Web sites started out as a separate program, called UltraDev. With Dreamweaver MX (the previous version of Dreamweaver), these features were incorporated into the program, and with the latest version, Dreamweaver MX 2004, these features are refined and enhanced to be more valuable than ever. In this part, you discover the benefits of creating a dynamic site, find out how to work with a database on the Web, and follow step-by-step instructions to build your first dynamic site.

Chapter 13

Building a Dynamic Web Site: Getting Started

Many Web designers farm out Web design work to programmers because the designers don't think that they have time themselves to find out all about databases and servers and ASP programming and all that complicated stuff, especially when they're trying to finish a project on a tight deadline.

But just as Web sites became more complicated to build, Macromedia released Dreamweaver UltraDev, which introduced a whole new level of integration to the world of Web development. Some designers call this wonderful tool their "developer-in-a-box."

You used to have to buy all those great features as separate programs, but with the release of Dreamweaver MX, Macromedia has integrated these tools right into Dreamweaver. Since this latest release, these features have become even more robust and versatile.

You may still need to give a hearty helping of work to the programmers, but Dreamweaver has definitely given you an easier time of taking care of more of this business on your own.

Dreamweaver now packs in all the UltraDev features, enabling you to write code and insert "developer speak" using buttons and simple on-screen instructions — so that you don't have to study high-end programming. With just a few clicks (and some patience while you take in all the nuances of what makes it work), you can create anything from a search engine for your Web site to an online catalog with thousands of products.

This chapter begins by introducing you to what a dynamic Web site and a database are and the many ways in which, through a dynamic Web site, you can display and edit information contained within a database. You also discover what you need to have in place in order to create a dynamic Web site.

A description of the more advanced Dreamweaver database features is beyond the scope of this book, but if you like what you find here, you can go on to find out more about the Dreamweaver advanced features on Macromedia DevNet (http://www.macromedia.com/devnet/mx/dreamweaver/) or in the *Dreamweaver MX Bible*, written by Joseph Lowery (published by Wiley Publishing, Inc.).

In Chapters 14 and 15, you find step-by-step directions to creating various dynamic features on a real-world Web site.

You also find on the CD-ROM a sample database that you can use as you follow the exercises in this chapter and Chapters 14 and 15.

Understanding the Dynamic Web Site

A *dynamic* Web site is usually connected to a *database,* which enables a Web site visitor to retrieve information relevant to his or her requests. The visitor (or sometimes a Web site administrator or content editor) can also make changes to the information that is displayed through a series of simple steps without ever leaving the Web browser. A good example of a dynamic Web site is a search engine on a Web site. You can type what you want to find and get instant results with information from within that site that is relevant (ideally, anyway!) to your search request.

A dynamic Web site has many advantages besides the ability to create a site-wide search. Suppose that you have a Web site where you sell 32 health-and-wellness supplements. On a *static* Web site, you would have to create 32 pages, one for each product. With a database in place however, you create just *one* page that contains special code where the product name, image, description, and any other pertinent information goes. The special code then communicates with the database, grabs each product's information from the database, and creates a page on the fly for each of those products.

Dynamic Web sites also allow changes and updates to be made with little effort. Through a Web browser, users can add or remove products and make changes to existing products without knowing much about databases or programming. They simply enter the information on a form in a Web browser and click Submit. The new information appears instantly the next time the page is loaded. Usually, you would limit the ability to make these changes to a few people on your staff. You don't necessarily want your customers making price changes or altering product descriptions, but you may want your sales staff to be able to easily make changes, even when they're out in the field. You can control this situation by setting up different levels of access to your site. That way, customers can search for information, and staff members with special access and the right passwords can make changes. The system you use to do both these tasks, however, is essentially the same.

Not all Web sites need to be dynamic. A three-page personal Web site can be static and run effectively. However, if the Web site includes hundreds of pages and consists mainly of similar content — for example, a news Web site, or an online catalog — going dynamic may be your best bet. I want to make clear that a Web site of that magnitude involves a significant amount of setup and pages before a data-entry person can make those quick and easy updates. The programmer could spend much more time setting up a simple content-management form than creating a couple of static pages. The big payoff (in both time and money) comes down the line, when it's time to update those pages.

Talking the Talk: Key Concepts

Before jumping into your first dynamic Web site, you should become familiar with a few concepts because they play an integral role in this show.

Exploring a database

A *database* is a collection of information compiled in one or more *tables* with *fields* organized in columns, and *records* in rows. What? Okay, picture a mail-order catalog, such as Pottery Barn. (Indulge me — it's my favorite.)

The catalog itself is the *database*. It contains a collection of information about various products. Each product is a *record* in the database. In this case, a particular product has an item number, price, and a color — and each of those is a *field*. A *record* in a database consists of a complete set of all fields in the database. Taking it a step further, within the catalog, the various products are organized in categories often because they have something in common (furniture, rugs, bedding, wall décor). Each category is a *table* — a grouping of various records from a database that have something in common.

This type of table isn't the same kind discussed in Chapter 6, where you find out how HTML tables are used to format information, much like you would use a spreadsheet program, such as Excel. Database tables aren't used for formatting; they're for grouping and organizing content.

How it works on the Web

Let's take this concept to the Web. It works in much the same way. Suppose that you go to www.penpal.net to find a new penpal. You can search by location, gender, and age: Starting on the www.penpal.net search page, you can click on the search by country link. On the next page you can click on France. The following page lets you choose gender and age range. You might choose Female, Ages 21 to 30, and on the last page you can choose a specific age, 25 for example. After you click 25, a list of potential penpals who match your requirements appears right before your eyes (see Figure 13-1).

When you submitted your criteria, some specific code on that page matched your information with information in a database that lists other people looking for a penpal. It looked through every field (individual criterion), trying to find records (penpals) with fields that matched your request. If you want, you could also list yourself as a potential penpal for others to find you, by entering your information and adding it to the database, directly from your Web browser!

Database applications

Various applications are made specifically for creating and managing databases, including Microsoft Access, SQL Server, MySQL, FoxPro, and Oracle. Novices most commonly use Access to create small databases (MDB files). Access is also commonly used to communicate visually with bigger databases, such as MSSQL.

The examples in this book were created in Microsoft Access 2000 running with Windows XP Professional system software. If you want to dig deeper into the world of databases, consider purchasing *Database Development For Dummies* and *SQL For Dummies*, both written by Allen G. Taylor; *Access 2002 For Dummies,* written by John Kaufeld; and *Oracle8i For Dummies,* written by Carol McCullough-Dieter (all published by Wiley Publishing, Inc.).

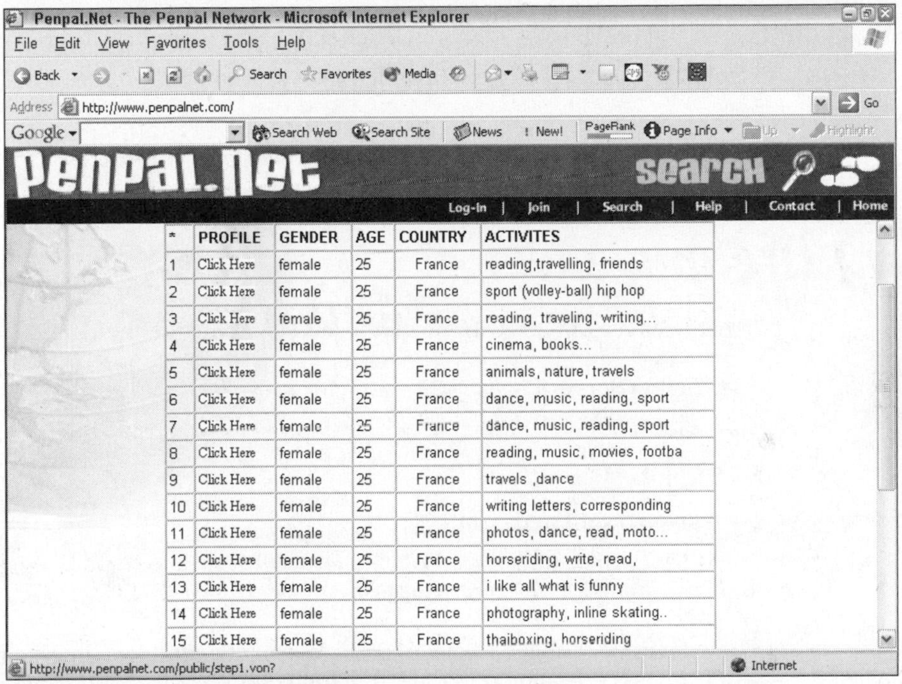

Figure 13-1:
The
Penpal.net
results
page.

Plugging in the data

Now that you have the database basics covered, you need to provide a way for the Web site and the database to communicate. In the next section, I show you how to set up a Web server and an application server step-by-step so that you can get started.

Setting up the Web server

While working with Web sites that are *static* (the content is entered by hand and isn't influenced by, nor does it interact with, the person viewing the site), you may be used to previewing pages directly from your local hard drive. It's not that simple when the content is dynamic because Dreamweaver MX 2004 adds some special code that needs to be processed by a server before content is published to the viewer. Having a Web server is crucial when you're working with a dynamic Web site, because you need to test your work along the way to make sure that you get the results you're shooting for.

A *Web server* is a system on which a Web site is stored or the software on that system that provides the server functionality. In this case, the Web server I'm referring to is the software installed on a system, not an actual system.

Server Technologies Supported by Dreamweaver

Dreamweaver MX 2004 supports these five server technologies:

- Active Server Pages (ASP)
- ASP.NET
- ColdFusion
- JavaServer Pages (JSP)
- PHP (which stands for PHP: Hypertext Preprocessor — a recursive acronym, for you wordsmiths)

The examples in this book use ASP in Microsoft Windows. In essence, all five work toward the same outcome: dynamic content on a Web page or Web site. They all provide the ability to generate HTML dynamically. Using server-side code, they can display information from a database and create HTML based on whether certain criteria are met or specified by a particular user. The following sections provide more detail on each of these scripting languages.

ASP

ASP is a server technology that comes, at no additional cost, built into Windows 2003 Server, Windows 2000, Windows XP Professional, and can be easily installed into Windows 98 and NT. Used in conjunction with Microsoft IIS or Personal Web Server, ASP isn't a standalone programming language because much of the code you write for ASP pages is in VB Script or JavaScript.

ASP.NET

ASP.NET is a relatively new server technology. It's not a revision of ASP 3.0, in fact, it's almost a complete overhaul of it. This latest installment of ASP isn't what 3.0 was to 2.0 — Microsoft has done more than add new tags. The language is more similar to traditional programming languages, like C++, where code is compiled. This arrangement suggests that applications written in ASP.NET will run faster than anything now available because Web servers will be working less. However, ASP.NET isn't as verbose as ASP 3.0, so it's much harder for novice programmers to read. ASP.NET is a Microsoft technology and more information can be found at `http://msdn.microsoft.com/asp.net/`. You can also check out this great site, to find out more about ASP.NET in what more closely resembles plain English: `www.4guysfromrolla.com`.

JavaServerPages (JSP)

JSP is from Sun Microsystems. Because its dynamic code is based on Java, you can run the pages from non-Microsoft Web servers. You can use JSP on Allaire JRun Server and IBM WebSphere. Using JSP, you can create and keep the dynamic code separated from the HTML pages (by using Java Beans), or you can embed the JSP code into the page. Unless you're a hardcore programmer, however, JSP is horribly complex.

ColdFusion MX

ColdFusion MX, owned by Macromedia, uses its own server and scripting language. ColdFusion is probably the easiest language to figure out and it offers built in XML processing and custom tags that also allow you to separate dynamic code from HTML, which makes it similar to JSP in a way.

PHP

PHP was originally native to Unix-based servers. However, you can now download Windows binaries from `www.php.net` to run Apache (a server software typically used with PHP) from any version of Windows as well as IIS on NT, 2000, XP Professional, and 2003 Server. You can even configure PHP to run on Personal Web Server (although it's rather tricky). The PHP scripting language is based on C, Perl, and Java. You can get more functionality with PHP right out of the box than you can with ASP. For example, virtually every ASP add-on that's on sale at `www.serverojects.com` comes built-in standard or is available for free from PHP.net.

To recommend one technology over the other really wouldn't be fair because they all offer similar functionality with slight variations in speed and efficiency. The most marketable language is ASP because of its widely used and mature features. If you dream of becoming a highly paid programmer, you can't go wrong with this one.

Check out these other titles, all published by Wiley Publishing, Inc.: *The Active Server Pages Bible,* by Eric Smith; *ASP.NET For Dummies,* by Bill Hatfield; *Java Server Pages For Dummies,* by MacCormac Reinhart; *ColdFusion MX For Dummies,* by John Paul Ashenfelter; and *PHP 4 Bible,* by Tim Converse.

Making the Data Connection

To set up a *Web server,* you need server software. A Web server, sometimes called an HTTP server, responds to requests from a Web browser by serving up Web pages based on those requests.

You also need to set up an *application server,* which helps the Web server to process specially marked Web pages. When the browser requests one of these pages, the Web server hands the page off to the application server, which processes it before sending the page to the browser.

I use ASP specifically for the examples in this section because it's much easier to set up than any of the other technologies. Assuming that you're rather new at this task, I wouldn't want to throw you into the deep end (not yet, anyway).

In addition to ASP, the server choices are Microsoft IIS or Personal Web Server (PWS). Either one of these servers works as both a Web server and an application server. PWS runs with Windows 98 or Windows NT, and you can install it from your Windows CD. If you have Windows 2000 Server, Windows NT 4, or Windows XP Professional, IIS is part of the package. If you can't find your CD, you can always download IIS or PWS for free from the Microsoft Web site.

At this point, if you're running Windows 95, Windows 98 SE, or Windows NT, make sure that you have PWS installed. If you're running Windows 2000 or Windows XP Professional, IIS is already in your system and all you have to do is make sure that it's started.

If you're running Windows 2000 or Windows XP Professional and IIS isn't enabled, you can install it by choosing Control Panel➪Add/Remove Programs➪ Add/Remove Windows Components. When the Windows Components screen appears, scroll down the list and make sure that a check mark appears next to the Internet Information Server option.

IIS doesn't work on Windows XP Home Edition. You must upgrade to Windows XP Professional to use it.

To download and install Microsoft Personal Web Server, go to `www.microsoft.com/downloads/` and search for *option pack.* Click the Download Windows NT 4.0 Option Packoption. If you're using Windows 98, choose Windows 95 from the list of operating systems — it's the same file — and follow the downloading instructions.

Setting up a DSN

A *Data Source Name,* or *DSN,* is basically a name associated with your database that helps you to keep your connection with the database intact even if the database changes to a new location.

Although you don't need a DSN to connect to a database using Dreamweaver, a DSN is the easiest way to get your dynamic Dreamweaver site to work.

To follow along with the steps in this section, you need to make sure that your Access Database Driver is installed. Follow these steps to ensure that it's already there and to create the DSN:

1. **In Windows XP Professional, choose Start⇨Programs⇨Administrative Tools⇨Data Sources (ODBC).**

   You see the ODBC Data Source Administrator dialog box (see Figure 13-2). On the first tab (User DSN), you see MS Access Database and Microsoft Access Driver (*mdb) on one line.

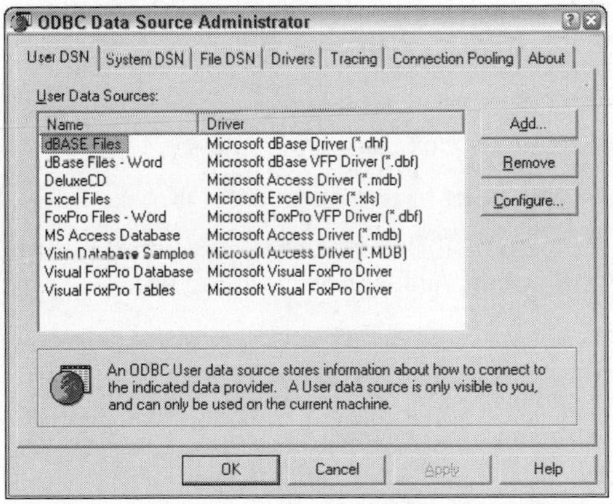

Figure 13-2:
The ODBC Data Source Administrator dialog box.

2. **Click the System DSN tab.**

   You see a list of database connections.

3. **Click Add.**

   A list of drivers appears (see Figure 13-3).

4. **Select Microsoft Access Driver and then click Finish.**

   The ODBC Microsoft Access Setup dialog box appears (see Figure 13-4).

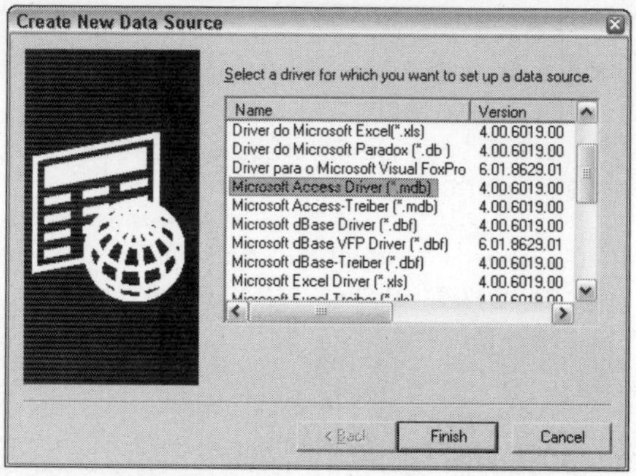

Create New Data Source

Figure 13-3:
The list of
drivers from
the Systems
DSN tab.

5. **Next to Data Source Name, enter a name for your database. (You can call it whatever you want, as long as you remember what you called it.) You don't *have* to type something in the Description box, but you can if you want.**

   Because the examples later in the chapter have to do with contacts, I assume that your database is called *contacts.mdb* and that you type *myContacts* as the Data Source Name.

6. **Click Select.**

   The Select Database dialog box appears.

7. **Find the database you want to use and click OK.**

   As you can see, the path to the database is now listed in the Database area in the ODBC Microsoft Access Setup dialog box.

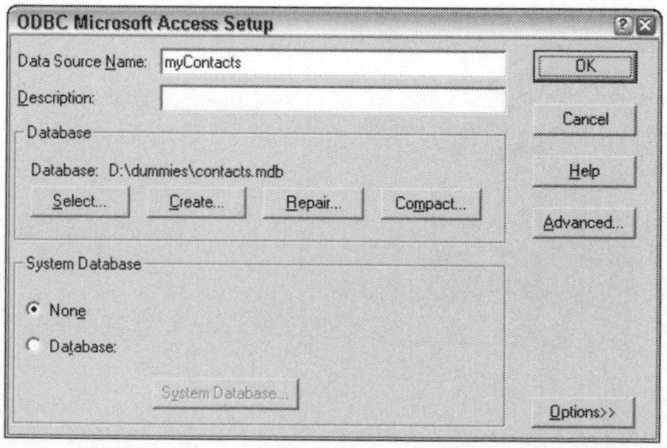

Figure 13-4:
The ODBC
Microsoft
Access
Setup
dialog box.

8. You can click Advanced to fill out authorization information if your database will require a username and password. Otherwise, don't worry about it.

9. Click OK in the ODBC Microsoft Access Setup dialog box to close it; then click OK to close the ODBC Data Source Administrator dialog box.

Setting up in Dreamweaver MX 2004 for Windows

Creating the data connection in Dreamweaver takes a few quick steps. You should start by setting up your site's local information and remote site information, which is explained in detail in Chapter 2. Check out that chapter to get reacquainted if you're not already comfortable with this process.

In this example, I assume that you're running IIS (or PWS) on the same machine you use Dreamweaver, so I show you how to set up a local connection.

If your IIS or PWS is enabled, when you go to your browser and type **http://local host** in the address bar, you see a page confirming that your Web server is up and running.

To get started, follow these steps:

1. **Create a new ASP Javascript page by clicking ASP Javascript on the Dreamweaver start page.**

    You have to have a document open to do anything with the Application panel.

2. **Click the Application panel to expand it and click the Databases tab (see Figure 13-5).**

    You can open the Databases tab by choosing Window➪Databases from the Dreamweaver main menu.

3. **Click the plus sign (+) and select Data Source Name (DSN) from the list.**

    You see the Data Source Name dialog box, as shown in Figure 13-6.

4. **Enter the name for the new connection.**

    For example, type **myContacts** and select the myContacts database that you created earlier in this section.

5. **Select your database from the list of DSNs. Make sure that you have indicated that Dreamweaver should connect using Local DSN.**

    If you want to use a remote application server, make sure, of course, that you have indicated that Dreamweaver should connect using DSN on the testing server.

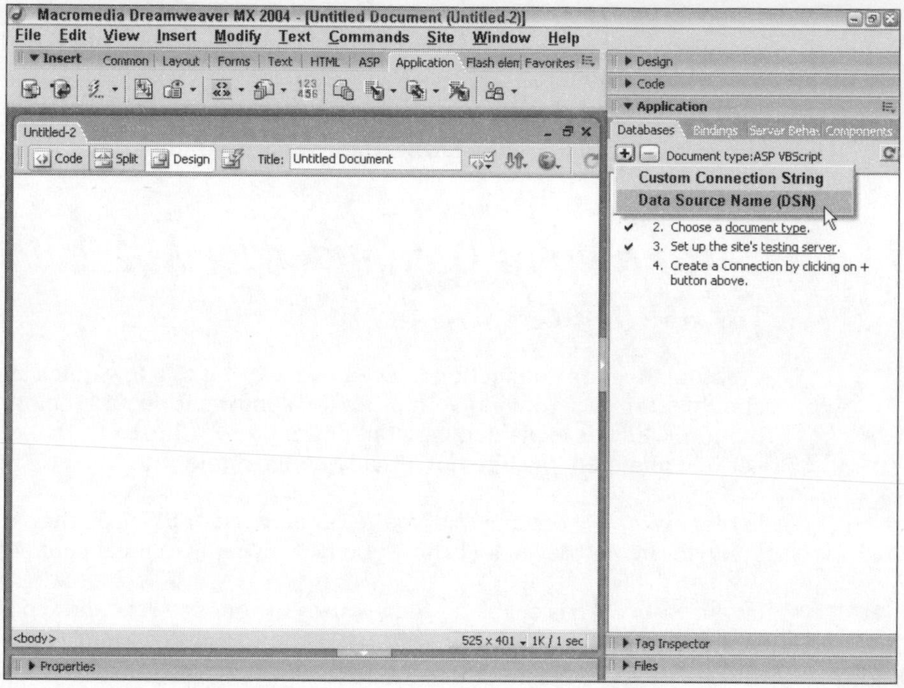

Figure 13-5:
The Data-
bases tab.

6. **Click the Test button.**

You see a pop-up message letting you know that the connection was made successfully, and you see your database listed on the Databases tab (see Figure 13-7).

In the Files panel, you also see on your local drive a Connections folder, which contains an ASP file with the connection information for this database. Dreamweaver automatically references this file on any page you create that uses this database connection, saving you from having to insert it by hand every time.

The ASP files in the Connections folder store necessary information that makes your page work correctly with the database. Upload this folder when you upload your site files to the application server.

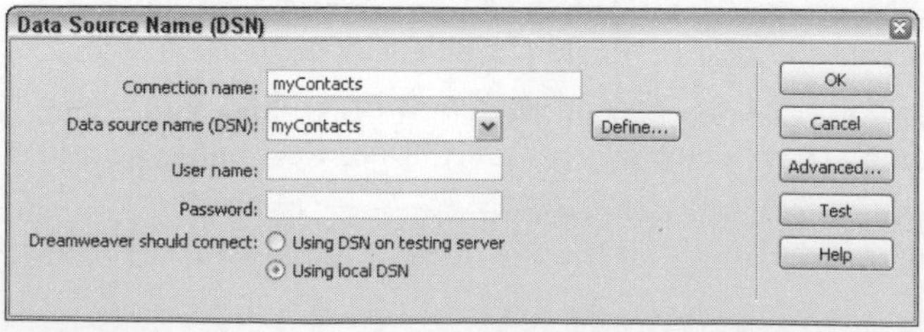

Figure 13-6:
The Data
Source
Name (DSN)
dialog box.

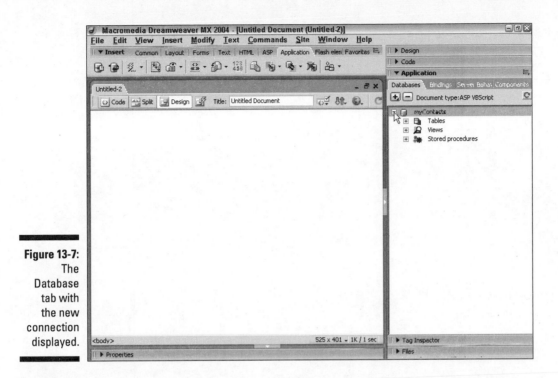

Figure 13-7:
The
Database
tab with
the new
connection
displayed.

If your connection fails, check your DSN again, and check the URL prefix for the application server. You can also check the Dreamweaver Help Index for other troubleshooting tips. Now you're ready to build a dynamic Web site. In Chapters 14 and 15, I get into more details so that you can put these great Dreamweaver features to use on your site right away.

Setting up Dreamweaver MX 2004 for Mac users

Setting up a data connection on a Mac is a little more complicated because you can't run a Web server or application server locally, unless you're running OSX; you must connect to a remote server. Ideally, you can connect your Mac to an NT server with permission to browse the Mac, and after you're networked, make the data connection. Dreamweaver includes information in its help files that specifically covers this process for Mac users.

OSX users can alternatively download Apache's HTTP server from `http://httpd.apache.org/`. However, anyone using OS9 and earlier is out of luck.

Chapter 14

Bringing Data into the Mix

● ●

In This Chapter

▶ Taking a look at the panels

▶ Covering the recordset basics

▶ Getting dynamic with your data

● ●

*I*f you've never used the dynamic development capabilities of Dreamweaver, you'll want to get familiar with a few windows and inspectors in the beginning of this chapter. In the rest of this chapter, you find out how these elements work together to create a Web site chock-full of dynamic features. For the purposes of illustration, each of the step-by-step exercises in this chapter is based on a contact management Web site that features contact information for various people — names, addresses, and pictures. If your site will feature another kind of data, such as product descriptions or articles, don't worry — these steps show you how to use Dreamweaver to create any kind of dynamic site. Just apply the lessons and features explained in this chapter to your own data and you'll be creating your own dynamic site in no time.

To help you follow along with the exercises in this chapter, you find a sample database on the CD-ROM called Contacts.

Make sure your Application Server is running and, because the examples in this chapter assume that you are using Internet Information Server or Peer Web Services for Windows, make sure that you save all the pages as ASP pages (*filename*.asp) so that the server parses the code correctly. For a quick reminder on how to set up the Application Server, refer to Chapter 13.

Exploring the Panel

In Dreamweaver, the most fundamental elements of creating a dynamic Web site are in the Application panel, which includes the Databases, Bindings, and Server Behaviors panels. In this section, I introduce you to these panels, which help you create your dynamic site.

The Databases panel

The Databases panel also lets you to look at the databases on your application server without creating a recordset. In the Databases panel, you can view your entire database structure within Dreamweaver — tables, fields, and stored procedures — without opening up the actual database.

You can find the Databases panel by choosing Windows⇨Databases on the main menu.

You can create a Data Source Name (DSN) or a custom connection string by clicking the plus (+) sign on the Databases panel (shown in Figure 14-1). To see how you can create a Data Source Name using the Databases panel, refer to Chapter 13.

The Bindings panel

The Bindings panel enables you to add and remove dynamic content data sources from your document. The number and kinds of available data sources can vary depending on whether you use ASP, JSP, or any other server technology (see Chapter 13 for a refresher on servers if you need to). A *data source* is where you get information to use on your dynamic Web page. An example of a data source is a recordset from a database, which you further explore in the next few sections of this chapter.

If you don't see the Bindings panel, you can open it by choosing Window⇨ Bindings in the main menu.

With the Bindings panel, you can access data sources in several ways. You can find out what data source objects you have available by clicking the plus (+) sign on the Bindings panel to get the Add Bindings pop-up menu (see Figure 14-2).

The Bindings pop-up menu includes

- ✔ **Recordset (Query):** A recordset stores data from your database for use on a page or set of pages. I explain recordsets in more detail in this chapter.

- ✔ **Command (Stored Procedure):** *Stored Procedures* are reusable database items that contain SQL code and are commonly used to modify a database (insert, update, or delete records).

- ✔ **Request Variable:** Commonly used wherever a search is involved, a Request Variable carries information from one page to another. When you use a form to submit data to another page, a request variable is created.

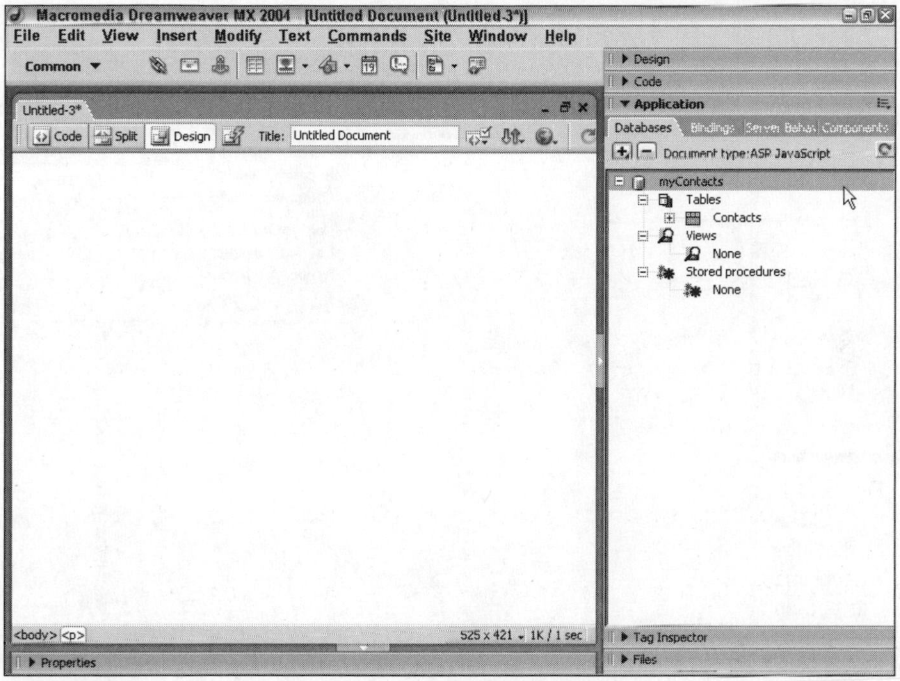

Figure 14-1:
The
Databases
panel.

- ✔ **Session Variable:** *Session Variables* store and display information for the duration of a user's session (or visit). A different session is created on the server for each user and is kept in use either for a set period of time or until a specific action on the site terminates the session (such as a log-out).

- ✔ **Application Variable:** *Application Variables* store and display information that must be present for all users and is constant throughout the lifetime of an application. These types of variables are commonly used for page counters, or date and time. Application variables are available only for ASP and ColdFusion pages, not for PHP and JSP.

- ✔ **Get More Data Sources:** Use this option to open Dreamweaver Exchange in your browser. You can use Exchange to download extensions for Dreamweaver. For more information about extensions, see Chapter 15.

The Server Behaviors panel

Server behaviors are server-side scripts that perform some type of action. Through the Server Behaviors panel, you can add server-side scripts to your pages, such as user authentication and record navigation, which you can read more about in this chapter and Chapter 15. Server behaviors available to you vary depending on the server technology you use.

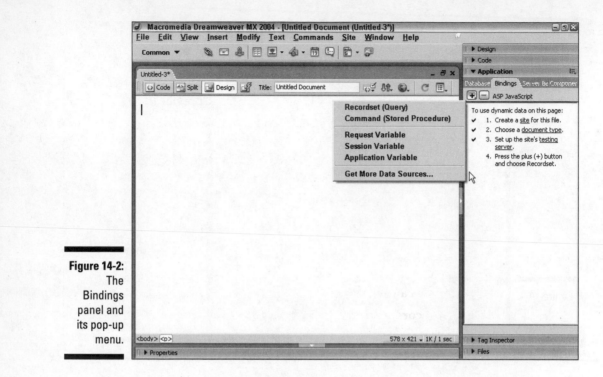

Figure 14-2:
The
Bindings
panel and
its pop-up
menu.

You can get to the Server Behaviors panel by choosing Window⇨Server Behaviors on the Dreamweaver main menu.

You can view the available server behaviors by clicking the plus (+) sign on the Server Behaviors panel to get the Server Behaviors pop-up menu (see Figure 14-3).

The Server Behaviors pop-up menu includes

- ✔ **Recordset (Query):** A recordset stores data from your database for use on a page or set of pages. I explain recordsets in more detail in this chapter.

- ✔ **Command (Stored Procedure):** Stored Procedures are reusable database items that contain SQL code and are commonly used to modify a database (insert, update, or delete records).

- ✔ **Repeat Region:** This server object is used to display multiple records on a page. Repeat Region is most commonly used on tables or table rows. You can see more about this behavior later in this chapter.

- ✔ **Recordset Paging:** If you have to display a large number of records, and are distributing them onto various pages, this set of behaviors allows you to navigate from page to page or from record to record.

✔ **Show Region:** With this set of server behaviors, you can show or hide record navigation based on the records displayed. For instance, if you have "next" and "previous" on the bottom of every page and your user is on the first page or first record of the recordset, you can set a behavior to display only the "next" link. The same goes if the user is on the last page or record — you can set it to display "previous" only.

✔ **Dynamic Text:** The Dynamic Text option allows you to display information from your recordset anywhere on the page.

✔ **Go to Detail Page:** Using this behavior, you can link each record in your repeated region to a detail page for that particular record. The behavior also tells the detail page which record's information to display.

✔ **Go to Related Page:** You can use this behavior to link a particular dynamic page to another page that contains related information, passing the parameters of the first page to the related page.

✔ **Insert Record:** Use this behavior on a page to add new records to a database via a Web browser.

✔ **Update Record:** Use this behavior on a page to update existing records in a database via a Web browser.

✔ **Delete Record:** Use this behavior on a page to quickly delete a record from a database via a Web browser.

✔ **Dynamic Form Elements:** This set of server behaviors turn text fields, list/menu fields, radio buttons, or check boxes into dynamic form elements, which you can set to display particular information from a recordset.

✔ **User Authentication:** The User Authentication set of behaviors allows you to log in a user, log out a user, check a user name against the information in your database, and restrict access to a page.

✔ **Edit Server Behaviors:** Use this option to customize or remove existing server behaviors. Unless you are very comfortable with coding or SQL, I advise you not to mess with this option. (If you're curious about SQL, see *SQL For Dummies,* 4th Edition, by Allen G. Taylor, published by Wiley Publishing, Inc.)

✔ **New Server Behavior:** Use this option to create new server behaviors and add them to the list of existing behaviors. Again, this option is for the more advanced users who are comfortable with coding.

✔ **Get More Server Behaviors:** Use this option to open Dreamweaver Exchange in your browser. You can use Exchange to download extensions for Dreamweaver. For more information about extensions, see Chapter 15.

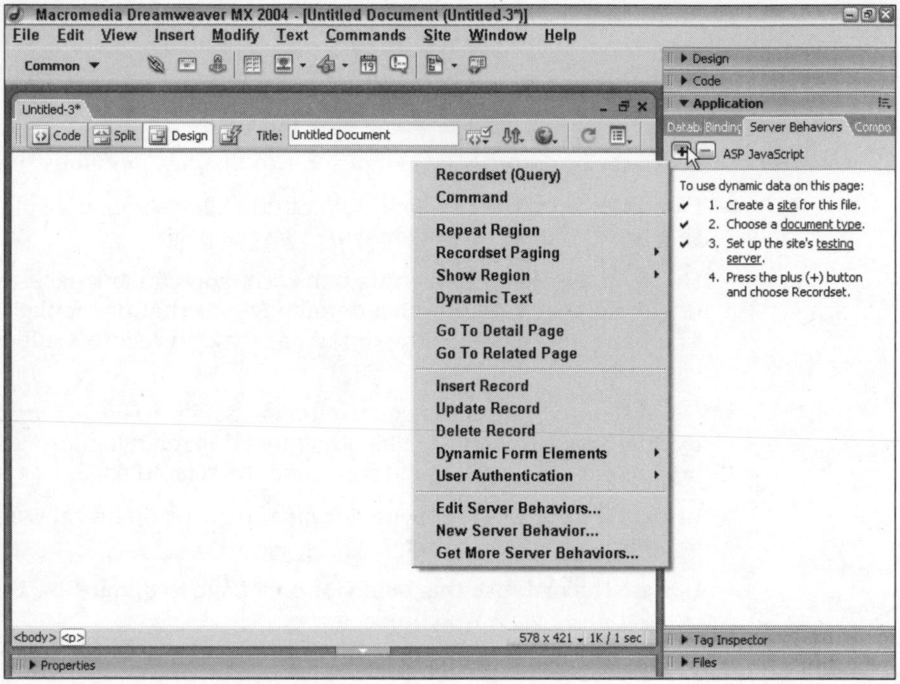

Macromedia Dreamweaver MX 2004 - [Untitled Document (Untitled-3*)]

File   Edit   View   Insert   Modify   Text   Commands   Site   Window   Help

Common ▼

Untitled-3*

Code   Split   Design   Title: Untitled Document

Recordset (Query)
Command

Repeat Region
Recordset Paging   ▶
Show Region   ▶
Dynamic Text

Go To Detail Page
Go To Related Page

Insert Record
Update Record
Delete Record
Dynamic Form Elements   ▶
User Authentication   ▶

Edit Server Behaviors...
New Server Behavior...
Get More Server Behaviors...

▶ Design
▶ Code
▼ Application
Datab Binding   Server Behaviors   Compo
ASP JavaScript

To use dynamic data on this page:
✓   1. Create a site for this file.
✓   2. Choose a document type.
✓   3. Set up the site's testing
        server.
    4. Press the plus (+) button
        and choose Recordset.

<body> <p>   578 x 421 ▾ 1K / 1 sec

▶ Tag Inspector
▶ Files
▶ Properties

Figure 14-3:
The Server
Behaviors
panel and
its pop-up
menu.

Creating a Recordset

The *recordset* stores data from your database for use on a page or set of
pages by creating a query. A *query* gathers information from a database to be
used on a page, using only the information in the fields you select for the particular query. The queries for a recordset are built with SQL (Structured
Query Language), but you don't need to know SQL in order to get the job
done. Dreamweaver writes it all for you.

With your recordset in place, you can display information from your database
in various ways.

Before you can create a recordset, you must first connect to a database.
Chapter 13 goes over this in more detail.

To define a recordset in Dreamweaver:

1. **Open the page that will use the recordset.**

2. **On the Bindings panel, click the plus sign and select Recordset (Query).**

   You see the Recordset dialog box, as shown in Figure 14-4.

3. **Enter a name for your recordset in the Name box.**

   Usually, it is recommended that you add the letters *rs* to the beginning of the name to distinguish it as a recordset in your code, but it isn't necessary. Example: *rsContacts*.

4. **Select your connection from the Connection drop-down list.**

   This list includes any data connections defined from the Databases panel. Chapter 13 explains how to create a connection.

5. **Choose a database table to collect the data for your recordset from the Table drop-down list.**

   You can select all the columns or only specific columns of data to be displayed.

6. **(Optional) If you want the available information to be filtered to show only records that meet specific criteria, fill out the Filter area.**

7. **If you want the displayed records to be sorted in ascending or descending order, specify it in the Sort menu by selecting the field by which you want the records sorted (Name, Phone Number, and so on).**

8. **To test the connection to the database, click the Test button.**

   If the test is successful, you see a window with the data in the recordset (similar to Figure 14-5).

9. **Click OK to close the Test screen.**

10. **Click OK to complete the Recordset dialog box.**

    You can now see the recordset displayed in the Bindings panel (see Figure 14-6). You can expand it by clicking the plus sign next to the recordset.

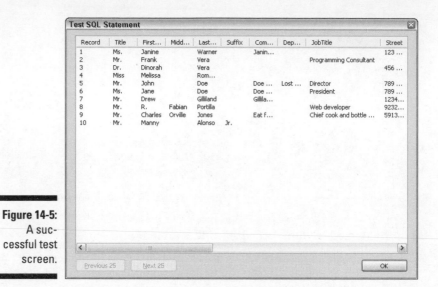

Figure 14-5:
A suc-
cessful test
screen.

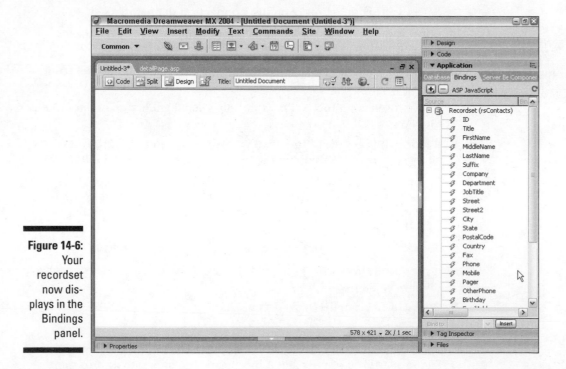

Figure 14-6:
Your
recordset
now dis-
plays in the
Bindings
panel.

Using a Recordset on Your Page

After you create a recordset, you can place the information on your page as you want. For this example, I make a basic list of all the contacts in the database, with a name, e-mail address, phone number, and Web site URL.

I already built a page with a table showing the appropriate number of columns for all the dynamic text that I'm inserting (see Figure 14-7).

After you have set up the document the way you want it, you can drag and drop each data source to its appropriate spot on the page.

1. **From the Bindings panel, select your first data source and drag it onto your page, dropping it where it's supposed to go.**

   The name of the dynamic text appears inside curly brackets. You can now format this piece of text any way you want, treating it like normal HTML text (see Figure 14-8).

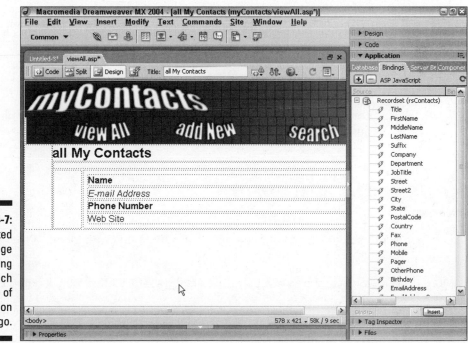

Figure 14-7:
I created a page showing where each piece of information will go.

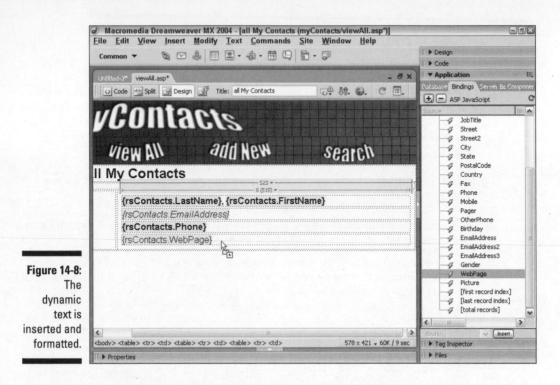

Figure 14-8:
The
dynamic
text is
inserted and
formatted.

2. **Test the result by clicking the Live Data button.**

   The first record of your database appears in place of the dynamic text code (see Figure 14-9). To show more than the first record, you need to define and repeat a region.

Repeating a Region

You probably want to show more than one record at a time on a page that's supposed to list all your contacts. You can do this by applying a server behavior to your region.

A *region* is any area of a page that displays information from a database on your page. After you define your region, you can apply a Repeat Region server behavior, which causes that area to be written to the page over and over, displaying every record, or as many as you tell it to, in the database defined by your recordset until all records display. Repeat Region is most commonly used on tables or table rows.

Live Data

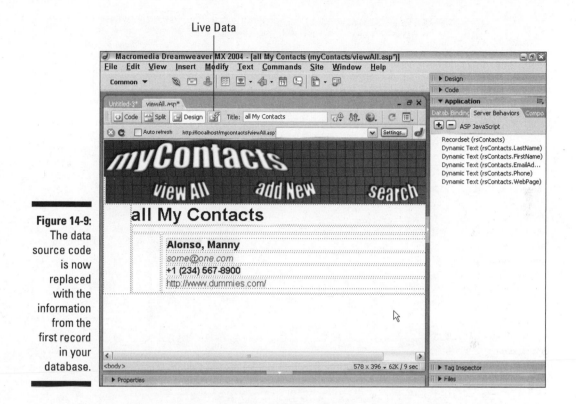

Figure 14-9:
The data
source code
is now
replaced
with the
information
from the
first record
in your
database.

To add a Repeat Region server behavior to your page:

1. **Select the area on your page that you want to define as a region.**

2. **Click the Server Behaviors panel, click the plus (+) sign, and select Repeat Region from the menu that appears.**

   The Repeat Region dialog box appears (see Figure 14-10).

3. **Select the number of records that you want to show on the page and then click OK.**

4. **Click the Live Data button to see the results (see Figure 14-11).**

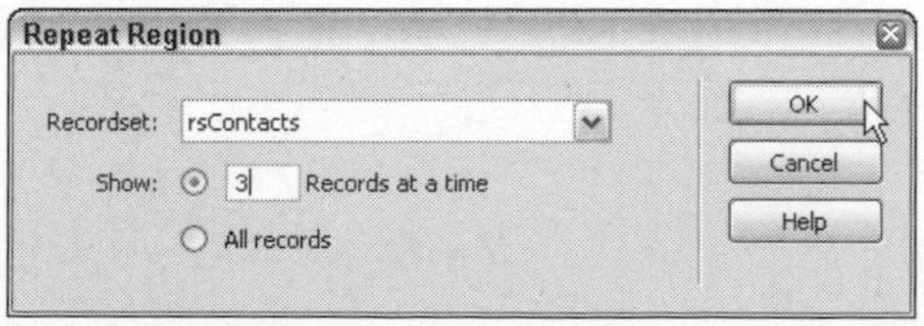

Figure 14-10:
Define a
region in the
Repeat
Region
dialog box.

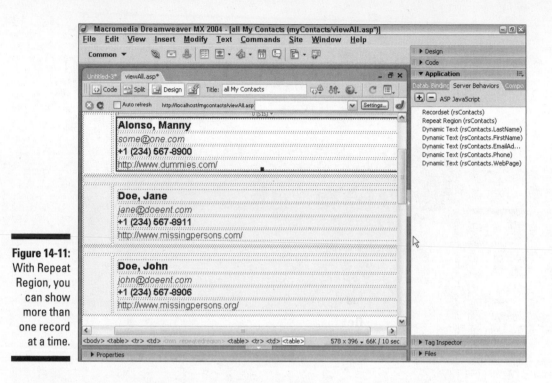

Adding a Dynamic Image

Whenever you have a dynamic Web site, images are usually involved, whether it is a catalog Web site or a news archive. You can bind an image to a recordset in various easy ways so that your images change depending on the other parts of the page that are bound to the same recordset. Before you bind the image, though, you need to take a few preliminary steps:

1. **Make sure that, in your database, you have a field for each record that lists the actual path of the image for that record.**

    For example, if your images reside in a folder called *images,* one level above your dynamic page, you enter the following in the image field in your database: **images/*imagename.gif***, remembering to replace the *imagename.gif* part with the actual filename for each image.

2. **Upload your image folder to the server, or you won't be able to preview the page with images in Live Data view.**

3. **Place a placeholder image in the spot that you want an image to appear for all the records.**

You can use any of the images in your image folder as a placeholder, or choose Insert⇨Image Object⇨Image Placeholder to use the built-in image placeholder. In the example I'm following, I use the Dreamweaver image placeholder. When you're done, you're ready to move on to the next section, "Binding the Image."

You can find out more about inserting images in Chapter 2.

Binding the Image

After you insert the placeholder image, you can bind images two easy ways — with the Bindings panel or the Properties inspector.

Follow these steps to bind images using the Bindings panel:

1. **Select your placeholder image in the open document.**

2. **Click the plus (+) sign to expand your recordset.**

3. **Select the field in your recordset that contains the name of the image file.**

   In my example, I called this field *Picture*, but you can call it whatever you want.

4. **Click the Bind button at the bottom of the Bindings panel (see Figure 14-12).**

Follow these steps to bind images using the Properties inspector:

1. **Click your placeholder image in the open document to select it.**

2. **Click the file folder icon in the Properties inspector next to the Image Src box.**

   The Select Image Source dialog box appears (see Figure 14-13).

3. **In the Select File Name From section (at the top), select the Data Sources option.**

4. **Select the field that contains your image information.**

5. **Click OK.**

   The image changes to a tree with a lightning bolt along its side.

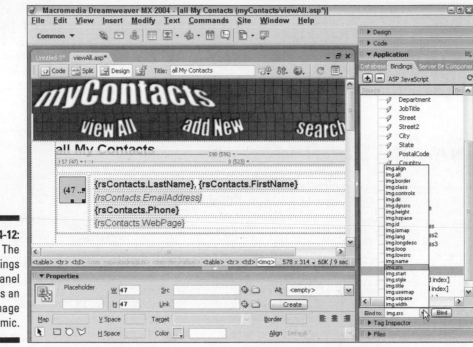

Figure 14-12:
The
Bindings
panel
makes an
image
dynamic.

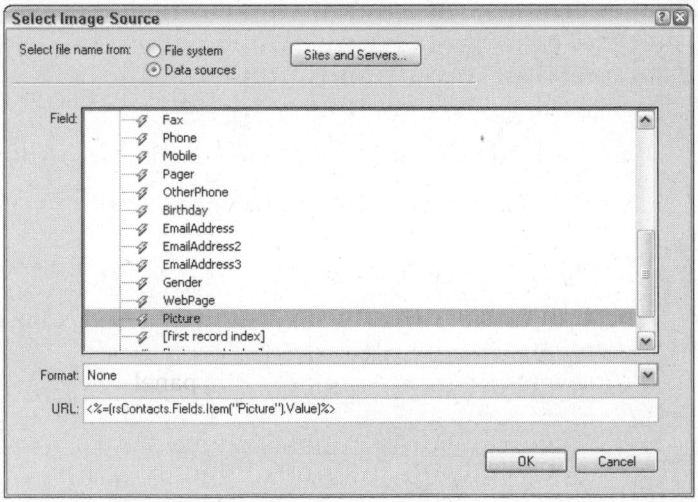

Figure 14-13:
The Select
Image
Source
dialog box.

After performing either of these two methods to bind your images to the page, click the Live Data button (the button with a lightning bolt) to check out the results (see Figure 14-14).

Figure 14-14:
You can test
your images
to find out
if they're
bound
correctly.

Adding Navigation to a Dynamic Page

If your database contains many records, you may opt to show only a small number of records per page, so that you don't overwhelm the user. The Dreamweaver Server Behaviors panel allows you to add navigation to your pages so that you can move forward or backward through records.

Define your Repeat Region, which I explain how to do earlier in this chapter, and make sure that you do not select to show all records. You can add button images or text links at the bottom of the page to indicate some kind of navigation, such as "Previous Page" and "Next Page." With the buttons in place, you can activate them by using the Server Behaviors panel.

For example, to add the navigation movements for the Next and Previous buttons:

1. **Select the Previous Page button you added in the Document window.**

2. **Open the Server Behaviors panel.**

   You can open the Server Behaviors panel by choosing Window⇨Server Behaviors in the main menu.

3. **Click the plus (+) sign and select Recordset Paging from the menu (see Figure 14-15).**

4. **From the submenu, choose the appropriate navigation movement (Move to Next Record or Move to Previous Record).**

   The Move to Record dialog box appears, and in most cases you can just click OK because the defaults are right.

5. **Follow Steps 1 through 4 for the Next button.**

6. **Choose File⇨Preview in Browser and select the browser you set up as your default preview browser.**

   You can now page through your records.

That's a pretty nifty trick. But did you notice that on the first page, the Previous Page button or link still appears, even though there is no previous page? Not to worry — a server behavior tells the navigation button when to show up.

1. **Click the Previous page button in the Document window to select it.**

2. **Click the plus (+) sign on the Server Behaviors panel, and select Show Region from the menu (see Figure 14-16).**

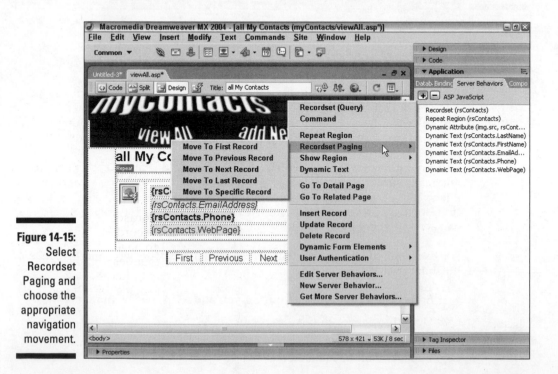

Figure 14-15:
Select Recordset Paging and choose the appropriate navigation movement.

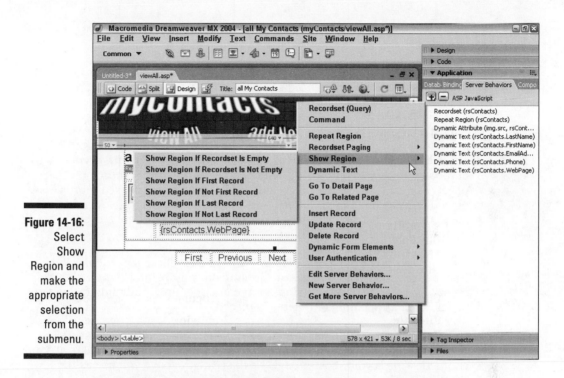

Figure 14-16:
Select
Show
Region and
make the
appropriate
selection
from the
submenu.

3. **If you are working with the Previous Page button, select Show Region If Not First Record. If you are working with the Next Page button, select Show Region If Not Last Record.**

   The Show Region dialog box appears. Usually the selected recordset is correct, so just click OK.

4. **Preview in your browser clicking the globe on the Document toolbar.**

   Notice that now when you're on the first page of records, the Previous Page button does not show, and when you're on the last page, the Next Page button does not show.

Now that you know how to add navigation to your recordsets, you can get really fancy and add buttons to go to the first or last record. So if you have, say, 100 pages of records, you can jump from page 1 to page 100 without having to click Previous Page or Next Page through countless other pages of records. The server behaviors for those two are Move to Record➪Move to First Record and Move to Record➪Move to Last Record. It's pretty useful stuff to know.

Creating a Master-Detail Page Set

A very common way to display information on a Web site is to show a list of records, such as a list of contacts, with a link to each individual record for more detailed information.

A master page displays a list of records and a link for each record. When a user clicks a particular link, a detail page appears with more information about that record. There are two types of master pages. The first type is a list of records determined by you. A user can't alter the list of records on this page; they can only click to view more information about those records displayed. The second type is a dynamically created master page. A good example of this type of master page is a search results page, where a user performs a search for specific records.

A detail page is the page that displays when a user clicks a particular link from a master page. This page can either display more information about a record (such as an online catalog), or it can be set up for administrative purposes, such as updating or deleting a record.

Creating a Master-Detail page requires just a few clicks of the mouse. Using the functions described earlier in this chapter, create a page that lists all your contacts. This is your master page. Next, create the page you use as the detail page. Now you're ready to create the Master-Detail Page Set.

1. **Open the page you created to be the master page and choose Insert⇨Application Objects⇨Master Detail Page Set.**

   The Insert Master-Detail Page Set dialog box opens (see Figure 14-17). The top part of the dialog box is for defining the properties of the master page. The bottom part is for defining the detail page.

2. **Select the recordset from the drop-down list that you will use for your master page.**

3. **Next to Master Page Fields, use the plus (+) and minus (–) signs to add or remove fields that you want or don't want to display on the master page.**

4. **Select the field from which you want to provide a link to the detail page for each record.**

   For example, if you list a bunch of contacts, you can use the contact's name as the link to the detail.

5. **In the Pass Unique Key drop-down list, usually the default is correct; if it is not, select the unique identifier that you want to pass on to the detail page.**

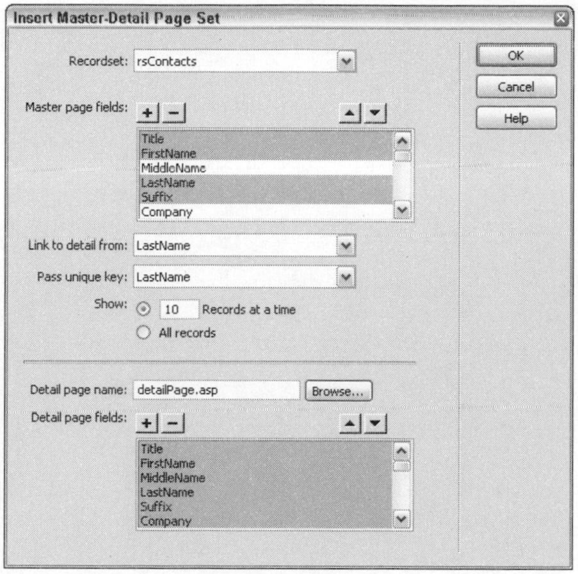

Figure 14-17:
The Insert
Master-
Detail Page
Set dialog
box.

6. **Select the number of records you want to show at one time on the master page.**

   It's okay to show only a partial listing because you can add navigation to view more records.

7. **For the detail page, browse for the page you created to be the detail page in this set, or type in the filename in the text box.**

8. **Just like with the Master Page section, use the plus and minus signs to add or remove fields that you want or don't want to show on the detail page.**

9. **Click OK.**

Dreamweaver automatically adds all the necessary recordset information and SQL code for you to begin using your Master-Detail Page Set. Everything from navigation to record status is in there.

After you create the master and detail pages, you may want to rearrange and format the fields in a way that is more aesthetic because Dreamweaver just plops the stuff onto the pages, which looks really generic. For example, you can change the column labels to read in a friendlier way. You can also format the font, color and size, add padding to the table cells, and change the order of the columns.

Chapter 15

Using Forms to Manage Your Dynamic Web Site

● ●

In This Chapter

▶ Setting up user authentication

▶ Creating a search page

▶ Editing a database

▶ Discussing the basic elements of e-commerce

● ●

Dynamic Web sites let you do a lot more than provide content and product listings to your Web site visitors. You can use Dreamweaver to create various types of forms that serve many useful purposes. Some examples include a login page so that users can register to use your Web site, a search page so that users can search your Web site for specific information, or a data entry form to allow nontechnical data-entry personnel to easily edit the content of a Web site.

Establishing User Authentication

One of the good things about a dynamic Web site is that you can retain a lot more control over it, from who can view it and how much they can view to who can edit it and how much they can edit. You can assign various users various levels of access depending on criteria that you determine. For example, you may have an employee directory online that all employees can access to obtain departmental information, titles, and phone extensions. However, if that directory also contains every employee's home phone number and home address, you wouldn't want the entire company to have access to everyone's personal information, right? The Dreamweaver User Authentication Server Behavior enables you to create different levels of access that restrict the kind of information a user can see; in this example, you can make the personal information something only department managers may access.

Creating a login page

In the first exercise for this chapter, you create a user login form that checks information against a database. I use a sample database of employees that contains the following fields:

- ✓ Employee number
- ✓ Password
- ✓ Last name
- ✓ First name
- ✓ Department
- ✓ Title
- ✓ Access level

If you want to use a pre-built database to complete this exercise, I have provided a sample database called `employees.mdb` on the accompanying CD. It was created using Access 2000.

After you have a database in place, create a page that contains a form with the following fields: a text box for User Name, a text box for Password, and a Submit button. Refer to Chapter 12 for more details on how to create a form. Next, create a Data Source Name (DSN), database connection, and recordset that contains your employee number, last name, first name, password, department, title, and access level. Check out Chapters 13 and 14 if you need a quick review on this stuff.

Now that you have everything in place, you're ready to add User Authentication to your form. For this exercise, I walk you through the setup for User Authentication on a company's employee directory. I use the employee number as the User Name.

1. **Select the form and click the plus sign (+) on the Server Behaviors panel (see Figure 15-1).**

   Selecting a form in Dreamweaver can be a little bit tricky sometimes. A quick way to select the entire form is to click anywhere inside the form and then select the word "form" from the status bar at the bottom of the Dreamweaver window. This selects the entire form.

2. **From the menu, select User Authentication and select Log In User from the submenu that appears.**

   The Log In User dialog box appears (see Figure 15-2).

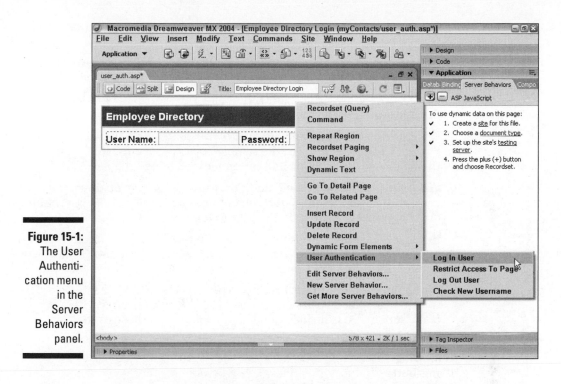

Figure 15-1:
The User
Authenti-
cation menu
in the
Server
Behaviors
panel.

3. In the Get Input From Form field, enter the form name.

Naming forms is good practice, especially if you have a page with multiple forms. Naming your forms makes each one easier to identify within
the code.

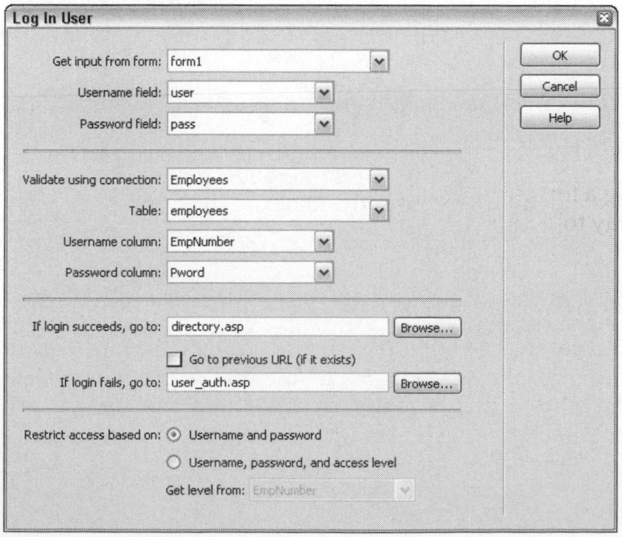

Figure 15-2:
The Log In
User dialog
box.

4. **Enter the name of the appropriate text box from your form next to Username Field and Password Field.**

In my example, the user name field is called *user,* and the password field is called *pass*.

5. **From the Validate Using Connection and Table drop-down lists, make the appropriate selections.**

Select the connection and table that corresponds to your user database. For example, if you're using the sample `employees.mdb` table, you'd use the Employees connection and the employees table.

6. **From the Username Column and Password Column drop-down lists, select the fields in your database that are used to verify the Username and Password provided by the user at login.**

Because I use the employee number as the User Name, I selected that field as my User Name column, but if you have a specific User Name field in your database you select *that* one instead.

At the time of this writing, Dreamweaver expects the user name field to be a text field. If you decide to use a field such as employee number, make sure that it is defined as a text field in the database or the page will not work.

7. **Enter the name of the page where users are redirected if the login succeeds.**

If you want to use this as a generic page for logins, then check the Go to Previous URL box as well. That way, after a user tries to access a restricted page and is sent to this login page, the user will be sent back to the restricted page after entering the correct user name and password. This covered further in the following section, "Restricting access to pages."

In my example, the page is `employees.asp`, which is the actual employee directory listing.

8. **Enter the name of the page where users are redirected if the login fails.**

They can be redirected to the same login page, or you can create a secondary login page that looks like the first one but contains an error message saying something like `That user name and/or password is incorrect. Please try again.`

9. **Select Restrict Access Based on *Username and Password*.**

If you restrict access only to certain users at a certain access level (say, Manager or Employee), you can define that in this area as well. The resulting effect is that only the users in the database whose access level matches what you specify are taken to the login success page. The rest are redirected to the login failed page.

10. **Click OK.**

You can now preview this page in your browser and test the form by entering a user name and password from your database.

Restricting access to pages

When you have a page you want to restrict, such as a user detail page, and a login page, you are ready to go. In the following steps, I assume that the name of the page that you want to restrict access to is *employeedirectory.asp*, that the name of your login page is `user_auth.asp`, and that Go To Previous URL was defined for the login page (see the previous section, "Creating a login page" for more information).

To restrict access to a Web page:

1. **Open** `employeedirectory.asp` **or which ever page you want to restrict.**

2. **On the Server Behaviors panel click the (+) button and select User Authentication⇨Restrict Access to Page from the menu.**

   This opens the Restrict Access to Page dialog box (see Figure 15-3).

   You can open the Server Behaviors panel by clicking Window⇨Server Behaviors from the main menu.

3. **Select Restrict Based on Username and Password.**

4. **Type user_auth.asp in the If Access Denied, Go To box.**

   When users try to access this page directly, they'll be sent to `user_auth.asp` to login before they can see this page.

5. **Click OK.**

6. **Press F12 to preview the page in your default browser.**

   Instead of the Employee Directory page, you see the user login page. Type in a valid user name and password to view the Employee Directory.

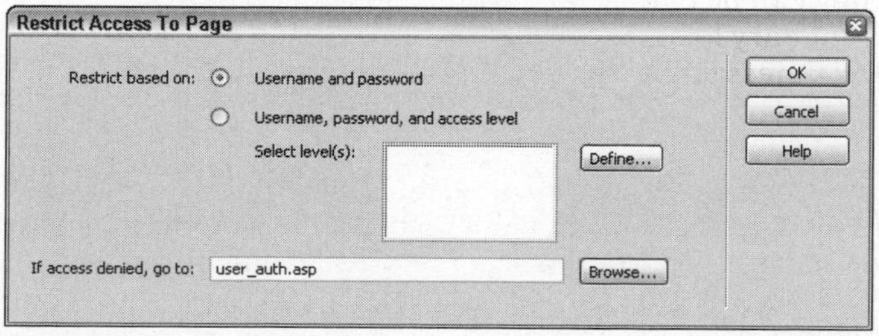

Figure 15-3:
The Restrict
Access to
Page dialog
box.

Restrict Access To Page

Restrict based on: ⦿ Username and password

◯ Username, password, and access level

Select level(s): [   ] Define...

If access denied, go to: [user_auth.asp] Browse...

OK   Cancel   Help

Securing Sensitive Information on Your Web Site

Here are some steps you can take that help make your sensitive information more secure on the Web. Some steps are for the more advanced users.

✔ **Carefully choose the passwords you use,** especially for your FTP, your database, and the admin login area of your Web site. Too often people use common words, names, and number combinations as passwords that are easy for hackers to figure out. An effective password consists of mixed letters and numbers — the more random the better — and is case-sensitive whenever possible.

✔ **Protect your development machine.** Many Web site break-ins are inside jobs, where someone from within the company itself obtains the sensitive information because he or she has access to the Web site files. If your development machine is on a network and you must grant access to it, grant only restricted access.

✔ **On your Web server, turn Directory Browsing** *off* so folders without an index page don't display everything that's in them. If you are not the administrator for your Web server, or don't know how to do this, ask a technical support representative at your hosting company to either walk you through it or do it for you. It's a fairly simple step.

✔ **Pages that require authentication, such as employees.asp from the previous example, should have code on that page that kicks out users who didn't log in to get into that page.** This way if someone happens to access the file without using the login page, they are sent elsewhere (see "Restricting access to pages," earlier in the chapter). One of the easiest ways to do this is with a cookie — of the ASP variety, not chocolate chip! In fact, this is how Dreamweaver's Server Behaviors do it behind the scenes. You can find out more about cookies and ASP in *Beginning Active Server Pages 3.0* by David Buser, et al (published by Wrox Press).

✔ **Don't use an Access database for a serious Web site.** Not only is it slow, but stealing the info is simple because it's typically a single file. Even if a person doesn't know SQL, he or she may be able to find it and read it off of your Web server. If you do use an Access database, make sure it is stored in a folder outside the root folder.

✔ **Keep your database on a dedicated machine, away from direct Internet access.** You can buff up database security by allowing only your Web server to access that machine through a local network infrastructure.

✔ **Use SSL technology to encrypt sensitive information sent back and forth from the server.**

✔ **Don't copy and paste complex snippets of code that you found on the Web unless you absolutely trust the source and checked out all the stops.** Sometimes hackers who look for this type of widely used code and know its specific vulnerabilities can easily pick it out.

Please keep in mind that the Dreamweaver Login Authentication can be a pretty basic method of restricting access to a page if you only follow the basic steps outlined in this book. An amateur hacker can easily find your database, figure out passwords, or bypass the login page altogether to get to the information he or she wants. If you are building a site that contains sensitive information, and you are not very familiar with Web site security, consider hiring a consultant to advise you. At the very least, read up on the subject so you can get a better understanding of the security risks you may encounter. *Web Security, Privacy and Commerce* by Simson Garfinkel (published by O'Reilly & Associates) provides a very thorough look into the subject.

Searching for Database Records

With Dreamweaver, you can create a form to search for records on your database using specific criteria. This is pretty useful if you have a large database. You don't want to make your users read through pages and pages of listings, whether they are employee records or products or anything else. Providing a search form allows your users to quickly find the information they want.

In this next exercise, you discover a simple way to implement a database search on your dynamic Web site.

Setting up the search page

The search page is the simplest part to set up. All you need is a form with an action that goes to the results page, a form text field, and a Submit button.

1. **Create a new page that contains a form with the fields you want your users to search.**

   Check out Chapter 12 to go over forms in more detail.

I use the same employee directory database from the first exercise, so my text field is *Lname*, which allows my users to search by employee last names.

2. **In the Action field in the Properties inspector, enter the name of the results page. (You create this page in the next example.)**

   My result page is called *search_results.asp*.

3. **Save this page.**

Setting up the results page

The results page is a little bit more complex. The search actually takes place on this page, behind the scenes on the server, and what you see is only the result of that search. The text field that you determine in the search page is referred to as the *form variable* in the results page. The information you enter in this form is passed on to the results page in order for the search to take place.

1. **Create a new page that contains a table with a column for each field you want to show in the results.**

2. **Create a connection and a recordset for this page using the database or table from which you want to bring in the results.**

   See Chapters 13 and 14 if you need more detailed information on how to do this.

3. **In the Recordset dialog box (see Figure 15-4), select the appropriate connection and table.**

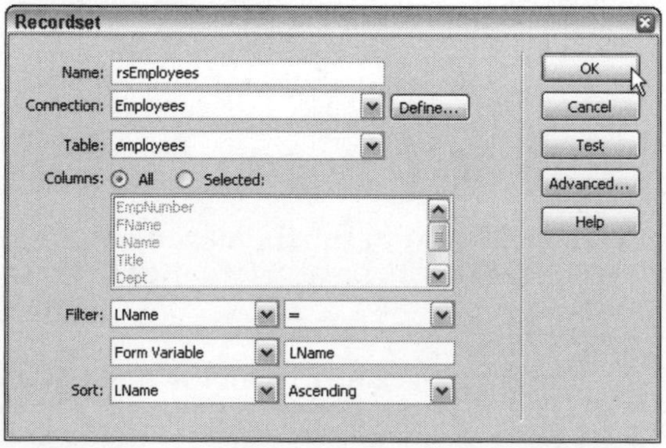

Figure 15-4:
The
Recordset
dialog box
prepared for
search
results.

4. Next to Filter drop-down list, select the column that corresponds with the field by which you want your users to search.

5. In the drop-down list directly below the Filter drop-down list, select Form Variable, and then enter the name of the text field element from your search form in the text box next to it.

6. In the Sort field, select the field by which you want to sort your results.

7. Click OK.

8. Drag each field from your recordset to the appropriate column on the table in your results page. (See Figure 15-5.)

   You can review the steps to do this in Chapter 13.

9. Transfer your pages to the server and open your search page in a browser. Try searching for one of the entries in your database.
   The search finds the entry and lists it in your search results page, showing every field you requested on the results page.

   I searched for *Hodges*, and Figure 15-6 shows my search results.

   If you want to return more than one matching row, you need to define a region and use the repeat region server behavior. You can find out more about this in Chapter 14.

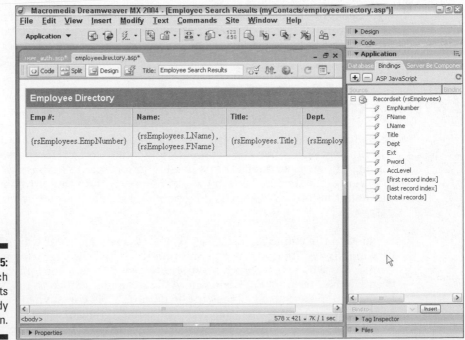

Figure 15-5: The Search Results page, ready for action.

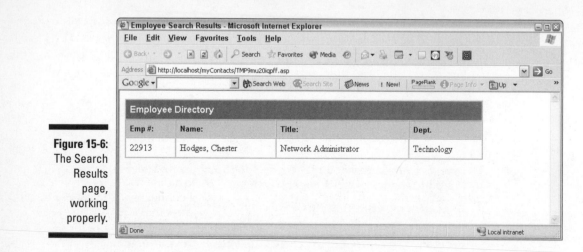

Figure 15-6:
The Search
Results
page,
working
properly.

That's it. Painless, right? This is a database search in its simplest form. The more advanced your understanding of Dreamweaver and the SQL language gets, the more complex you can make your search forms. Users with a basic understanding of SQL can enhance this page to search using multiple criteria, filter out search results, sort by various fields, and even display only certain results depending on the Access level of the person performing the search.

If you want to find out more about working with databases and SQL, I recommend *Database Development For Dummies* and *SQL For Dummies,* both by Allen G. Taylor (published by Wiley Publishing, Inc.).

Editing a Database from a Browser

Using forms is also an easy way to perform data-entry tasks on a database without having to open the database application. In fact, the person performing those tasks doesn't even need to know how a database works in order to use the form. All the work is done right on the browser window. Through the form, a user can add, update, or delete a record from the database.

Sticking to the employee directory example, say a manager wants to add a new employee and update some information in the directory for various employees who just received promotions. Using Dreamweaver, you can create a user-friendly interface where this manager can go to his browser, log in, and make those changes to the database. He can save his changes right there on his browser and view the updated information instantly, all without ever having to open a database application (such as Access).

You can secure content management pages (such as those discussed in this section) from the public by using the authentication features of Dreamweaver covered at the beginning of this chapter.

Adding a record to your database

A record in a database (a row) consists of a complete set of all the fields in the database.

In this next exercise, you use a form to add a record to a database. Before starting the exercise, you must create a new page and connect it to the database you are editing. Again, if you need to refresh your memory on how to do this, see Chapter 13.

After you create your page, you're ready to use the Dreamweaver Record Insertion Form Wizard Application Object. In one easy step, this Application Object Wizard creates a script that allows you to add a record to a database. It also creates the form, with which you make the addition.

An *application object* lets you create a more complex function in one easy step.

1. **Open your new page and place the cursor where you want the form to start.**

2. **Choose Insert⇨Application Objects⇨Insert Record⇨Record Insertion Form Wizard.**

   The Record Insertion Form dialog box opens (see Figure 15-7).

3. **Select the appropriate database connection, select the appropriate table from that database, and then enter the name of the page the user are redirected to after the new addition is made.**

4. **In the Form Fields section of the dialog box, verify that all the fields display.**

   In the Label column, you can change the actual name of the column by clicking a field from the list and editing the Label text. You can also determine what kind of form field and what type of formatting (numeric, text, and so on) is used for each field. If any field has a default value, you can define that in this dialog box as well.

   If your database table has an auto-number field (a field that the database automatically numbers sequentially for each record), it cannot be edited and needs to be removed from the Form Fields area.

5. **Click OK.**

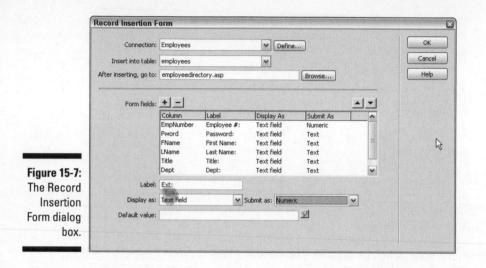

Figure 15-7:
The Record
Insertion
Form dialog
box.

You can now test your page (see Figure 15-8). Simply upload the page to your server, open it in your browser, and enter all the information for a new record. Click the Insert Record button. Did your new record show up in the database?

Upload the Connections folder when you upload your site files to the application server, otherwise you get an ASP `Include File Not Found` error message.

When you create the database connection (refer to Chapter 13), a Connections folder is added to your site on the local drive. The ASP files in the Connections folder store necessary information that makes your page work correctly with the database. This type of file is typically called an *include file* because its contents is referenced by the code in another page. Dreamweaver automatically *includes* the content of this file on any page you create that uses this database connection.

Updating a record via a browser

To edit or *update* a record from a database, you first need to create a search form to search for the record you want to update. After you find the record, the Update Record form appears, which is where you perform the actual update.

1. **On a new page, create a simple search form, with a text field element and a Submit button.**

   See the "Searching for Database Records" section, earlier in this chapter, if you need a refresher on creating search forms.

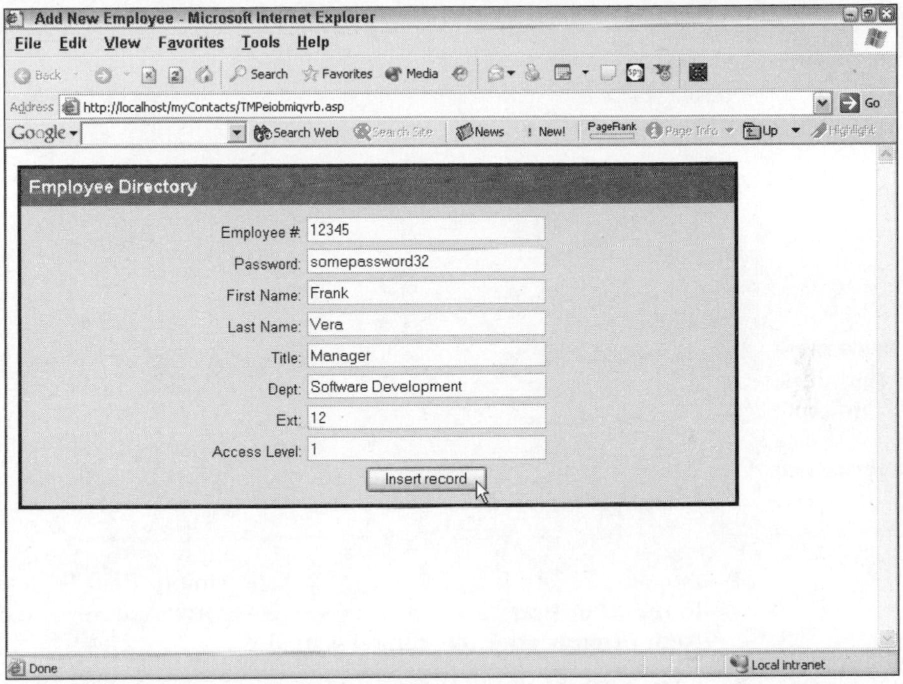

Figure 15-8:
The Record
Insertion
Form in
action.

2. **Select the text field on your page, and in the Properties inspector replace *textfield* with a more descriptive name. For example, *mysearch*.**

   This helps to differentiate one text field from another on a page that contains multiple fields.

3. **Create a recordset, and filter by the field that you use as your search criteria.**

   I use Employee Number (EmpNo) as my search criteria.

4. **From the drop-down list directly below the Filter list, select Form Variable. Next to Form Variable, type the name of the text field from your search form. In my case, I type *mysearch*.**

5. **Click OK.**

6. **Choose Insert➪Application Objects➪Update Record➪Record Update Form Wizard.**

   The Record Update Form dialog box opens (see Figure 15-9).

7. **Select the appropriate connection and table.**

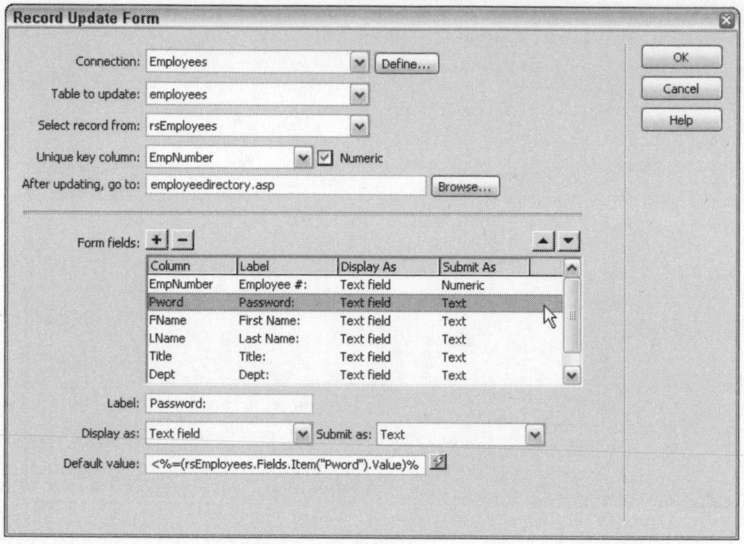

Figure 15-9:
The Record
Update
Form dialog
box.

8. **In the After Updating, Go To text box, enter the name of the page you want to show after the update is made.**

   I use `employeedirectory.asp`, which is my default employee directory page.

9. **In the Form Fields box, make sure that the field labels are correct, or rename them to what you want to display on the update form. You can rename them later on your page by selecting and replacing the text for each field directly on your page.**

10. **Click OK.**

    A new form appears on your page. You can format the look of the form (font, color, and so on) to make it match the rest of your site.

11. **Select the Server Behaviors panel and click the plus sign (+). From the menu, select Show Region, and from the submenu, select Show Region If Recordset Is Not Empty.**

    This last step ensures that you don't get an error if no recordset matches the criteria you enter into the search field.

Your Update form is now complete (see Figure 15-10).

You can test the new page by previewing it in your browser. Enter a value that you know exists in that field in your database and click the Submit button. The Update Record Form is now populated with the information for that record. You can now make any changes to that record and click the Update

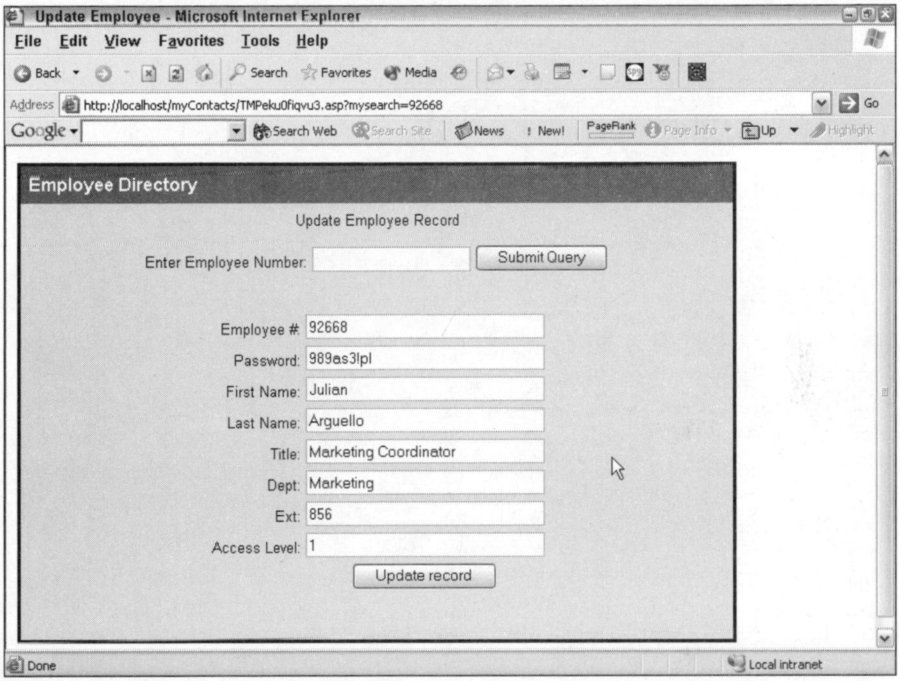

Figure 15-10:
The newly
created
Update
form.

Record button to save the changes to the database. The next time you view that record online, the changes are there (see Figure 15-11).

E-Commerce Basics

If there's one thing that's certain about most people who want a Web site, it's that they want to make money from it. The era of the "brochure" site is no more, my friends. People hawk everything from fine china to soil from the Holy Land on the Internet (I kid you not about that one). E-commerce helps bring together shoppers and sellers on the Internet.

In the next few paragraphs, I tell you more about what an e-commerce Web site is and what you need to have in place in order to create a fully functional e-commerce site. However, if you're looking for information on how to create an e-commerce site right out of the box with Dreamweaver, stop here. It's not going to happen. I don't know why the powers that be over at Macromedia haven't included this feature yet. To be quite frank, I think this is really one of the only major flaws I can find with Dreamweaver. You *can* create an e-commerce Web site using Dreamweaver, but it requires an extension, which I go into in just a moment.

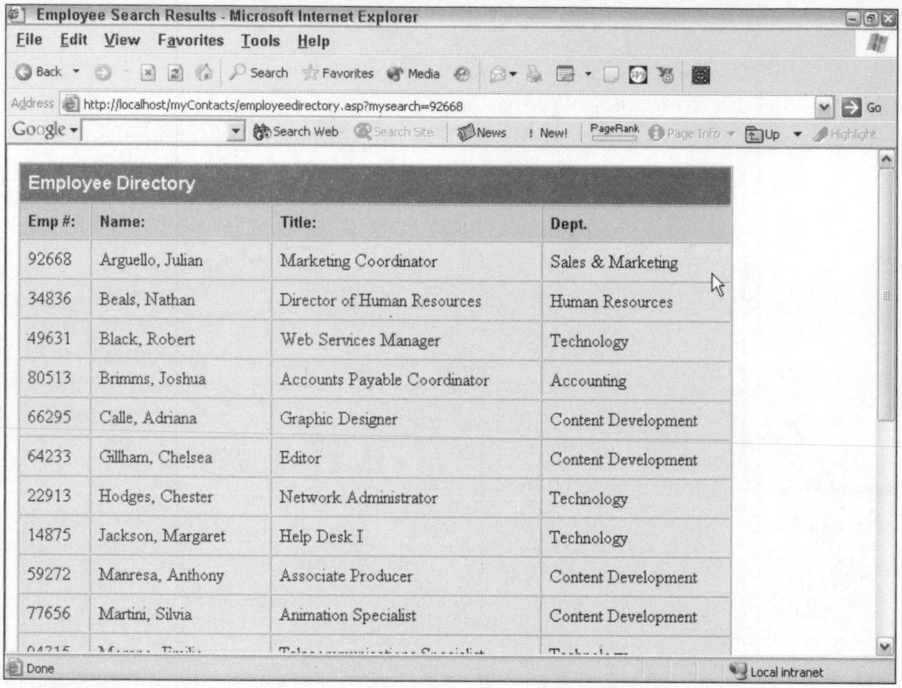

Figure 15-11:
The updated
record.

What puts the "e-commerce" into an e-commerce Web site?

An e-commerce Web site, in a nutshell, is a Web site that accepts real-time payments for goods and services. For example, if you're looking for a weight loss supplement you can log on to www.MetabolicNutrition.com, browse offerings in its weight loss product line, and have one shipped to you overnight.

Not all e-commerce Web sites are the same — many companies have built customized tools to aid users in the shopping process. For example, Metabolic Nutrition also allows you to store your shipping information so that you don't have to enter it every time you order. It also has a virtual "personal assistant" that recommends products based on your health, age, diet, and lifestyle.

The cost of an e-commerce Web site is significantly more than the cost of building a regular Web site because you have to figure in several third-party costs. Here's a quick run-down of the minimal (traditional) e-commerce requirements:

✔ **A shopping cart:** A shopping cart is a series of scripts and applications that displays items from your database, allows users to pick and choose which ones they want, and then collects payment and shipping information. Some Web-hosting accounts come with shopping carts included. A popular one is Miva Merchant (www.miva.com). Various Dreamweaver shopping cart extensions are also worth looking into. For example, PDG Software (www.pdgsoft.com) offers a Dreamweaver extension that provides full integration with PDG's Shopping Cart with a price tag of about $400 for a lifetime license.

✔ **A merchant account:** This is literally an account with a bank or a financial institution that allows you to accept credit cards from your clients. Many merchant account providers also offer payment gateways and virtual terminals as a suite, which can save you money and time. Costs and transactions fees vary, as service providers set their own prices. Online Data Corp (www.onlinedatacorp.com) is a good one.

✔ **A payment gateway and virtual terminal:** A payment gateway is what ties your shopping cart to your merchant account. A virtual terminal is like an electronic bookkeeper and cash register in one — you can view your Web site transactions, issue refunds, and manage orders. The two most popular packages are the VeriSign PayFlow Pro and PayFlow Link (www.verisign.com).

✔ **A secure site certificate:** This encrypts information between your Web site and the client's computer to protect the information from being stolen as you make your purchase online. This is commonly referred to as Secure Sockets Layer (SSL) technology. Verisign and Thawte's 128-bit certificates are popular picks. If you're on a shared Web-hosting account, you may be able to share the server's certificate to save money; however, this is often regarded as unprofessional, because the security certificate doesn't display your company name on it — shoppers who check it see your Web-hosting company's name instead.

The definition of what a "traditional" e-commerce Web site is continues to change as new technologies and application service providers emerge. Services such as Yahoo! Stores allow you to create a site without purchasing any of the previously mentioned items. PayPal.com offers all-inclusive e-commerce services with free shopping cart tools.

Pre-made shopping carts and e-commerce systems save you time and money up front, and buying one is the fastest way to get a business online. The downside of using a pre-made shopping cart is that you often can't make it look like an integral part of your Web site, meaning that you usually have limited control over the graphical elements on shopping-cart driven pages. Also, most shopping carts use their own database and give you limited access to the code (because a lot of it may be compiled CGI, which Dreamweaver can't read), so you may run into brick walls when trying to build new features that you didn't buy out of the box.

Considering the investment and risk, many companies prefer to hire a professional programming team to create a system from scratch that looks and functions exactly how they want it to. Amazon.com, for example, has spent millions on its system to make it the incredibly smart and easy to use system it is today. But you don't have to break the bank — many very successful custom-built e-commerce Web sites are created for less than the cost of a used '94 Toyota Camry.

Extending Dreamweaver one feature at a time

At last count, a few minutes ago, there were 49 e-commerce-related extensions for Dreamweaver on the Macromedia Web site, from standalone shopping carts to a PayPal extension that allows shoppers to pay you via PayPal directly from your Web site.

However, e-commerce is just the proverbial ol' tip of the iceberg when extending Dreamweaver. At the Macromedia Exchange Web site, you can download an extension for just about any functionality your Web site can have.

You can add extensions to Dreamweaver two ways. The first is by going directly to the Web site (`http://www.macromedia.com/cfusion/exchange/index.cfm?view=sn120`).

The other way to access Macromedia Exchange is through Dreamweaver itself. You must be connected to the Internet in order for this to work. This can be done from various points within the application:

- ✔ **From the Insert menu:** Choose Insert➪Get More Objects

- ✔ **From the Command menu:** Choose Command➪Get More Commands

- ✔ **From the Help menu:** Choose Help➪Dreamweaver Exchange

- ✔ **From the Server Behaviors panel:** Click the plus sign (+) and then select Get More Server Behaviors

- ✔ **From the Bindings panel:** Click the plus sign (+) and then select Get More Data Sources

- ✔ **From the Behaviors panel:** Click the plus sign (+) and then select Get More Behaviors

When you are on Macromedia Exchange, if this is your first time there, you must register before downloading any extensions. Also, you need to make sure that your *Extension Manager* (which comes with Dreamweaver) is installed and running.

If you register and have the Extension Manager on your system, you can search for extensions and download them to your system. You can also choose to download the extensions (.mxp files) onto your computer and install them using the manager, or you can choose to install them on the spot, which downloads and installs the extension from the Web without saving the installation file on your hard drive.

You can run the Extension Manager for installing an extension is various ways. In Dreamweaver, you can click Command⇨Manage Extensions. You must have a document open. In Windows, you can go to Start⇨Programs⇨ Macromedia Extension Manager⇨Macromedia Extension Manager. You can also launch it by double-clicking an .mxp file in Explorer.

When you open Extension Manager, you see all the extensions you installed on your system. To view the description for any of these extensions, simply click it once, and any pertinent information displays in the lower pane of the Extension Manager window.

Ready to add some extensions? Click File⇨Install Extension and follow the simple prompts to have your new extension up and running in no time. Uninstalling is just as simple: Click File⇨Remove Extension, and voilà!

Part VI
The Part of Tens

The 5th Wave   By Rich Tennant

"I'm not sure I like a college whose home page
has a link to The Party Zone!"

In this part . . .

The Part of Tens features ten great Web sites designed in Dreamweaver with descriptions about the tools and techniques used to make these sites work on the Web. You also find ten timesaving techniques to help you get the most out of Dreamweaver and ten great Web design ideas that you can use right away.

Chapter 16

Ten Great Sites Designed with Dreamweaver

Dreamweaver has become the clear choice of professional Web designers and is the program behind many of the best-designed sites on the Web.

Many of the sites featured in this chapter take advantage of the latest Web technologies, integrating Dynamic HTML, Flash, and more to create vivid animations and powerful interactivity.

The sites featured in this chapter provide an excellent overview of what you can do with Dreamweaver — and they're all great examples of what's possible on the Web today. Review the descriptions of these sites to discover what tools the designers used and how they made these great Web sites. Then spend some time online, visiting each site to appreciate the full impact of their design, navigation, and other features.

You can connect directly to these Web sites by clicking the appropriate hyperlink in the HTML interface on the CD that accompanies this book.

Hop Studios Internet Consultants

`www.hopstudios.com/`

Dreamweaver is the clear choice of most professional Web designers these days, including those at Hop Studios (shown in Figure 16-1), a Web design company in Southern California owned and managed by one of the coauthors of this book, Susannah Gardner.

Although Dreamweaver is great for large, complex sites, you can also use it for sites with a bent for simplicity. It should be no surprise that Hop Studios used Dreamweaver to develop its own Web site.

Susannah chose Dreamweaver because she wanted the site to be quick loading, easy to navigate, and fun to use. Using Dreamweaver as the primary production tool has allowed the designers at Hop Studios to focus their energy on making a site that shows off their clients and their skills.

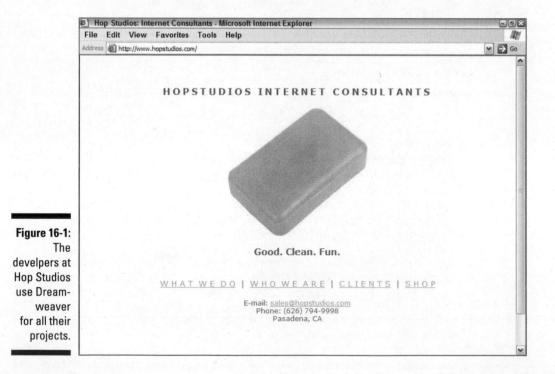

Figure 16-1: The develpers at Hop Studios use Dream-weaver for all their projects.

Chapter 16: Ten Great Sites Designed with Dreamweaver *361*

Bloom Art Walk Public Art Project

`www.usc.edu/publicart/bloomwalk/`

During the spring of 2003, the University of Southern California Public Art Studies Program was asked to supervise a public art project located on a campus pedestrian corridor called Bloom Walk (shown in Figure 16-2). Designing the site was a challenge because the competition had not been announced yet, and just what kind of art piece would be placed on campus is unclear. As a result, the site needed to be attractive and informative, without strongly suggesting a design focus or style that might influence the competition or have to be completely redesigned after a piece was chosen.

The site was designed by Hop Studios, where developers opted to create small Flash animations that showed possible sites for art pieces, and to keep other design elements to a minimum — to the point of using a very limited color and font palette. Dreamweaver was especially useful for creating pop-up windows to display photos of the site model and of the walkway.

Figure 16-2: The Bloom Art Walk project features small Flash animations to show off public art sites.

Coaching for CyberRomantics

www.kathrynblord.com/

Kathryn B. Lord is a psychiatric social worker who has branched out into the dot-com world to take advantage of the online romance market. Her site (see Figure 16-3) is a promotion piece for the coaching services Kathryn offers to men and women using the Internet to find relationships.

Kathryn was concerned about creating a site that looked like an elementary school Valentine's Day card — trite, sappy, and unconvincing. She needed a compelling concept that got across the idea of romance without turning people off. She and the designers at Hop Studios settled on a candy theme that makes her pages pop with visual appeal. It has some extra spice from the Dreamweaver rollover behaviors. She also integrated a third-party mailing list service to add the ability for her site visitors to sign up for her newsletter.

You find instructions to create your own rollover images in Chapter 9.

Figure 16-3: The Dreamweaver rollover behaviors help bring this online romance site to life.

Covering Crime and Justice, A Guide for Journalists

`www.justicejournalism.org/crimeguide/`

The Dreamweaver template feature was an essential element in the development of the Criminal Justice Journalists' guide to Covering Crime and Justice. The site (see Figure 16-4) was a fairly large project — more than 60 pages and 66,000 words, and the use of templates helped designers maintain consistency throughout the site.

The development of any complex Web site poses technical challenges — the challenge for the Covering Crime and Justice site was one of production. How do you put that much text on a site and keep everything looking consistent and professional? For Hop Studios, the answer was templates and style sheets. The site needs to be readable online and also printable, so the pages were laid out with that in mind. Content developers also made use of extensive cross-referencing in the text. Without a tool like Dreamweaver, developing a site of this size would have been much more difficult and time consuming.

Figure 16-4: The Dreamweaver template features helped designers maintain a consistent look and feel throughout this content-heavy site.

The Dreamweaver template features are covered in Chapter 4, and you can find out about Cascading Style Sheets and layers in Chapters 8 and 9.

Philip Matt Gardner, Artist

www.pmgardner.com/

If you've ever designed a Web site for an artist, you know how picky they can be about presentation. When Philip Matt Gardner, a recent Rhode Island School of Design graduate in illustration, decided to put his portfolio online, he had some very specific ideas about how it should look.

Matt designed some stunning artwork for the site (see Figure 16-5), and Hop Studios used Flash to produce a beautiful animation leading into the portfolio pieces. Dreamweaver was used to pull the whole site together. It was especially important to Matt that the pages display well on both Macs and PCs, so the Dreamweaver site testing tools were used extensively during production.

The Dreamweaver site testing tools are covered in Chapters 3 and 9.

Figure 16-5:
Artist Philip Matt's site was designed to display well on both Macs and PCs, something Dreamweaver is especially good at.

Looks Like Rayne

www.pattirayne.com/

Singer Patti Rayne needed a way to let her growing fan base know about her next show, and a way to make information about herself and her work available to the music industry. Her Web site (see Figure 16-6) does just that by providing dates and locations of her shows, photos, and downloadable music.

For Hop Studios designers, Macromedia Fireworks was particularly important in developing this site. The complicated layout on the front page of the site places several overlapping elements sitting on a heavily patterned background. Slicing proved to be a huge timesaver in producing this page. Dreamweaver was used to pull together all the elements on the inside pages.

You find lots of great information about Fireworks and how it is integrated with Dreamweaver in Chapter 10.

Figure 16-6: Singer Patti Rayne's site was designed and "sliced" in Fireworks, making it easy to pull together in Dream-weaver.

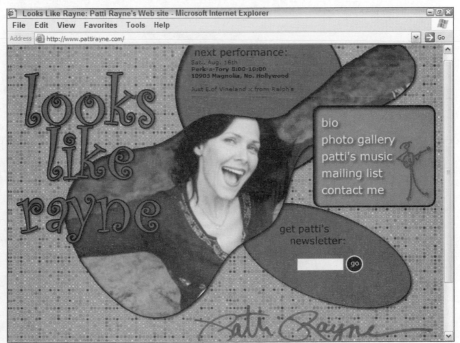

Michael S. Overing, A Professional Corporation

www.digitalmedialaw.com/

Lawyer Michael S. Overing wanted a Web site for two reasons — so that current and future clients can read about his firm and the work they do, and also to showcase the writing he and his partners do about Internet law.

The site (shown in Figure 16-7) is simple, professional, and elegant, relying heavily on Dreamweaver rollovers and easy table implementation for its clean design and readability. Additionally, Hop Studios used external Cascading Style Sheets, created in Dreamweaver, to keep text styles consistent from page to page.

To find out more about using tables to create complex designs, see Chapter 6.

Figure 16-7: The Cascading Style Sheets used on this legal site helps keep styles consistent from page to page.

A Natural Woman.com

www.anaturalwoman.com/

Lifestyle coach Suzanne Berg had a tough problem in designing her Web site. She runs her own business these days and coaches women in three different areas — natural lifestyles, natural menopause management, and active living. Although some of her clients want coaching in all three areas, not all do, and she needed a Web site that would work for each kind of client.

Suzanne and Hop Studios worked together to find a concept that would allow her to tie all three areas into a visual theme that worked across the site (see Figure 16-8). The oranges on the site convey the idea of health and enthusiasm that Suzanne brings to her coaching practice. The Dreamweaver site management features really helped in keeping track of the different sections of this site and managing navigation and other issues while the project was being developed.

Find out about the great site management features in Chapter 3.

Figure 16-8: The Dreamweaver site management features helped developers manage the three different sections of this site.

Bringing Humor

`www.marilynpittman.com/`

Marilyn Pittman is the leading voice coach for National Public Radio. Since 1989, she has worked with hundreds of radio and television professionals on their delivery. Trained as an actor at the University of New Mexico, she has played a variety of roles on the air for more than 25 years: news anchor, reporter, commentator, and talk show host.

On top of all that, she is also a professional comedian (look for her at the Improv in San Francisco and elsewhere) and she wanted that to come through in her Web site. Doing justice to someone like Marilyn is impossible on the Web, but as you can see in Figure 16-9, a design that features the many faces of Marilyn provides the flavor of her energy and glimpse into her personality.

Dreamweaver makes building sites such as this one easy, using tables to control the placement of images and other elements, and behaviors create the rollover effects and other dynamic elements. Dreamweaver also includes great multimedia features that allow you to load in sound files, such as those featured on this site.

Figure 16-9:
The Dreamweaver rollover effects and features for linking in multimedia helped bring this site to life.

You find behaviors covered in Chapter 9 and instructions for linking to sound files and other multimedia elements in Chapter 11.

Yours Truly

`www.JCWarner.com/`

I would love to take credit for the design of my own Web site (see Figure 16-10), but the truth is that my talented friend, Ivonne Berkowitz, developed my site using the great features of Dreamweaver to create a complex design that is simple to update and maintain. I can handle all the technical development on my site, but Ivonne is a much more talented designer.

As the Web has gotten more complex, and the design standards higher, most good Web sites require a team of experts to develop a truly great site. Don't expect to be able to do everything yourself — seek out better designers, programmers, writers, and editors to produce the best site possible. (My mom, Malinda McCain edits my site — she has her own copy editing business at `www.sharewords.com/copyedit`.)

Figure 16-10: My own Web site was, of course, built with Dreamweaver.

I use Dreamweaver to make regular additions to the site and handle site management when I want to add new sections or make more significant changes. (Just for the record, I really do think Dreamweaver is the best Web design program on the market, and I can't imagine using anything else on my own site.)

Chapter 17

Ten Web Site Ideas You Can Use

A ll good Web sites grow and evolve. If you start with a strong design and pay close attention to some basic rules about interface, navigation, and style, you have a better foundation to build on. The following design ideas can help you create a compelling Web site that grows gracefully.

Make It Easy

Creating a clear and intuitive navigational system is one of the most important elements in creating a Web site. Nothing is likely to frustrate your visitors more than not being able to find what they're looking for. Make sure that visitors can easily get to all the main sections of your site from every page in the site.

You can best do this by creating a set of links to each of the main sections and placing it at the top or side of every page. I call this set of links a *navigation row* or *navigation bar*, and it's a common feature on most well designed sites. If the pages are very long, consider including a navigation bar, or footer, at the bottom of the page as well. Often the navigation bar at the bottom of the page is just a list of text links. The bottom of the page is also an ideal place to include basic contact information. A set of graphical icons can make this navigational element an attractive part of your design. Your goal is to make sure that viewers don't have to use the Back button in their browsers to move around your site.

White Space Is Not Wasted Space

One of the best design features you can add to a page is nothing at all (also known as *white space*). Understand that white space, in this case, is not always white; it's simply space that you haven't crammed full of text or images. It can be any color, but it's usually most effective if it's the color or pattern of your background. White space gives the eye a rest, something readers need even more often when they're staring at a computer monitor. You can use white space to separate one type of information from another and to focus the viewer's attention where you want it most. Some of the most beautiful and compelling designs on the Web use only a few well-thought-out elements against lots of white space.

Design for Your Audience

No matter how technically sophisticated a Web site is or how great the writing, most people notice the design first. Make sure that you leave plenty of time and budget to develop an appropriate and attractive design for your Web site. The right design is one that best suits your audience — that may or may not mean lots of fancy graphics and animations.

Think about who you want to attract to your Web site before you develop the design. A gaming Web site geared toward teenagers should look very different from a Web site with gardening tips or an online banking site for adults. Review other sites designed for your target market. Consider your audience's time constraints and attention span, and, most importantly, consider your audience's goals. If you design your site to provide information to busy businesspeople, you want fast-loading pages with few graphics and little or no animation. If you design your site for entertainment, your audience may be willing to wait a little longer for animation and other interactive features.

Back It Up

Make sure you have a system in place to back up your Web site. Always keep a copy of all the files that are on your server in a separate location and update it regularly to make sure you have the latest version of your site backed up at all times. Even the best Internet Service Providers sometimes have technical problems, so you should keep a backup of your site where you have easy access to it and can get it back online quickly if something ever does happen to delete any or all the files you have on the server.

Also keep a backup of your original source files, such as Photoshop images. For example, when you develop images for the Web, you usually start in a program like Photoshop, creating a high-resolution image that may include layers and other elements. Before the image goes on your Web site, those layers get flattened and the image gets compressed or reduced and converted into a GIF or JPEG. If you ever want to go back and alter that image in the future, you'll want the original source file before it was compressed and the layers were flattened. Whether you create your own images or you hire a professional designer, make sure you develop a system for saving all these original elements when they are created.

Be Consistent

As you lay out your Web page, keep related items physically close to one another. You want your viewers to instantly understand which pieces of information are related. Give elements of similar importance the same weight on a page. Distinguish different kinds of information by their design, location, and prominence. This kind of organization makes following information visually much easier for your viewers. You can find many other design tips in Chapter 4.

Make sure that all similar elements follow the same design parameters, such as type style, banner size, and page background color. If you use too many different elements on a page or within the same Web site, you quickly have a very "busy" design, and you may confuse your viewers. Defining a set of colors, shapes, or other elements that you use throughout the site is a good way to ensure a consistent style. Choose two or three fonts for your Web site and use those consistently as well. Using too many fonts makes your pages less appealing and harder to read.

Inconsistency can also weaken your brand. A clean, consistent Web site goes a long way in building a user's trust. Sapient, a business and technology consulting firm, did a study in 1999 on how visual alignments affect user attention, trust, and interest. The study showed being consistent with color schemes and typefaces and keeping the design simple makes a significant difference.

Small and Fast

Despite all the promises that unlimited bandwidth was coming soon, the biggest problem on the Internet is still speed. Making sure that your pages download quickly makes your viewers more likely to keep clicking. You may create the best design ever to grace the Web, but if it takes too long to appear on your viewers' screens, no one will wait around long enough to compliment your design talents.

If your page designs take a long time to download, here are a few likely reasons and suggestions for how to make them load faster: First, take a look at multi-media elements and consider reducing the size or at least offering users the option to skip large multimedia files, such as Flash introductions. You especially don't want to make users wait too long for the first page of your site. If you suspect that static images are the problem, consider compression methods and use a program such as Fireworks or ImageReady that are designed for optimizing images for the Web (you find more on how to do this in Chapters 5 and 10). Finally, use the Dreamweaver code cleanup feature to get rid of extra tags that can contribute to a heavier page. To use this feature, choose Commands⇨Clean Up HTML.

Accessible Designs

As you design your site, keep in mind that viewers come to your pages with a variety of computers, operating systems, and monitors. Ensure that your site is accessible to all your potential viewers by testing your pages on a variety of systems. If you want to attract a large audience to your site, you need to ensure that it looks good on a broad range of systems. A design that looks great in Navigator 4.0 and higher may be unreadable in Internet Explorer 3.0. And many people still use old browsers because they haven't bothered — or don't know how — to download new versions.

Accessible design on the Web also includes pages that can be read (actually, converted to synthesized speech) by special browsers used by the blind. Using the Alt attribute in your image tags is a simple way to ensure that all visitors can get the information they need. The Alt attribute specifies a text alternative that displays if the image doesn't appear. It's inserted into an image tag like this:

```
<IMG SRC="CAT.GIF" ALT="A picture of a black and white cat.">
```

Follow the Three Clicks Rule

The Three Clicks Rule states that no important piece of information should ever be more than three clicks away from anywhere else on your Web site. The most important information should be even closer at hand. Some information, such as contact information, should never be more than one click away. You can make finding information easy for viewers by creating a site map (as I explain in the next section) and a *navigation bar* — a set of links to all the main sections on your site.

Map It Out

As your site gets larger, providing easy access to all the information on your Web site may get harder and harder. A great solution is to provide a *site map,* which is a page that includes links to almost every other page in the site. The site map can become a busy page and usually appears best in outline form. This page should be highly functional — it doesn't matter if it looks pretty. Don't put lots of graphics on this page; it should load quickly and provide easy access to anything that your visitors need.

Late-Breaking News

The Web provides a powerful vehicle for businesses and non-profit organizations to present their side of any story, and get the word out quickly when tragic events, bad press, and other crises arise.

But don't wait for an emergency to find out if you're prepared to add new information to your Web site quickly, and don't fool yourself into thinking that just because you don't manage a daily Internet newspaper you don't have to worry about speedy updates.

With a little planning and key systems set up in advance, you can be prepared for events that require timely information — whether an international crisis stops air travel, a potential strike prevents shipping, or an embarrassing event makes your CEO cringe and demand that the real story be told as soon as possible.

Most organizations develop Web sites that are updated on a weekly, monthly, or even annual basis. More sophisticated sites may link to databases that track inventory or update product listings in realtime, but even high-end sites are often ill prepared to update special information quickly.

Here are a few steps you can take to be prepared for timely updates on your site:

✔ **Make sure you can send new information to your Web site quickly.**

Many Web sites are designed with testing systems that safeguard against careless mistakes, but these systems can add hours, or even days, to the time it takes to add new information to your Web site. Work with your technical staff or consultants to make sure you can update your site quickly if necessary. This may require creating a new section you can update independently from the rest of the site or override the regular update system.

✔ **Make updating important sections of your site easy.**

Consider developing a content management system that uses a Web-based form to post new information to your site. Such a system can be designed to change or add information to a Web page as easily as filling out an online order form. You need an experienced programmer to develop a form-based update system. Many Web consultants offer this kind of service, and after it's developed, other kinds of updates can use it as well. For example, this method works if you are a real estate agent and need to change listings or you have a calendar of events. Password protection should be included so that you control access to the form. As an added advantage, a form enables you to make updates from any computer connected to the Internet. So you can update your Web site, even if you can't get back into your office.

✔ **Identify and train key staff to update the site.**

With the right systems in place, you do not need to have much technical experience to make simple updates to a site, but your staff needs some instruction and regular reminders. Make sure you also develop a schedule for retraining to ensure that no one forgets emergency procedures. Your most serious emergency could happen tomorrow or may not happen for years to come — you never know, so being prepared pays off in the end.

Chapter 18

Ten Timesaving Dreamweaver Tips

*W*ith each new version, Dreamweaver gets even better, which makes creating great sites easier and faster. As I put this book together, I collected tips and tricks and gathered them into this handy list. Take a moment to check out these tips and save tons of time in developing your Web site. Most of these tips apply to both Macintosh and Windows users.

Trying the New Interface

If you love the old interface, you can still stick with it, but Dreamweaver MX 2004 provides even more compelling reasons to give the new interface a chance. When you first turn on the program, you have a choice between the two interfaces — the old and the new. In the latest version, you can personalize menus and panels even more easily to ensure that the features you use the most are the most accessible.

The old interface still has all the floating panels (called *palettes* in previous versions), which provide quick access to the most popular Dreamweaver features. But, as you may have found in previous versions, those floating panels can clutter up the design area and get in your way. You can still use the F4 key as a shortcut to hide all visible panels at once and the F4 key again to get them back, but if you like that shortcut, you may be even happier with the new interface. Dreamweaver MX 2004 enables you to lock each panel into the work-space, keeping it handy without overlapping with the design area. You can move the panels around and change the icons that are visible on each of them to ensure that your favorite tools are where you like them. Macromedia changed the interface based on tons of feedback from professional designers, and you're likely to find it a better option as well. Even better, you can still use F4 to hide palettes, even in their new docked mode, so you get the best of both worlds.

Creating Dynamic Web Sites

Don't be intimidated by all the panels and options in Dreamweaver 2004. Much of what's been added are the features that were previously reserved for the Macromedia UltraDev program. These include high-end programming features for creating dynamic, database-driven sites using ASP, JSP, and ColdFusion. If that's all new to you, take your time getting into these advanced features in Chapters 13, 14, and 15.

And don't worry — if you aren't creating a database-driven site, you don't need to learn these features, at least not yet. But rest assured, they're ready for you when you want to take your site to the next level. Most of the best sites on the Web these days are dynamic and require a database and the power to connect it to the Web. Macromedia integrated these features into Dreamweaver and made sure you had them handy because you're likely to need them sooner or later.

Splitting the View: Working in the Code

If you like to switch back and forth between the HTML source code and the WYSIWYG (What You See Is What You Get) design view in Dreamweaver, you'll appreciate the option to split the window so that you can view the HTML source and the WYSIWYG design area at the same time. To split the window, choose View➪Code and Design or select the Show Code and Design Views button, located just under the Insert panel at the top of the work space.

Tabling Your Designs

HTML tables still offer the best way to create complex Web designs (because older browsers don't support layers, and even in new browsers, layers aren't supported consistently). Fortunately, Dreamweaver MX 2004 has made creating tables in its visual design area easier. In the Layout View, you can "draw" tables on a page, drag them into place, and even group cells in a nested table — without ever worrying about how many rows and cells you create. You can even use this feature to create tables that change with the window size, a great technique for ensuring your designs work on all monitors (even the tiny screens on Palm handhelds and Pocket PCs).

Choose View➪Table View➪Layout View to access Dreamweaver's special table-creation environment. But then make sure to switch back to the Standard View, which makes editing and formatting your table easier. You find cell and table layout options in the Objects panel when you select the table or cell. For more information about using Layout mode and working with HTML tables, check out Chapter 6.

Designing in a Flash

Flash rocks! The Macromedia vector-based design and animation program, Flash, is one of the hottest programs on the Web today because it makes creating fast-loading images and animations that dynamically adjust to fit any screen size possible. Now that the Flash plug-in is built into most current browsers, Flash has become a standard, and Dreamweaver has made adding Flash buttons and text to your Web pages easier.

To add premade Flash buttons to your site, just click the Insert Flash Button option in the Media tab of the Insert panel. The dialog box makes choosing a button design and editing the text that appears on the button easy, all from within Dreamweaver. You can even create your own buttons in Flash and add them to the list of available buttons.

You can add Flash Text the same way, by choosing the Insert Flash Text option from the Objects panel. For more on these integrated Flash features, read Chapter 11.

Making Fireworks with Your Images

The Dreamweaver integration with Fireworks, Macromedia's Web image program, makes editing images while you work in Dreamweaver easy. Need to change the text on a button or create a new banner? Just click the Edit image button in the Properties inspector to launch Fireworks. Any changes you make to an image automatically appear in the Dreamweaver page. If you always use another image program, such as Photoshop, this level of integration should at least get you to consider using Fireworks. It can save you a ton of time in your design work, especially when your pesky colleagues and clients are always asking for last minute changes. For more on using Fireworks and Dreamweaver in tandem, check out Chapter 10.

Finding Functional Fonts

Designers get so excited when they find out that they can use any font on a Web page. But, in reality, your viewers must still have the font on their computers for it to display. The more common the font, the more likely it is to display the way you intend. If you want to use a more unusual font, go for it — just be sure that you also include alternatives. The Dreamweaver Font List already includes collections of common fonts, and you can always create your own Font List by choosing Text➪Font➪Edit Font List.

And here's another tip: Windows is by far the most common operating system that people use to browse the Net. To ensure the best — and fastest — results for the majority of your users, list a Windows font first.

In an effort to make text easier to read on the Web, Adobe and Microsoft have both created fonts especially suited to computer screens. Visit their Web sites at www.adobe.com and www.microsoft.com respectively and search for Web fonts to find out more.

Differentiating DHTML for All Browsers

If you like pushing the technical limits of what works on the Web, don't overlook one of the most valuable features of Dreamweaver: the Convert option. This feature automatically converts your complex page designs that work only in 4.0 and later browsers into alternative pages that display in 3.0 browsers. The feature converts the CSS and DHTML tags into regular HTML style tags by converting CSS formatting into HTML formatting tags and recreating layers into HTML Tables.

To convert CSS and other features on a page, choose File➪Convert➪3.0 Browser Compatible. Beware that HTML is not capable of the complex designs you can create using DHTML, so your converted pages may not look as much like the original as you would like. For example, the conversion can't do justice to a layer that moves across the screen in a static table cell. Chapter 9 walks you through the process in detail. The conversion isn't a perfect science, but it is a relatively easy way to ensure your pages are at least presentable in older browsers.

I've heard too many good designers say that users should upgrade their browsers and that they don't care about users who are so lame they're still using an old version of AOL. Here's a word of caution: It only takes one really important viewer to get you in trouble for not doing multibrowser designs. Beware that one of the most likely people to be using an older browser is the president of the company who is traveling with his laptop that he's never upgraded the browser on because he only uses it from hotel rooms on the road. Don't take the risk that your paying clients, your boss, or worse yet, your investors, are the ones with the old browsers. Make sure your designs work well for everyone — it's the sign of a truly high-end Web designer.

Directing Your Viewers

Creating multiple pages is the most fail-safe solution for making sure that all your viewers are happy when you use cutting-edge page designs filled with DHTML and CSS. That means you create two or more sets of pages: one that uses the latest features and one that uses older, more universally supported HTML tags. But how do you ensure that viewers get to the right pages? Use the Check Browser behavior.

The Check Browser behavior is written in JavaScript and determines the browser type that each viewer who lands on your site uses. The behavior then directs users to the page design best suited to their browser version. To use this feature, choose Window⇨Behaviors to open the Behaviors panel. You can also find this panel by clicking the Design panel in the top right of your screen and choosing the Behaviors tab.

Select the plus sign (+) to open the drop-down list of options on the Behaviors tab and choose the Check Browser option. In the Check Browser dialog box, specify what browser versions should be directed to what pages on your site. When users arrive at your site, they are automatically directed to the page of your choice, based on the browser type and version that you specify.

Keeping Frequently Used Items Handy

Ever wished you could keep all of your favorite Dreamweaver features in one convenient place? Now you can with the Favorites tab.

When you launch Dreamweaver, the Common tab is visible at the top of the Workspace. Click the arrow to the right of it, and you find a pull-down menu with several options, including Layout, Forms, and HTML. At the bottom of that list is the newest addition of Macromedia, the Favorites bar.

Select the Favorites bar and you can customize it with all your favorite objects with right-click ease. Use this as a convenient way to keep all your favorite features handy. You can even change it for special projects that require a series of steps or elements.

Appendix

About the CD

. . . .

. . . .

*T*he CD-ROM that accompanies this book contains the following goodies:

- ✔ Trial versions of Dreamweaver, Fireworks, and Illustrator (all from Macromedia)

- ✔ Lots of extra trial versions of software (see the "What You Find on the CD" section, later in this appendix) that can help you become more efficient in many aspects of Web design

- ✔ Templates to make building your Web site easier

- ✔ A Flash file for you to use when you try out the Dreamweaver plug-in features

- ✔ A few extra GIF and JPEG images for you to use while you become familiar with building Web pages in Dreamweaver

- ✔ A glossary that can help you become familiar with Web design and Dreamweaver lingo

System Requirements

Make sure that your computer meets the minimum system requirements shown in the following list. If your computer doesn't match up to most of these requirements, you may have problems using the software and files on the CD.

- A PC with a Pentium III or faster processor and 600+ MHz; or a Power Mac 500+ MHz computer or faster processor.

- Microsoft Windows 98, 2000, NT, or XP; or Mac OS system software 9.1, 9.2.1, or OS 10.2.6

- At least 128MB of available RAM on your computer; for best performance, I recommend at least 256MB.

- At least 275MB of available hard drive space if you want to install all the software from this CD; you need less space if you don't install every program.

- A CD-ROM drive.

- A sound card for PCs; Mac OS computers have built-in sound support.

- A monitor capable of displaying at least 256 colors or grayscale, 800 x 600 resolution. (1024 x 768, millions of colors recommended. Thousands of colors required for OS X.)

- A modem with a speed of at least 14,400 bps.

If you need more information on the basics, check out these books published by Wiley Publishing, Inc.: *PCs For Dummies,* by Dan Gookin; *Macs For Dummies* and *iMacs For Dummies* by David Pogue; *Windows 98 For Dummies, Windows 2000 Professional For Dummies, Microsoft Windows ME Millennium Edition For Dummies,* and *Windows XP For Dummies,* all by Andy Rathbone.

Using the CD with Microsoft Windows

To install items from the CD to your hard drive, follow these steps:

1. **Insert the CD into your computer's CD-ROM drive.**

2. **Click the Start button and choose Run from the menu.**

3. **In the dialog box that appears, type** d:\start.htm.

   Replace *d* with the proper drive letter for your CD-ROM if it uses a different letter. (If you don't know the letter, double-click My Computer on your desktop and see what letter is listed for your CD-ROM drive.)

   Your browser opens, and the license agreement displays.

4. **Read through the license agreement, nod your head, and click the Agree button if you want to use the CD.**

   The Main menu appears, where you can browse through the contents of the CD.

5. **To navigate within the interface, click a topic of interest, which takes you to an explanation of the files on the CD and how to use or install them.**

6. **To install software from the CD, simply click the software name.**

   You see two options: to run or open the file from the current location or to save the file to your hard drive. Choose to run or open the file from its current location, and the installation procedure continues. When you finish using the interface, close your browser as usual.

Note: I included an "easy install" in these HTML pages. If your browser supports installations from within it, go ahead and click the links of the program names you see. You see two options: Run the File from the Current Location and Save the File to Your Hard Drive. Choose the Run the File from the Current Location option and the installation procedure continues. A Security Warning dialog box appears. Click the Yes button to continue the installation.

Using the CD with Mac OS

To install items from the CD to your hard drive, follow these steps:

1. **Insert the CD into your computer's CD-ROM drive.**

   In a moment, an icon representing the CD you just inserted appears on your Mac desktop. Chances are, the icon looks like a CD-ROM.

2. **Double-click the CD icon to show the CD's contents.**

3. **Double-click** `start.htm` **to open your browser and display the license agreement.**

   If your browser doesn't open automatically, open it as you normally would by choosing File⇨Open File (in Internet Explorer) or File⇨Open⇨Location in Netscape (in Netscape Navigator) and select *Dreamweaver For Dummies*. The license agreement appears.

4. **Read through the license agreement, nod your head, and click the Accept button if you want to use the CD.**

   The Main menu appears. This is where you can browse through the contents of the CD.

5. **To navigate within the interface, click any topic of interest and you go to an explanation of the files on the CD and how to use or install them.**

6. **To install software from the CD, simply click the software name.**

What You Find on the CD

The following sections are arranged by category and provide a summary of the software and other goodies on the CD. If you need help with installing the items provided on the CD, refer to the installation instructions in the preceding sections.

Shareware programs are fully functional, free, trial versions of copyrighted programs. If you like particular programs, register with their authors for a nominal fee and receive licenses, enhanced versions, and technical support. *Trial, demo,* or *evaluation* versions of software are usually limited either by time or functionality (such as not letting you save a project after you create it).

Software programs

Acrobat Reader 6.0, from Adobe Systems

For Mac and Windows. Evaluation version.

This program lets you view and print Portable Document Format (PDF) files. Many programs on the Internet use the PDF format for storing documentation because it supports assorted fonts and colorful graphics.

To find out more about using Acrobat Reader, choose the Reader Online Guide from the Help menu, or view the Acrobat.pdf file installed in the same folder as the program. You can also get more information by visiting the Adobe Systems Web site at www.adobe.com.

Dreamweaver MX 2004

For Mac and Windows. Tryout version.

Dreamweaver MX 2004 is the latest version of Macromedia's award-winning Web design program, which is covered in detail in this book. The tryout version of Dreamweaver included on the CD is a fully functional version of the program that works for 30 days after installation — an ideal trial period during which you can find out for yourself how great Dreamweaver is for designing Web pages. Use the trial version as you explore the lessons in this book. To purchase Dreamweaver and continue using it after the 30-day period, visit www.macromedia.com.

Fireworks MX 2004, from Macromedia

For Mac OS 10.2.6 or later and Windows 98, or NT (with Service Pack 3) or later. 30-day tryout version.

This graphics program is designed for creating images, animations, and complex design elements for the Web. The program is integrated with Dreamweaver to make it easier to edit images even after they are placed on your Web pages. Check out the Macromedia Web site at www.macromedia.com.

Flash MX 2004

For Mac and Windows. Tryout version.

If you've ever seen motion or animation on the Web, it was likely created with Macromedia Flash. This powerful animation and design program has become the most popular way to animate banner ads, create online games, bring life to static graphics, and so much more. The tryout version included on the CD is a fully functional version of Flash that works for 30 days. If you want to purchase Flash, visit www.macromedia.com.

Illustrator 10, from Adobe

For Mac OS and Windows 95 and 98. Tryout version.

Adobe's advanced vector-drawing program enables you to create complex images with powerful precision. To learn more, check out the Adobe Web site at www.adobe.com.

Webspice 3-D Animations

Looking for a little motion for your Web site? Check out the animation samples from Webspice on the CD. This company provides a variety of 3-D animations especially designed for business Web sites. If you like what you find on the CD, you'll find lots more at www.webspice.com.

Webspice Objects

If you need images for your Web site, check out the samples from Webspice on the CD. This company provides a variety of images especially designed for business Web sites in the medical, legal, real estate, and education fields. If you like what you find on the CD, you'll find lots more where they came from at www.webspice.com.

Templates

Dreamweaver gives templates high-end functionality, such as the power to automatically update many pages at once if you change the template they are designed with. You can also control what areas of a template are edited by designers and what areas cannot be changed — a great way to maintain quality control when you work with a team of developers. You find several templates on the CD.

Glossary

Don't forget to check out the glossary on the CD. It can be your first resource when you stumble across unfamiliar Web-design lingo.

Author-created material

For Windows and Mac.

All the examples provided in this book are located in the Author directory on the CD and work with Macintosh, Linux, Unix, and Windows 95/98/NT and later computers. These files contain much of the sample code from the book. The structure of the examples directory is

```
Author/Chapter1
Author/Chapterx
```

Troubleshooting

I tried my best to compile programs that work on most computers with the minimum system requirements. Alas, your computer may differ, and some programs may not work properly for some reason.

The two likeliest problems are that you don't have enough memory (RAM) for the programs you want to use, or you have other programs running that affect installation or running of a program. If you get an error message such as Not enough memory or Setup cannot continue, try one or more of the following suggestions and then try using the software again:

- ✔ **Turn off any antivirus software running on your computer.** Installation programs sometimes mimic virus activity and may make your computer incorrectly believe that a virus is infecting it.

- ✔ **Close all running programs.** The more programs you run, the less memory is available to other programs. Installation programs typically update files and programs; if you keep other programs running, installation may not work properly.

- ✔ **Have your local computer store add more RAM to your computer.** This is, admittedly, a drastic and somewhat expensive step. However, if you have a Windows 95 PC or a Mac OS computer with a PowerPC chip, adding more memory can really help the speed of your computer and allow more programs to run at the same time. This may include closing the CD interface and running a product's installation program from Windows Explorer.

If you still have trouble installing the items from the CD, please call the Customer Service phone number at 800-762-2974 (outside the U.S.: 317-572-3994) or send and e-mail to techsupdum@wiley.com. Wiley Publishing provides technical support only for installation and other general quality control items; for technical support on the applications themselves, consult the program's vendor or author.

Index

Wiley Publishing, Inc.
End-User License Agreement

5. **Limited Warranty.**

    (a) WPI warrants that the Software and Software Media are free from defects in materials and workmanship under normal use for a period of sixty (60) days from the date of purchase of this Book. If WPI receives notification within the warranty period of defects in materials or workmanship, WPI will replace the defective Software Media.

    (b) WPI AND THE AUTHOR(S) OF THE BOOK DISCLAIM ALL OTHER WARRANTIES, EXPRESS OR IMPLIED, INCLUDING WITHOUT LIMITATION IMPLIED WARRANTIES OF MERCHANTABILITY AND FITNESS FOR A PARTICULAR PURPOSE, WITH RESPECT TO THE SOFTWARE, THE PROGRAMS, THE SOURCE CODE CONTAINED THEREIN, AND/OR THE TECHNIQUES DESCRIBED IN THIS BOOK. WPI DOES NOT WARRANT THAT THE FUNCTIONS CONTAINED IN THE SOFTWARE WILL MEET YOUR REQUIREMENTS OR THAT THE OPERATION OF THE SOFTWARE WILL BE ERROR FREE.

    (c) This limited warranty gives you specific legal rights, and you may have other rights that vary from jurisdiction to jurisdiction.

6. **Remedies.**

    (a) WPI's entire liability and your exclusive remedy for defects in materials and workmanship shall be limited to replacement of the Software Media, which may be returned to WPI with a copy of your receipt at the following address: Software Media Fulfillment Department, Attn.: *Dreamweaver MX 2004 For Dummies,* Wiley Publishing, Inc., 10475 Crosspoint Blvd., Indianapolis, IN 46256, or call 1-800-762-2974. Please allow four to six weeks for delivery. This Limited Warranty is void if failure of the Software Media has resulted from accident, abuse, or misapplication. Any replacement Software Media will be warranted for the remainder of the original warranty period or thirty (30) days, whichever is longer.

    (b) In no event shall WPI or the author be liable for any damages whatsoever (including without limitation damages for loss of business profits, business interruption, loss of business information, or any other pecuniary loss) arising from the use of or inability to use the Book or the Software, even if WPI has been advised of the possibility of such damages.

    (c) Because some jurisdictions do not allow the exclusion or limitation of liability for consequential or incidental damages, the above limitation or exclusion may not apply to you.

7. **U.S. Government Restricted Rights.** Use, duplication, or disclosure of the Software for or on behalf of the United States of America, its agencies and/or instrumentalities "U.S. Government" is subject to restrictions as stated in paragraph (c)(1)(ii) of the Rights in Technical Data and Computer Software clause of DFARS 252.227-7013, or subparagraphs (c) (1) and (2) of the Commercial Computer Software - Restricted Rights clause at FAR 52.227-19, and in similar clauses in the NASA FAR supplement, as applicable.

8. **General.** This Agreement constitutes the entire understanding of the parties and revokes and supersedes all prior agreements, oral or written, between them and may not be modified or amended except in a writing signed by both parties hereto that specifically refers to this Agreement. This Agreement shall take precedence over any other documents that may be in conflict herewith. If any one or more provisions contained in this Agreement are held by any court or tribunal to be invalid, illegal, or otherwise unenforceable, each and every other provision shall remain in full force and effect.

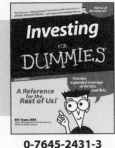

FOR DUMMIES®

A world of resources to help you grow

TRAVEL

0-7645-5453-0

0-7645-5438-7

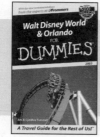

0-7645-5444-1

Also available:

America's National Parks For Dummies
(0-7645-6204-5)

Caribbean For Dummies
(0-7645-5445-X)

Cruise Vacations For Dummies 2003
(0-7645-5459-X)

Europe For Dummies
(0-7645-5456-5)

Ireland For Dummies
(0-7645-6199-5)

France For Dummies
(0-7645-6292-4)

Las Vegas For Dummies
(0-7645-5448-4)

London For Dummies
(0-7645-5416-6)

Mexico's Beach Resorts For Dummies
(0-7645-6262-2)

Paris For Dummies
(0-7645-5494-8)

RV Vacations For Dummies
(0-7645-5443-3)

EDUCATION & TEST PREPARATION

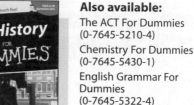

0-7645-5194-9

0-7645-5325-9

0-7645-5249-X

Also available:

The ACT For Dummies
(0-7645-5210-4)

Chemistry For Dummies
(0-7645-5430-1)

English Grammar For Dummies
(0-7645-5322-4)

French For Dummies
(0-7645-5193-0)

GMAT For Dummies
(0-7645-5251-1)

Inglés Para Dummies
(0-7645-5427-1)

Italian For Dummies
(0-7645-5196-5)

Research Papers For Dummies
(0-7645-5426-3)

SAT I For Dummies
(0-7645-5472-7)

U.S. History For Dummies
(0-7645-5249-X)

World History For Dummies
(0-7645-5242-2)

HEALTH, SELF-HELP & SPIRITUALITY

0-7645-5154-X

0-7645-5302-X

0-7645-5418-2

Also available:

The Bible For Dummies
(0-7645-5296-1)

Controlling Cholesterol For Dummies
(0-7645-5440-9)

Dating For Dummies
(0-7645-5072-1)

Dieting For Dummies
(0-7645-5126-4)

High Blood Pressure For Dummies
(0-7645-5424-7)

Judaism For Dummies
(0-7645-5299-6)

Menopause For Dummies
(0-7645-5458-1)

Nutrition For Dummies
(0-7645-5180-9)

Potty Training For Dummies
(0-7645-5417-4)

Pregnancy For Dummies
(0-7645-5074-8)

Rekindling Romance For Dummies
(0-7645-5303-8)

Religion For Dummies
(0-7645-5264-3)

Available wherever books are sold. Go to www.dummies.com or call 1-877-762-2974 to order direct

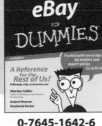